D1068145

Catholic Radicals in Brazil

The Royal Institute of International Affairs is an unofficial body which promotes the scientific study of international questions and does not express opinions of its own. The opinions expressed in this publication are the responsibility of the author.

The Institute gratefully acknowledges the comments and suggestions of the following who read the manuscript on behalf of the Research Committee: Raymond Carr, Professor R. P. Dore, and the Reverend François Houtart.

Emanuel de Kadt

Catholic Radicals in Brazil

Issued under the auspices of the
Royal Institute of International Affairs

OXFORD UNIVERSITY PRESS

LONDON   NEW YORK

1970

37303

Oxford University Press, Ely House, London W.1

GLASGOW NEW YORK TORONTO MELBOURNE WELLINGTON
CAPE TOWN SALISBURY IBADAN NAIROBI DAR ES SALAAM LUSAKA ADDIS ABABA
BOMBAY CALCUTTA MADRAS KARACHI LAHORE DACCA
KUALA LUMPUR SINGAPORE HONG KONG TOKYO

SBN 19 214984 9

F2538.2
.D45

© Royal Institute of International Affairs 1970

HARVARD UNIVERSITY
GRADUATE SCHOOL OF EDUCATION
MONROE C. GUTMAN LIBRARY

May 14, 1973

Printed in Great Britain
by Ebenezer Baylis and Son, Ltd.
The Trinity Press, Worcester, and London

Acknowledgements

VARIOUS sections of this book were read in draft by Alan Angell, Julieta Calazans, Padre Sena, and Francisco Weffort, and I am most grateful for their constructive criticisms. I recall with much pleasure a number of long discussions with Pierre Furter. I benefited greatly from his intimate knowledge of and sympathy for the movements discussed in this book. Raymond Carr and Ronald P. Dore read the entire final draft, which was presented as a Ph.D. thesis in the University of London. Their often detailed comments were extremely helpful and resulted in substantial changes in the structure of the book. François Houtart was also kind enough to read the final version; his reaction to the text was of great importance to me.

Generous financial assistance, which enabled me to travel to and in Brazil on more than one occasion, was provided by Chatham House, under the Latin American grant made available by the Ford Foundation.

Various persons gave me different forms of 'technical assistance'. Frank Gattoni enlightened me in matters statistical. Sueli Ghivelder's indexing labours on my field notes proved invaluable in the early stages of the analysis and writing up. Daphne Rodger typed parts of various drafts and saved me from a number of linguistic inaccuracies through her flawless knowledge of Portuguese. The index was made by Katharine Duff and has benefited from her long-standing interest in Latin America. Hermia Oliver edited the final typescript. She approached this task with a splendid mixture of sympathy and firmness, and executed it with meticulous care, giving help well beyond that which I would have expected of an editor. The heaviest burden fell on Angela Strickland, who typed and re-typed successive drafts often under the greatest of time pressure. She was a solid support in many other ways, with her sensible views, her capacity to undertake many varied research tasks, and in general with her never-ending helpfulness.

The greatest of all debts I owe, no doubt, to the cadres of MEB. In the first place for allowing me total freedom in my inquiries, for making available any document I wished to see, and for answering my many questions. More important, perhaps, for letting me become one of them during the fieldwork, and for extending their trust and friendship to me. I hope that I have not abused that friendship by publishing a book which is, no doubt, in various respects different from the one they would have written, or liked to see written. The comments on successive drafts made by past or present members of the organization were extremely useful. But especially with them in mind, I must state with emphasis that the views expressed in this book remain entirely my own and that they in no way express official or even informal views held by the present leadership of MEB.

November 1969   E. de K.

Contents

Acknowledgements   v

Abbreviations   xi

1 Introduction   1

2 Aspects of Brazilian Social Relations   9
Introduction, 9; Social relations in pre-twentieth-century Brazil, 10; The position of the peasants in 'traditional' rural areas, 16; The traditional political processes, 19; Recent changes in grass-roots rural politics, 22; The *ligas*: reflections on 'leaders' and 'followers', 24; Urban changes, 31

3 Aspects of National Politics and Government since 1930   34
The first Vargas era (1930–45), 34; The first postwar decade (1945–54), 37; From Vargas to Goulart (1954–64), 41; Politics and the rural masses, 47

4 The Church and the Stirrings of Catholic Radicalism   51
Brazilian Catholicism: historical introduction, 51; The setting up of Catholic Action, 58; The early years of JUC, 60; The radical turning point in JUC, 65; JUC and the university, 68; The point of view of the Brazilian hierarchy, 72; Growing friction between JUC and the hierarchy, 77

5 The Heyday of the Catholic Radicals I: Theory and Ideology   81
AP and its philosophy of history, 81; The 'personalist' element in the radical Catholic *Weltanschauung*, 90; An excursus on populism, 94; Further comments on the radical Catholic analysis of society, 98

6 The Heyday of the Catholic Radicals II: Activity and
   Praxis   102
   The theory and practice of *conscientização*, 102; The beginnings
   of rural *sindicalismo*, 107; The Catholic radicals move into *sindicalismo*, 111; *Massificação* in the rural areas, 113; AP in the
   political arena, 118

7 MEB: Its Scope, Operation, and Cadres   122
   The origins of MEB, 122; The radio schools and the *sistemas*, 125;
   Overall co-ordination: *Nacional* and *Estaduais*, 134; Characteris-
   tics of MEB's cadres, 138; MEB and its bishops, 143

8 Aspects of MEB's Development until April 1964   149
   Earliest formulations of MEB's aims and methods, 149; MEB
   radicalizes: the *I Encontro de Coordenadores*, 152; The affair of
   the 'subversive *cartilha* of the bishops', 156; MEB and the
   sindicatos, 162; Notes on *sindicalismo* in one *sistema*, 167

9 Some Observations on the *Zona da mata*   172
   MEB frustrated, 172; A North-Eastern sugar plantation, 175;
   Difficulties between *usina* and *sindicato*, 179; The cane workers,
   182; Lack of leadership and intimidation, 187

10 MEB after the Military Take-Over of 1964   190
   The April coup and its repercussions: the bishops step in, 190;
   The second *cartilha*, 200; MEB's centre of gravity shifts to the
   North, 205; MEB settles down to new realities, 208

11 The Fusion of Populist Ideology and Non-Directive
   Techniques   212
   Animação Popular (AnPo), 212; The introduction of non-directive,
   techniques, 215; The changing interpretation of non-directiveness,
   217; The *III Encontro Nacional de Coordenadores*, 220

12 Populism and Non-Directiveness at the Grass-Roots, I   230
   A view of Franqueira, 230; Non-directiveness at the *equipe* level,
   231; Peasants and landowners in the Franqueira area, 235;
   Conscientização in a discouraging environment, 240

13 Populism and Non-Directiveness at the Grass-Roots, II   245
   Fernandópolis and Lagoinha, 245; *Animação Popular* in Lagoinha,
   247; Lagoinha runs into trouble, 251; Peasants and politics, 254;
   Politics in Lagoinha and populist non-directiveness, 259

14 Conclusions   260
    Community development and class confrontation, 260; Populism
    and power, 266; By way of epilogue, 270

Appendices
    1. Results of the Survey of MEB's Cadres   275
    2. Notes on Fieldwork at São Pedro   286

Glossary   289

Select Bibliography   291

Index   297

Abbreviations

ACO	*Ação Católica Operária*
AnPo	*Animação Popular*
AP	*Ação Popular*
Arch. sociol. relig.	*Archives de sociologie des religions*
CDN	*Conselho Diretor Nacional*
CIDOC	Centro Intercultural de Documentación
CNBB	*Conferência Nacional dos Bispos do Brasil*
CONSIR	*Commissão Nacional de Sindicalização Rural*
CONTAG	*Confederação Nacional de Trabalhadores na Agricultura*
CPC	*Centro Popular de Cultura*
Cr $	Cruzeiro
D.	Dom
ECLA	(UN) Economic Commission for Latin America
Fr.	Frei
IBRA	*Instituto Brasileira de Reforma Agrária*
Int. Soc. Sc.J.	*International Social Science Journal* (now *Bulletin*)
ISEB	*Instituto Superior de Estudos Brasileiros*
JAC	*Juventude Agrária Católica*
JEC	*Juventude Estudantil Católica*
JOC	*Juventude Operária Católica*
JUC	*Juventude Universitária Católica*
JUC, *Ideal Histórico*	JUC, *Boletin* 4/1—*Ideal histórico*
MEB	*Movimento de Educação de Base*
Mons.	Monsenhor
PCB	*Partido Communista Brasileiro*
Pe	Padre
PSD	*Partido Social-Democrático*

PTB	*Partido Trabalhista Brasileiro*
R. bras. cien. soc.	*Revista brasileira de ciências sociais*
R. bras. estud. polit.	*Revista brasileira de estudos políticos*
RENEC	*Rede Nacional de Emissôras Católicas*
SNI	*Serviço Nacional de Informações*
SORPE	*Serviço de Orientação Rural de Pernambuco*
SUDENE	*Superintendência do Desinvolvimento do Nordeste*
UDN	*União Democrática Nacional*
ULTAB	*União de Lavradores e Trabalhadores Agrícolas do Brasil*
UNE	*União Nacional de Estudantes*

1

Introduction

FEW periods in Brazil's recent history can have seemed so full of omens of change to contemporaries as the decade from the mid-1950s to the mid-1960s. On the one hand it saw, in a sense, the apotheosis of the political and social system first implanted by Getúlio Vargas in the 1930s. On the other it witnessed the rise of groups and movements, most of them numerically quite small, yet clearly visible (and especially audible) on the political scene, which demanded a radical change in the system, and promised a better life to those vast groups of Brazilians who had hitherto been refused participation in whatever benefits society had to offer. Among these radical groups, those whose 'pedigree' is, broadly speaking, Christian are of particular interest, in view of the potential influence they have on the Roman Catholic church as such.

People who boast of Brazil as the greatest Catholic nation may be failing to take into account the weaknesses of institutional Catholicism in that country; at the same time there is no doubt that the Catholic church is a body of uncommon significance in a country where most of the structurally important organizations with a nation-wide character have extremely limited effective authority outside the main centres of political life. The church has always had a remarkable capacity of assimilating substantial parts of all but clearly heretical dissenting points of view; during the years of Pope John's *Aggiornamento* and the Second Vatican Council, critical and innovating ideas were even more likely to make some kind of impact, however great the hostility with which they might at first have been received.

It was considerations such as these which prompted me to attempt to throw some light on the ideas and activities of that small minority among Brazil's committed Catholics who could be called 'radicals' in the social and political spheres. This book is the outcome of that attempt. It does not purport to be a definitive discussion of the subject. On the contrary: by choosing to concentrate primarily on a case study,

1

I have *ipso facto* foregone the opportunity of presenting a detailed over-all picture.

This case study is of the *Movimento de Educação de Base* (Movement for Basic Education, MEB) and its development from its beginnings until the second half of 1966. MEB is a church-sponsored, government-financed organization which from early 1961 has been active in the rural areas of Brazil's less developed states. The earliest emphasis in its educational programmes, which are transmitted by radio, was on literacy training and various forms of peasant self-improvement; gradually it became more interested in the social structure which had led to and perpetuated the peasant's plight, and its main thrust came to be specifically directed to changing that structure. But after the military coup of April 1964 the radical impetus was lost, and basic structural change, though still accepted as a long-term necessity, was no longer given the central place it had previously occupied in the Movement's educational programmes and was no longer discussed and striven for with the same sense of urgency.

At this point it is necessary to give a brief account of the situation which has developed in Brazil since 1964. It would have been an exaggeration—as Chapters 2 and 3 will show—to describe Brazil before the coup as a democracy in the full sense of the word. But superimposed on a social structure at the grass-roots of politics that in many areas lacked all characteristics of, or even prerequisites for, democratic processes, Brazil had a set of formally democratic institutions which, despite relatively frequent interventions by the military, worked tolerably well. It certainly had a long and proud tradition of non-violence at the higher levels of the political system, of bloodless coups and very limited use of physical aggression or harassment of political opponents. It also had maintained, again at those higher levels, a soundly functioning set of mechanisms guaranteeing individual civil liberties and a respected independent judiciary.

The military coup of 1964 changed all that. For a year or two afterwards zealously-pursued political inquiries by the military (IPMs) hunted many of those supposedly compromised with the 'subversion' prevalent during the years of Goulart's presidency, and numerous persons of high or low position lost their jobs, elected offices, or political rights. Then, after Marshal Costa e Silva had taken over from Marshal Castelo Branco—in March 1967—the situation seemed to ease a little, when the former attempted to fulfil his promise of 'humanizing' the '*Revolução*' (the term by which its supporters designate the coup and the political processes set in motion by it). A series of events, which included student disturbances, unrest among the progressive clergy, and a seemingly minor challenge to the military by a young federal deputy elected after 1964 on the opposition ticket culminated in the abrupt end to Costa e Silva's compromise line, when the military staged a further 'coup within the coup' on Friday, 13 December 1968.

Since then, the Brazilian scene has become increasingly unrecognizable. A very rigid and highly effective censorship of all mass media of communication has been instituted, and thus no reports appear of the increasingly severe repression and growing use of violence by the authorities. Widespread dismissals have occurred in the universities; virtually all traditional legal safeguards have been abolished; the rule of law and the existence of normal civil liberties are a nostalgic memory of the past; right-wing terrorists intimidate, attack, and murder; arbitrariness reigns. The revolutionary Left has responded with an ever bolder series of armed attacks, especially on TV stations and banks. The successful kidnapping by an 'urban guerrilla group' of the American Ambassador to Brazil in September 1969, and his release after the government had fulfilled the group's demands of publishing their manifesto and releasing fifteen political prisoners, was followed by the institution of the death penalty for certain kinds of 'subversive' and revolutionary acts. And so the impetus in the upwards spiral of violence and counter-violence gathered steady momentum.[1]

My last visit to Brazil in connection with this book started on that fateful Friday, 13 December 1968. I shall not attempt to describe the effect on many of my friends. Though interested in my research they were doubtful of the advisability of publishing a book on events, people, and ideas which have become taboo to the country's new rulers. In this respect I have had to make a very difficult judgement, but the fact that the book treats of matters which by now are clearly 'historical', and that the nature of MEB's activities, as well as its personnel, have undergone so fundamental a transformation, has made me decide that the story should be told. Needless to say I have taken even greater care than is usual for sociologists to protect the anonymity of my informants (who were all exceptionally co-operative, frank, and open, and allowed me access to anything I wished to see) by using fictitious

---

[1] These may seem sweeping statements, but they can all be extensively documented from reports which appeared during the first half of 1969 in such diverse sources as the *New York Times*, *Le Monde*, *The Times*, and *Latin America*. A cursory inspection of any file of press cuttings would confirm this.

names for people and places throughout those parts of the book that
are directly based on field data.

The main task I set myself was to make some contribution to a
better understanding of the way in which ideologies develop in inter-
relation with social action and the limitations placed on action by external forces; I have tried to do this primarily by tracing the evolution
of ideas in MEB and the changes in its performance. Thus this is by
no means an exhaustive study of MEB: many aspects of its work, many
specific problems encountered, many achievements accomplished are
excluded. My attention was drawn to MEB because it was so much
part of the radical scene before 1964, while it was simultaneously
formally under the aegis of the Brazilian hierarchy. It was, therefore,
an almost ideal *locus* for the study of the multifarious interrelations,
influences, and conflicts which went with the emergence of a specifically
Christian radicalism in Brazil. But academic consideration could not
prevent me from being interested in the wider aspects of the Movement's work, or from becoming closely identified with its personnel
and their truly dedicated labours on behalf of Brazil's neglected,
unprivileged, and usually exploited peasantry.

I should like to draw attention to a few of the more important
themes with which this book will deal. In the first place there is a
general discussion of those aspects of Brazil's social, economic, and
political structure which are most relevant to an understanding of the
plight of Brazil's rural population. Though Brazil's peasants and rural
workers are, of course, a 'class', both in Max Weber's sense of sharing
economically determined life chances, and in the Marxist sense of
sharing a common fate of exploitation at the hands of those who own
the basic means of production, some of the most persistent features of
their behaviour can only be satisfactorily explained by focusing on the
'*patron–dependant*' relationships—and their gradual modification in
more recent times—which have enveloped them in most spheres of
life. Only once the tenacity of those relations has been fully appre-
ciated will it be possible to understand the difficulties encountered by
the Catholic radicals, and particularly by MEB, in their efforts to
ameliorate the plight of the peasantry.

In the second place there is the theme of *populism*. This concept is
used extensively throughout the book to refer to certain characteristics
the Catholic radicals came to share once their views of man and society
had been fully developed. As urban intellectuals (in the broadest
sense of the term), concerned with the most exploited sections of the

population, they became thoroughly hostile to any 'manipulation' of the people, whose potential for choosing their own economic and political destiny was given great prominence in populist thinking—rather like the situation prevailing among Russia's nineteenth-century *Narodniki*, the proto-typical Populists.

An excursus on populism (in Chapter 5) deals with this matter after the presentation of the ideas and activities of those groups of Catholic radicals who, preceding or contemporaneous with MEB, exercised much influence on the evolution of the Movement, often providing the prototypes of concepts or laying the groundwork for activities which were to become central in MEB. Special attention is paid to the radicalization of the students' branch of Catholic Action, *Juventude Universitária Católica* (JUC). For while, towards the end of the 1950s, new ideas were undoubtedly current in many Catholic circles in Brazil, it was in JUC that these ideas were first forged into a more or less coherent and articulate world-view and programme for action. And although some bishops and priests could be found among JUC's most enthusiastic supporters, conflict with the hierarchy is very much part of the story. Largely as a result of this a new movement, *Ação Popular* (AP), without any ties with the church, was set up in 1961–2, and until 1964 the radical impulse was mainly carried forward by this movement.

I should explain, however, that no attempt has been made to give a comprehensive historical account of movements such as JUC or AP. They are analysed only for the periods which have relevance to subsequent events or developments in MEB, for especially since 1964 the views held by members of these movements has changed sharply. It must, moreover, constantly be borne in mind that the actual power or even influence of these radical groups was in no way commensurate with their quite high 'visibility' in the Brazil of the early 1960s. Even in their heyday their impact on the wider Brazilian political scene was very small indeed; and although they became prominent and powerful in the student movement, most of the student body remained aloof from all activity or commitment.

Another point to which I must draw attention is that because of my interest in MEB and in the *Catholic* church, I have not referred to the radical views which were developing—though on a far smaller scale—within Brazil's Protestant churches. No doubt influenced by developments among Catholic radicals, a special commission for church and society of the Evangelical Confederation of Brazil (the non-Pentecostal

2

churches) organized a conference on the North-East in 1962, at which many radical views were expressed.[2] But the commission in question was soon disbanded, and the face of Protestantism in Brazil remained almost solidly conservative until some ecumenical efforts began to bear fruit after 1964. The most notable of these was the bi-monthly journal *Paz e Terra*, to which Christian as well as non-Christian radicals of many shades contributed.[3]

The second part of the book deals with MEB, with the way in which it became part of the wider radical movement of Catholic inspiration in the years leading up to the coup of April 1964, formulating its own specific contribution to the Catholic radicals' prescriptions for the 'Brazilian Revolution', then with the vicissitudes of MEB after the coup, the kinds of pressures—and attacks—to which it was subject, and the manner in which it responded. When the hopes for the 'Brazilian Revolution' had been dashed by the *'Revolução'* of April 1964, and its advocates were being persecuted by the victors of the *'Revolução'*, changes were inevitable. For a time the laymen of MEB maintained their determination not merely to side with the *pólo dominado* (dominated pole) in Brazilian society, but also to continue the effort to awaken (*conscientizar*) the peasantry to the fact that their situation was likely to improve only—or mainly—through a united struggle with the *pólo dominante* (dominating pole), and the resulting transformation of society.

The change from this perspective of conflict between classes to one of co-operation within a class (the peasantry), the change from *class confrontation* to *community development*, may be seen as the third major theme of the book; special attention will be paid to the role played in this process by MEB's bishops, who, after 1964, transformed their hitherto largely ornamental presence in the Movement into a highly

---

[2] Confederação Evangélica do Brasil, Setor de Responsabilidade Social da Igreja, *Cristo e o processo revolucionário brasileiro* (1962).

[3] Most discussions of Protestantism in Brazil omit the political dimension—largely because hitherto it has been so insignificant; thus, for instance, Emilio Willems's otherwise important book *Followers of the New Faith* (Nashville Tenn., 1967). Two exceptions are the article by Jovelino Pereira Ramos, 'Protestantismo brasileiro: visão panorâmica', *Paz e terra*, no. 6, and the paper by Waldo A. César, chief editor of *Paz e terra*, 'Situação e crescimento do Protestantismo na América Latina', in César, *Protestantismo e imperialismo na América Latina* (1968). Some discussion of Protestants in politics may also be found in Marcio Moreira Alves's *O Cristo do povo* (1968), a committed journalist's valuable account of much of the radical Catholic scene in Brazil, which came to my notice after this manuscript had been completed.

active one (see particularly Chapter 10). This theme is also developed in the discussion of my fieldwork experience, which took place in two broadly speaking 'traditional' areas—the kind of area which still predominates in the portion of Brazil at one time or another covered by MEB.[4]

Two years after the coup, when I was engaged in the fieldwork which took me into the rural areas, anyone discussing the realities of class conflict was liable to be in trouble with the authorities as a bringer of 'subversion'. Even the promotion of peasant co-operation or community development was regarded with suspicion by many powerful men. No wonder that the focus of MEB's approach changed. Yet, with the new approach came new limitations in (potential) achievements: central to the elaboration of this third theme is the question of MEB's diminished effectiveness as a catalyst of change under the post-coup political circumstances (last three chapters).

The chapters on MEB also take up the two earlier themes, on patron–dependant relations (fieldwork discussion), and on populism. The Movement, in fact, developed its own highly distinctive version of populism,[5] resulting from the conjunction of three factors. These were the ideological views which MEB came to share with the rest of the Catholic radicals in Brazil; a methodological stress on non-directiveness—i.e. the principles derived from group dynamics of non-intervention by the group leader in the process whereby the group reaches decisions; and, finally, the peculiar political circumstances that made effective action impossible and put a premium on lengthy, non-directive discussions whose results were likely to be minimal.

If the Conclusion is somewhat pessimistic regarding any likely alleviation of the most pressing problems in Brazil's rural social structure,

[4] These areas were, of course, not 'typical' of the social reality faced by MEB: Brazil is too large and heterogeneous a country for any limited area to be 'typical'. An attempt at capturing something of the existing diversity was made by spending some time in the *zona da mata*, the North-Eastern coastal sugar-zone, with its rural proletariat (ch. 9). MEB's experience in this area, where some of its best *equipes* (i.e. teams of teachers, supervisors, etc.) were to be found, contributed greatly to the formulation of its radical perspective in the years preceding the coup d'état, and some awareness of the social situation there is indispensable to an understanding of the different approaches that came to prevail within the Movement. The Amazon region, a part of the country that became increasingly important for MEB after 1964, could unfortunately not be visited due to lack of time. A few general paragraphs on the socio-economic position of the peasantry in the North are, however, included in ch. 10.

[5] The term, incidentally, was never used in MEB, and my application of it to the Movement caused distinct uneasiness among one or two of its cadres who read the earliest drafts of this book.

if doubts are voiced regarding the role of MEB when measured against its own aspirations before the fall of Goulart in April 1964, no disparagement is meant of the profound dedication which the Movement's cadres brought to their work, no underestimation is suggested of their sustained efforts to try and help to raise the peasants' sense of human dignity or unlock their creative potential. In areas such as the North, moreover, where the confrontation between 'haves' and 'have-nots' is (as yet) on the whole less sharp and immediate, MEB's 'humanizing' work among the peasantry may well help lay the foundation for healthier socio-political relationships in the future.

It must be clearly stated from the outset that my fieldwork involved me at least partially in participant observation; as a participant, I came to see the world through the eyes of my many friends in the Movement, and to share their hopes and their fears. Up to a point, I also participated in their disagreements and quarrels, although the existence of tensions and conflicts prevented me from becoming too fully identified and so helped me preserve what measure of objectivity this study possesses. I hope that that objectivity has not been too much diminished by my sense of gratitude, for it would be hard not to feel grateful for the privilege of working with people so deeply committed to the betterment of the least privileged members of their society.

Aspects of Brazilian Social Relations

Introduction

A BOOK such as this, which deals to a large extent with attempts to change the social and political attitudes of sections of the Brazilian masses (especially in the rural areas), must begin by looking at some of the basic principles which underlie the Brazilian social structure. A limited examination of those principles—obviously *not* a wholesale analysis of 'key sociological concepts' or a total examination of Brazilian society—is necessary for the understanding of various 'practical' problems encountered by the Catholic radicals, and particularly by MEB, both before the coup of April 1964 and afterwards. This background is, I believe, so unfamiliar even to many who have some acquaintance with Brazil that such a preliminary general discussion is necessary, and the more so because the full implications of these principles have not always been clearly understood by the people who are the protagonists of this study.

In recent years an increasing number of studies have pointed out that the concept of 'patron–dependant' or 'patron–client' relations offers a fruitful approach to the understanding of certain significant and widespread patterns of social behaviour in Brazil, which have seemed to defy analysis when discussed *solely* in terms of social class.[1]

Of course, this is not to suggest that the concept of social class is irrelevant in Brazil. However one defines it, in Marxian terms as having to do with the ownership of the means of production and the potential dynamic of change inherent in the 'dialectic' between opposing classes, or in Weberian terms as relating to the differential 'life chances' resulting from the economic power in the market of different social strata, social class is a crucial concept in all stratified societies—and Brazil is hardly classless. The point, however, is that class consciousness among the masses is still rudimentary in Brazil, even in the large cities; and that social or political action oriented to class interests

---

[1] An excellent synoptic discussion can be found in Bertram Hutchinson, 'The Patron-Dependant Relationship in Brazil: a Preliminary Examination', *Sociologia ruralis*, vi/1 (1966).

has so far been insignificant among workers and peasants. Given this fact, all analysis in terms of social class remains almost entirely on the level of *potential* developments—consistently failing to account for the continual strength of structural patterns which seem to have nothing to do with class whatsoever.[2] This is significant in terms of the concern of this book because, certainly until April 1964, the Catholic radicals in general, and MEB in particular, had oriented much of their activity to the stimulation of action and consciousness centred in class interests. Some of the major obstacles they have encountered can best be understood via an examination of the dynamics of patron–dependant relations.

Social relations in pre-twentieth-century Brazil

Many writers who have wished to distinguish the most significant differences in colonial times between the social and political structure of Hispanic and Portuguese America respectively—differences which have left a permanent imprint on the contemporary societies—point to the much more limited effectiveness of the central colonial authorities in Brazil.[3] Partly this was no doubt a result of the sheer size of the Brazilian territory, and of the growing economic and military weakness of metropolitan Portugal almost from the start of its colonizing venture in America. Of greater importance was probably the fact that no gold or precious stones were discovered in Brazil till a century and a half after colonization began. Portugal's interests in the country were thus for a long time almost wholly agricultural, and the scattered plantations producing mainly sugar, with the aid of African slave labour, were left almost entirely to their own devices. In that way the colonial administration remained even farther removed from the reality of local power in colonial Brazil than in Hispanic America.

Colonial Brazilian society has consequently to be seen primarily in terms of a fairly large number of discrete units: the plantations. It has been largely thanks to Gilberto Freyre's monumental work of social history, *The Masters and the Slaves*,[4] that we have become aware

[2] Most enlightening is the comparison in this respect with Japan. See John W. Bennett & Iwao Ishino, *Paternalism in the Japanese Economy* (1963). The analysis of patron–client relations presented there contains many insights equally applicable to Latin America.

[3] Two papers by Richard M. Morse may be consulted on this matter: 'The Heritage of Latin America', in Louis Hartz, *The Founding of New Societies* (1964), and 'Some Themes of Brazilian History', *S. Atlantic Q.*, Spring 1962. Most standard histories of Latin America will make the same point; see e.g. Hubert Herring, *A History of Latin America*, 2nd. ed. (1963), ch. 12.

[4] Trans. by Samuel Putnam (1946).

of the importance of these units. Since then other writers have followed
suit, notably Fernando de Azevedo, who laid much greater stress on the
importance of the structure of power on the plantations and the implications of social relations there for the wider social structure.[5] There now
exists a fairly detailed picture of life on these patriarchial family domains.
They have been mainly described for the sugar-planting zone of the
North-East, but as the frontier shifted, the social patterns first established
in that area spread southwards and inland.

The sugar plantations, self-sufficient and virtually autonomous,
were hardly ever interfered with by the central colonial authorities.
Their social centre, the extended family, might include unmarried
aunts or sisters, nephews, nieces, and godchildren. It was surrounded
by slaves, servants, and dependants of all kinds, and fulfilled all the
economic, social, and political functions necessary for its survival;
functions which only at a much later stage were separated out, spread
over a number of formally independent units in a process of differentiation.[6] The *engenho* (plantation) was in the first place an economic
unit of production, based on slave labour. The 'relations of production'
in this economic system were characterized by the exercise of near-
absolute power, with the chain of subordination following from the
master of the plantation, usually through his sons, to the slave-
overseers and then to the slaves themselves. The *engenho* was also a
'clan' or extended family unit, once again based on relations of submission and domination, in which the patriarchial family head exercised powers over the other family members which, though obviously
not totally arbitrary, were extremely extensive and despotic. Wife
and sons were expected to submit passively to husband and father;
in their turn they 'tyrannized' other members of the household or
dependants.[7]

Finally the *engenho* was a political unit, in that no independent
agencies existed which exercised power or dispensed justice locally.
Power derived wholly from the ownership of land and slaves, and
(even much later) the landowner had to 'obtain for himself and his
family a justice that, were it left to the state to provide, would not be
forthcoming'.[8] The relationship between *engenhos* in the same area

---

[5] *Canaviais e engenhos na vida política do Brasil*, 2nd. ed. (1958).

[6] One of the most interesting sociological analyses of such a process is to be found in
Neil Smelser, *Social Change in the Industrial Revolution* (London, 1959)—and that despite
the quite unhelpful jargon.

[7] de Azevedo, p. 67.

[8] Hutchinson, *Soc. ruralis*, vi/1 (1966), p. 11.

was thus fairly similar to that between feudal holdings in medieval Europe, with politics, or public life, as an extension of private life; and the master of the *engenho* both 'ruled' over his family, dependants, and slaves, and protected them from outside interference. In the social structure formed by these units it was not the individual who counted, but the family, the clan, of which he was a member.

The one exception to this was the *senhor de engenho* himself. His overwhelming individualism found ample scope in his authoritarian role as *pater familias*, and in his activities as an entrepreneur, who was piloting a complex economic enterprise under decidedly difficult circumstances. Those who operated in his shadow, the minor masters and the dependants, were all bound to him by the principle of personal loyalty. That principle was accepted and internalized by all involved, thereby bestowing the quality of legitimacy on the master's exercise of power, despotic though it may have been. His commands were seen as perfectly proper by himself as well as by those subordinated to him, his position was one of generally accepted authority, within a framework of values accepted by all.[9] 'Authority entails voluntary compliance in contrast to coercion, since the influence of the superior on subordinates rests on their own social norms.'[10] This, then, is one of the bases of the dependence relationship.

Another aspect of this relationship—which, as will be seen, gradually assumed greater importance in modern times—is the element of genuine exchange between master (patron) and dependant, whereby each stands to gain something from the arrangement. Peter Blau has defined exchange relations as those involving 'voluntary actions of individuals that are motivated by the returns they are expected to bring and typically do in fact bring from others'. He has specified further that action 'compelled by physical coercion is not voluntary, although compliance with other forms of power can be considered a voluntary service rendered in exchange for the benefits such compliance produces.'[11] It is clear that in the present case this exchange is asymmetrical—that the 'benefits' for the dependant are conditioned by the very existence

[9] On the legitimation of power see Max Weber, *Wirtschaft und Gesellschaft* (1956), pp. 122 ff. The problems of value consensus and of social integration by means of internalized norms are central to the functionalist school in sociology, perhaps best exemplified in the 'middle period' of Talcott Parsons. Cf. his *The Social System* (London, 1951). I have dealt with some of the criticisms of this approach in 'Conflict and Power in Society', *Int. Soc. Sc. J.*, xvii/3 (1965).

[10] P. M. Blau, *Exchange and Power in Social Life* (1964), p. 209.

[11] Ibid., pp. 91 & 92. Blau's work in this area follows up the earlier ideas of George Homans. See espec. the latter's *Social Behaviour* (New York, 1961).

of the system of unequal distribution of power and resources which operates to the advantage of the master. 'Once superiority is firmly rooted in political or economic structures, it enables an individual to extract benefits in the form of tribute from subordinates without any peril to his continued superiority over them.'[12] Nevertheless, within such a system, the dependant does receive certain gains from a close relationship with a benevolent master. In exchange for his services and his loyalty he can expect protection, occasional special help, and relative security in a very insecure world.[13] As Hutchinson has remarked:

a man who lacked patronage, who failed to recruit himself to some land-owner's following, was then, and in most part remains, in an unenviable position. Consequently, to the enforced dependency of slavery there was added in Brazil the voluntary but prudent dependency of the freeman.[14]

It would, however, be absurd to portray the essential features of this plantation micro-society exclusively in terms of the consensus which existed between its (free) members on the value of personal loyalty and on the legitimacy of the near-arbitrary authority of the head of the unit on the one hand, and of the benefits of exchange relations on the other.[15] All that authority and all those feelings of loyalty rested on the master's control of the main economic resources: land, capital (not unimportant in the sugar mills), and slaves. The latters' dependence was most clearly the result of the exercise of power—in this case naked physical force—and arguments in terms of loyalty and exchange are irrelevant. But also for the formally free dependants there was no way to flee from the superior power of the masters, whose control over all alternative sources of life support was virtually complete. As Blau has argued, the capacity to provide unilateral services that meet basic needs is the 'penultimate source of power', only surpassed by actual physical coercion.[16] With the penultimate as well as the final means of power at their disposal, the masters could always ensure compliance with their wishes should the built-in psychological mechanisms of obedience and loyalty fail to function.[17]

[12] Blau, p. 113.

[13] For a discussion of the changing position of the free dependants from early colonial times to the present day see Manuel Correia de Andrade, *A Terra e o homem no Nordeste* (1963), pt. 3.

[14] Hutchinson, *Soc. ruralis*, vi/1 (1966), p. 12.

[15] On the role of the church in underpinning this social structure see below, pp. 51–2.

[16] Blau, p. 22.

[17] A similar point, stressing the precedence of economic dependence over loyalty or exchange, is made for the Japanese case by Bennett & Ishino, p. 75. For an explicit comparison with Latin America: ibid., pp. 237–9.

This, then, is what the colonial structure looked like 'at the bases'. As for the top, the colonial government was a 'patrimonial' system,[18] in which the king claimed full personal power over the domain. He was concerned to prevent the emergence of a feudal-style independent landed aristocracy with inherited *political* rights, privileges, and positions; hence the royal administrative apparatus was made up of people bound to the king through personal, non-hereditary 'benefices', bureaucrats rather than feudal lords. As has been mentioned before, the efficacy of the central system of government in colonial Brazil was minimal, and for all practical purposes the king's power stopped at the gates of the plantations. But it is important to keep in mind the manner in which that power was exercised and the principles on which it rested: this has a bearing on the type of political structure that emerges after independence, when the functionaries of the central government come to hold their 'benefice' first from the Emperor, then from 'the state'. It was the peculiar meeting and meshing of the two levels, of the patriarchal local landholding units with the patrimonial central government, which gave Brazil's socio-political structure many of its most salient characteristics—ones which were retained until the middle of the twentieth century.

After independence, from the first half of the nineteenth century, some of the areas of activity which had hitherto been covered exclusively by the patriarchal family unit began to be taken over by formally independent structures. A differentiation of functions was taking place, with new organs coming into being which were given special tasks in the fields of government, politics, and religion. With the growth of the towns an urban upper class made its appearance. *Some* of its members—they usually came from landowning families—were used by the centralizing monarchy in the latter's attempts to strengthen its power at the expense of the rural patriarchate. Under the Empire,

the graduate—magistrate, provincial president, minister, chief of police— would be, in the almost mortal battles between imperial justice and the jurisdiction of the rural *pater familias*, the ally of the government against his own father or grandfather.[19]

[18] See Max Weber, ch. ix, espec. pp. 593 ff.; also Morse, in Hartz, *Founding of New Societies*, pp. 140 ff.

[19] Freyre, *Sobrados e mucambos* (1951), i. 139. This massive work describes the decadence of the rural patriarchate and the development of its urban equivalent, but, as the present quotation also shows, it does not sufficiently stress the continuities in the rural power structure.

A decentralized local-government machinery was set up, and political parties were formed as vehicles for the channelling of 'public' opinion. This was, of course, very limited indeed and expressed little more than the views of 'a few thousand landowners, lawyers, physicians, engineers, priests, officials, and businessmen', an electorate of not more than 1 per cent of the total population by the end of the Empire.[20]

In all, the change was less profound than might have been expected. The power base in the backlands had shifted only slightly, and the heads of the patriarchal families were neither inclined nor constrained to let things slip out of their control. To a large extent the upper class in the provincial towns remained closely identified with the rural patriarchate, through outlook, family ties, and economic connections. The Emperor seems to have been far less successful in securing the personal allegiance of those in the local-government bureaucracy than Freyre or Herring appear to suggest; after independence

the economically and socially dominant class ... appropriated the bureau-cratic apparatus which had been mounted by the Portuguese, and after changing its personnel put it at their own service without ever changing its original characteristics.[21]

Then they proceeded in the same way to 'take over' the new structures that had been created—and they became mayors of municipalities, judges, and political party bosses.

Outside the urban centres—and even to a large extent in the towns— those political parties were from the start vehicles for the expression of the personal power and the fulfilment of the personal ambitions of the heads of 'patriarchal clans'. They were never anything other than convenient receptacles for the captive votes of the dependants of the locally powerful. These parties gave Brazil an intensely personalist political system, which it retained throughout its modern history; their goal became that of raising the more powerful local men to the higher formal command posts of the political system. In its local mode of operation that political system came to be characterized by principles and mechanisms taken straight from the patriarchal plantation or *fazenda*. Foremost was the principle whereby authority was upheld and legitimized: it was again based on the expectation of personal loyalty. The holding of a formally established office, legally endowed with certain powers which gave its incumbent authority over other

---

[20] Herring, p. 734; also de Azevedo, pp. 77 & 93 ff.
[21] de Azevedo, p. 94.

men, was not itself enough to ensure compliance. The new functionaries or political leaders were but patriarchal masters in disguise; they expected—and rewarded—personal loyalty from those beneath them, and used their office (and their subordinates) to further their own interests, relying where necessary on their dependants to provide support.[22]

The position of the peasants in 'traditional' rural areas

Though slavery has disappeared, and the wheel of fortune has brought up some new landowning families and pushed some old ones down, many features of the system which developed in the course of the nineteenth century out of the multi-functional plantation unit are still recognizable in the more isolated rural areas today—despite the many significant changes which have come about, especially in the last twenty to thirty years. There are no more slave masters; the *senhores de engenho* producing sugar in the North-East *zona da mata* have given way to the managers of the highly mechanized and capitalized central sugar mills; and the relations of production have become those between agrarian capitalists and a landless proletariat. But elsewhere in the rural areas away from the South, such as in Minas Gerais, in Goiás, and in large parts of the North-East—in fact in most of the areas where MEB has operated—the large landowners (*fazendeiros*) and the substantial middlemen (*comerciantes*) form the pivots of the patron–dependant system, a network of relationships similar in countless ways to the one already described. A system which has, moreover, shown a remarkable capacity for expansion into the 'modern' urban areas, albeit in a somewhat modified form.

Like the society of patriarchal plantation units before it, the power upholding the present system of social relations in the rural areas outside the *zona da mata* is based on the ownership of the means of production and exchange—there is no need here to modify Marx's classical analysis. Landowners and storekeepers control the peasants' means of livelihood, and the locally available credit, and they act as gatekeepers[23] or communication filters between the peasants and the

[22] Ibid., p. 93.

[23] Also in the literal sense of the word. Benno Galjart, referring to Caio Prado Jr., remarks that the owner of a *fazenda* 'could manipulate to some extent the social contacts [of the peasants living on his land]; a visitor whom he did not like was not admitted' (Class and "Following" in Rural Brazil', *América Latina*, vii/3 (1964), p. 4 n. 4). Even on a modern sugar plantation this can still be true: see the incident with the *sindicato* described below p. 180 in the section on the Usina São Pedro.

outside world—including the government agencies dispensing credits for development, and the business interests from the towns linked in one way or another to the production or distribution of foodstuffs or export crops. No doubt many aspects of patron–dependant behaviour must be 'ultimately' traced back to these economically determined relations in the market. This is the brunt of the argument of Andre Gunder Frank, who rejects all analyses of the Brazilian agrarian structure which focus on 'feudal relations', and suggests that the behaviour of peasants and landowners is understandable only as part of the dynamics of monopoly capitalism. The types of tenancy or sharecropping arrangements, even the crops that are to be grown, vary in the same area 'at the pleasure of the farm owner or manager', a pleasure that is 'determined by hard economic and technological considerations' within a system where 'everything . . . is monopolized to an extreme degree'.[24] 'The monopolization of land [and credit] forces non-owners, and even small owners, to buy access to, or the fruits of, that key resource.'[25] Such considerations have come more to the fore as mobility from the countryside to the towns, and even more so that within the rural areas, has increased over recent years.[26]

These economic aspects of monopoly power have found their counterpart in political monopoly power. Before this is examined, it will be useful to describe the nature of the day-to-day relations of landowner and peasant, with their intermingled 'exchange' and 'consensual' or 'solidarity' aspects. The peasant's patron is the landowner on whose land he squats or with whom he has a sharecropping arrangement (rent-tenancies are less widespread in the traditional areas), or the merchant on whom he depends for the sale of his crop. The patron must protect the peasant from hostile outsiders (such as government officials), and come to his aid in the case of unexpected setbacks resulting from natural or economic causes. As most peasants still live at, or very near, subsistence level, little is needed to force them

[24] *Capitalism and Underdevelopment in Latin America* (1967), pp. 234 & 248; cf. also p. 259. In fact this is hardly an argument for rejecting the analogy with social conditions under feudalism: in the Middle Ages, too, such variations, dictated by the economic interests of the lord of the manor, occurred. See M. Postan, 'The Chronology of Labour Services', *Trans. Rl. Hist. Soc.*, 1937, pp. 169–92.

[25] Frank, p. 265.

[26] Ibid., p. 273. See also Galjart, *América Latina*, vii/3, p. 8. Though Gunder Frank does set up the occasional man of straw in his critique of the concepts of 'feudalism' or 'dual society', and fails to examine the 'consensual' and 'exchange' aspects of social relations in the countryside, his analysis is a healthy reminder of the *primacy*, under these circumstances, of economic power—of class.

to petition the patron for such a special favour. Other more usual 'favours' include the granting of a piece of land on which to plant subsistence crops, or that of allowing the dependant to buy necessities on credit between harvests—a doubtful privilege, which effectively binds the peasant to the patron in debt-peonage.

But not in all aspects of the relationship is the exchange so unequal, and in recent times the dependant has increasingly been seeking to maximize the exchange advantages inherent in those aspects of the relation built on the patron's traditional 'solidarity' obligations. One way of doing so is to ask the landowner to become godfather to his children. This creates at least certain socio-religious obligations to reinforce those of a socio-economic nature, and at best emotional bonds which make the patron genuinely interested in and concerned for the well-being of his dependant's family.[27]

In return the peasant has various duties.[28] In the first place he is expected to provide certain labour services for the landowner. This may either be free of charge (not so frequent nowadays), at a reduced wage, or at the locally accepted, standard working conditions—with wages frequently not reaching the legally prescribed minimum. But one of the most important expectations resting on the peasant is the fulfilment of certain *political* obligations in support of the patron. Formally this can only operate if the peasant is literate—a qualification for his participating in elections—but in fact electoral boards influenced by the locally powerful have been known in many instances to accept the registration of illiterate or semi-literate dependants.[29] These, then, can be relied upon to support the patron in his quest for political office, or to vote for the patron's candidates.

---

[27] Hutchinson (*Soc. ruralis*, vi/1, 1966, p. 14) notes that while previously 'the institution of *compadrio* merely ensured that none should be at a disadvantage in comparison with the average of the community ... the current movement is ... towards an expectation of exceptional advantage for the godchild', so that seeking the best godfather tends to be like looking for the most powerful patron.

[28] Richard N. Adams has defined paternalistic relations (as opposed to personalistic or impersonal ones) as those in which the employer has rights, the employee only privileges. See his 'Rural Labor', in John J. Johnson, ed., *Continuity and Change in Latin America* (1964), p. 69. Though the use of the term paternalistic is perhaps unfortunate, Adams has pointed to an important distinguishing characteristic of social relations. Lack of symmetry characterizes patron–dependant relations, especially as the traditional *mutual* obligation element begins to disappear: dependants know what is expected of them, what *duties* they have; patrons know under what circumstances they *might* give help and grant favours.

[29] Cf. Marcos Vinicios Vilaça & Roberto Cavalcanti de Albuquerque, *Coronel, coronéis* (1965), p. 38.

The traditional political processes

This aspect of the patron–dependant relation is usually referred to as *coronelismo*,[30] a word derived from *coronel* (colonel), the rank granted to the local commander of the National Guard, an auxiliary military force in the *municípios*, established in 1831, which gave the local men of power the legitimate command over para-military forces. During its heyday—roughly until 1865—the National Guard was, whatever its formal duties, in fact concerned with maintaining internal order rather than with defending (or enlarging) the national territory. After the demise of the National Guard—formally disbanded in 1918—the term *coronel* remained in use as a designation of the locally powerful: the *coronel* is a kind of local super-patron, who dominates not only his own direct dependants, but also his independent neighbours with less land than himself.[31] He secures the election of trusted lieutenants (very often members of his family) to the local political posts such as mayor, town councillor, or president of the town council.[32] He knows he can depend on the compliance of his dependants to cast their votes for the right candidates: this is part of the 'exchange' bargain, and part of the patterns of 'solidarity'. Peasants not 'voluntarily' convinced of the need to comply with the wishes of their patron are easily intimidated by a more blatant exercise of power. Even under ideal circumstances of secret balloting the *coronel* could have made the peasant believe that a 'wrong' vote would be found out. But in reality circumstances are far from ideal. Candidates present the voters with their own, differently printed, perhaps even differently coloured (and therefore easily recognizable) ballot-papers.[33] An area securely in the grip of a *coronel* can be virtually sealed off at election time, so that opposition ballots never reach the voters. If they do, pressure and intimidation at the ballot box is quite open, while secrecy hardly exists. When all these

[30] On the historical background see Nélson Werneck Sodré, *História militar do Brasil* (1965), espec. pp. 116–35. The classical discussion of the political operation of patron–dependant relations in Brazil's traditional rural areas is Victor Nunes Leal, *Coronelismo, enxada e voto* (1948).

[31] Vilaça & Albuquerque, p. 30 and Galjart, *América Latina*, vii/3 (1964), p. 4.

[32] The situation pertaining in 1966 in the Franqueira area, analysed in ch. 12, is instructive, also in respect of the relations with the higher level of the political system shortly to be discussed.

[33] One of the significant and positive innovations of President Goulart's administration was the introduction of the so-called *cédula única*, the ballot paper with all candidates' names printed on it. Marshal Castelo Branco, however, reintroduced the *cédula avulsa*, the separate ballot paper, in 1966 for the rural areas.

expedients fail, some political bosses have on occasion not hesitated to resort to the destruction of electoral documents or the annulment of urns with unfavourable returns. Finally the fear of post-election reprisals will tend to keep voters of doubtful loyalty in line. Individuals may have been handed specially marked ballot papers 'which had better turn up in the urn', or whole communities can be victimized if their votes are not homogeneously in line with the *coronel*'s wishes.[34] No wonder dependants think twice before voting against their patron's candidates.

As in the case of the social and economic aspects of the relationship, some sort of reciprocity or exchange operates in the political sphere. Again, as against the dependant's *duties*, often enforced by powerful sanctions, the patron allows the dependant to enjoy certain *privileges* and dispenses *favours*. Dependants will be rewarded individually with minor jobs in the municipal bureaucracy or public service: to be made municipal street sweeper or park attendant is a real favour in a world of poverty and insecurity. Lieutenants—also, of course, dependants— will be given more substantial posts; their children may be made school teachers. The more rewarding teaching posts, especially in the second- ary schools, are state rather than municipal appointments: these, too, are usually at the disposal of the local political chieftain. How this comes to happen must now be examined: it points to one of the most significant aspects of the political operation of patron–dependant relations.

A local political boss not only secures the election of his own men to municipal posts, thus giving him a secure grip over the political machine in his domain. He also delivers the votes of his dependants upwards, so to speak as a ready-made parcel contributing to the election of a state or federal deputy, of the state's governor, or even of the President of the Republic. If the *coronel* is a powerful man, with many votes at his disposal, the state deputy may in fact be someone with whom he has close and intimate links, a man who knows that under the system of proportional representation he can get elected on nothing more than the support which the *coronel*'s electoral herd provides. In that case the deputy will be indebted to the local boss, little more than a tool in the latter's hands. More frequent, however, is the case where the regimented votes of the *coronel* are not sufficient to

---

[34] For a description of the various fraudulent or coercive practices see Vilaça & Albuquer- que, p. 38. Cf. also the discussion of pressure on the community in the Franqueira area, below, pp. 236–7, 240.

elect a state deputy (let alone a federal deputy). Then a certain amount of bargaining will go on between the party managers at the state level and the local bosses, with votes of dependants being exchanged for leverage on the state power structure, where both funds and decisions are controlled, affecting the *coronel* and his *município*.[35]

Almost taken for granted will be the right of the local boss to nominate his candidates for certain state-controlled posts, certainly those within his *município*. But bargaining will also be concerned with broader decisions: whether a particular road will be paved, a state school founded, or the electricity grid extended to the *município*.[36] In the drought-ridden North-East the building (and precise location) of dams and reservoirs has been a traditional instrument of political bargains; by this means large numbers of big landowners with political influence have been enabled to increase the value of their *fazendas*, often in total disregard of the interests of the other inhabitants.

Some of this political bargaining does, of course, lead to benefits for the *município* as a whole, but even then they are usually concentrated in its administrative centre. Marshall Wolfe has remarked that in general in Latin America public services are concentrated in this urban nucleus, and that 'any financial aid received from the higher authorities is spent there, largely on projects that will constitute lasting monuments to the administration of the time—public buildings and parks.'[37] Thus even there improvements are to the advantage of the local upper class of landowners, merchants, and professional men, who usually live, or have a second house in 'town'.

It must be noted that, at least to some degree, this process of exchange of votes for state or federal favours is self-reinforcing. Once a political boss has secured some 'co-operation' from the higher authorities, he is enabled to use the extra power at his disposal to fortify and solidify his loyal clientele. But, in turn, a loyal following of dependants secures for the *coronel* the control of administrative positions which hold the keys to unlock access to the state level of power.

[35] A truly splendid example of the way in which the votes were delivered upwards is given in Vilaça and Albuquerque., p. 90. In 1947 the state leadership of the Pernambuco PSD cabled just before the elections to one of their men, a *coronel* in the *município* of Bom Conselho: 'Please reserve entire vote Bom Conselho for Barros Barreto'.

[36] An interesting case study with many data of relevance to this discussion is Belden H. Paulson, *Local Political Patterns in Northeast Brazil* (1964).

[37] 'Rural Settlement Patterns and Social Change', *Latin American Research R.*, i/2 (1966), p. 22.

The lines of communication between the legally constituted public entity, the *município*, and the higher levels of public authority pass through him or his representatives in the local government. It becomes extremely difficult, if not impossible, for the *município* to take actions or formally make reports which jeopardize his position.[38]

In fact in pre-1930 Brazil, the *only* significance of electoral struggles in areas where rival *coronéis* disputed each other's supremacy lay in the privilege of backing the state government and, as a result, receiving its all-important support.[39]

Recent changes in grass-roots rural politics

In some areas things have hardly changed since the political functions previously fulfilled by the plantation or *fazenda* were taken over by formally separate public organizations. In others political patron-dependant relationships have been modified in important respects, especially in the course of the last thirty years. Certain aspects of traditional patron–dependency, as described above, have been transferred into the presumably non-traditional spheres of urban politics, trade unionism, industry, and the civil service. But it would be foolish to suggest that politics and social relations, even in the traditional areas of Brazil, can be understood without introducing some modifications to the structure as outlined so far.

In many places peasants no longer regard as legitimate the demand of *patrão* or *coronel* that their vote should be cast for him, as part of a generalized obligation of dependant to patron. Despite the power of local landowners and *coronéis* to 'punish' those who do not vote 'correctly', the peasants usually no longer simply *give* their vote as a matter of course. They have learned that votes are valuable merchandise, and that one can make use of one's eligibility to participate in elections and at least tacitly demand a price for the exercise of the vote in the required way. In the most traditional areas of the countryside this new-found power may as yet amount to very little, based as it is on no more than a vague stirring of consciousness on the part of the peasant, and a vague uneasiness about changes occurring elsewhere on the part of the *coronel*. It may mean that voters are not only transported to the polls and treated to some kind of entertainment, but

[38] Paulson, p. 51.

[39] Juarez R. Brandão Lopes, 'Some Basic Developments in Brazilian Politics and Society', in Eric N. Baklanoff, ed., *New Perspectives of Brazil* (1966), p. 69. See also p. 70 n. 18, where Lopes refers to the earlier-cited pioneer study of Leal.

that they are given meals, shoes, clothing, or even money.[40] It may also mean that at election time individuals or peasant communities are more likely to be successful in their quest for 'favours'.[41] Vilaça and Albuquerque have described this change as one from the *voto-de-cabresto* (loosely translated: cattle vote) to the *voto-mercadoria* (vote-as-merchandise)—'the vote begins to be a business proposition'.[42] But although these changes result in the raising of the cost to the *coronel* of a vote, by themselves they do not yet constitute a fundamental change in the nature of the exercise and acquisition of political power.

There are, however, places where outside influences have penetrated to a larger extent. This is mainly a result of the increasing complexity of the political structure at the state level, which is obviously more responsive to the overall changes occurring in the society, felt in the first place in urban centres such as state capitals. This increasing complexity means that political groups in opposition to the ruling party can no longer be simply disregarded in matters of appointments, the use of state funds or federal aid, or the drawing up of public-works programmes. Such changes complicate the previously existing 'arrangements' between the *coronel* and the party bosses, who now have to take more account of the formal rules of the political game. It thus becomes increasingly difficult to preserve the *coronel*'s 'fief' from some encroachment by outsiders, people not directly subordinated to him in a patron–dependant relationship, especially through increasingly independent appointments to the judiciary, or because of the proliferation of federal agencies operating throughout the country.[43] It is only a short step to the appearance of vote-collecting newcomers in what has so far been the *coronel*'s preserve. Such a development does herald an important change, for it effectively breaks the previous automatic monopoly of the exercise of political power and increases the peasant's awareness of his value in the whole procedure, even if initially this involves little more than competitive bidding for his support. It may be helpful to distinguish this new situation by reserving another term for it, frequently used in this context: that of *patron–client* as opposed to patron–dependant relationship. This indicates the element of personal choice now entering into the relation which a person establishes with *a*

---

[40] See Vilaça & Albuquerque, p. 39.
[41] See below, pp. 31–3, 159, 239–40, 250.
[42] Vilaça & Albuquerque, p. 39.
[43] Cf. Lopes, in Baklanoff, p. 70.

patron, with the patron he has *chosen*.[44] In recent times another development has been occurring, especially in the towns—as will be seen later—but also in the countryside, which has started to undermine the wholly personal nature of the relationship between (political) patron and client. Though politicians may still seek to secure votes by such procedures as the provision of a job or a bed in a hospital, they now also present 'platforms' which, if in no sense ideological, are at least political by being concerned with promises from which individuals would benefit only indirectly, through their community—promises of electricity, paved streets, new roads, and so on.

The *ligas*: reflections on 'leaders' and 'followers'

By taking the traditional patron–dependant relationship as a starting point (rather than the common-class position of the peasantry, which objectively is equally relevant), the changes that have come about in the rural areas appear in their proper perspective—although, as will shortly be seen, the continuity with traditional structures can also be over-emphasized. One of the most widely discussed developments is the appearance in the countryside from the mid-1950s onwards of various peasant movements and peasant organizations, at first the peasant leagues or *ligas camponeses*, later, largely in reaction to them, the rural trade unions or *sindicatos rurais*. The *ligas*, especially, have been regarded by various observers as a major break-through into non-traditional, class-oriented, patterns. Thus in a recent paper Aníbal Quijano has classified the *ligas* as an example of revolutionary agrarianism, seeing them as successful organizations led by the peasants themselves. He has suggested that the *sindicatos* are also peasant-controlled, and that both phenomena show that the peasants are well on their way to developing class-consciousness.[45] Hence a brief examination of their activities, and particularly of their leadership patterns, should be of interest in this context. The *ligas* will be discussed in this section, but the examination of the *sindicatos* (so much more important in relation to Catholic initiatives) must be postponed till Chapter 6. Both *ligas* and *sindicatos* certainly represented a challenge to the unbridled 'rule' of the *patroës*. The question that must be con-

[44] Another way to distinguish the new situation would be to call it one of 'achieved', as opposed to the previously existing 'ascribed', relations of patronage.

[45] Aníbal Quijano Obregón, 'Contemporary Peasant Movements', in S. M. Lipset & A. Solari, eds., *Elites in Latin America* (1967).

sidered more closely is whether they presented the peasants (as clients) merely with an alternative *patrão*, or whether their presence in the countryside heralded a totally new mode of consciousness and organization.

The emergence in 1955 of the first peasant league, out of a friendly society on the Fazenda Galilea in the *município* of Vitória de Santo Antão, thirty miles west of Recife, has been extensively documented, and only a very brief recapitulation follows.[46] A mutual-benefit association of the share-croppers of that *fazenda* came to be regarded by the landowner as potentially dangerous and 'communistic', even though he had earlier agreed to become its honorary president. The dissolution of the association was demanded, and the peasants were threatened with eviction from their lands, something the landowner had apparently also wished to proceed with for economic reasons.[47] The ensuing conflict assumed a legal character, and the peasants went for advice and help to Francisco Julião, at that time an unknown lawyer and politician from Recife, who was alternate deputy for the small *Partida Socialista do Brasil* (PSB) in the state Assembly. He fought the case not only in the courts but also, later, in the political arena—and eventually obtained in 1959 a decree from the state Assembly expropriating the property on behalf of the peasants.

Julião gained a certain amount of fame as a result of this episode. Soon he began, with a gradually growing number of helpers, to promote similar organizations among other groups of peasants, whose living conditions were similar to those on the Fazenda Galilea. The aims of the new organizations, now generally known as *ligas*, were at first relatively modest.[48] The *ligas* sought to 'mobilize' the peasants for certain limited objectives. The most important of these was to strengthen the peasants' rights of property over or occupation of the land they worked. This in itself was already a significant departure from the central conception of patron–dependant relations, where the landowner had given *favours* in exchange for tasks performed as *duties* by the peasants. The *ligas*, then, fought for greater security of tenure

---

[46] For the origins and developments of the *ligas* see Galjart, *América Latina*, vii/3 (1965), pp. 10 ff.; Robert E. Price, *Rural Unionization in Brazil* (1964, mimeo.), pp. 41–4; Cynthia N. Hewitt, *An Analysis of the Peasant Movement of Pernambuco, Brazil, 1961–4* (1966, mimeo.), *passim*; de Andrade, pp. 243 ff.; and of course Julião's own account: Francisco Julião, *Que são as ligas camponeses?* (1962).

[47] de Andrade, p. 108.

[48] Cf. Julião's 'Ten Commandments', as reproduced in de Andrade, pp. 247 ff.; or the 'Charter of Enfranchisement of the Peasant', reproduced as App. A. in Julião.

(and the supposedly better living conditions that would go with it), and attempted to achieve this by legal as well as political means. They regarded it as essential that the peasants should be able to organize—another major change from the reality of dependency relations, where each peasant is in an active relationship only with his own *patrão*, and the peasantry as a whole is completely atomized—but the right to organize was often disputed by the landowners, who used the local police to break up meetings or intimidate the peasants. Another demand of the *ligas* was the vote, from which most peasants were excluded because of the requirement of literacy; not, of course, in order to vote for the candidate of the *patrão*, but in order to elect genuine representatives of their 'class'. Local peasant organization was to be coupled with local political pressure: the latter, it was hoped, would break the landlords' hold over administration, justice, and the police.

The *ligas* also had certain specifically economic demands, regarding the 'relations of production' under which most peasants had to live. They came out strongly against the traditional system, which was discussed earlier in this chapter and which involved labour performed without payment or at a very low wage in exchange for a plot of land on which to plant subsistence crops. They argued that these traditional labour duties, as well as share-cropping in general, simply kept the peasants ignorant of the real price paid by them for the 'privilege' of working a piece of land. Similarly they turned strongly against the practice of payment by means of *vales de barracão*, coupons to be exchanged in the *fazenda*'s own store, where prices were always considerably higher than in the local market. Later the demands of the *ligas* became more revolutionary. Although Julião never achieved a consistent and really well-elaborated ideological position, the tone of his statements, books, and articles—effectively the sole expression of the ideology of the *ligas*—gained in stridency in the early 1960s. New slogans appeared: 'Liberation of the peasants', 'Land to the tiller'. From a reform of the tenure system the *ligas* moved to demand its wholesale transformation.[49]

When Julião began to organize other groups of peasants on the lines of the original association at Galilea, he concentrated on those living under traditional tenure and labour relations and had little to do with the growing landless proletariat in the sugar zone of the North-East.

[49] See the extensive interview with Julião published in Lêda Barreto, *Julião, Nordeste, revolução* (1963), pp. 86 ff.

This decision was based on legal, financial, and economic considerations: on each count, he felt, the landless workers lacked the means to conduct their struggle.[50] Even though the legal relationship between peasant and landowner may have been unclear, the former could attempt to use the civil code—accepted as the foundation of social and economic relationships by the landowner—to improve his position.[51] Again, this was a step in the direction of getting the peasant to shift from thinking in terms of privileges and favours granted by the *patrão* to seeing himself as a citizen with rights under the law.[52] His landholding, moreover, did provide him with a basis for subsistence, however meagre, and surplus produce could be sold in the local market. The landless labourer, on the contrary, was totally dependent upon the wage he received, and more often than not indebted to his employer through his purchases at the *barracão*.

Julião, therefore, thought he had good reasons for expecting success among the more traditional peasants, and judging from the publicity he received at the time, there is little doubt that his impact was substantial.[53] But it must be asked what 'success' really meant. Thus one returns to the original question, namely whether the *ligas* should be seen as representing a fundamental break with traditional social relations in the rural areas, or whether they involved no more than some kind of internal transformation—and perhaps evolution—of these. In this connection it is necessary to consider the ideas of Benno Galjart, who has held with some insistence that the *ligas* were nothing but the 'followings' of the old *coronéis* in a new form, with the leaders of the *ligas*—and, incidentally, also of the *sindicatos*—acting in ways equivalent to those of the *patrões* whom they replaced.[54] The point has also been made by Anthony Leeds, who has specifically examined Julião's case.[55] Leeds has, in fact, accused Julião of using the cause of the peasants merely to further his own political career. He suggests that

[50] See Julião, pp. 50 ff.

[51] Cf. Comité Interamericano para el Desarrollo Agrícola, *Posse e uso da terra e desenvolvimento socio-económico do setor agrícola: Brasil* (1966), p. 346, where it is suggested that once a suit was filed, the situation was frozen, and the peasant could not be moved from his land until judgment had been pronounced: a matter which might take years.

[52] This is further discussed below, pp. 37, 48, 112, 264.

[53] References to some of the many contemporary accounts in newspapers as well as journals and reviews can be found in Diana C. Dumoulin, *The Rural Labor Movement in Brazil* (1964, mimeo.), p. 4, and in Anthony Leeds, 'Brazil and the Myth of Francisco Julião', in Joseph Maier and Richard W. Weatherhead, eds., *Politics of Change in Latin America* (1964), pp. 224 ff.

[54] Galjart, pp. 18 ff. The discussion of the *sindicatos* is taken up in ch. 6.

[55] Leeds, in Maier & Weatherhead.

Julião acted as a new-style benevolent *coronel* whose political power rested on the support of his followers. Leeds argues further that Julião used this power to obtain favours for himself and for his followers by manipulating the traditional network of politicians of which he became a member. Leeds arrived at this evaluation of the leadership of the *ligas* after discovering, as a result of his interest in career patterns, the operation of high-level patrimonial networks in Brazilian society.[56] For him Julião was just another typical upper-class Brazilian careerist, pursuing his goal of fame and power through a series of opportunistic steps which lacked consistency from a professional as well as from an ideological point of view—a careerist in contact with others similarly engaged, who all used each other for their reciprocal self-promotion.

Leeds received indirect support for some of his views though not for his imputation that Julião consciously 'used' the peasants for his own ends, an assessment which I too regard as incorrect, from a rather unlikely source. In a most perceptive analysis of the state of affairs among the North-Eastern peasantry in the sociological journal supported by the Brazilian Communist Party, Fragman Carlos Borges argued late in 1962 not only that Julião underestimated the importance of struggling to achieve limited but real successes for the peasants—he was subordinating everything increasingly to his broad revolutionary demands—but also that he addressed himself less and less to the peasantry, and more and more to students in the towns.[57] Julião's 'constituency' was apparently shifting, his 'career' better served by politicking in town than by helping the peasants in the countryside.

Looked at from the perspective of leadership, then, Galjart and Leeds are stressing the continuity with traditional behaviour and saying that nothing much has really changed: *plus ça change, plus c'est la même chose*. But what about the other party to the relationship—the peasants themselves? Did they act as a mere 'traditional following', did they act as a 'class', or did they perhaps act as something in between? Galjart has also argued that peasant behaviour in the emerging peasant movements should be considered as essentially continuous with their behaviour as dependants. He contends that they saw these organizations—and the *sindicatos*—fundamentally as providers of personal services of various kinds: medical, legal, economic,

---

[56] See his 'Brazilian Careers and Social Structure: an Evolutionary Model and Case History', *Amer. Anthropol.*, Dec. 1964.

[57] 'O Movimento Camponês no Nordeste', *Estudos sociais*, Dec. 1962, p. 259.

even educational, and hardly as entities which promoted their collective class interests.[58] Lêda Barreto, in her sympathetic journalistic portrait of Julião, remarks that the peasants regarded him as 'um doutor seu', a man who was compared with the messianic leader Antônio Conselheiro, or the bandit leader Lampião, both clear exponents of pre-political (and traditional) challenges to the social structure.[59] Galjart seems to be right in his suggestion that the peasants hardly acted politically, with a view to their collective interests. One can go further: in most areas the peasants were only very dimly beginning to see their interests as a class; they were, in Marxian terms, no more than an incipient 'class for themselves'.

And yet in most cases it is also misleading merely to classify them as traditional followings, a point which has been forcefully made by Gerrit Huizer.[60] He has suggested that one may well be able to arrange 'followings' on a continuum. At one extreme he places a type corresponding to the traditional patron–dependant relationship, where a 'traditional following' consists of a number of dependants in relation to one patron. The latter's position is, according to Huizer, ultimately backed by force. But at the other end of the continuum one finds the 'rational following', made up of a group of people who have freely chosen to follow a particular leader. Such a following is likely to disintegrate once the leader no longer produces the desired and expected results.[61] Earlier, the situation in which one patron is chosen from a range of possible ones has been called one of patron–client relations. The choice of the same person as patron (or leader) by a large number of people does not necessarily mean anything beyond the fact that they all act individually, from enlightened self-interest (the Galjart argument, further discussed below, in relation to the urban areas). But such a collective choice *may*—perhaps only gradually—lead to an awareness of common interests among the people who, in Huizer's terminology,

---

[58] *América Latina*, vii/3 (1964), p. 13. A similar point is made even for industrial unions by Juarez Brandão Lopes, *Sociedade industrial no Brasil* (1964), pp. 56 ff. & 160.

[59] Barreto, p. 113. For a brief discussion of Brazilian messianic movements see my 'Religion, the Church and Social Change', in C. Véliz, ed., *The Politics of Conformity in Latin America* (1967), p. 197; the broader problems of messianism and banditry as traditional responses may be approached through Eric Hobsbawm's classic *Primitive Rebels* (Manchester, 1959), or through Yonina Talmon's 'Millenarian Movements', *Eur. J. Sociol.* vii/2 (1966). Very useful is also Maria Isaura Pereira de Queiroz, *Réforme et révolution dans les sociétés traditionnelles* (1968).

[60] 'Some Notes on Community Development and Rural Social Research', *América Latina*, viii/3, (1965).

[61] Ibid., p. 142.

make up the 'rational following'. The common interests of which they become aware may be those of citizens demanding compliance with the laws, they may be those of local community members who would benefit from 'community development', but they may also come to be those of members of a class collectively exploited by another class.[62] Huizer does not seem to have taken the first two possibilities into account: he implies that as one moves on the continuum towards the 'rational following', one approaches a situation in which a 'class-for-itself' can be said to exist. Though this does not appear to be valid in all circumstances, Huizer may well have been right for the landless plantation workers not organized in *ligas*: much of the evidence points to the fact that they were increasingly beginning to perceive their interests in collective terms as a class.

Returning to the nature of the transformation of rural social relations wrought by the appearance of the *ligas camponeses*, there is no doubt that Julião's 'agitation' caused more than a stir in the national press, and more than a passing scare among conservatives and mild reformists alike. The accounts of peasant enthusiasm at the meetings held all over the country to found new *ligas* bear witness to Julião's impact—though one must, of course, beware of the exaggeration which was grist to the mill of those who wished to emphasize the dangers in the development. Few data exist about what happened to the *ligas* once they had been founded. A certain amount of peasant violence and the illegal occupation of estates continued to be reported throughout 1963 and the early part of 1964. Despite the general paucity of evidence I am inclined to conclude that in most areas the *ligas* led a rather shadowy existence, especially after Julião had been elected one of the federal deputies for Pernambuco late in 1962. The *ligas* no doubt helped the peasants further along the road of emancipation from patron–dependency (though not always from patron–clientage). But I would argue that under non-revolutionary circumstances this road is both long and arduous, and does not lead directly to class-consciousness, let alone class action. Certain conditions have to prevail for a certain period of time for this to happen. One of these conditions is real grass-roots participation. But that seems to have been fairly limited in most *ligas*.[63] Hence the difficulty in accepting Quijano's view that the

[62] This problem is discussed further in the Conclusions.

[63] In this connection it is worth noting what Julião himself remarked to the journalist Antônio Callado: 'Agitating is wonderful. But organizing—that's what is difficult' (Antônio Callado. *Tempo de Arraes, padres e comunistas no revolução sem violência* (1965), p. 58).

ligas had developed into a revolutionary agrarian movement—despite the change in the professed aims of the leadership.[64] And it will be seen in Chapter 6 how similar considerations apply to the rural *sindicatos*. It is, therefore, very doubtful whether these organizations had gone far in laying a solid foundation for peasant *mobilization*, for the creation, that is, both of commitment to action and of appropriate organizational forms to translate that commitment into observable behaviour.[65]

Urban changes

Although this study will not be directly concerned with the situation among the urban masses, in the present context a rapid examination of developments in the towns provides useful comparative material. Among the urban poor, where many are relatively recent migrants from the backlands, the transformation from a docile herd of voters to a collection of individuals who shrewdly calculate the advantages to be gained for themselves from the political game is virtually complete. Previously, casting his vote for the candidate of the *patrão* was one of the unquestioned means by which the dependant fulfilled his side of the bargain; now the vote is used to strengthen his bargaining position. Apparently a good deal of bargaining occurs.

The electors request the candidates to provide all kinds of things: a job, a dwelling, water, light, medical help, legalization of one's shack and even a telephone. The candidate is mainly seen as an intermediary in regard of services and favours, as an agent of the shanty-town dwellers *vis-à-vis* the negligent authorities.[66]

Of course a candidate who can deliver any of these goods *before* the election (rather than promise them for *afterwards*) does have an edge on his opponents.

In the large cities, where election procedures are on the whole fair, with secret balloting and the use of a single ballot paper for all candidates, voter intimidation is not easy. Nor can one hope to find out with any degree of certainty how a man cast his vote: the most one

---

[64] Quijano, in Lipset & Solari, espec. pp. 312, 322.
[65] See the seminal study by J. P. Nettl, *Political Mobilization* (1967), espec. pp. 32 f. & 70.
[66] Carlos Alberto de Medina, *A Favela e o demagogo* (1964), p. 82. See also Lopes, in Baklanoff, p. 65.

can do is go by his behaviour during the campaign. That behaviour may have been intentionally ambiguous: an elector, to be on the safe side, may have provided himself with a plausible claim on more than one candidate, in order to be sure that after the election he will be able to benefit from the advantages which the man in power can offer to his clients or followers.[67] On the other hand he who wants to gamble on the success of a particular candidate, and ensure a relatively secure position of privilege and relative certainty in the flow of significant favours, will have to demonstrate his loyalty rather than merely protest it. He must give public demonstrations of esteem, supply information on potentially helpful or harmful third parties, and be willing to be used for certain 'jobs' by his patron.[68]

Here, then, as in the countryside, the almost automatic operation of patron–dependant relations (especially from the side of the dependant) is breaking down with the availability of potential alternative patrons. And yet in the towns, as in the rural areas, the basic mechanism on this level—from which a departure has only recently begun to occur[69]—remains that of the exchange of support for *favours*, for a reciprocation to which no *rightful* claim exists. This results from the structurally conditioned highly unequal access to scarce resources on the one hand, and the very low average income of the masses on the other. Eric Wolf has suggested that such a situation is in general conducive to the emergence or perpetuation of patron–client ties, which should 'prove especially functional in situations where the formal institutional structure of societies is weak and unable to deliver a sufficiently steady supply of goods and services, especially to the terminal [i.e. lowest] levels of the social order'.[70]

The candidates who do manage to gather sufficient votes to get themselves elected as municipal councillors, state or federal deputies, as a result of their deeds, cash, or promises, usually represent fairly narrow economic interests—perhaps even those of one particular enterprise.[71] These narrow interests are then pursued in further complex wheelings and dealings, mutual promises of help, coalitions and higher clientage structures, with legislative power being forged around limited transactions of give and take, and executive power

---

[67] See de Medina, pp. 83 ff.
[68] Eric R. Wolf, 'Kinship, Friendship and Patron-Client Relations in Complex Societies', in M. Banton, ed., *The Social Anthropology of Complex Societies* (1966), p. 17.
[69] See below, pp. 36–7.
[70] See Wolf, in Banton, p. 17.
[71] See Lopes, in Baklanoff, p. 65.

being used for particularistic purposes.[72] The relationship of those people to the *cabo eleitoral*, the vote-getter in the electoral district—a person rather like the precinct captain in boss politics in the United States—continues very much in a clientelistic vein. The *cabo eleitoral* will work for his candidate in the expectation of extra rewards if the latter is successful in his quest for office—money, of course, but more importantly some kind of position which will increase his own potential for distributing patronage, and raise his own power and prestige.

In this system election is obviously neither the results of ideological commitments, nor of the *class* interests of the electorate. It is a system which has contributed greatly to party political weakness in Brazil. In town and countryside alike party support is on the whole quite irrelevant to the creation of an electoral base. On the contrary: parties exist by virtue of the votes which politicians are willing to bring to them. Thus before its extinction in 1965 the *Partido Trabalhista Brasileiro* (PTB) used to command the loyalty of many workers in the cities more as a result of the 'paternalistic' policies of its founder, Getúlio Vargas, than for ideological reasons or because of the existence of 'class-consciousness'. This becomes clearer in the context of the emergence of *populismo* as a political style in Brazil, a development which will be analysed in the next chapter.

---

[72] On the higher clientage structures see the excellent second part of the paper by Anthony Leeds cited in n. 56 above. See also F. H. Cardoso, *Empresário industrial e desenvolvimento econômico no Brasil* (1964), espec. pp. 105–6, 126 ff., 133 ff., 165 ff.

3

Aspects of National Politics and Government since 1930

The first Vargas era (1930–45)

WITH the reference to Getúlio Vargas at the end of the preceding chapter, the point has been reached at which the focus of this discussion must change. The analysis of Brazil's socio–political structure that has been given so far proceeded from the bases of society upwards. The present chapter will look again at this structure, but this time from the vantage point of national government and politics. Its historical discussion is mainly intended as a brief guide for readers who are not familiar with those political developments which are referred to again and again in subsequent chapters, and obviously has no pretensions to serious historiography, being entirely based on secondary sources.[1]

Vargas had come to power in 1930, after an armed insurrection which brought to an end the political system of the so-called Old Republic. Till that year effective national power had been shared by the two most important states, São Paulo and Minas Gerais; the presidency had been held alternately by a representative of one or the other. The formal institutions of democracy hardly functioned; elections were rigged, and the federal government operated on behalf of nothing but a small section of the nation's politically articulate forces. The revolutionaries of 1930 represented those groups and interests which had so far been deprived of the benefits of support from the federal government—a government which had seemed to run

---

[1] Until recently there existed no single satisfactory account of the period since 1930, in Portuguese or in English. Various sources, such as José Maria Bello, *A History of Modern Brazil*, trans. by James L. Taylor (Stanford, 1966), Charles Morazé, *Les trois âges du Brésil*, (Paris, 1954), Nelson Werneck Sodré, *História militar do Brasil* (1965), had been consulted when Thomas E. Skidmore published his excellent *Politics in Brazil, 1930–45* (1967). It is to Skidmore's account, by far the most complete, accurate and accessible, that reference is mainly made in the following pages.

the country largely in the interest of the Paulista coffee planters and their landowning allies in Minas Gerais.[2]

In the first place they acted for the states left out by the political and economic schemes of Paulistas and Mineiros: those in the North-East as well as those in the South—but especially Rio Grande do Sul. In the second place they represented the urban middle class, which had greatly increased in numbers and importance during the first decades of the twentieth century, and which formed the backbone of the liberal constitutionalists. Their chief political goal was more 'authentic' representation: 'voting must be honestly supervised and the ballots honestly counted'.[3] Another important group were the younger professional military (the *tenentes*), who were 'semi-authoritarian nationalists', concerned with 'national regeneration' and modernization.[4]

Vargas juggled masterfully with the support of the various groups that had backed him in 1930. Some got more than might have been expected at the time of the Revolution—the coffee planters, for instance[5]—others got less. The man who gained most of all was Vargas. He managed the Brazil of the 1930s—even after his assumption of full powers as dictator in 1937—by means of a series of compromises between various politically and economically important groups in the country. The coffee planters were given continued financial support; the military were given promotion and a larger establishment; the middle classes were given real political participation and a fast growing bureaucracy in which they could find employment at the expense of the state;[6] and, finally, the traditional landowners were given the privilege of being left alone—which meant the abandonment of the rural masses (at that time still over two-thirds of Brazil's total population)

---

[2] Skidmore (p. 335 n. 21) contests the view that the revolt was against the dominance of the coffee planters; he suggests that they were equally dissatisfied with the federal government. This may have been true in the year immediately preceding the Revolution, but it seems to be quite well established that they had exclusively benefited from federal policies for years, and that resentment against them had been building up for a long time.

[3] Ibid., p. 13.

[4] Ibid., p. 9.

[5] The classical analysis of how Vargas's policies helped both coffee planters and industrialization is contained in Celso Furtado, *The Economic Growth of Brazil* (1963), chs. 31–2. A brief summary is found in his 'Political Obstacles to Economic Growth in Brazil', in C. Véliz, ed., *Obstacles to Change in Latin America* (1965), pp. 146–7.

[6] The transformation in the structure of the state as a result of this growth of the public bureaucracy (the emergence of the 'cartorial state') has been described briefly by Hélio Jaguaribe, *Economic and Political Development* (1968), p. 144, and in more detail (though also with considerably more obscure and obscuring jargon) by Cândido Mendes de Almeida, *Nacionalismo e desenvolvimento* (1963), espec. ch. 4.

to their lot of dependence and exploitation. The power base of none of the sectors was sufficiently great to enable it consistently to impose its views on the government and have its interests prevail, and one group was deftly played off against another. But Vargas did not rest content with relying on this type of shifting support. In order to keep a substantial measure of control over the bargains he had to strike with these 'dominant' groups, he needed a power base of his own. This he found in the urban working class.[7]

At the time when Vargas came to power, the urban working class was still relatively insignificant.[8] Various factors, among them the spurt of industrialization brought about by the need for import substitution resulting from the Great Depression, led to a large influx of rural migrants into the towns. There is no need to stress again that the early behaviour and attitudes of these new urban masses were largely derived from the patron–dependant complex. The significant development which occurred in the course of the late 1930s and early 1940s was that the actions of Vargas—and of the state apparatus identified with him—came to be calculated to make him appear as the super-patron of the workers and the poor, especially in the towns. On the one hand he saw to it that whenever possible his favours came to specific people, direct from him (a sewing machine, a job), so that he played the role of patron in the traditional, well-established manner. But on the other hand he transformed the personal patron–client relationship into one between himself and whole categories of people, whole classes. In this new mode of operation, which Brazilian political analysts, including Weffort, have called *populismo*, his 'favours' consisted in social security and labour legislation, very advanced for their time.[9] In 1937 a new trade union structure

---

[7] Francisco C. Weffort has been engaged in a sociopolitical analysis of this period for some years. His latest—and most successful—formulation, 'Le Populisme dans la politique brésilienne', can be found in *Les Temps modernes*, Oct. 1967. The following analysis is much indebted to Weffort's ideas.

[8] Even in 1940 the proportion of the labour force in secondary activities was no higher than 9 per cent—with primary activities accounting for 71 per cent. See Octavio Ianni, *Industrialização e desenvolvimento social no Brasil* (1963), p. 143.

[9] Though Vargas differed in certain respects from other *populistas* who only appeared on the scene after 1945—men such as Adhemar de Barros, João Goulart, and, in his own quixotic way, Jânio Quadros—he did fit into the category. Skidmore (p. 83) suggests that although he had occasionally 'struck the populist pose', his approach 'remained essentially paternalistic, reflecting his own estimate of the growing but still limited political consciousness of urban workers.' Skidmore's use of the term paternalist seems to imply that Vargas operated on the traditional lines of personal patron–client relations, which was certainly partly true.

was set up, in corporatist fashion, and all unions came under the direction of the Ministry of Labour. A pyramid of urban clientage relations was thus created in the *sindicatos*, and the unions became instruments by which the government could manipulate the masses.

Brazil's working class was, therefore, handed its rights 'on a silver platter'.[10] It did not have to fight for them; there had been no agitation among the urban masses, hardly any strikes, no situations in which being engaged in a struggle helped them see the world in a different light. For a long time these acquisitions were regarded by most workers more as traditionally 'guaranteed' favours than as anything so abstract as legally enforceable rights. Gradually, however, the meaning of the 'rights' they had acquired through the labour and social-security legislation was apprehended by the urban working class. And it was this changing 'consciousness' which led to the transformation of the urban masses at least into a potentially autonomous force on the Brazilian political scene. For once the conception of 'rights' spreads, two further things can happen. People who have rights can demand that these be respected, that the law be fulfilled, that the gap between statute book and reality be closed. In the second place, rights can come to be regarded as dynamic—new rights can be won, old rights, perhaps, relinquished. In Brazil's larger cities, among the more established sectors of the working class—if not among recent migrants —there slowly emerged, in contrast to a consciousness of self inextricably bound up in the individualistic relations of patron and dependant or client, a sense of citizenship, 'the recognition of their fundamental equality within the institutional system'.[11] The urban workers may not have been very clear about their position as members of a 'class', they may have been far from constituting a 'class-for-itself', in the Marxian sense. But the *populismo* fostered initially by Vargas did make them aware of their rights (and, to some extent, also of their duties) as citizens of the state. The state became an ally which could be mobilized against bosses, employers, or politicians, whether lapsed patrons or new 'exploiting' capitalists.

The first postwar decade (1945–54)

The contradictions inherent in the existence side by side, within one

10 Henry A. Landsberger, 'The Labor Elite: Is It Revolutionary?', in Lipset & Solari, p. 260.

11 Weffort, *Les Temps modernes*, Oct. 1967, p. 642. See also the classic discussion in T. H. Marshall, 'Citizenship and Social Class', in his *Sociology at the Crossroads* (1963).

political framework, of the mechanisms of the traditional politics of ('ruling class') compromise and those which were emerging around the new-style *populismo* led gradually to greatly increased tensions in the Brazilian polity. Before examining those tensions and their eventual 'resolution', some other general developments on the Brazilian political scene must be briefly discussed, as they constitute the backdrop to the eventual emergence of a specifically Christian radicalism.

The end of World War II, which Brazil had joined on the side of the Allies in 1942, saw the demise of the dictatorship of Vargas under the 1937 Constitution of the *Estado Nôvo*.[12] Vargas's manœuvres to carry through the 'redemocratization' of the country under his own auspices, and no doubt, to his own benefit, were foiled by the War Minister Góes Monteiro, who deposed the President on behalf of the armed forces in October 1945. Vargas was, however, allowed to organize his support and to participate in the December elections. Two ('Getulista') parties were formed to tap the vote of those who had hitherto been the 'ins': the PTB and the *Partido Social Democrático* (PSD). The former aimed at the urban working class, or at least at the literates among them, and extended the embryonic principles of *populismo* into the political sphere. The latter was a—traditional—monster of incompatibility, which united support for Vargas among the middle class and state-oriented industrialists in the cities, with the machines built up by Getúlio among the—*coronelista*—politicians of the states of the interior. The PTB and PSD launched the candidacy of General Dutra for President. In December 1945 he easily defeated Brigadier Gomes of the *União Democrática Nacional* (UDN)—another unholy coalition, in this case of the anti-Getulista urban middle class with those political bosses from the backlands who had become the 'outs' during the *Estado Nôvo*. Vargas himself remained an active politician, as senator elected on a PSD ticket for his home state of Rio Grande do Sul, though he was heard of more outside the legislature than in it.

Dutra, who seemed concerned above all to see the country return to 'tranquillity', was to prove 'a blandly non-political President'.[13] After less than a year of co-operation the UDN went formally into opposition, and in December 1946 Vargas also decided to break with the executive. Dutra's government is usually discussed in connection with its handling of economic affairs, which in the opinion of all observers

---

[12] The following discussion is largely based on the account in Skidmore, ch. 2.
[13] Ibid., p. 65.

adds up to a staggering record of mismanagement. Brazil's foreign-currency reserves, which had been much boosted during the war, almost entirely disappeared as a result of economic *laissez-faire* 'policies' under which no restriction whatever was placed on imports, which consisted to a large extent of luxury and consumer goods for the wealthier sections. By mid-1947 the government was forced to change its course. A period followed of ever more elaborate import and exchange controls, but these did little to overcome the country's fundamental economic problems.

Vargas's aloofness from the government during most of the Dutra presidency enabled him to re-emerge on to the national scene when the presidential elections of October 1950 approached. Now with the blessing of the military, to whom he promised good constitutional behaviour, he stood as joint candidate of the PTB and the *Partido Social Progressista* (PSP)—the personal *populista* instrument of the governor of São Paulo, Adhemar de Barros—against Christian Machado, the PSD candidate of President Dutra, and Eduardo Gomes, who once again represented the UDN. During his campaign Vargas, not surprisingly, managed to make a large number of semi-private deals with PSD politicians throughout the country, despite the party's official commitments to Machado; in the towns he campaigned on a mixture of *populista* welfare-statism, and promises to use the state's powers to promote a far-reaching programme of industrialization. He was elected by a surprising margin over Gomes, the runner-up, and polled almost half of the total vote.

Once in office, Vargas did indeed attempt to push ahead with the kind of policy that would later be called 'developmentalist'. But the concrete proposals did not (yet) jell into a clearly structured overall development programme, nor were they underpinned by a coherent ideology. In fact Vargas inaugurated his second government at a time when three principal development formulas were *beginning* to appear: the neo-liberal, which largely followed the prescriptions for economic and fiscal policy laid down by the central bankers of industrialized countries (and by the International Monetary Fund); the develop-mental–nationalist, which Brazilian intellectuals developed in parallel with the UN Economic Commission for Latin America (ECLA); and the radical-nationalist, which came to be held by the Left, and not only the Marxist Left.[14]

Nationalism, then, began to play an increasingly important part on

[14] Ibid., pp. 37–92.

the Brazilian political scene from this time. At first this nationalism was blurred and diffuse; it took some years for the three positions just mentioned to become clearly stated and contending alternatives. But the emphasis was, from the start, placed on economic matters. An early manifestation of this was the controversy over the nationalization of the oil industry which raged for two years from late 1951. Support for the nationalist position was found in fairly wide sections of the politically articulate population, among the middle class, the urban working class, and the military, and it seemed an excellent means for constructing a public consensus.[15] After January 1953 the hand of the more radical sectors of nationalist opinion was strengthened when, with the change-over in the United States from President Truman's administration to that of General Eisenhower, a new approach to Latin America's economic problems emerged in that country. The emphasis shifted from economic co-operation and aid to the creation of a proper 'climate' for private US investment.[16]

Vargas was now found vacillating between aggressive nationalism and the more orthodox economic and financial policies expected abroad, while on the home front he increasingly seemed willing to abandon his attempts to continue a politics of compromise. He switched his attention more and more to the urban working class, hoping, according to some observers, to base a new political era for Brazil on a solid alliance between the industrial bourgeoisie, the middle class, and the urban masses.[17] If Vargas ever had this intention, he certainly failed.[18] He found the military increasingly opposing his policies and criticizing his appointments; he was finally requested to resign after a scandal, which involved a member of his closest entourage in a political assassination attempt. When, in August 1954, he chose a suicide rather than resignation, he left a note which declared that 'the underground campaign of international groups joined that of the national groups which were working against the regime of assuring employment', and which spoke of profits of foreign companies 'reaching as much as 500 per cent per annum', and of the 'spoliation of Brazil' which he had fought.[19]

---

[15] Ibid., p. 109.
[16] Ibid., pp. 116–17.
[17] Ibid., p. 134. For the latter view see Jaguaribe, p. 148.
[18] For a brief discussion of the reasons, see my 'The Brazilian Impasse', *Encounter*, Sept. 1965.
[19] John W. F. Dulles, Jr., *Vargas of Brazil* (1967), pp. 334 ff.

From Vargas to Goulart (1954–64)

Vargas's suicide had a profound emotional impact in the country, and gave a new lease of life to the political system which seemed to be tottering towards the end of his presidency. After an interim period new elections were held, and Vargas's political heirs, Juscelino Kubitschek of the PSD and João Goulart of the PTB, were elected respectively to the presidency and vice-presidency. Military pressure to prevent their inauguration was thwarted by a constitutionalist 'preventive coup' led by General Lott. They took office in January 1956.

If any President of modern Brazil attempted to make an 'alliance' work between the elusive 'national bourgeoisie' and the urban working class it was Kubitschek, the man who more than any other can be seen as the representative of the former. Not that he tried to break with the Getulista politics of compromise—he owed too much to the PSD in the backlands—but he did go all out for development. He attempted to open up the bottlenecks in the economy by means of his famous *Programa de Metas* (Target Plan),[20] and he encouraged discussion and research about Brazil's development problems by granting government support to the *Instituto Superior de Estudos Brasileiros* (ISEB), which brought together such nationalist intellectuals as Cândido Mendes, Hélio Jaguaribe, Álvaro Vieira Pinto, and Roland Corbisier.[21] He boosted both economic growth (he had promised 'fifty years of progress in five') and national confidence by the gigantic enterprise of building Brasilia. His nationalism was much less 'exclusivist' than that to which Vargas had been drawn in the end; he gave substantial encouragement and incentives to private foreign capital, which invested on a large scale in the production of such goods as motor vehicles, other consumer durables, and pharmaceuticals.[22]

But during the later years of Kubitschek's presidency the debate on nationalism sharpened markedly, again spurred on by antagonism to the demands for financial orthodoxy, stipulated as a condition of aid by the IMF.[23] Nelson Werneck Sodré, another teacher at ISEB, held

---

[20] Jaguaribe, ch. 11.
[21] For a valuable general discussion (which does, however, somewhat underplay the differences which later developed in the group) see Herminio Martins, 'Ideology and Development: "Development Nationalism" in Brazil', in Paul Halmos, ed., *Latin American Sociological Studies* (1967).
[22] Skidmore, p. 165.
[23] Ibid., pp. 185 ff.

that nationalism was the political expression of the struggle of both bourgeoisie and working class against external economic forces, against international capitalism, and thus a positive factor.[24] Not all, however, were willing to 'believe in a kind of idyllic communion of the national bourgeoisie with the proletariat',[25] something of which Hélio Jaguaribe could perhaps be accused with more reason than Werneck Sodré. For Marxist sociologists such as Octavio Ianni nationalism represented 'the ideological expression of a specific class', and a negative factor in so far as it was

a means of numbing the political consciousness of the proletariat. . . . The manipulation of nationalism in terms of a conjunction of class interests or in terms of the overcoming of the contradictions between the national bourgeoisie and the working class can transform the workers into docile elements in the hands of those interested in appropriating the product of their labour.[26]

Here Ianni indirectly draws attention to a phenomenon discussed explicitly by Francisco Weffort: the fact that the concept of *povo* (people), used both by nationalists to contrast the whole nation with the exploiters from overseas, and by *populistas* to bind widely divergent sectors of the population together in the political system, is ambiguous and even misleading.[27] 'Nationalism proposes, on a theoretical level, essentially the same ideas as those which the *populistas* propose concretely in the demagogy of public meetings; both have their nucleus in the idea that the *povo* is a community. . . .'[28] But concretely this is far from being the case: such talk merely masks the existence of conflicting interests. Even though, says Weffort, 'there is no doubt that the radical nationalist policies strive to defend the interests of the most sacrificed strata of the population', the concepts used in their formulation result in 'ideological mystification' and the

[24] Ianni, p. 63.
[25] Ibid., p. 64.
[26] Ibid., p. 65.
[27] As Nettl and many others have shown, the attempt to present the interests of the entire people as homogeneous, and to play down the cleavages that exist in society, occurs in many developing countries. In other parts of the world, however, and perhaps especially in Africa, this is both more necessary and less absurd objectively than in Brazil. In Brazil a more solid historical foundation exists for a sense of nationhood, while on the other hand class-based cleavages are much more deeply engrained there than in Africa (see Nettl, chs. 5, 7, & 8).
[28] Weffort, 'Política de massas', in Ianni and others, *Política e revolução social no Brasil* (1965), p. 188.

delaying of the emergence of class consciousness among the masses.[29] 'Public consensus', then, based on a nationalism capable of pleasing everyone, was no longer possible, and a rift developed among the intellectuals of ISEB. Jaguaribe increasingly became the ideologue of the (potentially) nationalist bourgeoisie; others, such as Álvaro Vieira Pinto, moved very sharply left.[30]

The debate, soon the conflicts, over nationalism penetrated the student milieu, and *populista* politicians of the Left, such as Leonel Brizzola—the brother-in-law of Goulart and governor of Rio Grande do Sul, elected on a PTB ticket—were beginning to build up a following by their appeal to radical nationalism. But it had no great influence on the bulk of the party politicians: as has been seen in Chapter 2, the operation of political parties hardly depended on ideological factors. The party system, operative at the bases only at election time, was effectively little more than the complex structure of clientage, spiced with some demagogic promises to the masses; and each party displayed various ideological hues in different areas of the country.

This was as true for the *Partido Democrata Cristão* (PDC)—the one party which would seem to have especial relevance to the subject-matter of this book—as for any of the others, and there was no one identifiable Christian Democratic ideology in Brazil. One could not even speak of a theme with variations. The party lacked significance not only because of its limited impact (its representation in the Federal Chamber of Deputies in the early 1960s was never higher than 5 per cent), but even more because of its heterogeneity. In the southern states of Brazil, and especially in Rio Grande do Sul, the party was conservative to the bone and its leadership enthusiastically endorsed the coup of April 1964. On the other hand the São Paulo PDC brought forth some of the state's and the country's most radical non-communist politicians, such as Paulo de Tarso and Plínio de Arruda Sampaio, men whose rather fuzzy political views did not differ very

---

[29] It is obvious that in a society as divided in class terms as Brazil, *interest articulation* is likely to become a more prominent feature of political processes than *authority legitimation*. In fact, the very nature of the hitherto existing authority legitimation (based on class interests) is challenged. Cf. Nettl, espec. pp. 131 ff. See also the conception, developed by Ralf Dahrendorff, of class conflict as representing a conflict over the *legitimacy* of the existing authority relations (*Class and Class Conflict in Industrial Society* (Stanford, 1959), p. 176).

[30] See also the very well-informed analysis of Michel Debrun, who discusses various other important political figures such as Celso Furtado, as well as the more or less nationalist economic position developed in CEPAL (ECLA): 'Nationalisme et politiques du développement au Brésil', *Sociol. du Travail*, vi/3 & 4 (1964).

much from those held by the more radical sectors of Catholic youth.[31] Finally, in Rio de Janeiro (Guanabara) the party's line became both individualistic and moralizing, and it developed close ideological as well as personal links with Moral Rearmament—although even there more radical individuals were active in the party.[32] Party politics, then, did not on the whole present any attractions for the emerging young Catholic radicals.

Gradually the euphoria of the early years of the Kubitschek era made way for a more sober assessment of the consequence of his presidency in terms of inflation and 'corruption'.[33] This brought a reaction against the view that mere economic growth, any kind of economic growth, would automatically solve all the country's problems. And it ushered in a period during which the need for 'basic reforms' came to be widely discussed.

Kubitschek had left the agrarian sector alone—partly because he was the heir to the old Getulista system of balancing conflicting interests, which made him most reluctant to attack a landowning class so powerfully represented in Congress, partly because he felt that the change for which he was working in the urban industrial sector would 'inevitably provoke a corresponding change in the rural agricultural system, by unleashing the natural economic forces that would unify the internal market'.[34] But nothing of the sort happened; on the contrary, the discrepancies between town and country merely became more pronounced.[35] Of all the basic reforms demanded, land reform

[31] See chs. 4 & 5.

[32] In general there were various states in which the internal tension between the different factions had steadily been rising when the party was abolished, together with all other existing parties, by the Castelo Branco government in October 1966. For a statement of the ideology of the São Paulo group see Paulo de Tarso, *Os Cristãos e a revolução social* (1963). Cândido Mendes devotes some pages of his book on the Catholic Left in Brazil to the PDC: *Memento dos vivos, a esquerda católica no Brasil* (1966), espec. pp. 42–45. It is a very interesting work, but inadequate as a scholarly analysis of the subject. Mendes has been deeply involved in the whole movement, as a kind of young elder statesman and moderating ideologue. This fact has given the book its value, but at the same time has produced its lack of objectivity. That in itself should not exclude *Memento dos vivos* from the realm of contemporary historiography or political science; what is more disturbing is that Mendes moves continuously and without warning between (incomplete) historical data and his own ideological prescriptions. On the PDC he does not mention the differences in orientation between the various branches.

[33] Skidmore writes (p. 173): 'The overnight construction of Brasilia . . . gave the President an unprecedented amount of leverage in dealing with opponents susceptible to the attractions of profitable participation in the new enterprise'.

[34] Jaguaribe, pp. 163–4.

[35] The arguments of Andre Gunder Frank (see espec. pp. 9–12, 190 ff., 258 ff.) are worth remembering in this context: metropolis-satellite relations characterize the nexus between

was the most often mentioned and discussed, and was considered the most urgent.[36]

Administrative reform, the hacking through the jungle of the *Estado Cartorial*, was also a 'necessity'. Kubitschek, however, preferred to leave existing structures as they were. He did not wish to stir up a hornet's nest, and therefore attempted to cope with administrative problems by adding new organs, by a process of accretion. The same was true of Jânio Quadros, Kubitschek's successor: he too tried in his own very unorthodox manner to find a way through the bureaucratic maze which he had inherited. But he as little as Kubitschek realized or overcame the institutional limitations which had been inherent in previous policies and in the structures set up to carry them out.[37]

The brief presidency of Jânio Quadros does not present a consistent pattern and is difficult to assess. He resigned after seven months in office in August 1961 in a maverick move—after he had begun to arouse opposition to his policies and style of government—probably in the vague hope that a wave of 'popular feeling' in his support (which he never even attempted to mobilize) would force Congress to refuse his resignation. He clearly wanted to break with the Getulista politics of compromise. His obvious contempt for the run-of-the-mill politicians, his inclination to govern without them, certainly without the usual bargaining at the top, without the clientage, the wire-pulling, and so on, represented a new style of politics in Brazil: a novel approach which no doubt in many ways helped convince the disenchanted younger generation—Christians and others—that things could be different. Whether this conviction was justified is altogether another matter; Quadros's failure to grasp or tackle the institutional and structural obstacles has already been mentioned. His 'independent foreign policy' made him unpopular with, and dangerous to, influential sectors of the armed forces, strongly oriented to the United States. It did, however, create a favourable climate for the anti-imperialist aspect of the new Christian ideology.

But one of the most important factors (even though it was essentially

the developed and less developed parts of the country, with the former appropriating—through monopoly power—some of the surplus generated by the latter; for these the result is that they will simply 'underdevelop' further. Though one can argue that Frank's model is too determinist, it does fit the case of Brazil during this period.

[36] A few years later João Goulart's clumsy and largely demagogic agrarian proposals of 1964 were among the direct causes of his removal by the army; then, for half a decade, the subject was, for all practical purposes, ignored.

[37] Skidmore, pp. 182, 193, 197 ff.

a fortuitous one) in the crystallization of radical groups and radical
politics in Brazil—emphatically not only among Christians—was the
situation created by Quadros's resignation. The events of that time
need not be rehearsed in detail here: Quadros's Vice-President, João
Goulart, was allowed to take over early in September after a tense
period of threats and counter-threats from different sections of the
armed forces.[38] The outcome was a compromise solution drastically
curtailing presidential powers and interposing a Prime Minister
between the President and Congress. For the next fifteen months or
so Goulart's main objective was to regain full presidential powers by
means of a plebiscite. He realized that success on that occasion would
depend largely on an awareness in the country that the parliamentary
system could not function properly in Brazil. And Goulart saw to it
that it did not work: from September 1961 till January 1963, when
the presidential regime was restored by a massive majority, the political system of Brazil presented a picture of complete frustration and
ineffectualness.

In one sense this ineffectualness was nothing new: it has been seen
how for some time the whole political system had been straining under
the contradictions imposed on it by the politics of compromise (from
which Quadros had seemed to promise redemption). As Skidmore
put it: 'Goulart . . . was about to reap the harvest of the prolonged
political deadlock',[39] with 'extremists' at either end of the political
spectrum urging 'anti-democratic solutions'.[40] What *was* new was the
total lack of direction, the unqualified absence of effective government
for a year and a quarter, the complete sense of drift. Even more than
the hitherto existing strain of the political institutions, the circumstances
of the interim period created a situation extremely favourable to the
emergence of radical political movements promising a total break not
only with the past but also with the present.[41] Then again, in the
second half of 1963, Goulart's government found itself repeatedly
deadlocked in battles with a Congress unwilling to co-operate with

[38] Ibid., pp. 205–20.

[39] Ibid., p. 223.

[40] Ibid., p. 224. This remark typifies the way in which Skidmore's liberal American ideology ultimately prevents him from drawing the apparently obvious conclusions from his own
material. It is—to me—quite impossible to envisage what 'democratic' solution would have
been a *practical* possibility, given the forces and interests involved. See also below, pp.
49–50, 265.

[41] It is one of the many valuable generalizations in Neil J. Smelser, *Theory of Collective
Behaviour* (1962), that radical political movements tend to crystallize in such circumstances.
See espec. pp. 325 ff.

'democratic' solutions to change, after the failure of the six months of reformist government of the 'positive Left' (Santiago Dantas; Celso Furtado).[42] The last two years before the 1964 coup constituted the period which saw the most extensive development of radical and revolutionary groups and grouplets in Brazil.[43] Unquestionably the most important of these was *Ação Popular*, the movement of Christian inspiration founded during the period of parliamentarianism, which is considered in Chapter 5.

Politics and the rural masses

All this suggests clearly that after a relatively successful final showing during the Kubitschek years, when economic development ensured a growing share of the cake for almost everyone, the attempt at a continued politics of compromise began to break down irrevocably by the beginning of the 1960s. On the one hand Brazil's economic difficulties increased, and her growth-rate slowed down considerably. On the other hand pressure developed from the least privileged groups: in the towns through the growing importance of urban *populismo* and a measure of mass militancy, in the countryside with the emergence first of the *ligas* and later of the *sindicatos*—though the extent to which the leaders' stridency was matched by a *tomada de consciência* (emergence of political consciousness) at the grass-roots is, certainly in retrospect, open to serious doubt.[44] It became increasingly clear that the interests of some fundamentally conflicted with those of others; the time had passed when government could consist of little more than arbitration between different claims, of judicious giving in to different pressures at different times. And it was no longer possible to ignore the existence of 50 per cent of Brazil's population—the peasants and rural workers—when the political deals were made and the economic cake was shared out.

Heralds of change in the countryside were not only the fame of the *ligas* and the slow spread of the *sindicatos* in the first years of the new decade. Of substantial importance in the calculations of the federal

---

[42] Skidmore, pp. 239–50.

[43] Skidmore (p. 398 n. 40), quoting Robert Alexander's *Today's Latin America* (1962), refers to them as the 'Jacobin left': those who 'favor social revolution at whatever cost, and . . . are excessively nationalistic to the point of xenophobia'.

[44] Whatever there was, there was no proper organization: the 1964 coup did, after all, fail to arouse any active opposition from the masses at all. See also Skidmore, pp. 253 ff, and the present volume, espec. pp. 29–31 above and chs. 12 & 13, *passim*.

government was also the rising strength, in various of the backward states of the country, of politicians who no longer fitted into the traditional pattern of rural politics. They had managed to attract support, despite that traditional (and still very strong) political structure, on the basis of more or less radical appeals to the under-privileged part of the electorate—in the cities as well as in the rural areas. The most formidable of these rising stars was no doubt Miguel Arraes, elected Governor of Pernambuco in October 1962. His advantage over the UDN candidate in the capital of the state had been enormous. But he did extremely well even in the interior, where the electorate was presumably more docile and amenable to the suggestions of the violently anti-Arraes landowners; he polled there almost as many votes as his opponent, João Cleofas.[45]

Once in office, Arraes, in the eyes of the established powers a dangerous subversive supported by the communists, set about to bring the realities of citizenship to those groups which had hitherto lived under the shadow of landowners and *coronéis*. Henceforth the latter could no longer assume that the apparatus of the state, including its police force, would always and without question be at their disposal for the intimidation of peasants, strike-breaking, or the eviction of illegal squatters. Henceforth laws, which had never been enforced outside the cities, began to take on 'significance' for the peasants. In the *zona da mata*, on the sugar plantations, the minimum wage had nearly everywhere remained a legal fiction: the decision as to how much work was required in order to earn that minimum wage had rested almost entirely with the employers. Arraes forced them to sit down with the unions and his own representatives, in order to work out clearly-defined norms, the official *tabela*, which could be unambiguously applied and which specified how much payment was due for different kinds of labour.[46] In this way at least some peasants and rural workers began to discover in the state a potential ally. They also developed a new sense of legitimacy for their economic demands—and one can say that, at least for the cane workers, wages finally lost all association with 'favours' from the *patrão*. All this represented a serious menace to the federal government. The awakening of the countryside, hitherto simply ignored in Brazilian politics, threatened to upset the balance on which the successful operation of the system depended. And the emergence of Arraes as a popular and uncompro-

---

[45] Figures in Adirson de Barros, *Ascensão e queda de Miguel Arraes* (1965), pp. 91 f.
[46] The Pernambuco *tabela* is reproduced in Callado, App. I.

mising politician, who might find widespread mass support for possible presidential ambitions, menaced the very system which had brought men like President Goulart to positions of prominence.[47] The latter did not fail to react.

Goulart had for some time been proclaiming the necessity for 'basic reforms' of the agrarian structure.[48] He put various bills before Congress, including a constitutional amendment which would allow payment for expropriated land in government bonds. Throughout 1963 he failed to get the necessary majorities. But he seemed to be more successful in his moves to strengthen his own power base in the countryside, which involved trying to transplant to the rural areas the urban *populismo* with which he was familiar.[49] He thus hoped to shore up the rickety structure at the top of which he was precariously perched. His best chance came after Congress, also in response to the growing restlessness in the backlands, had passed the Rural Labour Statute (*Estatuto do Trabalhador Rural*) in January 1963: it led to a massive drive at organizing the peasants and rural workers by government-sponsored agencies.[50]

The preceding analysis should have left no doubt—certainly not with the hindsight now available—that the old political mechanisms could no longer cope, and that the system was heading for a breakdown. It was, however, by no means clear at the time *how* that breakdown would occur. Despite the numerous instances of direct and indirect interference by the military in politics since the end of the *Estado Nôvo*—in themselves signs of the tensions in the political system—few people thought about a military coup on behalf of the classes whose

[47] On Arraes, see Skidmore, pp. 275–6 & 281–2.

[48] On Goulart's proposals for 'basic reforms' see ibid., pp. 237–47. Skidmore suggests (p. 237) that they could have had three purposes: (1) to eliminate a series of new bottlenecks in economic development; (2) to achieve a more equitable distribution of wealth and income; (3) to alter the 'political balance'. 'What was dangerous was the President's continual emphasis upon the need for "reforms" without calming the growing suspicions of the center about his third purpose.' Skidmore obviously means dangerous to the survival of formally democratic political processes—something to which he appears committed above all else. His subsequent analysis makes clear that he regrets the military take-over of April 1964. But he fails to appreciate that the circumstances which led up to it were the result of growing—though as yet largely unarticulated—*class* antagonisms, and that the post-1964 regime itself acted to safeguard some of the class interests which had seemed most seriously threatened: those of the landowning groups, but also those of the urban middle class and bourgeoisie.

[49] For a general discussion of such attempts at broadening the bases of power see R. N. Adams, 'Political Power and Social Structures', in Véliz, *Obstacles to Change*, pp. 33 ff.

[50] Goulart and those around him did not manage to maintain control of this drive. See the further discussion in ch. 6, pp. 113–18.

dominance seemed threatened.[51] Those on the Brazilian Left, secular and Christian, were convinced by the political developments of these years that the revolution, *their* revolution was, if not around the corner, at least around the next one. How the radical Catholics saw this revolution will, I hope, become clear as the analysis proceeds. The next chapter opens the discussion by examining the sources of radical Christian thought in Brazil and the emergence of radical movements of Christian inspiration.

[51] See, for a notable exception to this statement, the little book by Wanderley Guilherme, *Quem dará o golpe no Brasil?* (1962).

4

The Church and the Stirrings of
Catholic Radicalism

Brazilian Catholicism: historical introduction

SEEN in historical perspective, the Catholic church in Brazil has never been a particularly powerful institution—certainly not when compared with most other Latin American countries, where a strong and above all rich church was entrenched near the top of the colonial structure of domination. It has, consequently, never generated the passionate kind of anti-clericalism found elsewhere. During the colonial period the secular clergy, usually ignorant and of lax morals, were mainly scattered in the rural areas, subject more to the domination of the sugar-planters and other landowners whose plantation chapels they served than to the authority of their own bishop. Through their teaching and preaching they supplied a theologically-anchored ideology which justified and underpinned the existing socio-economic patterns. Apart from the Jesuits, writes Gilberto Freyre, the

clergy, including the friars, grew big-bellied and soft in fulfilling the functions of chaplains, ecclesiastical tutors, priestly uncles and godfathers to the young ones, and they proceeded to accommodate themselves to the comfortable situation of members of the family or household, becoming allies and adherents of the patriarchal system.[1]

Plantation chaplains virtually became the ideologues of the *senhores de engenho*, calling down heavenly blessings on anything the latter requested, and transmitting the prevalent ideas on social organization to the next generation in their role as teachers. Church and planter thus put their respective powers at each other's disposal.

In this community of shared life and interests, with its exchange of services and system of mutual concessions, which even reached the level of indulgence for, if not complicity with, each other's faults, shortcomings, or

---

[1] *The Masters and the Slaves*, p. 192.

crimes, priest and master, living in solidarity under the same roof, benefited from the forces which each represented, and which were put at the service of one another. Thus religion did not raise a single obstacle against the master's crude and autocratic power. . . .[2]

And the alliance was not only one of habitat, education, and religion. It was fortified by shared material interests, as the church itself was involved in the exploitation of the land: monasteries were among the largest landholders and slave owners in colonial Brazil.[3]

Some religious orders, and especially the Jesuits, represented Catholicism as an institution independent of society's powerful men. They opposed the *bandeirantes*, the roaming bands of adventurers, in their enterprise of enslaving Brazil's Indians, and carried out extensive missionary activities among the latter.[4] The Jesuits also played an important educational role: their schools represented all that existed in the way of a structured educational system during the first two centuries of the colonial period.[5] They were in fact the only well organized and purposeful ecclesiastical force in the country, maintaining a moral self-discipline which was not seen elsewhere in the Brazilian church, and a wide margin of independence from the civil authorities.

The hierarchy itself was weak and totally subordinated to the Crown, especially by means of the *padroado*, the arrangement which had gradually emerged as a result of concessions wrung by the Portuguese kings from successive Popes in the fifteenth and sixteenth centuries, making church appointments dependent upon secular patronage rather than upon ecclesiastical necessity.[6] The domination of the church by the state was sealed by the 'regalist' reforms of Pombal, the centralizing and despotic representative of the Enlightenment in Portugal, who expelled the Jesuits in 1759.

Shortly after Independence (1822) the Emperor took over the ecclesiastical prerogatives which had previously been those of the Portuguese kings, a situation accepted *de facto* by the Vatican. The control of the state over the church was well-nigh complete during the Empire, and almost the entire secular clergy supported the regalist

[2] De Azevedo, p. 70. The last comment is clearly exaggerated: cf. the following discussion on the role of the Jesuits.

[3] Ibid, pp. 71 ff. See also Freyre, *New World in the Tropics* (1963), p. 70.

[4] See Sérgio Buarque de Holanda, ed., *História geral da civilização brasileira, a época colonial*, i. 265; ii. 12 f.

[5] Ibid., ii. 71.

[6] Ibid., ii. 52–7. The chapter by Américo Jacobina Lacombe, 'A Igreja no Brasil colonial', to which this and the previous footnote refer, contains further valuable material on the position of the church in colonial Brazil.

organization in which they were enmeshed. A prominent example was Fr. Diogo Antônio Feijó, at one time Regent of the empire. There was much flaunting of independence from Rome, formally expressed in the Imperial consent needed for the promulgation of Papal proclamations: the Vatican's desire for a direct line of authority to the Brazilian church was seen, not only by the government but also by most churchmen, as 'interference by the Holy See in the affairs of state'.[7] The secular clergy were paid by the state, which collected the tithes due to the church. Broadly speaking, bishops and priests were regarded as agents of the Executive; church affairs were regulated by state decrees. In 1854 the Emperor carried regalism to an extreme by declaring that he had the right to nominate candidates to all ecclesiastical offices and benefices without taking advice or counsel from the prelates, the hitherto accepted custom. Repeatedly the question was raised of the abolition in Brazil of clerical celibacy (an institution in any case hardly adhered to in practice). The influence of liberal thought and Masonry in the church was great, even after the latter's condemnation by Pope Pius IX in 1864.[8]

Sporadic Catholic calls for undoing the bonds that bound God and Caesar in Brazil began to be heard from the early 1870s under the 'ultramontane' influence of the Papal encyclical *Syllabus Errorum* of 1864 and of the proclamation, at the Vatican Council, of papal infallibility in 1870. An open clash over the issue of Freemasonry between the government and two bishops in 1873–4, leading to their condemnation by a civilian court and their imprisonment, was an indication of mounting tensions. The *questão religiosa* agitated the country for a couple of years, but it appears that when a new government declared an amnesty in 1875 and released the bishops from prison, most of Brazil's churchmen were quite willing to let bygones be bygones, and to revert to the regalist *status quo ante*. As Pe Júlio Maria lamented:

The church had recognized and loudly proclaimed that it had been enslaved [by the state]. But the amnesty led to everything being forgotten, even the duty of the church not to tolerate [a reversion to] this state of affairs. The

<hr>

[7] Pe Júlio Maria, 'A religião; ordens religiosas; instituições pias e beneficentes no Brasil: Memória', in *Livro do Centenário, 1500–1900* (Rio, Imp. Nac., 1900), p. 67.

[8] Ibid., pp. 66–71. See also J. Lloyd Mecham, *Church and State in Latin America*, rev. ed. (1966), pp. 264–71. The most detailed discussion of the situation of the Brazilian church in this period, as in the last years of the empire, is contained in João Dornas Filho, *O padroado e a igreja no Brasil* (1938). He is especially concerned with the relations between church and state, and has incorporated many of the relevant documents of the period.

episcopate, renewing the bonds of friendship, made its peace with regalism. The clergy, imitating their pastors, returned to their old submission.[9]

Nevertheless, the question of church–state relations remained a bone of contention between the Empire and the Vatican, with a slowly growing number of Brazilian churchmen being 'won over' to the point of view of Rome. The solution came at one stroke shortly after the proclamation of the Republic in November 1889: the new leadership of the country, in this respect much influenced by positivist ideas, had no use whatever for the *padroado* and all that went with it. In January 1890 the formal separation of church and state took place. Two months later, in a collective pastoral letter, the Bishops welcomed the new situation with the statement that 'the Catholic church in Brazil has been assured of a certain range of freedoms which were never achieved during the monarchy'.[10]

The new freedoms had to be put to use. The institutional separation of church and state had to be made meaningful in human terms. The earliest efforts at independent Catholic thought are therefore devoted to the problem of 'revitalizing' the church as an institution: to the improvement of the standing and standard of the clergy after centuries of decadence resulting from its subordination to the interests of the state. Credit during this largely pre-ideological phase must go to Pe Júlio Maria, whose life and writings constitute a *tour de force* aimed at helping the church over the hurdles of transition to its independent status. In 1900 he still found it necessary to castigate the clergy for their inability to act in new ways. Old habits die hard: the past ties which bound the priests to the apparatus of state lingered on in a predilection for personal involvement in politics, and in a failure to establish true links with the mass of their own parishioners. Under the influence of Leo XIII's *Rerum Novarum* (1891) Pe Júlio urged the clergy to concern themselves with social and economic questions relating to the interests of the nation and its people. He told them that they should be 'social reformers', instead of ministering to a small 'aristocracy of the devout' in whose service they provide 'feasts for the living and funerals for the dead'.[11] They should show the simple folk, the poor, the proletarians that they 'were the first ones to be called by the Heavenly Master'.[12]

[9] Maria, p. 102.

[10] Ibid., p. 108. A general discussion of relevance to the church in this period may be found in João Cruz Costa, *A History of Ideas in Brazil* (1964), chs. 3 & 4.

[11] Maria, respectively pp. 127 & 128.

[12] Ibid., p. 125.

Pe Júlio Maria may, in a certain sense, be regarded as an early example of the progressive 'opposition' from within the Brazilian church. But to regard him as a forerunner of radical Catholicism in Brazil could be a misleading interpretation if it were not placed in a proper perspective. What he called for was an acceptance and application by a church, which had, till quite recently, openly dissociated itself from Rome, of the teachings of Leo XIII—and the teachings to which he demanded obedience referred to the conditions prevailing in Europe at the zenith of *laissez-faire* capitalism. Pe Júlio's call to his fellow priests to get out of their churches, whence they 'contemplate the people from a distance', may have been both relevant and appropriate; his concern with the fate of 'proletarians', with 'christianizing the workshop' and 'humanizing the factories, where men are absorbed by machines'[13] had little meaning in the Brazil of 1900: even at the time of the first industrial census seven years later, the number of 'industrial establishments' (most of them very small workshops indeed) in the whole country was hardly over 3,000, and the total number of people employed a mere 150,000.[14] No wonder the impact of *Rerum Novarum* was so small as to be negligible from a social point of view. In fact, even Pope Pius XI's follow-up of 1931, *Quadragesimo Anno*, caused scarcely more than a ripple in Brazil. The 'ruling ideas' of the country remained very much those of the country's small élite.

During the late Empire and early Republic those 'ruling ideas' were a confused imported mixture of positivism, Darwinism, and other less coherent systems of thought. This general situation of intellectual disorientation continued until the beginning of the 1920s. It was not until then that the hitherto isolated expressions of a specifically Brazilian culture in literature and the arts began to be seen, by their protagonists, as a new movement—incoherent though it may have been, and still much in debt to contemporary European trends. In 1922, the year of the centenary of Brazil's independence, a 'Week of Modern Art' was organized in São Paulo, an event which so to speak formally announced the existence of the new ideas to the country.[15] It was also the year which saw the famous revolt of the Copacabana fort, the first open sign of dissatisfaction with the general state of society and politics among the younger officers, whose expressions of rebelliousness,

---

[13] Ibid.

[14] Dorival Teixeira Vieira, 'The Industrialization of Brazil', in T. Lynn Smith & A. Marchant, *Brazil, Portrait of Half a Continent* (1951), p. 249.

[15] See Cruz Costa, pp. 249–57. For a detailed study see Mário da Silva Brito, *Antecedentes da semana de arte moderna* (1964).

flaring up throughout the 1920s, became known as the *tenentismo* movement.

This is not the place for an analysis of the Brazilian cultural or political scene during the first quarter of our century. But it is not without interest to note that the earliest appearance of a distinctively Catholic ideology was negative in character. Though it was promoted by one man (Jackson de Figueiredo), it did have a certain amount of impact on a wider circle. It developed as a reaction against the still isolated, disparate, and far from coherent impulses expressed in the 'Week of Modern Art' and the *tenentes*' revolts, the first stirrings of innovation in the country after decades of political stagnation and cultural and intellectual confusion.[16] Jackson's ideology, inspired by the ideas of Bonald de Maistre and of Maurras, was very precisely a reactionary one—in fact he himself took pride in the epithet. The journal he founded, *A Ordem* (Order), proclaimed the virtues not only of order, but also of authority, morality, Catholicism, and nationalism. His nationalism looked back to a pure Catholic past, when Brazil was not yet threatened by Protestantism, or by international Freemasonry, capitalism, and Judaism. Order and authority would safeguard the country against revolution—not only the mild kind with which the *tenentes* seemed to threaten, but also that which had engulfed Tsarist Russia in 1917.

Jackson had gradually been converted to Catholicism, taking the final step of confession in 1921 at the age of 30 after an interview with the Archbishop (later Cardinal) of Rio de Janeiro, D. Sebastião Leme. D. Leme stood in the background of much that happened on the Brazilian Catholic scene from his appointment to Rio in 1921 until his death in 1942. As Archbishop of Olinda (Recife) his first pastoral letter (1916) had dealt with the problems of religious indifference in Brazil, with the agnostic, secularist, and positivist frame of mind of most Brazilian intellectuals, and with the lack of doctrinal foundation of the ideas of those who called themselves Catholics.[17] Once in Rio he stimulated study groups and associations of Catholic laymen; he was fully behind Jackson's activities in the Centro D. Vital, from which *A Ordem* was published, activities which he saw as part of the effort to christianize the Brazilian intelligentsia. D. Leme was a man who

[16] See the enlightening article by Francisco Iglésias, 'Estudo sôbre o pensamento reacionário: Jackson de Figueiredo', *R. bras. cien. soc.*, 2 July 1962, to which my discussion of Jackson, and that of Alceu Amoroso Lima, which follows, are much indebted. See also Cruz Costa, pp. 256–61.

[17] See the massive biography, written with all the love—and some of the bias—of a disciple, by Irmã Maria Regina do Santo Rosário, *O Cardeal Leme* (1962), pp. 61–84.

vigorously promoted what he considered to be the interests of the Catholic church on the national political scene, but he resolutely opposed Jackson in the latter's desire to found a Catholic political party. He left him full freedom as director of the Centro D. Vital, however; and it is quite possible that the views promoted by the Centro and published in *A Ordem* received their polemical imprint as a result of the frustration of Jackson's political ambitions.[18]

Jackson died suddenly in 1928. His successor as editor of *A Ordem* and as director of the Centro D. Vital was Alceu Amoroso Lima, also known by his *nom-de-plume*, Tristão de Athayde. He resolutely steered the Centro away from the all too open involvement in politics it had pursued under Jackson. Amoroso Lima's views on man and society were from the start rather different from those of his predecessor. It is true that he opposed the Revolution of 1930, the political culmination of the *tenentes* movement, and that late in 1932 he became the secretary-general of the *Liga Eleitoral Católica* (LEC), D. Leme's answer to those who were still pressing for a Catholic political party. The LEC acted as a pressure group to ensure the acceptance of 'Catholic principles' by candidates from all parties in the elections of 1933, and to see to it that these principles (e.g. sacredness of the family, i.e. no divorce; religious instruction in schools) were incorporated in the 1934 Constitution—which they were.[19]

Alceu also flirted for a few years in the early 1930s with the *Integralistas*, whose para-fascist ideology had been more than foreshadowed by Jackson. From the middle of that decade, however, he definitely turned away from reaction. He became the main channel for Brazil of the ideas of Jacques Maritain—whose *Humanisme intégral* (1937) was a landmark on the road towards what we now know as progressive Catholic social thought. Amoroso Lima has shown a consistent intellectual openness and a true capacity for philosophical and ideological dialogue. He directed the Centro D. Vital for over three and a half decades.[20] Under his direction it played an important role in laying the groundwork for the 'renewal' that came about from the late 1950s. The study groups and discussion circles at the Centro during the 1930s

---

[18] Ibid., pp. 173–88.

[19] Ibid., pp. 309–22. This method has been followed in elections ever since. For a recent example cf. my 'Religion, the Church, and Social Change in Brazil', in Véliz, *Politics of Conformity*, p. 207.

[20] Eventually, after the 1964 coup, the Centro D. Vital came to be directed by Gustavo Corção, a man close to the extreme right of the present political spectrum in Brazil.

and 1940s brought together many people who would later play a significant part in the promotion of progressive ideas in the church. A number of those who, as young priests, had discussed at the Centro D. Vital the need for a return to the liturgical sources, the significance of Christian humanity, or the role of the laymen in the church, were later to be found, as bishops, battling hard to get the church actively involved in the process of development, and squarely behind the under-privileged in society.[21] In this sense, the Centro D. Vital was clearly an early catalyst in the process which eventually led to the emergence of a radical Catholic ideology. But the Centro never actually became the focus from which a specific ideology spread, never became the pivot of a social movement *engagé* in society. Its links with the diocese of Rio, since 1943 directed by Cardinal D. Jaime Câmara, a very conservative prelate, made that impossible.

The setting up of Catholic Action

The social movement from which, after many years without any clear direction, a truly radical social Catholicism emerged was another organization in which Alceu Amoroso Lima played a leading role: Catholic Action. Catholic Action is a form of 'lay apostolate' which has been stimulated by various Popes from the beginning of the present century, and which was given formal status by Pius XI in the mid-1920s. By the early 1930s it was well established in Europe: in Italy the emphasis being on a general mass movement with branches for men and women, adults and youths, while in France and Belgium greater stress was placed from the beginning on a 'specialized' lay apostolate as a result of the success of the organization of working-class youth in *Jeunesse Ouvrière Catholique*.[22]

D. Leme had accompanied the gradual development of the idea of Catholic Action. The charter and guide-lines for the co-ordinating body of lay Catholic organizations he had founded in 1923, the *Con-federação Católica*, had in fact been called *Ação Católica*. In 1929 he had set up a university group in his diocese, *Ação Universitária Católica*, and three years later a working-class movement, the *Con-*

[21] Among the most prominent one can name the present Archbishop of Recife, D. Helder Câmara, and the Brazilian bishops' specialist on education, the Bishop of Lorena, D. Cândido Padim.

[22] A general discussion of Catholic Action can be found in Yves Congar, OP, *Lay People in the Church* (1957), espec. ch. 5. A book devoted to the situation in Australia also contains valuable background information: cf. Tom Truman, *Catholic Action and Politics*, rev. ed. (London, 1960).

federação Operária Católica. When the establishment of branches of Catholic Action was formally encouraged for all dioceses in Brazil, the movement followed the Italian pattern, with which D. Leme was personally familiar. At the same time the students' branch in Rio was re-named *Juventude Universitária Católica* (JUC), and the youth branch of the working-class movement JOC: *Juventude Operária Católica*. A branch for secondary school students, *Juventude Estudantil Católica* (JEC) was also organized in the Rio diocese.[23] Alceu Amoroso Lima became the first national chairman of the over-all organization.

Catholic Action was organized on a large scale. It sponsored mass rallies and pilgrimages, and had thousands of members who enthusiastically wore their badges and turned out in public places for demonstrations of faith. But its impact was not very deep, and the enthusiasm did not last. It languished during the 1940s, an organization impressive on paper but virtually non-existent in reality. The beginnings of change came towards the end of that decade, when specialized movements on the French and Belgian pattern—particularly among youth—were given greater prominence. The first to be officially recognized by the hierarchy on a nation-wide scale was JOC in 1948. Then, in July 1950, the other branches were nationally launched: JAC (*Juventude Agrária Católica*), for the agrarian youth; the two student branches, JEC and JUC, which had been in existence for various periods in several of the more important dioceses; and a kind of catch-all for the residual category of 'independents', JIC (*Juventude Independente Católica*). Each (except JUC, which had both men and women members) had a separate branch for women. JIC never really established an identity of its own, let alone an ideology or a recognizable mode of action in its hazy, vaguely middle-class 'milieu'. But the other four were all to play a part in the development of Catholic radicalism in Brazil.

Least effective in the early years was JAC. Its weakness was partly the result of a certain lack of interest and support on the part of the hierarchy. Perhaps even more important were the backward conditions in the rural areas, the fact that in a sense 'rural youth'—as a separate social category—simply did not exist where young people had to share most of the burdens of adult life at an early stage and where, moreover, the adults themselves usually formed no more than an embryonic 'community' in the sociological sense of the term. From the leadership of JAC there did, however, eventually emerge a number of people who came to occupy positions of often national influence in progressive

[23] See Santo Rosário, pp. 299–308 & 334–49.

lay and ecclesiastical circles. This was true to an even larger extent of JOC. In the beginning JOC's role depended much on local conditions and on the attitude of the *assistente*, the ecclesiastical adviser appointed by the diocesan bishop (which was, incidentally, also true for the other youth movements of Catholic Action). Where he was a progressive, a person with an outlook not dissimilar to that of the French worker-priests, the branches of JOC and its adult equivalent ACO (*Ação Católica Operária*) could be quite aggressive organizations, stimulating the urban workers into a strong defence of their existing rights and the conquest of new ones. With *assistentes* more concerned to preach co-operation and understanding between the sides facing each other in capitalist industrial enterprises, the impact of JOC and ACO was not very great. But they followed developments in other Catholic circles, and gradually the overall tone of the workers' movement became more radical. After 1964 different sections of JOC and ACO increasingly presented open challenges to the post-coup government which, with its economic policies, bore heavily on the working class.

The secondary-school branch, JEC, should not be underestimated, especially in its impact on the pupils in schools run by the church. Towards the end of the pre-coup period they had developed their own socio-political activities and even ideas; but it was in the nature of things that their influence as a movement did not reach as far as that of the university students—although one must remember that many of the latter had been members, or leaders, of JEC. Thus the really crucial movement was the one in the universities, JUC. Catholic radicalism in Brazil has many sources and had, no doubt, been fermenting for some time when it first emerged as a *coherent* body of ideas and activities. But when this happened it occurred among one particular generation of students active in JUC. Therefore an analysis of the evolution of JUC's ideology is a *sine qua non* for the understanding of the phenomenon as a whole.

The early years of JUC

JUC hardly started as a movement with a remarkably radical bent. Its motto was the same as that of similar Catholic Action organizations elsewhere: 'see, judge, and act.' It was oriented towards the spreading of generally accepted Catholic ideas and the stimulation of religiously approved behaviour, by means of the active participation of Catholic

'militants' in their own milieu, that of the university. At the first
national congress in 1950 the themes of commissions ranged from
internal administrative matters to religious teaching in the university;
they also took in sex education, the family, spiritual life, and the
cinema.[24] From that year onwards the movement's national council
met annually to discuss problems and policies, and to review the
achievements of the year just passed. These achievements seemed to
lie mainly in the spheres of the spiritual: Easter retreats, pilgrimages,
courses on Catholic culture, and the provision of religious services in
the universities. But almost everywhere the movement failed to grow
sturdy roots in its milieu. It neither reached many people nor did it
seem to have a particularly profound effect on those who had participated in its activities, not even on the so-called militants. Dissatisfaction among the successive cohorts of leadership increased, especially
from 1956 onwards, and at the 8th National Council in 1958 the mull-
ings over a vague sense of unease made way for a more concerted
effort at self-criticism.

JUC, it was felt, had become a movement which discussed, especially
at the level of the annual National Councils, well-prepared and well-
sounding texts, which, however, meant very little indeed in the concrete life of the movement.[25] The terse report of the 1958 discussions,
in which the various *assistentes*, as was usual, took an active part, almost
gives a feeling of desperation with the working of the movement, which
—outside one or two areas which formed a significant exception—
seemed unable to influence anyone but those most centrally engaged
as leaders.[26] The cause of JUC's ineffectiveness was sought in the
'lack of life' within the movement, its excessively abstract theoretical
discussions and orientation, its lack of engagement in concrete reality.

It is not by chance that this problem came to the fore in JUC at this
time. Juscelino Kubitschek was just half-way through his period of
office, and the problems of 'Brazilian reality' were already being
widely discussed in the country at large. The first important pronouncement on these matters from within the church, the declaration of the
bishops of the North-East, had been made more than two years before.[27]

[24] See Fr. Romeu Dale, *JUC do Brasil, uma nova experiência de Ação Católica* (1962,
mimeo.), p. 4. This historical analysis, prepared at the time of JUC's crisis with the
hierarchy, discussed below, has been a helpful guide.
[25] Ibid., p. 8.
[26] Secretariado Nacional da JUC, *Anais do VIII Conselho Nacional de Dirigentes* (Rio,
1958), pp. 107–8.
[27] See below, pp. 74 ff.

Most to the point was probably the fact that a more 'practical', socially committed, orientation had been embraced by JUC in Pernambuco. With the example before them of the Recife *JUCistas*, who had concentrated in the years 1957 and 1958 on such topics as university and society, social factors in health and sickness, and the problem of hunger, and who were already in 1958 beginning to act on their ideas by going into the city's slums, the participants in the National Council could not fail to see the aridity of the activities elsewhere. Nevertheless, as the 1958 report of JUC's Council remarks, 'engagement' creates problems for the movement: a switch to activity which has deeper roots in concrete reality and its problems raises the issue that, as an apostolic organization formally subordinated to the hierarchy, JUC cannot take specific positions on socio-political matters. In fact it was the awareness of this restriction which had kept the movement on more theoretical ground in the first place.

This report of the Council of JUC in 1958 was the first significant airing of the central 'existential problem' of JUC: to find a course between the Scylla of excessive theorizing and the Charybdis of concrete political commitments.[28] Pe Almery, one of the *assistentes*, then suggested that a compass for safe sailing could be found in the more systematic development of a body of thought within the movement, which would provide the basic ideas to orient all action. A year later, at the 1959 Council, this would emerge as his proposal for the movement's *ideal histórico*.[29] It is clear that the movement had been groping towards this for some time, and it must be remembered that JUC's quest for consistency and coherence was not exceptional on the Brazilian university scene of those years. A growing concern with the problem of university reform would soon prompt militants of many shades of opinion to re-examine their basic premises and to re-formulate their central ideas around the views on 'Brazilian reality' and the 'Brazilian Revolution' which were then beginning to crop up.

At the Council of JUC in 1959 Pe Almery read a paper which was to have a profound influence.[30] He began by stating that for Christian

[28] Readers accustomed to the deeply engrained scepticism displayed towards almost all 'philosophizing' in Anglo-Saxon countries may be reminded of the fact that in Brazil—and in Latin countries in general—the search for a coherent *Weltanschauung* in itself is *not* regarded as excessive theorizing.

[29] The concept *ideal histórico* had, as will become clear, obvious affinities with the existentialist-derived *projeto histórico*, very much in the air during this period. The latter was popularized through the publications of the ISEB.

[30] Almery Bezerra, 'Da necessidade de um ideal histórico', *JUC, Boletim Nacional No. 2, Anais do IX Conselho Nacional*, Dec. 1959, pp. 37–40.

militants it is not sufficient to know that they have a task to fulfil in this world, a task which would involve such matters as 'creating a Christian social order', 'bringing salvation to the social structures', or 'restoring all things to Christ'. They needed much more specific guidance in order to apply such no doubt excellent precepts to the situation here and now. Though a Christian will find the *ultimate* meaning of history in his faith, faith is not necessarily of any help in enabling him to make sense out of the history of his own time and society. On the one hand the teaching of the church and the speculations of theologians have provided him with the universal principles by which to guide his action. Social scientists, on the other hand, have supplied many facts and some theories about society, but these facts and theories are usually not connected with an explicit philosophical, let alone theological, concern. Pe Almery therefore concluded that

it is absolutely necessary, if we aim at an effective Christian commitment in the temporal order, to reflect amply and carefully in the light of reality . . . so that we may arrive at certain *principia media* [intermediate principles] which express what one might call a Christian historical ideal.

He added, however, that knowledge and reflection by themselves are not enough for the emergence of such intermediate principles; reality must also be experienced personally, by living in it actively and with commitment.

Pe Almery's discussion of the *ideal histórico* was based on the ideas of Jacques Maritain; even though this parentage was not explicitly mentioned in Pe Almery's published paper, the fact was known in the movement. Almery followed Maritain's formulation quite closely, when he stated that the *ideal histórico* was not only to be conceived as intermediate principles, but as a 'realizable ideal essence'. These had been Maritain's words:

A *concrete historical ideal* is not an *ens rationis*, but an ideal *essence* which is realizable (with more or less difficulty, more or less imperfectly, but that is another affair; and not as a finished thing, but as a thing in process), an essence able to exist and called to exist in a given historical atmosphere, and as a result corresponding to a *relative* maximum (relative to that historical state) of social and political perfection.[31]

In sociological parlance it may be called an 'ideal type', and it has affinities with a utopia, understood as an ideal construct which 'helps

[31] Jacques Maritain, *Humanisme intégral*, Engl. version: *True Humanism*, tr. by M. R. Adamson (1938), p. 122.

to prepare public opinion for certain possible realities'.[32] The availability of such an *ideal histórico* should, according to Almery, prevent
one from arguing in a relativistic manner 'that the iniquities of this
world should be accepted with tranquillity'. But there is the danger
that it may lead people to 'fall prey to the illusion that the Kingdom
of God can be established on earth', an illusion against which Pe Almery
warns with some insistence. His fears were to prove to be well-founded.
For, even though the more sophisticated intellectual and philosophical
leaders of the young Catholic radicals never succumbed to blatant
millennarianism, a 'utopic' streak,[33] based on assumptions which
from all past experience would seem unrealistic in human and social
terms, developed among the second string of ideologues and diffusers
of ideas, once they had brought together Christian principles and
social analysis based on empirical data of history and society.

This social analysis has been rumbling in the wings for some time.
It erupted into Catholic circles in July 1960, with a series of articles
by the French Dominican Friar Thomas Cardonnel in *O Metropolitano*,
the paper edited by the Students' Union of the state of Guanabara,
the *União Metropolitana de Estudantes*, UME. These articles generated
a heated polemic, and led to an increasingly visible separation of
viewpoints on social organization between 'progressives' and 'conservatives'. They marked the watershed between the thought of two
generations, and for the first time led a large number of students to
protest *as Christians* about the shape of their society. It is true that one
could by then point to the beginnings of episcopal pronouncements
concerned with the injustices suffered by the mass of the Brazilian
people. But these did not in any essential point deviate from that

[32] Pierre Furter, *Educação e reflexão* (1966), p. 39—an excellent analysis by a sympathetic
outside observer of educational problems related to the present discussion.
[33] For a long time social scientists have failed to see the distinction between a 'utopia',
seen as an ideal construct based on certain political or philosophical notions, which can serve
as a guide for purposeful social change, and 'utopics', the belief in the *actual* possibility of
the construction of an ideal society, free from evil, power, 'contradictions', etc. They have
usually either attacked all utopias or engaged in utopics themselves. Martin Buber implicitly
made the distinction in his *Paths in Utopia* (1958), p. 10; more recently Wilbert Moore
proposed an act of rehabilitation in his 'The Utility of Utopias', presidential address to the
American Sociological Ass. in 1966, reprinted in the *Amer. Sociol. R.*, Dec. 1966. Extremely
useful are also the excellent discussions of the topic by Pierre Furter. See his 'Utopie et
Marxisme selon Ernst Bloch', *Arch. sociol. relig.*, no. 21, 1966, ch. 3 of his *Educação e
reflexão*, and his outstanding discussion of the thought of Ernst Bloch, 'L'Imagination
créatrice, la violence et le changement social', *CIDOC Cuaderno*, no. 14, 1968. The seminal
ideas of Bloch do not fundamentally clash with the distinction made here between 'utopic'
and 'utopian'. I have looked at the problem in relation to a few other Latin American cases
in 'Paternalism and Populism: Catholicism in Latin America', *J. Contemp. Hist.*, Oct. 1967.

interpretation of Christian social thought which had almost exclusively emphasized the need for social harmony, had promoted the idea of inter-class solidarity in opposition to the Marxists' acceptance and even furtherance of class conflict, had seen in co-operation between all the sectors (classes) of the community the solution for the nation's social problems. It had revolved around the elusive concept of the 'common good', always presented as something clear-cut in philosophical terms and obvious in practice. Even in 1963 Pe Fernando Bastos Ávila, SJ, one of the more progressive representatives of this viewpoint, which predominated till the very end of the 1950s, proclaimed in the *Manifesto Solidarista*: 'The community is the natural place where men think and will together, where they plan and decide together in function of the common good'.[34] How different a note do we hear from Cardonnel:

We can never insist enough on the need to denounce natural harmony, class collaboration. God is not so dishonest, so false as a certain kind of social peace, consisting in the acquiescence of all in an unnatural injustice. Violence is not only a fact of revolutions. It also characterizes the maintenance of a false order.[35]

The radical turning point in JUC

Thus various factors had combined to swing JUC into a more radical mood. There was the growing dissatisfaction, inside the movement, with its lack of success, and with the failure to relate itself to the concrete problems facing its potential membership. The changing outlook of European Christian circles was reflected in Brazil not only in Cardonnel's articles, but also in the writings of Lebret, Mounier, and other 'advanced' Catholic thinkers, increasingly available in Portuguese.[36] Of importance was also the French Christian existentialist journal, *Esprit*, founded by Mounier. This coincided with a growing active concern among students—Catholic and other—with social problems in cities such as Recife, Belo Horizonte, and Natal, where they began to set up various educational or organizational projects among the urban masses, and with a shift towards the social sciences among the subjects read at university. Thus the discovery of 'Brazilian

[34] Fernando Bastos de Ávila, *Neo-capitalismo, socialismo, solidarismo*, 2nd ed. (1963), pp. 11–12.

[35] Reproduced in H. J. Souza, ed., *Christianismo hoje* (1962), p. 21.

[36] Cf. Leonard D. Therry, 'Dominant Power Components in the Brazilian University Student Movement, prior to April 1964', *J. Inter-Amer. Studies*, Jan. 1965, pp. 33–4, who lists these translations.

reality' was coming about not only by means of academic study and evaluation reflected in the growing sociological output mainly emanating from the Universities of São Paulo and Belo Horizonte and from the ISEB, but also through direct contact and the indignation it provoked. There was widespread fermentation in the universities at large,[37] and finally, of course, the social and economic transformations, and the political tensions, which were gripping Brazil in the years following Juscelino Kubitschek's inauguration as President, greatly contributed to the radical tone the discussion was beginning to acquire.

JUC's National Council had decided to make the search for and elaboration of an *ideal histórico* into the centre-piece of its tenth anniversary Congress, to be held in July 1960. That Congress was both exceptional and of substantial importance: it brought together 500 delegates from all over the country, in contrast with the usual score or so at the annual councils. A long analysis, meant as a kind of working draft for such a project, was presented to the Congress by the *equipe* from Belo Horizonte, one of a number of texts which had been earlier discussed (and criticized, but *not* amended) in a meeting of the National Council immediately preceding the Congress. JUC was strongly represented in Belo Horizonte among students in the Faculty of Economics and Social Science, and the main outlines of their analysis of social reality will provide some feeling of the way the radicals' ideology was developing.[38]

The basic options for Brazil are considered to be three. In the first place, there is the need to overcome underdevelopment. Secondly, the freeing of the country from the 'gravitational field' of capitalism, as the continued existence of capitalist institutions is an impediment, in Brazil, to development. Finally there is the need to break the inter-

---

[37] Background information on both the Christian and the secular Left may also be found in the article by Therry referred to in n. 36. While containing useful data, the paper suffers greatly from the distortions arising out of Therry's incapacity to see politics in terms other than those of American 'democracy'. He seems antipathetic to the concept 'united front', greatly overplays the part played by the communists, and never fails to be critical of any organization to which he cannot comfortably attach the label 'democratic'. As a result his judgements, and occasionally even his facts (e.g. on the relation between MEB and AP), are unreliable. Here is a sample from his Conclusion: 'Among the major actors described in this study one finds no independent left in the true sense of the word, however. All are compromised, to one degree or another, with external interests: the MRT [*Movimento Revolucionario Tiradentes*] with Castroism, the POLOP [*Política Operária*] with the Peking variety of Communism, and the JUC and AP with the PCB, which in turn is linked to Moscow' (p. 47).

[38] Regional Centro-Oeste, 'Algumas directrizes de um ideal histórico Cristão para o povo brasileiro', in JUC, *Ideal histórico*, pp. 27–32.

national equilibrium generated by capitalism, shamefully based on the complementarity of the metropolitan and the colonial nations. Thus, in a negative sense, development involves disengagement from the free play of international exchanges, the rules of which are set by the economically dominant countries and the 'egotistical policies of the monopolies (trusts, cartels, holdings, etc.)'. In a positive sense it is seen to involve the creation of a solid infrastructure of basic industry, the development of an efficient transport system, the elimination of regional disparities and the enlargement of the internal market. One of the pre-conditions for the last requirement is the carrying out of an agrarian reform, which is to lead to the modernization of agriculture as well as to the creation of co-operative and 'socialized' agrarian institutions.

The economy must be planned so that its workings reflect priorities based on the needs of the people; it is to be organized within the total perspective of the personalist ideas of Mounier, to become a 'personal economy, of persons and for persons, using means which are appropriate to persons'. That would mean the acceptance of the principle of the primacy of labour over capital, 'the substitution of the institution of private property . . . by an effective instrument of personalization for all Brazilians, with due regard to the higher requirements of the common good'. The commanding heights of the economy are to be nationalized, i.e. put under state control; in other sectors of industry worker co-management should be instituted. The anonymous nature of capitalist property, with its great and powerful limited companies, should be eliminated; the abolition is called for of the 'proletarian condition', a term used to refer to the situation in which the Brazilian masses, whose work produces the national riches, are robbed of the benefits of this production.

Even in such a short, and necessarily inadequate, summary it can be seen how ideas from very different sources are mixed together in this first tentative statement of the reality component of the *ideal histórico*. Socialist ideas and Marxist slogans intermingle with barely digested lumps of personalist philosophy, whose implications for practical policy are hardly considered. Apparently the project was debated with such gusto that its publication after the Congress was followed in the JUC bulletin by a page of cautionary observations from the national leadership, mainly based on the as yet not incorporated criticisms voiced at the preceding National Council. These pointed out that the ideas were merely provisional, that the paper had been written somewhat in haste, and used at times intemperate language (though not intemperate ideas). Moreover these ideas at many points went beyond the intermediate principles which constitute the essence of any *ideal histórico* into the formulation of specific lines of policy, the choice of which ought to be left to the individual. More about this later; the goings-on at the Congress greatly strengthened the chorus of those raising the hue and cry of Marxist infiltration.

JUC and the university

As a specialized section of Catholic Action, JUC's primary concern was meant to be its own 'milieu', the university. JUC participated actively in general student politics, and, like other student movements, developed a specific concern for university reform. The Latin American university reform movement, which originated in 1918 in Córdoba, Argentina, had till then completely by-passed Brazil. A Latin American seminar on the issue held in Salvador, Bahia, in May 1960, in which a majority of participants were Marxists, marked the beginning of growing agitation in the universities.[39] Early in the following year the *União Nacional de Estudantes*, UNE, organized a national seminar also in Salvador. This time a large proportion of the participants were *JUCistas*. The reformers' demands were aimed not only at giving students a say in the running of the universities, but also at the 'de-alienation' of the whole system of education with its archaic curricula irrelevant to development, and its gross inequalities of opportunity which effectively excluded from a university education all but an insignificant number of students from the urban masses. Students thus began by denouncing the internal university set-up, but soon moved on to look at the social functions which the university fulfilled. They realized that it turned out graduates who would become part of a small and highly privileged minority—a minority which lacked the qualifications as well as the capacity to tackle the country's problems of development. 'Questions of the purpose of a university education led to others on the role of the intellectuals and the élite in society; then finally, to doubts about the very course of that society.'[40]

[39] Dale, p. 14. For a theoretical statement of the position held on the secular left of the student movement, see Álvaro Vieira Pinto, *A questão da universidade* [1962]. A Catholic view on the subject can be found in JUC, *Boletim informativo*, no. 2, [1963], pp. 18–21.

[40] Pierre Furter, 'Caminhos e descaminhos de uma política da juventude', *Paz e terra*, no. 3 (1967), p. 37.

It did not take JUC long to realize that the centres of learning are not islands isolated from the rest of society. Already at the 1960 Congress the university milieu was defined as 'comprising all the micro-structures of the university, and the macro-structures of society in so far as they influence, or are influenced by, the university micro-structures, and are closely linked to them'.[41] During the next two years the struggle for university reform which JUC waged, together with other student organizations (mostly representing varieties of Marxism), achieved nothing, despite strikes, demonstrations, and other forms of militancy. This only strengthened the students' convictions that changes in the university and in education would result from, rather than bring about, a basic restructuring of society. Early in 1963 this point was made as follows in a JUC bulletin:

At the present time the student movement, and particularly its leadership, is becoming conscious of the fact that university reform is part of the [more general] Brazilian process, intrinsically articulated with the socio-economic and political structures. This being so we could not simply start with university reform and move on to achieve [changes in the wider society]; university reform has to become part of the Brazilian Revolution.[42]

Here, then, is another road which turns out to have led to a more general revolutionary position, a position which drove all students, Catholics and non-Catholics alike, out of their own 'milieu' into the wider society. Student politics, as will presently be seen, provided one bridge between university and society. But as the conviction grew that no change would be seen in the university until radical changes had been brought about in society, students increasingly participated in, rather than merely talked about 'Brazilian reality'. They joined or set up organizations whose focus of activity was outside the universities, which were engaged in political or educational work with the masses in town or countryside, such as the *Centros Populares de Cultura* and *Ação Popular*. These will be further discussed below. (Of course, MEB also fits into this list.) First a few lines on student politics, which brought Catholic students in contact with others acting in the universities.

Catholic participation in student politics did not *formally* involve JUC. It was more a matter of involvement by a number of individuals who shared a common set of views and beliefs, acquired through their

[41] JUC, *Ideal histórico*, p. 6.
[42] JUC, *Boletim informativo*, no. 2, pp. 19–20.

membership in JUC. But of course it was difficult to draw the line: individuals who stood for office were known to belong to certain groups, and votes were cast for candidates in view of the label attached to them, however invisible, at least as much as because of their personal characteristics.[43] JUC had always attempted to participate in student politics at the local (faculty) level, but only gradually did the movement widen its 'militance' to the regional and national spheres. The latter occurred with *éclat* in 1960, when the UNE Congress took place shortly after that of JUC. On that occasion a left-wing candidate, Oliveiros Guanais, was elected to the presidency of UNE with the support of JUC and the Marxists. In 1961 an actual militant of JUC, Aldo Arantes of the Catholic University of Rio de Janeiro, captured the highest office in UNE. Arantes's success no doubt owed something to the furore caused by a manifesto published early that year by the students' council of his university, in which he played a prominent part. This manifesto, coming from the students of a Catholic university, shocked established Catholic opinion not only because of its denunciations of the alienating bourgeois university, the class nature of the state, and the vacuousness of the constitutionally guaranteed liberties, but also because of its very daring theology of history, which was far 'in advance' of anything commonly accepted as progressive in Brazil. Arantes was, in fact, expelled from JUC after his election to UNE by the Cardinal of Rio de Janeiro. The Catholic students' manifesto owed much to the thought (and on that occasion to the active help) of Pe Henrique de Lima Vaz, SJ, a brilliant young philosopher and theologian, whose influence during this period on the entire generation we are considering was profound.[44] He had emerged into the limelight during the controversy over the Cardonnel articles, and had participated in a seminar of 80 JUC leaders from all over the country which was held in Santos, in February 1961, where he had laid the groundwork for the later transition from the concept *ideal histórico* to that of *consciência histórica* (historical consciousness).[45]

The massive entry of JUC into national student politics brought it

---

[43] See Sonia Seganfreddo, *UNE, instrumento de subversão* (1963), pp. 6 ff. Though this is a polemical, thoroughly reactionary, and at many points inaccurate account of the history and activities of UNE, the careful reader can benefit from the information it contains. It touches at various points on the role of *JUCistas* in UNE.

[44] The manifesto is reproduced in Souza, *Cristianismo hoje*, pp. 89–98. See, in the same volume, Pe Vaz's defence both of the manifesto and of his own indirect role in its formulation, pp. 55–68.

[45] See below, pp. 87 ff.

into closer contact than hitherto with other student groups, including those of the secular Left, with which it collaborated on an increasing scale. In 1962 only one candidate to the UNE presidency was nominated, backed by all major groups, from communists to JUC. JUC's experience at the 'bases' of university life, the concentration of its efforts in the actual *faculdades*, had stood the movement in good stead when it moved up to the national level. Its concern with actual students 'of flesh and blood' became an example to others who participated in UNE: before the turn of the decade UNE had consisted almost exclusively of a *cúpula* (top leadership group) and had had little contact with the people it purported to represent. In the early 1960s financial support dispensed with largesse by the Ministry of Education gave UNE substantial room for manœuvre, and some possibility of exercising influence on the national scene. Its pronouncements on and incursions into national politics multiplied; it became headline material in the national press. But politicking once again removed the leadership from contact with the student bases, and even in JUC some problems of this kind seem to have developed. Action, any kind of action, became good in itself. A little later, in the middle of 1963, an article in a JUC bulletin dealing with the movement's involvement in student politics was to muse: 'We in JUC lost the habit of seeing and judging. Thus our action became poor in humanizing and salvation-bringing content, often even lacked it altogether.' Another writer, in the same issue, had this to say:

A sudden awakening to a reality which required a response from Christians . . . [led to] . . . an over-valuation of socially oriented activity and the reform of structures, while the structure of the movement itself was neglected. As the movement grew, took up coherent positions, came to be believed in in the student milieu, gradually became committed, it came to lack depth, reflection and organization. The most diverse commitments were entered into which had virtually no apostolic meaning. The movement thus denied its own *raison d'être*.[46]

Almost certainly these criticisms did not reflect the feelings of the majority of JUC's membership, for whom the opening which had at last been achieved to social and political reality was only to be welcomed. But they were very similar indeed to the complaints of the hierarchy two years earlier, which had led to a major conflict between

---

[46] JUC, *Boletin informativo*, no. 2, respectively pp. 15 & 7.

students and bishops. That conflict had been caused in the first place
by the fact that JUC was obviously developing a view of the proper
role of the church in the world, and of the layman in the church, which
was not at all shared by the vast majority of bishops. The other, and
more immediately visible, cause of the conflict was to be found in the
bishops' disagreement with JUC's public position on socio–political
matters. To understand that disagreement we must spend some time
in examining the position of the bishops themselves.

I have, so far, ignored the pronouncements of members and organs
of the hierarchy, and it would, indeed, be difficult to see in them direct
sources of the radical ideas with which we are here concerned. But
Brazil's bishops have never been homogeneous in their socio–political
views, and various episcopal statements in the decade preceding the
awakening of JUC must have helped to prepare the ground for a radical
position which was specifically Christian. The following account,
though it inevitably constitutes a digression, should provide at least
some indication of the degree to which the Brazilian bishops contributed to create the atmosphere in which the 'radical explosion' of the
turn of the decade occurred. It should also illuminate the extent to
which that radical explosion had left the bishops behind.

The point of view of the Brazilian hierarchy[47]

On 10 September 1950, shortly after JUC had been launched as a
national movement, the Franciscan bishop of the small and ancient
town of Campanha, in Minas Gerais, published a pastoral letter on the
occasion of a rural (study) week, which brought together 60 rural
parish priests, 250 landowners, 270 rural teachers, and various people
in religious orders working in secondary schools. Its title was: 'With
us, without us, or against us the rural milieu will be reformed'. After
reminding his audience that the church 'lost' the urban workers in
nineteenth-century Europe, D. Inocêncio Engelke stated that a similar
danger threatened the church in respect of the rural workers of his day.
While 'their situation is sub-human amongst us,'[48] the

[47] I am grateful to Pe Raimundo Caramuru for making available to me much of the
documentation on which the present section is based. As that documentation was largely
in typewritten, mimeographed, or pamphlet form, quotations cannot be cited with precise
page numbers.

[48] It is not without interest to find already in this first public church document of recent
times on the life of Brazil's rural population, the term 'sub-human situation', a term which
in the mid- and late 1960s came to be so strongly identified with D. Helder Câmara.

agitators are reaching the fields. If they act with intelligence they will not even have to invent anything. They merely need to comment on reality, to lay bare the situation in which the rural workers live or vegetate. Far be it from us, Christian employers, to do justice moved by fear. Anticipate the revolution. Do from a spirit of Christianity what the directives of the Church indicate...

and that means not just the giving of alms but the doing of justice. D. Inocêncio went on to say that one did not have to wait for the passing of social legislation in order to fulfil one's Christian duty; he spoke of social action which could not be postponed, of the need to de-proletarianize the rural workers. 'The terrible picture challenging sociologists, legislators . . . and the Christian apostolate is that of an enormous mass of workers without lands and of enormous areas of land without workers.'

From then on other pastoral letters, individual or collective, related to social problems begin to make their appearance. The next year three bishops from the state of Rio Grande do Norte put out a document—of a thoroughly traditional kind—on the occasion of another study week on rural problems. In 1952 two meetings were held, respectively in July and August, of bishops whose dioceses were in 'development areas'—the Amazon region and the region of the São Francisco valley. They were apparently requested by *Ação Católica*, and formally called by the Papal Nuncio—the National Bishops' Conference of Brazil, the CNBB, which would later become the organizational focus for such meetings, was not founded until later that year.[49] The discussion of the prelates from Amazônia arose out of the government's Plan for Economic Improvement of Amazônia,[50] which broadly discussed some of the problems peculiar to the region (such as health, education, migration and colonization, the rubber gatherers). The prelates stressed the pioneer role which the church might play, especially in education, the provision of hospitals, etc., and gave warning of the dangers of giving a supposedly Marxist-inspired primacy to the economy.

[49] The CNBB (*Conferência Nacional dos Bispos do Brasil*) was the brainchild of D. Helder Câmara, then auxiliary bishop of Rio, who became the CNBB's first secretary-general, a post he held until his appointment to the See of Recife in 1964. D. Helder apparently also had a hand in the organization of the two meetings under discussion here: he signed the São Francisco document as secretary of the *Encontro*.

[50] The *Superintendência do Plano de Valorização Econômica de Amazônia* (SPVEA) had been created by the Dutra government in 1948 and had been leading a more or less hibernating existence ever since. Vargas, early in his second government, made some attempts at infusing new life into the Plan (see Skidmore, p. 71).

A similar concern was expressed in the declaration of the bishops of the São Francisco valley, also related to a governmental development plan.[51] The absence of any provision for religious assistance was criticized, as was the small proportion of the 1951–5 budget (2·5 per cent) earmarked for education, and the lack of emphasis on co-operation with private entities, especially schools and hospitals. The bishops then called for human as opposed to 'mere economic' development—a call from then on repeated again and again in all conceivable contexts by groups of bishops or Catholic laymen. The São Francisco bishops went on to discuss problems of health, education, and migration, and then plunged into an examination of agrarian problems and land reform. In this area the specific recommendations remain very cautious: although (partial or total) expropriation of a *latifúndio* which no longer fulfils its social functions can be justified provided 'reasonable indemnification' is given, basically the bishops place their hope in the colonization of empty lands. As for occupied property, 'it is utopian in our milieu and circumstances to think of large-scale expropriation (we lack resources, psychological climate and political maturity for this)'. But already in 1952 these bishops were speaking of the need for a new educational orientation in the countryside, for the formation of local rural leaders, who are to take over from the 'urban lawyers'.[52]

Four years later a meeting of considerable importance took place in Campina Grande in Paraíba. In May 1956, under the auspices of the CNBB, the bishops of the North-East met as a group for the first time, to discuss the region's socio–economic problems, together with lay experts, including representatives of various ministers who had actively co-operated in the preparation of the *Encontro*. After the meeting, which lasted six days, and was closed by President Kubitschek himself, a lengthy document was published.[53] The bishops' declaration—obviously the work of specialists—analysed both the region's social and economic life and the manifold official organs involved in aspects of its development, and presented detailed proposals

---

[51] The *Comissão do Vale do São Francisco* had also been established in 1948, and again it was the 2nd Vargas government which tried, late in 1951, to rescue it from ineffectiveness. This would, incidentally, be to no avail: the CVSF continued to lead 'a wholly undistinguished existence'. (See A. O. Hirschman, *Journeys Toward Progress* (1963), espec. pp. 50–5.)

[52] This concern came strongly to the fore once the rural *sindicatos* were organized—but 'urban lawyers' apparently maintained their predominant positions. See ch. 6.

[53] It was reissued in 1960 by the government, together with the various presidential decrees which were a direct result of the meeting. Cf. Brazil, Presidência, Serviço de Documentação, *I Encontro dos bispos do Nordeste* (1960).

for various community projects in the region. Again a 'paternal warning to the economists' about their purely economic goals, and the need for a broader perspective on man is heard.

The church has no technical and temporal solutions to the problems of an economic and social nature which it presents as specifically its own. It examines the concrete data and attempts to analyse these from a moral point of view. It is in the religious and moral field, and moreover in the direct or indirect repercussions of social and economic problems, that we find the mode of action peculiar to the church. . . . The church can help to set the obviously important methods and techniques of development in the context of the natural requirements of a Christian humanism.

The bishops from the North-East went on to say that 'in the present socio–economic structures which constitute our political organization and the system of our private economy there are tremendous injustices', injustices for which the church bears no responsibility, and which it cannot condone. 'The church . . . places itself on the side of those unjustly treated, so that it may co-operate with them in a task of recuperation and redemption.' The most significant conclusion was that which pointed out that the technical and administrative needs of the North-East could no longer be met by the multifarious state organs operating in the area: a new 'higher-level plan', designed to bring the various public authorities, private initiatives, and the church into closer co-operation, was urgently required. This point was further elaborated in the appended suggestions by the working groups. One of these, after analysing the predominance of personal and sectional interests, and the ubiquity of political machinations, in the bidding for federal financial support for the region, called for 'a great national programme for the North-East'. Over three years were to pass before that great national programme finally crystallized in the shape of the Superintendency for the Development of the North-East (SUDENE), established after a presidential bill had been passed by Congress in December 1959. Many forces helped to give birth to this important agency—forces of a natural (the 1958 drought) as well as of a political kind. One of these was, no doubt, the enthusiasm for such an agency among the bishops of the North-East, which was even more pronounced at their second meeting in May 1959 (by which time unrest in the region was clearly growing).[54]

By now the Kubitschek era, with its general exaltation, its great

[54] See Hirschman, p. 85.

developmental plans, and, significantly, the growing signs of 'troubles' in some of the country's rural areas had opened. The bishops of Amazônia met a second time late in 1957, those of the North-East, as has been stated, in mid-1959. The former concerned themselves with little else but internal church problems, but the latter focused once again mainly on the socio–economic structure. Nevertheless, all these pronouncements remained, as one would expect, firmly circumscribed by the traditional doctrine of the church. Those from the North-East bishops did seem to anticipate a more activist line in the pursuit of social justice; generally, however, the stress on 'harmony between the social classes' (CNBB declaration of 1958) remained the dominant note, tempered by 'appeals' to those in positions of privilege or authority. Thus on the occasion of the tabling of a state bill on land reform, the São Paulo episcopate, much more conservative than the prelates from the North-East, appealed late in 1960 to the rural landowners to be 'of open mind and open heart'. In the same declaration they appealed to the rural workers to seek an 'enlightened and Christian person' to tell them about the scope of the agrarian reform, as the danger of misunderstanding would arise should they 'be informed about it in a tendentious way by agitators interested in exploiting the issue'; and they were told to 'remain alert to communist infiltration'.

In July 1961 Pope John published his encyclical *Mater et Magistra*, the first major pronouncement on social matters by a ruling pontiff since Pius XI's *Quadragesimo Anno* of 1931. Although *Mater et Magistra* makes no startling new departures—this was much more the case with Pope John's second social encyclical, *Pacem in Terris*, of April 1963—it did provide a progressive gloss on the church's traditional social doctrine. The Central Commission of the CNBB referred to this encyclical in a document it released in October 1961, but there was no sign that its impact had been very profound. The CNBB's document discusses, among other matters, the rural situation. This is done in terms which are both fairly general and merely cautiously reformist: the document speaks of developments in infrastructure, new agricultural techniques, tax policies, credits, price controls, and agro-industry. But land reform is not mentioned, let alone expropriation. MEB, which was then just starting, is paternally patted on the head as 'a providential instrument in our hands for the . . . expansion of JAC, of rural unionization, and of the *Frentes Agrárias*'. Finally, the communist menace is once again paraded before the faithful. Not only are communists not interested in solutions—for them, the worse the better

—but 'red agitators on various fronts prepare for guerrilla tactics, in accordance with the best Cuban or Chinese examples'.[55]

Growing friction between JUC and the hierarchy

It was in this mood that the hierarchy finally met the 'challenge' from JUC head-on in 1961. The conflict had been simmering ever since the Congress of July 1960, after which a number of prominent Catholics had apparently 'denounced' the movement to various bishops. The large-scale participation of *JUCistas* in the UNE seminar on university reform (Salvador, early 1961) had created further problems, especially with D. Eugênio Sales, then Apostolic Administrator of the diocese of Natal, a churchman with reformist social views, but a paternalist in his approach to ecclesiastical matters, and reluctant to allow much freedom of movement to laymen in Catholic organizations. When the National Council of JUC met for the first time since the tenth anniversary Congress, in July of 1961 in Natal, the tensions found expression in the announcement of the national *assistente*, Fr. Romeu Dale, that he intended to resign. Though he did not say as much, his consistent defence of the movement had produced stresses and differences between himself and the hierarchy which had become hard to bear.

By this time it had become increasingly apparent that JUC's conception of its place within the church, of the extent of freedom it might expect from ecclesiastical control, and of its proper sphere of action, diverged substantially from the thinking dominant among the hierarchy. This thinking was shared by D. Eugênio, who was present at the 1961 Council meetings as an observer. Various specific points of view expressed during that Council meeting disturbed him greatly, and he raised the matter of JUC's position with the episcopal commission for Catholic Action when it met shortly afterwards.[56] His strictures met with much sympathy among other members of the commission who had also been outraged by the manifesto of students in Rio's Catholic University, made public a few months before, in which JUC was believed to have had a hand. They decided to take the bull by the horns, and after officially forbidding the publication of any text discussed or agreed upon by the 1961 Council of JUC, they issued an extremely strongly worded directive to JUC's national and regional

---

[55] For further references and important statements by the Brazilian bishops in 1963 and 1964 see below, pp. 84 f, 190 ff.

[56] Dale, p. 18.

directorates and their *assistentes*, which roundly forbade the movement
to make radical pronouncements or to engage in what the bishops
considered undesirable political activities.[57]

JUC then found itself in the crisis of legitimacy which had been
looming ever since it embarked upon the uncharted seas of *ideal
histórico*. The crisis had been present in embryonic form in the very
concept, which was, after all, made up of two ideas whose practical
implications were very different. The first one, the notion of 'intermediate principles' supposed to guide the individual in his specific
choices under concrete circumstances, is indeterminate and ambiguous,
vague enough to leave much freedom to individual judgement
regarding those circumstances. This characteristic it shares with much
of Catholic social thought, serviceable to a wide range of opinions and
policies.

But the second element of the *ideal histórico* tends to make it like a
utopia, concrete and specific, spelling out the details of an ideal, yet
potentially realizable, social order. Utopian blueprints for the future
have much greater specificity—and persuasiveness—than intermediate
principles guiding behaviour in a general direction; they underpin
one, rather than a variety of socio–political viewpoints. Utopias allow
less room for choice, and lead to wider areas of commitment. This
apparent commitment of JUC, an official organ of the church with a
mandate from the hierarchy, to specific social and political options for
Brazil first of all brought about some internal tensions in the movement: as has been seen, not all members approved of the ideas and
actions which almost came to be regarded by the majority as JUC's
'official line'. But of greater consequence was the fact that it brought
down the wrath of the bishops—partly, no doubt, because the options
did not coincide with their more conservative ones, partly as a result
of pique over the trespassing on their authority.

One cannot say that the students had not been aware of this problem.
It had been put to them at the 1960 Congress by one of their *assistentes*.
Pe Sena had remarked: 'The hierarchy has the task of governing the
church . . . from them we must finally receive the authentic interpretation of Revelation and Tradition; to them we must submit our
experience and our conclusions.' And although he had pointed out
that 'the task of Christian initiative falls to the faithful [the laymen],
who are the front-line soldiers', he had added: 'When the hierarchy

[57] The full text may be found in the *Revista ecclesiástica brasileira*, vol. 21, fasc. A, Dec.
1961.

approves our conquests, it is as if they are canonized and inserted into the tradition of the church'.[58] The laymen, however, showed little inclination meekly to submit for approval to priests or bishops the social and political judgements they had arrived at as Christians. They had become aware—as another of their *assistentes*, Fr. Romeu Dale, explained in a document which appeared shortly after the bishops' restrictive directives were issued—that 'the authority of the clergy normally is limited' and that it does not belong to the task of the hierarchy to organize the structures of society. They also resented the often very 'authoritarian and distant' exercise of authority by bishops, who treated all laymen 'as if they were minors'. Such behaviour does not go down well with a generation that has struggled hard to free itself from the weight of parental authority in Brazil's traditional patriarchal family.[59]

All this was true and important, and yet there was force in the argument, formulated by Fr. Romeu, that the work of JUC could have no meaning without a vital link with the bishops. Catholic Action was a movement of the church; as part of it, JUC was subordinated and owed obedience to the hierarchy. The problem was that its members had, in a sense, run away with the organization.[60] As members of JUC, the only nation-wide Catholic organization in the universities, the students had embarked together on an exciting journey of discovery. On this journey they had met others, non-Catholics, similarly engaged, and they were proud of what they had found and committed to hold on to it.[61] Too bad that the hierarchy had originally given them a mandate; intolerable that the bishops now wanted to control them. JUC was their organization, they had shaped it into what it now was, they made use of its structures to think and act together. In short they *were* JUC.

To the *assistentes*, the problem did not present itself in such a simple light. Many of them had fully identified themselves with the new course of the movement, and wanted as much as the membership to use the organization for the promotion of a social revolution in Brazil, to which they felt the Church should give its blessing. But they were priests, after all, specifically appointed by their bishop to a position of trust, and they were torn by a dilemma of loyalties until precise instructions

[58] Pe Sena, 'Reflexões sôbre o ideal histórico', JUC, *Ideal histórico*, p. 15.
[59] Dale, pp. 34–5.
[60] It will be seen in ch. 8 how a very similar process occurred in MEB.
[61] For a general view of the dynamics of an emerging 'youth-consciousness' in Brazil, see Furter, in *Paz e terra*, no. 3 (1967).

had been received from the hierarchy. They were preparing the following question for the bishops when the latter intervened:

Would it befit JUC, *as a movement*, to assume the responsibility for organized work in the political field? Or would it be better for the members who are militants in university politics to organize themselves on their own behalf, in a separate group, acting on their own responsibility, as Christians—but including others who are not from JUC, and even not Christians?[62]

The *assistentes* looked at the matter from the point of view of its appropriateness. The members of JUC, who were thinking in similar terms even before the hierarchy forced them to take their politics elsewhere, had clearly begun to question the very nature of what was appropriate to the movement. This occurred within the framework of a wider reappraisal of the relationship between the hierarchy and the laymen in the church, the division of labour between them, and the extent to which their relationship should be governed by authority or co-operation, by a requirement to obtain permission at least for the outlines of action (and thought), or by freedom to develop under their own steam and on their own responsibility. *JUCistas* were also beginning to feel, as they moved from student politics to activities outside the universities, that they should broaden their base to include others— intellectuals, workers, and peasants. At that stage JUC, though already considering that possibility, was not yet willing formally to break with Catholic Action and the hierarchy and to declare itself an independent lay movement (a step that was to be taken in mid-1966). Instead, as a result of internal necessities and the bishops' external pressure, a new movement, *Ação Popular*, was born. Once this alternative vehicle for social and political action—which was joined by most of the more active members of JUC—had come into being, the preoccupation of JUC itself turned more and more to reflection about the question that had originally sparked off the crisis: the role of the layman in the church, and the theological and philosophical analysis of his action in the world *qua* member of the church.[63]

[62] Dale, p. 27.

[63] At the Vatican Council the problem of the role of the laity was given a thorough airing, and the discussions, where fairly radical opinions on the matter were expressed, had an influence among the laity at least as great as the more 'equilibrated' final document, the *Decree on the Apostolate of the Laity*, or the relevant sections in the *Dogmatic Constitution on the Church*, also known as *Lumen Gentium*. Together with the other texts promulgated by the Vatican Council, they may be found in Walter M. Abbott, SJ, ed., *The Documents of Vatican II* (1966). For a discussion which clearly reflects the views of the people we have been concerned with in these paragraphs, by someone who was greatly involved during the whole period, see Luis Alberto Gomes de Sousa, *O Cristão e o mundo* (1965).

5

The Heyday of the Catholic Radicals I:
Theory and Ideology

AP and its philosophy of history

AÇÃO POPULAR had been informally started sometime late in 1961, but was officially launched on 1 June 1962, a political movement rather than a political party. Many of its initiators were drawn from among the most active JUC militants, though from the start it attracted people from outside Catholic student circles. By now no trace was left of the lack of social engagement prevalent in the Catholic student movement at an earlier stage.[1] Hence this chapter will deal with the most decisive phase for the non-Marxist radicals of the pre-coup period.

It is essential to remember throughout that views and activities obtaining until April 1964 are under review here. Especially for AP no extrapolation from these to the years after its violent repression at that date is permissible. The history of AP in the most recent years remains to be written—that history will, I believe, show fundamental, even essential, differences from the pre-coup days. Thus the specific period examined here gives no guidance to AP's own later orientation: the movement seems to have lost virtually all connections with its own roots in specifically *Christian* radical thought, a development that had its beginning even before the coup. But this pre-coup period does remain of seminal importance for an understanding of the ideas in

---

[1] The lack of wider social relevance of that previous orientation may be glimpsed from an article written in a pamphlet commemorating the fifth anniversary of JEC in Belo Horizonte: *5 Anos de JEC* (Belo Horizonte, 1958), pp. 18–21. Then, the main preoccupation was clearly religious. Student readers were urged to deepen their faith. The list of authors suggested as fundamental to a more humane vision of Christianity is instructive. Of 21 names 2 are younger contemporary Brazilian priests, who had a direct influence on the movement; 7 are saints, church fathers, or founders of holy orders. Most of the others are such Catholic literary figures as Graham Greene or Chesterton; only three, Jacques Maritain, Simone Weil, and Father Lebret, were people whose main concern was with the social rather than the personal or spiritual.

MEB in particular, which did continue to function openly after the coup, and without any kind of repudiation of its own past. The period examined in the following pages was, as will be seen in Chapter 8, a momentous one for MEB, and many of its own principles emerged both under the influence of, and in reaction against, the views to which I will shortly turn.

From mid-1962 until its forcible removal from the political scene it seems that AP gathered substantial support outside the few universities which had been the centres of JUC radicalism—although it is interesting to note that at first AP was apparently not very successful in Recife, where a good deal of 'committed' activity of one kind or another had been going on for some time—from SUDENE, through the municipally-sponsored programmes of *cultura popular*, to the literacy efforts promoted by the university under the direction of Paulo Freire. It seems to have found new adherents in the first instance in the lesser universities and colleges, among young intellectuals and professionals, and among older secondary-school students. Most of these people must have come from backgrounds which were at least middle class.[2] Later AP created something of a following among the more articulate workers and peasants, but their numbers never reached significant proportions and their commitment never seems to have gone very deep. Thus AP remained till the coup essentially a 'populist' movement, namely one of intellectuals for the people.[3]

No trustworthy information exists on the size of AP's membership, or on the area in which it effectively operated.[4] 'Membership', moreover, is a somewhat misleading term in this context. There was in AP a small core of perhaps twenty to thirty ideologues and activists, a

[2] On the social composition of AP there is an almost complete lack of reliable evidence. The coup of 1964 scattered the movement and its documentation, and scotched all moves to obtain objective statistical data on it. One thus has to rely largely on those who remember their contemporary impressions, hardly a reliable method for the gathering of statistical evidence. One of those impressions was conveyed to me by Mrs Maria Brandão, a sociologist from the University of Bahia. She suggested that the young AP militants hailed mainly from traditional upper- or middle-class families. To them the movement represented an 'acceptable' protest, however radical, because of its implicit Christian label. These considerations about social background almost certainly apply *a fortiori* to JUC.

[3] For a discussion of the origins of this concept and a justification of its use in this, for Latin America, unusual manner, see below, pp. 94–8.

[4] Thomas G. Sanders, in his excellent paper 'Catholicism and Development: the Catholic Left in Brazil', in Kalman H. Silvert, ed., *Churches and States* (1967), p. 96, states that in early 1964 AP had about 3,000 members—without, however, giving any source. Leonard D. Therry (*J. Inter-Amer. Studies*, Jan. 1965, p. 36) suggests that at that time active membership was estimated to be between 2,000 and 3,000.

group neither monolithic in views, nor constant in membership, throughout the period. This was the *cúpula*. They produced, often after long discussions and arguments, the movement's general lines of orientation and action. Beyond the *cúpula* was the actual membership: those who formed part of some specific AP 'group', often centred on the common work-place of a number of people.[5] These members committed themselves to the lines of action elaborated at the top. But those lines were accepted also by others, who never came to belong to a specific AP 'group'. The somewhat 'floating' co-operation with AP of those 'adherents' seems to have substantially enlarged the scope of a movement which in itself was probably rather small. Certainly until 1964 the movement represented less a political force resulting from disciplined organization, than a 'state of mind' broadly shared by its adherents. When, in the following pages, I refer to AP rather than to other manifestations of Christian radicalism, it is merely because AP was the most articulate of them, and the most important in terms of its scope.

From the start AP was careful to avoid giving the impression that it was in any sense a *Christian* movement. It had no formal ties with the church, nor did it wish to be known as a movement of Christians. Religious or theological references were self-consciously omitted from its documents; nowhere could one find a mention of its antecedents in the Catholic student movement.[6] Nevertheless at the time it was regarded by many as a kind of para-Christian organization, because of the presence in it of so many who had earlier been active in JUC. But perhaps especially because of the difficulties which JUC had experienced with the hierarchy, AP wanted to have nothing to do with bishops *qua* bishops, and mistrusted other organizations which maintained formal links with the church. Needless to say it declared war on the more accommodated, or reformist, Catholic organizations (such as many of the church-sponsored *sindicatos*), but it also joined issue with MEB (especially in the early days of both movements) and even with JUC. Moreover a good number of those identified with AP gradually appear personally to have moved away from religion and Christianity.

The attitude of the hierarchy towards AP was, at first, one of 'wait

---

[5] For further discussion of the operation of AP, see below, pp. 118 ff.

[6] An understandable, but despite that no less absurd, confusion between JUC and the embryonic AP may be found in Seganfreddo, pp. 102 ff., where she cites preparatory documents for AP's founding meeting as referring to JUC.

and see'. Themselves influenced by the climate of radicalization among Brazil's Catholics as well as in the country at large, the Central Commission of the CNBB had been persuaded, while still under the spell of Pope John's encyclical *Pacem in Terris* (published in April 1963), to release a declaration at Easter of that year which went further in subscribing to the need for radical change than anything that had gone before. Prepared in collaboration with a group of prominent Catholic laymen who at least at that stage were far from unsympathetic to the ideas then being formulated among the most radical sector of Catholic opinion, the declaration began by referring in glowing terms to *Pacem in Terris*. It went on to speak of the 'profound aspirations of the *povo*' in this 'underdeveloped country, where the popular masses do not participate in the Brazilian process'. Later it referred to the 'static order, vitiated by the heavy burden of a capitalist tradition', the kind of order in which 'the minority, who have the means, find all doors open to them . . .' and in which 'the majority, who do not have any means, are for that very reason deprived of many of the fundamental and natural rights enunciated in *Pacem in Terris*'. The declaration then went on to refer specifically to various 'urgent transformations'. On the rural question the bishops spoke among other things of 'expropriation in the social interest'; this should be subject to 'just indemnification', but 'with due regard to the possibilities of the country and the demands of the common good'—a formulation that left the door wide open to a much more radical land reform than the church had hitherto been willing to support. Further paragraphs spoke of reform of industrial enterprise, so that increasingly all in industry could effectively participate in its ownership, profits, and decision making; of tax reform; reform of the public bureaucracy; electoral reform (praising the *cédula única* introduced by Goulart); and of reforms in the educational system.[7]

But, as 1963 passed by, the initially neutral attitude of the bishops towards AP was transformed into one of suspicion and even hostility. Developments in AP's ideology, and particularly in its activities, resulted in the Central Commission of the CNBB addressing another pastoral letter in December of that year to those responsible for the youth movement of Catholic Action. They pointed to 'the incompatibility [with Catholic Action] of certain ideological currents in vogue among the lay sector', calling particular attention to the need for extreme care in regard of AP and forbidding Catholic militants to

[7] *Manifesto da Comissão Central da CNBB*, Easter 1963.

enter into united fronts with Marxists. The bishops sought entirely to prevent *JECistas* from entering AP, and carefully circumscribed the conditions under which *JUCistas* could join. One of those conditions would be the militant's 'intent of substantially modifying AP towards an authentic Christian line'.[8] For all that, AP cannot be excluded from the present discussions: despite conflicts with other Christian organizations, despite personal religious doubts, no one could really deny the origins of the movement. In his discussions of this period Cândido Mendes in fact regards AP as *the* expression of the Catholic Left; and though one may quibble with this characterization on formal grounds, there can be little doubt that AP bore the imprint of radical Catholicism until the coup of April 1964.[9]

This imprint can be found in its philosophy of history, the link of which with Catholic theology is no less noticeable for being merely implicit. For AP the central line which runs through history is that of the process of socialization, understood as the increasing density and ubiquity of social (as opposed to individualistic) arrangements of human intercourse. This concept was given prominence in Pope John's encyclical *Mater et Magistra* of 1961, where it was defined as the 'progressive multiplication of relations in society, with different forms of life and activity, and juridical institutionalization'.[10] Previous Popes had used the term 'socialization' in a pejorative fashion, to refer to the encroachment of the state on the private lives of its citizens in economic, social, and political matters. Gradually, however, during the decade before Pope John issued his encyclical, these overtones were lost, and with *Mater et Magistra* the concept finally became 'respectable' in the church—though even then not without encountering substantial opposition from conservative quarters.[11] Pope John regarded socialization 'at one and the same time [as] an effect and a cause of growing intervention of the public authorities', but also as

[8] Quoted in Therry, pp. 39 f.

[9] Mendes (*Memento dos vivos*, p. 51) fails to discuss the historical relationship between JUC and AP. The former is only once mentioned in passing in the book, and negatively at that.

[10] John XXIII, *Mater et Magistra*, para. 59. The English version is the one issued by the Vatican Polyglot Press, reproduced in the *New York Times* of 15 July 1961. It is a pity that this process is designated by 'socialization', a term which has a wholly distinct meaning in standard sociological terminology. In the following paragraphs I shall follow the Catholic usage.

[11] The excellent Brazilian edition, *As encíclicas sociais de João XXIII* (Rio, José Olympio, 1963), contains the Portuguese texts of *Mater et Magistra* and *Pacem in Terris*, with extensive scholarly commentaries to each paragraph from the hand of Luís José de Mesquita. For the point under discussion, see pp. 170-7.

7

'the fruit and expression of a natural tendency, almost irrepressible, in human beings—the tendency to join together to attain objectives which are beyond the capacity and means at the disposal of single individuals.'[12]

Well before Pope John inserted the concept into the main stream of Catholicism, 'socialization' had been an important element in the complex thought of Pierre Teilhard de Chardin, whose ideas had begun to influence the philosophical outlook of the future intellectual leaders of Brazil's radical Catholics by the beginning of the 1960s. Teilhard, a Jesuit, who became a distinguished palaeontologist, developed an early interest in evolutionary theory, and wrote profusely on the subject during his lifetime—without, however, being given permission by his superiors to publish any of his major philosophical works. After his death, in April 1955, his *oeuvre* gradually saw the light of day. It caused a veritable flood of secondary publications— critiques, exegeses, and defences—and soon became a major influence in the Catholic world. Teilhard presented a unified and integrated view of the universe. In Sir Julian Huxley's words, Teilhard considered that the 'different branches of science combine to demonstrate that the universe in its entirety must be regarded as one gigantic process, a process of becoming, of attaining new levels of existence and organization, which can properly be called a genesis or an evolution'.[13] Within this evolution 'socialization' relates to the growth of solidarity among mankind and its unification.[14]

Teilhard's views on this process were only marginally incorporated into Catholic social doctrine by Pope John. For Teilhard, socialization was apparently the result of an ultimately inevitable and irreversible dynamic grounded in the biological and psycho-social nature of man, in the ever closer 'compression' of the world's inhabitants, *and* in the 'pull' exerted on mankind by the 'point Omega', the final state to which the universe is tending. 'For Teilhard this Omega, final point, God, is also Christ—the Man-God whose second coming will bring about the plenitude of the universe of persons.'[15] The unprecedented impact

---

[12] *Mater et Magistra*, para 60.

[13] 'Introduction' to P. Teilhard de Chardin, *The Phenomenon of Man* (1959), p. 13.

[14] For an analysis of the development of Teilhard's thought on the subject, see Robert Coffy, 'Teilhard de Chardin et le socialisme', *Chronique sociale de France* (Lyon), 1966— which despite its title deals exclusively with the idea of socialization. A relevant bibliography is found there on p. 15.

[15] This quotation, one of many possible ones, comes from André Ligneul, *Teilhard et le personnalisme* (1964). I have used the Brazilian edition, in the translation by Marina Bandeira (Petrópolis, Vozes, 1968), p. 42.

of Teilhard's ideas was no doubt largely due to this fusion of science—
Teilhard speaks, for instance, of his reflections on evolution as constituting 'a serious scientific proof that ... the zoological group of
mankind ... is in fact turning ... towards a second critical pole of reflection of a collective and higher order'[16]—and of history, philosophy,
and theology ('For a Christian believer it is interesting to note that the
final success of hominisation (and thus cosmic involution) is positively
guaranteed by the "redeeming virtue" of the God incarnate in his
creation').[17] In that respect Teilhard is a kinsman of Marx, whose
appeal rests to such a large extent on the fact that *scientific* status is
claimed for a *Weltanschauung* which contains both explanations of the
past as well as predictions regarding the future of mankind.[18] AP, not
surprisingly, was influenced by both. Thus AP's *Documento Base*,
elaborated towards the end of 1962 by its co-ordinating team, stated:
'The fact of socialization presides ... over the emergence of human
history, and appears as the fundamental matrix for the interpretation
of its evolution.'[19] Socialization, however, is not in AP's view a simple
evolutionary process; it is a dialectic one (and here we meet the other
mainstream of inspiration, that of Hegelianism mediated through Pe
Vaz), a process in which struggle plays a part of overwhelming
importance.

Before examining this dialectical aspect of socialization it is necessary
to devote some lines to another important philosophical development.
Under the influence of Pe Vaz the previously central notion of *ideal
histórico*—as has been suggested, from the start an ambiguous concept
—was gradually replaced by that of *consciência histórica*. The former
suggested the task of elaborating an image of the future which was a
'realizable ideal essence', something rather like a specific utopia to be
striven for. Historical consciousness, in contrast, is seen to result from
conscious and critical reflection about the historical process (with the
present understood as a result of the past and as a potentiality for the
future), and about the contradictions, conflicts, and *un*desirable
aspects of reality, as much as about man's hopes or ideals, or the highly
valued aspects of his concrete existence. Historical consciousness

---

[16] *Phenomenon of Man*, p. 306.
[17] Ibid., p. 308 n.
[18] See D. G. MacRae, 'The Bolshevik Ideology', in his *Ideology and Society* (London,
1961), pp. 182 ff. Teilhard is also a kinsman of Marx in that many scientists are attracted by
his philosophy but have doubts about his science, while many philosophers or theologians
are impressed by his science while having reservations about his other views.
[19] AP, *Documento base*, Jan. 1963, s. I/1.

emerges when man starts looking critically at his world, and becomes aware of the fact that 'history unfolds in an empirical time-span, which is given substance by the action of man in the form of historical initiative; action, that is, which transforms the world'.[20]

Transformation of the world: that was the general message contained in the call for historical consciousness. A transformation which is based on an understanding of the real conditions found in the here and now (and their historical roots),[21] a transformation which *humanizes* the world.[22] This humanization is also more specifically what modern Christianity demands of man: 'man, in his freedom and in his action, must shoulder the destiny of creation: to refuse this, or to make his appropriation of the world into an egoistical gesture, that is original sin, the fount of evil.' And, radically surmounting religious 'naturalism', Vaz maintains that God should not be regarded as

a cosmic power operating in mythical time, but [as] a Word which unpredictably breaks the regularity of worldly time ... and provokes man to accept a historical destiny which reorients his time so that it comes to be aimed at the historical realization of the Kingdom of God.[23]

Man has the ability to shape history; 'the great sin of the Christian will be today the sin of historical omission'.[24]

Vaz has also examined the problem of the dialectic in history. History, he argues begins to exist only when one man communicates to another the meaning he gives to the world, a meaning more likely than not to be in terms of the domination of man over man. In a significant near-quote he suggests that 'history, till today, has always been this: one man who dominated another, or human groups which dominated other groups, in the most varied ways possible'. But a dialectical 'solution' in terms of domination 'is not the final synthesis of history, its ultimate meaning'. Through this dialectic of domination 'little by little a more profound meaning to history manifests itself: the synthesis in terms of recognition, reconciliation, acceptance of man by man ... as a person'. Although domination and conciliation will always coexist in history,

[20] H. de Lima Vaz, 'Consciência e responsabilidade histórica', in Souza, *Cristianismo hoje*, p. 72.
[21] This, says Vaz, is Marx's contribution (ibid., p. 75).
[22] Ibid., p. 79.
[23] Ibid., p. 80.
[24] Vaz, quoted by Sanders, in Silvert, p. 93. Sanders's discussion of the philosophy of historical consciousness may be profitably consulted.

the problem of the advance of history is that of the permanent overcoming, in ever wider and more universal circles, of domination by reconciliation. This shows us history as a kind of asymmetrical movement, tending towards final reconciliation. That moment, for the Christian, is situated in an historical perspective; the eschatological hope of the final manifestation of God to man.[25]

Vaz had thus carefully formulated his final hope in eschatological terms, commended a hope outside history, a hope—as Karl Rahner would later put it—of the *absolute* future, which man may strive to bring nearer, but can never reach 'in' history.[26] Vaz had recognized the difficulty in this formulation for a wholly secular philosophy of history. Finding no obvious secular equivalent to the 'final manifestation of God to man', he suggested hesitantly to those who could not base themselves on an explicitly Christian standpoint that this asymmetrical tendency of history—the universalization of relations of conciliation—might just be simply accepted. Accepted, he seems to have meant, as an article of faith without a theological anchoring, rather like the Marxist credo of the classless society. And so, indeed, it happened: in the secularized context of AP the eschatological hope became an inner-worldly one. The hope beyond history became transformed into a belief in the actual possibility of utopia.

The dialectic of History presents a hard countenance of strife: it is the multiplication of forms of domination on all planes of human reality. But only a desperate and absurd vision (which is still an extremely subtle form of domination of the other) can give History's final word to the relation which alienates, depersonalizes, negates man. More profoundly, and decisively, it is the movement of recognition, of personalization, and of solidarity which orients History. It is this movement which gives meaning to History, and provides the ultimate standard for historically valid options, and the very measure of the human being.[27]

Though this formulation was somewhat ambiguous in regard to the possibility of fully realizing a non-dominant society, and regarding the period needed to achieve it, there is no question how this ambiguity was resolved in the movement at large. Many adherents of the new Christian radicalism did come to believe that it was possible to achieve

[25] Vaz, 'Uma reflexão sôbre ação e ideologia', transcript of a lecture given in 1962 (typescript).

[26] Karl Rahner, 'Christentum als Religion der absoluten Zukunft', in Erich Kellner, ed., *Christentum und Marxismus—Heute* (1966), pp. 202 ff. See also Vaz's own subsequent article 'O absoluto e a história', *Paz e Terra*, no. 2 (1966).

[27] AP, *Documento base*, s. II/3.

a final 'purification' of the world, and to eliminate all that was 'evil', power-seeking, dominating, individualistic, and alienating. After the revolution, and after the new theory and praxis would have had time completely to permeate social relations, the contradictions which society had known so far would disappear, and all men would become 'subjects of their own history'.

This 'utopic' streak in the radical ideology[28] probably owed as much to Marx's unwillingness to consider the possibility that social problems might continue to plague the world after the advent of communism as to Teilhard's ambiguous formulation of mankind's chances of reaching the 'point Omega'. As for the latter, there appear to be contradictions, or at least ambiguities, on this point in his works.[29] He does, of course, repeatedly stress that man must freely choose either to collaborate with the evolutionary process, or to oppose it; that the risk of failure exists; and that the 'time of history' is the 'time of evil'. But the earlier quoted passages from *The Phenomenon of Man*[30] do seem to argue that 'point Omega' is reached as a result both of 'natural' evolution and of 'supernatural' salvation, and hence that it is not an exclusively eschatological phenomenon. In the final analysis, Teilhard does seem to invest the process with inevitability, so that his views are quite consonant with the kind of utopic—or millenarian—hopes to which I have just referred. Mankind has to transverse 'critical points on its road'; individuals can err and fall—but *ultimately* 'interruption, or regression, appear to be impossible'.[31]

The 'personalist' element in the radical Catholic *Weltanschauung*

Christian radicals in Brazil shared with the members of many other postwar radical movements in the world a profoundly humanistic orientation. For the elimination of 'evil' and 'contradictions' would come about as a result of promoting, in the most general sense, the well-being of the Brazilian people, of the downtrodden *povo*, of Brazilian man.

[28] See ch. 4, n. 33.

[29] These are difficult to unravel for a person who, like myself, cannot claim even to have begun to familiarize himself with a sufficiently wide range of Teilhard's writings.

[30] See above, p. 87.

[31] Ligneul, p. 66. The 'exegetical' views on this point are very diverse. Those who wish to defend Teilhard's 'orthodoxy' simply deny the ambiguity in his thought—cf. Hubert Cuypers, *Pró ou contra Teilhard* (1967), p. 38. Others, who are more critical, will reject the attempt of Teilhard to 'base the "hopes" of mankind on experimental grounds' (cf. P. Smulders, SJ, *Het visioen van Teilhard de Chardin* (Utrecht, 1964), p. 227).

Our only obligation is towards man. Towards Brazilian man, first and foremost—he who is born with the shadow of premature death over his cradle; who lives with the spectre of hunger under his wretched roof, his inseparable companion as he stumbles along the path of those who travel through life without hope or direction; who grows up stupid and illiterate, an outcast far from the blessings of culture, of creative opportunities, and of truly human roads of real freedom; who dies a beast's anonymous death, cast down on the hard ground of his misery. Thus we struggle for man with man. Our struggle is the struggle for all.[32]

Man and the full development of his potential were the chief devices on AP's banner. Such full development would be possible only after the structures of domination had been eliminated. In the present era that would mean essentially the elimination of capitalism, which was leading the world into an impasse of ever-increasing alienation and domination, both within nations and between them. Its structures would have to be replaced by others, in which each person could affirm himself in freedom and co-operation with his fellow men. AP was convinced that only structures with a socialist cast would make that possible—but the ideology which was to guide their functioning was far removed from Marxism–Leninism.

AP's interpretation of history owed much to Hegel in its stress on dialectical movement in history; to Marx in its emphasis on relations of domination; to John XXIII in its use of the concept of socialization; and to Teilhard in its optimistic and utopic interpretation of what is generally possible in the future. But the basic—but vague—principles which would guide social relations after the great transformation were derived largely from yet another source, which also accounts for the movement's emphasis on 'man' and the unfurling of his potential: the 'personalist' Christian existentialism of Emmanuel Mounier.[33]

Mounier stresses in his philosophy the paramount importance of person-to-person relations, of openness to 'the other', rather like the emphasis found in the work of Jaspers, Marcel, and Buber.[34] While

[32] AP, *Documento base*, Introd.

[33] In an interesting and valuable article, 'Existencialismo e juventude brasileira', *Paz e terra*, no. 3 [1967], Conrado Detrez notes the convergence of various currents of thought, also in the wider context of the ideas prevalent among Brazilian youth today. His affirmation that existentialist doctrines did not find specific Brazilian formulations (as did Comtean positivism and Marxism) seems contradicted by his own analysis, as well as by the fragmentary evidence which I have presented here.

[34] See his *Le personnalisme* (1950), espec. ch. 2. I have used the Portuguese translation by João Bénard da Costa, *O personalismo* (Lisbon, 1964). For an excellent analysis of the thought of Mounier see Roy Pierce, *Contemporary French Political Thought* (1966), ch. 3.

accepting the reality value of Sartre's description of human relations as being those of subject to object, of tyrant to slave, and of his view that man may 'look at' his fellow man in a hostile, paralysing way, Mounier is emphatic in denying that man's existence is exhausted by these modes of relation. Real communication is possible, and the individual only becomes a person in so far as he manages to transcend the limitations of his individualism through making himself 'available' to others (Marcel). Man must strive in co-operation with others, to create a society of persons, a society which will rest on 'a series of original acts which have no equivalent in any part of the universe'. Such acts would include efforts to place oneself in the position of others, to understand them, and to make oneself available to them. It also comprises a funda-mental reorientation of our relationships from a concern with claims, demands, and struggles, to a focus on generosity and gratuitousness. 'The economy of the person is an economy of gifts, not one of compensa-tion and calculation.'[35]

Mounier wrote much about society and about the 'established disorder' brought about by capitalism and strengthened by parlia-mentary democracy.[36] Ultimately, however, his focus was on persons, not on institutions, on the goal of changing the nature of man rather than on the methods for achieving this, or on the institutional context which might make it possible.[37] 'He had no sociology, although he recognized the need for one.'[38] And in so far as the Christian radicals culled their view of the future from Mounier, it suffered from these shortcomings.

Mounier's ideas on economy, state, and society remained sketchy, though he repeatedly affirmed his faith in socialism.[39] At times his views on the transition to the new socialist, corporately organized, and decentralized social order expressed a revolutionary romanticism which dangerously skirted the real problems of revolutionary violence and the corrupting effects of absolute power: 'Our fundamental belief is that a revolution is an affair of men, that its principal efficacy is the internal flame which is communicated from man to man, when men offer themselves gratuitously to one another. . . .'[40] His writings, however, also remonstrate against the rhetoric of the revolutionary and the all-

[35] *O personalismo*, respectively pp. 65 & 66.
[36] Pierce, pp. 51–2.
[37] Ibid., p. 71.
[38] Ibid., p. 55.
[39] *O personalismo*, pp. 56 ff., 103 f., 121, 140.
[40] Quoted in Pierce, p. 76.

too easy condoning of violence or dictatorship for the sake of 'future generations'.[41]

Mounier voiced frequent warnings that the perspective of personalist philosophy could not be expected to become the world's exclusive reality. His was a 'tragic optimism', one fully aware of the inevitable obstacles to generosity and love, of the tension between social structures and personal relations, of the permanent character of force in the world.

The real problem lies in the fact that while we are engaged in a struggle of force for as long as humanity will exist, we have simultaneously the vocation to struggle against the reign of force and against the installation of a state of force.[42]

Nevertheless most Catholic radicals seem to have believed that the reign of force and other 'unpersonalist' aspects of society could be exorcized for ever.

There is a further aspect of Mounier's thought which has been of great influence on the Catholic radicals. With other existentialists Mounier expresses a deep concern for a life of 'authenticity', through careful and honest choice between the options that present themselves from day to day. 'Whenever I make a choice between this or that, I indirectly choose what I am to be. Through such choices I am edified.'[43] By living with full consciousness man comes to be what he is: he has no other essence apart from his existence. It is this aspect of existentialism which has given new weight to history and to the making of history, and which has further strengthened the importance attached by the Catholic radicals to *consciência histórica*. Moreover, the emphasis on authenticity through free options provided the philosophical underpinning of another very important characteristic: their populist horror of any action which curtailed the freedom of choice of the people, which forced them into directions which were not genuinely their own. The contribution of the *povo* to the elaboration and construction of the new society was seen as essential.[44] And although the Catholic radicals were conscious of the need to organize the masses, this was to occur after these masses had been made aware of the problems involved (*conscientização*) and had opted for change. The movement, in theory

[41] Ibid., p. 75.
[42] *O personalismo*, p. 104. See also p. 56.
[43] Ibid., p. 22.
[44] AP, *Documento base*, s. IV.

at least, resolutely opposed the *populista's* modern techniques of 'superficial' mass mobilization, and it accused Goulart as well as the Marxists of *massificação*, i.e. manipulation, as opposed to guidance that would make free choice possible.

An excursus on populism

As the concept of populism is important in the rest of this chapter and in the later analysis of developments in MEB, it is, I believe, necessary to explain why it is introduced into the discussion. And further, some justification is needed for my decision to attach to this term a meaning so radically different from its Brazilian linguistic equivalent, *populismo*.[45] I have hesitated on two grounds to challenge outright the Brazilian usage—which is also the usage of Hispanic America[46]— in the first place because this is invariably to compound the terminological confusion, already pervasive enough among social scientists, in the second place because haggling over terms seems a senseless and sterile exercise. I have done so from the conviction that the radical Catholic movements in Brazil have resembled in many crucial respects certain movements which have occurred, or are occurring, elsewhere in the world, movements which have, in fact, been referred to by political scientists as 'populist'. Hence by using this term the present material can be seen (and criticized) from the comparative perspective which is thereby opened up.[47]

The term populism was first used in connection with the *narodnik* movement which arose in Russia in the 1870s.[48] The *narodniki* were intellectuals who developed an ideology which was an expression of the class position of the downtrodden Russian peasantry, then begin-

[45] See above, pp. 36–9, 42–3.

[46] See, for instance, Torcuato Di Tella's 'Populism and Reform in Latin America', in Véliz, *Obstacles to Change*, an article which introduced Hispanic America's *populismo* as 'populism' to the English-speaking academic community. In the concluding chapter, however, I shall suggest that one can point to certain—limited—similarities between the phenomena covered by the definition of populism adopted here and those usually referred to as *populismo*.

[47] This comparative perspective was first brought to my attention during a conference on populism held at the London School of Economics in May 1967. The collected papers have appeared in a volume edited by Ghiţa Ionescu and Ernest Gellner, *Populism* (1969). For a summary of the proceedings see 'Populism', *Government and Opposition*, Spring 1968, pp. 137–79.

[48] The following account is based mainly on the most valuable analysis by A. Walicki, in Ionescu & Gellner.

ning to be exposed to the effects of Russia's capitalist development.[49] The populists were in agreement with Marx and his followers in regarding capitalism as an evil which had to be fought, but in contrast to the latter they saw no need for all societies to go through a capitalist phase. They developed a theory of non-capitalist development for Russia which looked at once backward and forward. The institutions of the village commune, the *mir*, in decadence by that time, were to form the basis for the building up of new communal (co-operative) institutions appropriate to an industrial society. Socialist planning would bring about the transition to industrial society in a more 'humane' way than the individualistic market mechanisms of capitalism; socialism would be ushered in by a social revolution—i.e. a basic change of the structure of society, as opposed to a 'bourgeois' political revolution merely directed against the institutions of the Tsarist state. In this way the proletarianization of the Russian peasant would be avoided, as would the proletarianization of Russia as a nation in relation to the advanced West.

This latter point is of considerable importance. The intellectuals, who formed an island of sophistication in an archaic, and in many senses brutal, country, were acutely aware of the backward position of Russia *vis-à-vis* the rest of Europe, whence they had imported their very culture. They were Westernized, but objected to their country being exploited by the advanced nations of the world. Being Westernized, they were also alienated from their own society and its values. Significantly, this alienation in turn produced a guilt-ridden reaction which rejected the imported ideas, and led to the glorification of the simple people, the peasants. 'To the people' became the rallying cry of the populists. The people will know what is good and just ('The people will rise and justice will reign'); the people will transmit their values to the intellectual élite, who, being neither manipulative nor élitist, will simply help to bring about such social structures as the people desire. That those structures would have a strong co-operative flavour (derived from the *mir*), and that the state would have to play an important role in the future society, was clear to the populists; apart from that they had few ideas about how to build those structures, or about what they would actually look like.

I have treated the *narodniki* in some detail—and even so the account has greatly simplified historical reality, especially in relation to the

---

[49] For a brief but excellent account of this period see A. Gerschenkron, *Economic Backwardness in Historical Perspective* (1965), chs. 6–7.

evolution of the populist ideas—both because they constituted the
first significant movement to which the name populist has been applied
and because in many ways they were more closely analogous to the
Brazilian case than were most subsequent 'populist' movements. As a
generic term 'populism' obviously carries a broad spectrum of meanings:
one need only scan the pages of the Ionescu and Gellner volume[50]
to become aware of this.

Thus in Eastern Europe, where the doctrines of the peasant-oriented
populists were at least in part direct descendants of those of their
Russian counterparts, at an early stage the movements became politicized into peasant parties. They never developed a communitarian
outlook equivalent to that generated in Russia by harping back to the
institutions of the *mir*, even though much emphasis was placed on the
advantages of co-operatives for small peasant owners. In the relatively
small countries of Eastern Europe, 'Denmark was and remained the
model [of society].'[51]

In discussions of contemporary Africa, the term populism has been
used with an almost bewildering variety of connotations—some of
them so general as to be well-nigh meaningless. But by including
certain modern African political movements in the category, it is
possible to acquire some very useful insights into the 'degeneration' of
populism once it reaches power, when the movement's leadership has
to grapple with the problems of governing—in contrast to attacking
the authorities and 'the system' from the outside. Africa also provides
a potent reminder of the possible clash between populist rhetoric and
empirical social reality.[52]

In North America, perhaps the most deviant case of them all,
populism was a mass movement of farmers in which urban intellectuals
played virtually no role; but it did represent those who under late
nineteenth-century American conditions were just as much the 'common people' as were the Russian peasants in their society. America's
small capitalist farmers, too, were caught in the process of social change:
the advance of large-scale 'trustified' capitalism. Understandably,
however, their response was not communitarian but individualistic.

Finally, for Latin America, as has already been seen, the term
populismo has been applied predominantly to urban movements,
clearly transitional phenomena, largely manipulative, 'in which the

[50] See n. 47.
[51] G. Ionescu, 'Eastern Europe', in Ionescu & Gellner, p. 104.
[52] See the excellent analysis of John S. Saul, ibid., ch. 5.

genuine voice of the people finds little chance for expression'.[53] Hennessy calls this 'urban populism', and he contrasts it with rural populism. The older, rural variety, which focuses mainly on the Indian population, is found in Mexico as well as in Peru (Belaúnde's *Acción Popular* party). New rural populism is exemplified by certain important aspects of the Cuban Revolution, both in its ideology, and in its practice (e.g. Castro's reluctance to institutionalize the Revolution, and his inclination to invoke 'the people' against the bureaucracy). Lastly, Hennessy concurs with my application of the term to the recent radical Catholic movements. These, he writes, 'are distinguished by their strong populist strains, particularly among their younger supporters . . . whose concept of revolution is one of change brought about by the people on behalf of themselves'.[54]

This rapid review of some of the so-called populist movements will have confirmed that the term covers a very heterogenous set of cases, as is also the case with certain other concepts used in political and social science.[55] Before I proceed to clarify the *specific* sense in which I am using the term, one last point should be made. It may be true that 'communism' or 'socialism' are vague terms, but, as Peter Worsley points out, the people categorized as 'communists' or 'socialists' commonly 'see themselves as part of a shared tradition or organized movement, or trace their ideological descent to a distinct source'.[56] That is emphatically not the case for those who find themselves assigned to the category of 'populists' by the cold logic of the social scientist.

Typically, there has never been a Populist International and many movements which others have labelled 'populist' have never themselves used any such label to describe themselves. They have not even been aware that other—to us—analogous movements . . . existed; even less did they have any organizational contact with them.[57]

Not surprisingly, therefore, the populist label may be experienced by

---

[53] Alistair Hennessy, 'Latin America', ibid., p. 28.

[54] Ibid., p. 51. For a brief discussion of such movements outside Brazil, see my 'Paternalism and Populism', *J. Contemp. Hist.*, Oct. 1967.

[55] Peter Worsley remarks at the end of his admirable general analysis in the Ionescu and Gellner volume that 'populism' is no looser a term than labels such as 'capitalism' or 'communism', and that for 'the eternal attempt of people to claim politics as something of theirs' (yet another short-hand definition), ' "populism" is as good as any terminological neophilism' ('The Concept of Populism', pp. 247 f.).

[56] Ibid., p. 218.

[57] Ibid.

the people involved as a distortion of the 'true nature' of the movement to which they belong.[58]

Obviously, no single term can capture the 'true nature' of any movement or describe it 'exhaustively'. 'Populist' will be used here only to emphasize certain important aspects of the movements with which this book is concerned, a cluster of characteristics to which attention would not be drawn by the less specific term 'radical'.[59] Basically, I describe these movements as 'populist' in so far as:

1. They are made up of intellectuals (and students), concerned with the life-situation of the down-trodden masses in society, the 'people', who apparently cannot by themselves assert their interests;

2. these intellectuals have a deep-seated horror of the manipulation of the people: their central credo is that solutions to the problems lived by the people must ultimately come from the people themselves, that their own ideas and visions, developed in a wholly different milieu, may at most serve as a sounding board for, but never as signposts to the people.[60]

Further comments on the radical Catholic analysis of society

No exploited or down-trodden people is able to take its destiny into its own hands until after it has become aware of its situation in the world. Such awareness constitutes the basis for action. Hence the importance which Brazil's radical Catholics attached to *conscientização*. This involved in the first instance the presentation of certain facts and theories—an ideology—to the people, hitherto ignorant of the situation in which they found themselves. The ideology of AP was rather similar in its views of past and present to those proposed in the draft *ideal histórico* presented two years earlier by the Belo Horizonte team

[58] At worst, it can be regarded as offensive. I did, in fact, encounter a certain amount of resistance to the use of the term 'populist' among some of my Brazilian friends who read one of the early drafts of this book. I hope that no uneasy feelings remain over the present, revised, version.

[59] When all the characteristics of the cluster are present, the movement would correspond to the 'ideal type'.

[60] See, in the summary of the conference on populism in *Government and Opposition*, the summing up of Sir Isaiah Berlin (pp. 173–8). The short definition of George Hall (p. 179) was as follows: 'Populist movements are movements aimed at power for the benefit of the people as a whole which result from the reaction of those, usually intellectuals, alienated from the existing power structure, to the stresses of rapid economic, social, cultural or political change. These movements are characterized by a belief in a return to, or adaptation of, more simple and traditional forms and values emanating from the people, particularly the more archaic sections of the people who are taken to be the repository of virtue.'

of JUC. But AP's views had been better worked out and were more elegantly worded and more consistent in analysis. The central tool for the dissection of Brazilian reality became the conceptual pair, *pólo dominante* and *pólo dominado* (dominant and dominated pole), obviously derived from the historical principle of the dialectics of domination. The discussion owed much to the Marxist analysis of class conflict. It also owed much to Marx in another sense: the central principle of the system of domination was thought to lie in the fact that the means of production, distribution, and opinion-formation were in private hands.

The *Esbôço Ideológico* (Ideological Outline) presented at the founding meeting of AP contains a description of interrelated institutional orders, of the different sectors which make up the *pólo dominante*—such as landowners, 'financial bourgeoisie', 'industrial bourgeoisie', 'international bourgeoisie'—not seen as one class with identical interests, but rather as various groups whose interests overlap. The *Documento Base* contains sections not only on the course of world history, socialism, and philosophy, but also on the historical background of Latin America's present situation in the world, as well as on the socio-economic situation in Brazil.

The section on world history takes the communist movement to task for having altered but not 'radically transformed' the power structure of the countries that have become communist. Because of the new role allotted to the state, the revolution 'has lost the perspective of overcoming alienation, and has created a new pole of (state) domination with the rise of a dominating bureaucracy'; what is missing is 'real, plural, participation'.[61] AP obviously shared the post-Stalinist disenchantment of the world's neo-Marxists and socialist humanists with the results of the Russian Revolution.[62]

In the section on the socio-economic situation of Brazil there are various barely disguised attacks on the *Partido Communista Brasileiro* (PCB), mainly for its lack of a true revolutionary perspective. The policy of the communists focused on 'piecemeal economic improvements' and on collaboration with a 'national bourgeoisie, with interests [supposedly] antagonistic to international capitalism'; a distorted view, according to AP, which could only be sustained by those who did not go to the trouble of testing their theses through a 'concrete verification

[61] AP, *Documento base*, s. III.
[62] For a representative collection of such views see the papers in Erich Fromm, ed., *Socialist Humanism* (New York, 1965).

of reality'. Empirical work had demonstrated 'the tendency of imperialism to lodge itself in the dependent economic structures through
bourgeois [and neo-capitalist] developments'.[63]

There is, in this case, no doubt that from a sociological perspective
AP was right, and the communists were wrong. Their conception of
collaborating with 'all nationalists and democrats' in a united front,
which would bring together the 'largest number of patriots, irrespec-
tive of their class position or party affiliation'[64] certainly overestimated
the 'patriotism' of the bourgeoisie as a whole, and their willingness to
oppose 'imperialism', as evidenced, for instance, in the 'denationaliza-
tion' of Brazilian industry and its progressive incorporation into
'international capitalism'.[65] The error in their judgement was relatively
visible even before April 1964; it became much more evident after
the military had taken over the government.

But in other ways the communist view was more realistic, if ideologically less attractive to those who yearned for rapid radical change.

Marxism [states the PCB-oriented *Estudos sociais*] does not conceive of
social development as if it consists solely of a leap towards a new regime,
but as a process in which the revolution is preceded by gradual changes in
the old order. The gesture of the petit-bourgeois radical, who refuses to take
note of the need for reforms and considers all struggle in this field as oppor-
tunism, is nothing but revolutionary infantilism.[66]

And not only were such reforms valuable in themselves—though they
were emphatically *not* supposed to lead to a strengthening of the
status quo—but they were, according to the communists, the *only*
type of political action that could be pursued with any real hope of
success in the circumstances of Brazil of the early 1960s: the forces
ranged against revolution were still considered to be too strong. Thus,
although the communists would have been delighted to benefit from
any revolutionary upheaval, they did not really expect it. AP, on the
other hand, badly underestimated the strength of the existing power

[63] AP, *Documento base*, s. IV.

[64] Almir Matos, 'Aparências e realidades do panorama político', *Estudos sociais*, Apr. 1962,
p. 403. This journal generally expressed the viewpoint of the PCB.

[65] There is a growing body of literature on this problem. An excellent article by Osvaldo
Sunkel, 'Política nacional de desarrollo y dependencia externa', *Estudios internacionales*
(Santiago), Apr. 1967, marshalls many of the general arguments. For Brazil, see Fernando
Henrique Cardoso, 'Hégémonie bourgeoise et indépendance économique', *Les temps
modernes*, Oct. 1967.

[66] Mario Alves, 'A burguesia nacional e a crise brasileira', *Estudos sociais*, Dec. 1962,
p. 244.

structure, and especially the determination of the military to come to the rescue of the landowners or the middle classes once these regarded themselves as threatened in their fundamental interests.[67]

AP also seemed to be entirely unaware of the deep-seated nature of the ubiquitous patron–dependant relationships. Although the *Documento Base* briefly pointed to the difficulties to be expected in the most backward areas of the country, 'where the population is dispersed and the peasantry highly conformist', it was again the communists, in their analysis if not in their activity, who were more realistic about the obstacles to be expected in the rural areas.[68] AP, in general, believed that old structures and mentalities would not constitute major difficulties, and that they would disappear fairly easily in the wake of its activities.

[67] The mood in AP is well reflected in the earlier-mentioned discussion of university reform by Álvaro Vieira Pinto, the Director of ISEB, in *A questão da universidade*—a book that, having grown out of the mood among radical university students discussed in ch. 4 above, subsequently had a good deal of further influence on these students. There we read: 'the climate in which the general need for social reforms presents itself is pre-revolutionary . . . that means . . . that these objectives *will not be frustrated*' (p. 12), or: 'From now on the students' demands tend to grow. Today they raise the banner of university reform which will, without a shadow of doubt, *be very shortly triumphant. . . .*' (p. 93). [Italics added.]

[68] See, for instance, the very interesting article by Borges, 'O movimento camponês no Nordeste', *Estudos sociais*, Dec. 1962.

6

The Heyday of the Catholic Radicals II: Activity and Praxis

The theory and practice of *conscientização*

FOR all those who participated in one or another of the radical movements of Christian inspiration activity was of the greatest importance. Their militants did not merely sit and debate the general evils of capitalism, or the wickedness of the imperialists. Marxists acknowledge the 'unity of theory and practice'; the Catholic radicals shared the principle with them, not only as a result of the common roots of their respective philosophies in Hegelian dialectic, but also as a result of the concern for 'commitment' in existentialist thought. The principle had various important corollaries, not least the psychologically sound idea that learning (*conscientização*) could not occur unless it was accompanied by a testing out of the newly acquired knowledge (the achievement of practical socio-political results).[1] But even under prerevolutionary circumstances this was a slow process. Only in a few areas, notably in Pernambuco, had such testing-out gone so far as to lead to permanent results in *conscientização* before the coup ended almost all 'radical' praxis.

Conscientização was mainly attempted by means of two instruments: the various mass literacy efforts, and the more general movement for popular culture (*Movimento de Cultura Popular*). In both, Catholic radicals played a prominent part, though the latter was also strongly influenced by the Communist Party.

MEB, of course, was one of the organizations concerned with an adult literacy campaign, but before turning to a detailed examination of that Movement, it is necessary briefly to turn to another one of considerable interest. This was the *Método Paulo Freire*. In its short period of existence it gathered substantial momentum, although at the

[1] A point well made by Mendes (*Memento dos vivos*), pp. 178–85. This problem, as encountered in MEB, will be extensively discussed below. See chs. 12 & 13.

time of its repression in April 1964 it was still characterized by potential rather than actual achievements, by promise more than realization.[2] The *Método Paulo Freire* expressed the educational philosophy of Paulo Freire, a professor of education in the University of Recife, a philosophy elaborated independently from AP yet in many respects closely related to their views. Education as the Practice of Freedom: this is the title of the book in which Freire expounds his ideas, and a neat summary of its main thesis.

Freire has no use for adult education which is not based on wholehearted respect of teacher for student, which does not start from the idea that education must make man aware of his freedom in the world —his possibility of choice and option—and stimulate a critical attitude towards the world. There were in his method no schools or classes, but *círculos de cultura*; no teachers, but co-ordinators. The road by which literacy is reached must go through the heartland of a man's existential problems. It is futile to try and teach people who have been hard at work all day to read and write with traditional Brazilian school phrases like *Eva viu a uva* (Eva saw the grape); people who have probably come across few Evas and have never eaten *uvas*.[3] Literacy must be taught at the same time that *conscientização* is promoted. Words such as *favela* (shanty town), *arado* (plough), *terreno* (plot of land), *comida* (food), or *govérno* (government), chosen from the actual vocabulary of the people concerned, are to be the basis of the learning process. Discussions around such words, and around pictorially represented 'existential situations', start from a man's immediate life situation: his community, neighbourhood, or place of work, the boss from whom he receives his wage or the authorities with whom he has to deal. Slowly students become aware of their own environment, both as it *is* and as it *could* be. Then they can venture to begin thinking about the wider society, about 'the world at large', and become aware of their place in the world, of their creative potential as 'makers of culture',[4] as people actively engaged in *transforming the world*.[5]

Freire was considered 'subversive' by the post-coup military

---

[2] In Guanabara alone 6,000 people were registered for the training courses for 'co-ordinators' of literacy groups between mid-1963 and the coup; plans for 1964 spoke of reaching 2 million illiterates (Francisco Weffort's Introduction to Paulo Freire, *Educação como prática da liberdade* (1967), p. 11).

[3] Ibid., p. 104.

[4] Ibid., pp. 108 ff.

[5] Cf. the discussion of the concept of *consciência histórica*, above pp. 87 f. The same concepts became important in MEB (see ch. 8).

authorities; he was imprisoned and later went into exile in Chile, where he wrote his book. Francisco Weffort points out in his admirable Introduction to the book that a pedagogy of freedom may carry the germ of revolt, because *conscientização* brings out the reality of a man's life situation in which struggle and violence are frequently the most significant facts. 'If *conscientização* prepares the way for the expression of social dissatisfactions, it is because these [facts] are real components of a situation of oppression.'[6] Nevertheless, incitement to revolt was never Freire's direct objective as an educator, though democratization was; thus he rejected authoritarian methods in education, the social palliative of *assistencialismo* (welfareism), and the stifling of political expression through *massificação*. The latter make man into an object rather than a subject; they impose on him silence and passivity, they stifle his consciousness and his sense of criticism, and imprison him in a kind of 'anti-dialogue'.[7] Ultimately what matters in helping man 'is to help him help himself'.[8] All in all, as will be seen, a populist approach not fundamentally different from that proposed and practised by MEB.

The second and equally important instrument of *conscientização* was the more general movement for popular culture. From the start students played an important part in its development. This was especially so in various of the more important state capitals. In Recife a *Movimento de Cultura Popular* had been started by the municipality at the time when Miguel Arraes was mayor. From its inception in 1960 many of those who helped to direct its activities were members of JUC. And although the leadership remained in the hands of Catholics, members of the Communist Party became increasingly influential among the rank and file as time went by. It was at least partly in reaction to this development that Paulo Freire transferred his (populist) *método* to the Cultural Extension Service of the University of Recife.[9] In Rio both the local student union and UNE sponsored centres concerned with *cultura popular*. Similarly in São Paulo various student organizations had committees for popular culture.

By mid-1962 these, and a further number in other states, had ex-

---

[6] Freire, p. 12. Cf. the similar views expressed by D. Távora, MEB's President, when defending the primer *Viver é lutar*, below p. 158.

[7] Freire, p. 57.

[8] Ibid., p. 58.

[9] This happened around the same time that MEB 'radicalized' at its *I Encontro de Coordenadores* in Dec. 1962 (see below pp. 152 ff.). There is some reason to believe that Freire was influenced by this development.

panded to autonomous organizations financed with public funds. Many of them came under the control of members of the PCB. These organizations tried to reach and stir the masses by means of plays, films, leaflets, and other cultural manifestations which focused on the people's own problems and had a clear socio-political content. Brazilian culture in general and the existing popular culture in particular were seen as imposed and alienated culture: 'The work of *cultura popular* is the work of all who want the de-alienation of culture, and consequently national emancipation.'[10] One of the papers read during the first Congress of *cultura popular* formulated the matter as follows: '*Cultura popular* assumes the character of a struggle. Apart from forming an authentic national culture, this struggle promotes the integration of Brazilian man in the process of socio-economic and politico-cultural liberation of our people.'[11] The struggle against imperialism figured prominently in the declarations emanating from the *Centros Populares de Cultura* (CPCs) which mushroomed all over Brazil. But many of these *Centros* seem to have had little substance, being made up mainly of enthusiastic but not very efficient (or persevering) students—often, away from the few main population centres, secondary school students.

Catholic radicals who dedicated themselves to *cultura popular* regarded it, in the words of Cândido Mendes, as a 'continuous process of feedback between action and consciousness, one transcending the other in the effective open construction of a new historical experience'.[12] *Cultura popular* was concerned with the life situation of the *povo*, and with their 'true' beliefs and values which had come to be obscured by the superimposed elements of alienated culture. One task of *cultura popular* was to restore vigour to those pristine values. In this respect the views of the Catholic radicals—which fit so well into their wider populist orientation—had an appeal that went beyond their own circles. Thus one reads in the *Revista brasiliense* that the CPC intends to

open the way which will lead to an authentic popular culture by learning from popular aesthetics, and by identifying with the aspirations, the emotions, the problems, the anguish, and the thought of the popular masses.

[10] First resolution of the *I Encontro Nacional de Cultura Popular*, Recife, Sept. 1963. MEB was one of the movements which participated—certainly one of the best organized ones.

[11] Paper presented by *Movimento de Cultura Popular* of Dept. of Education of the *Município* of Natal at the *I Encontro Nacional de Cultura Popular*.

[12] *Mementos dos vivos*, p. 190.

Starting from this . . . the CPC hopes [to help in] the formation of a [real] Brazilian culture.[13]

But the opinions on *cultura popular* which were prevalent in the year or so immediately preceding the coup only partially crystallized into clearly distinctive positions, and a good deal of confusion as to its real objectives remained among those engaged in the various activities. The public definitions and statements largely tended to reflect the point of view of the communists; the Catholic radicals, however, had considerable reservations about certain ideas of the Marxists. The latter, in general much less concerned with the philosophy of *conscientização*, seem to have believed that mere awareness, mere 'de-alienation', would suffice to bring about the necessary climate for a change in structures.[14] Moreover, they regarded *cultura popular* as an instrument to be forged by the political leadership, out of the latter's interpretation of how best to utilize a particular cultural phenomenon in the political struggle: *cultura popular* to them was a political tool in the hands of the élite, to be used for speeding up the course of history. For the orthodox Marxists the truths of *cultura popular* were relative ones, relative to 'specific political objectives'.[15] Any kind of debate, play, exhibition, or course of instruction could be 'transformed into cultural means capable of developing the political consciousness of the masses. For this all that is needed is that such events are not limited exclusively to the aims they [openly] proclaim.'[16] *Cultura popular*, therefore, is about 'the appropriation for political ends of the cultural means of production'.[17]

In a valuable article Uchoa Leite discusses some of these differences between the Catholic populists and the communists (without, however, identifying the two approaches as such). For the latter *cultura popular* was something that was done *for* the people, and it involved introducing a 'politicizing content into the popular forms of artistic expression'. But, as Uchoa Leite quite rightly points out,

if *politização* is a manner of opening up the consciousness of the people and of creating the conditions under which the *povo* . . . can choose their own

---

[13] Camila Ribeiro, 'Novos caminhos do teatro universitario', *R. brasiliense*, Sept.–Oct. 1962.

[14] Ibid., pp. 182 ff. For an orthodox Marxist view of the subject see Carlos Estevão, *A questão da cultura popular* (1963).

[15] Estevão, p. 24.

[16] Ibid., p. 35.

[17] Ibid., p. 33.

political road, then the appropriation of their artistic forms in order to offer them a new political *content* is implicitly a denial of their capacity to judge.[18]

For those with a populist orientation *cultura popular* and *alfabetização* (literacy training) were intimately linked. The whole literacy effort of those working with Paulo Freire—and of those in MEB—was directed at making man aware of his *social* situation in order to enable him to make the valid *political* choices. *Cultura popular* had to fit into this conception. It could not simply present the people with concrete solutions—that would be *massificação*; if it did it would moreover, as any kind of mere propaganda effort, lack the roots of real culture and hinder rather than help the emergence of real social and political awareness.

The beginnings of rural *sindicalismo*

The area of activity in which the Catholic radicals were probably most successful was in the organization and penetration of already existing rural trade unions. A brief discussion of the relevant legal and political antecedents will make it easier to follow subsequent events.

The organization of rural trade unions had been legal in Brazil since 1944. Article I of a decree enacted towards the end of that year provided: 'All those who exercise rural activities, whether as employer or employee, are permitted to form associations for the purpose of study, defence and co-ordination of their economic or professional interests.'[19] The first official Instruction issued by the Ministry of Labour to implement the 1944 decree appeared in the following year. The legislation, however, had effect only in the more developed agricultural areas of Brazil's South. In the backward parts of the country it took some fifteen years for rural unionization to become a reality. This was the result of a number of interrelated factors. In the first place, as has been seen, until very recently most peasants in the backward states of the North-East or Centre West could not be described as a rural proletariat, and the framework of traditional patron–dependant relations did not provide conditions favouring the development of peasant organizations. Secondly, the landowners were strongly opposed to any kind of peasant organization—both as individuals *vis-à-vis*

---

[18] Sebastião Uchoa Leite, 'Cultura popular: esbôço de uma resenha crítica', *R. civilização bras.*, Sept. 1965, p. 279 (italics in original).
[19] Price, p. 8.

their own dependants, and collectively *vis-à-vis* the government. In fact in 1954, when João Goulart, Minister of Labour in Vargas's second government, had proposed to push ahead with the establishment of rural unions, the Brazilian Rural Confederation (the landowners' association) objected strongly to this plan. It had sent a memorandum to the *Conselho de Segurança Nacional* (the National Security Council) which stated among other things 'that apart from political reasons there is nothing to justify rural syndicalism', 'the rural proletariat is not sufficiently mature to understand the political rights that Minister João Goulart wants to grant them', and 'the Minister of Labour's action is imprudent'.[20] Finally, apart from the above-mentioned exceptional incident, the Ministry of Labour, whose official recognition was necessary for the operation of any trade union, was in no hurry to promote the extension of trade unionism into the countryside. The Ministry was part of a government structure whose power rested, until the end of the 1950s, on a series of compromises which left the rural structure essentially untouched. Antagonizing the landowners was studiously avoided, as their political strength in Congress remained massive. Goulart alone, had, in 1954, presented them with a challenge; two weeks after he had done so he was forced to resign.[21] Consequently the Ministry of Labour had recognized very few rural *sindicatos* by the end of the decade. This had not prevented the setting up of various peasant organizations under the civil as opposed to the labour code. Especially the communists had attempted to create such associations in various parts of the country, including the North-East, at first in the late 1940s, then again from the early 1950s.[22] In most cases these were little more than phantom organizations, usually tightly controlled by a very small urban-based leadership— but they did later turn out to be quite convenient for conversion into *sindicatos* once legislation had made the foundation of unions easier.

Slowly the government became interested in promoting such legislation. There were various reasons for its increasing concern, most of which have been discussed before: the emergence of the *ligas*, seen by 1960 as a 'reflection' of the revolutionary situation in Cuba; the generally growing feeling in the country that the rural areas could no longer be completely left to their own devices; and the development of

---

[20] Quoted by Mary E. Wilkie, *A Report on Rural Syndicates in Pernambuco, Brazil* (1967, mimeo.), p. 37.

[21] For other actions which influenced his forced resignation, see Skidmore, p. 126.

[22] See Borges, p. 253.

an interest in the fate of the peasants on the part of various groups in the Catholic church.

The first of these Catholic efforts had started in the state of Rio Grande do Norte, where as early as 1949 the then Bishop, D. Eugênio Sales, had founded the *Serviço de Assistência Rural* (SAR).[23] In the first decade of its existence the orientation of this organization had been essentially paternalistic and ameliorative: it had focused on various small-scale projects of community development and education in the rural areas. Late in 1960, however, SAR began to take a more active interest in the possibility of organizing the peasants into *sindicatos*. The emphasis in SAR's work began to shift towards leadership training, and its role was conceived more and more as that of a midwife to rural trade unions. The first *sindicato* led by SAR people was founded in November 1960. Other members of the hierarchy followed suit. Early in 1961 the Archbishop of Recife appointed a small number of priests to occupy themselves with the problem of *sindicalização* (the preparation and founding of rural trade unions).[24] SORPE, the *Serviço de Orientação Rural de Pernambuco*, was set up under the direction of Pe Paulo Crespo. Its primary task was to occupy itself with the training of potential peasant leaders versed in Catholic social doctrine, capable of withstanding the lures of Marxist ideologies and of revolutionary political organizations.[25] Although these church-sponsored organizations were no doubt also genuinely interested in helping the peasantry, in *promoção humana*, the new interest in working with rural trade unions had primarily resulted from the notoriety which the *ligas* had by then achieved. The *sindicatos* seemed a means of simultaneously combating the evils of Marxism and keeping the rural masses 'within the church'.

As the church became involved in the foundation of rural *sindicatos*, the attitude of the government, and especially of the Ministry of Labour, increasingly changed from that of an unsympathetic bystander to that of an interested party. The second official Instruction, referring to the decree of 1944 and dealing with the founding and operation of rural *sindicatos*, was sent out in the middle of 1959. At this time the Minister of Labour was a member of the small PDC, a man keen to help along the earliest embryonic efforts of church-linked organizations.

[23] See Price, pp. 47 ff.
[24] See Wilkie, pp. 42 ff.
[25] See the article by Paulo Crespo, 'O problema camponês no Nordeste brasileiro', *SPES*, 17 (1963).

In 1962 the heightened activity and interest of the Ministry of Labour was reflected in three further Instructions.[26] By then the Ministry, no longer occupied by a PDC politician, was more concerned with its own role in and influence on the process of rural unionization than with helping the Christian unions to grow. Nevertheless, at first these Instructions were of concern almost exclusively to church-sponsored unions: in Rio Grande do Norte, in Pernambuco, and soon in various other states of the North-East. Other organizations, not linked to the church, did not seriously begin their efforts in the field of rural unionization until after the middle of 1962.

What, then, were the characteristics of these early church-sponsored *sindicatos*, and how did their characteristics compare with those of the *ligas*? The latter, from an early reformist position, had moved to a more revolutionary stand, if not in terms of visible activity, at least in terms of the ideology—or rhetoric—of their leadership. That ideology became, as the Brazilians would say, *marxisante*—that is not fully Marxist, but inspired by and sympathetic to Marxist revolutionary ideas. The church-sponsored *sindicatos* were meant to set Christian social doctrine over and against the 'materialism' of the *ligas*. The efforts of *sindicatos* operating in areas with a rural proletariat were first of all directed at ensuring compliance with the labour laws on the part of the employers. Most of those laws had so far remained a dead letter in the countryside. Thus, although the law recognized trade unions as legitimate means of defence of the workers' interests, many employers denied the very right to organization. Employers hardly ever paid the legally prescribed minimum wage, nor did they proceed honestly in the allocation and evaluation of the daily tasks. These were situations requiring immediate action. Then came economic bargaining, meant to lead to an improvement in the living conditions of the rural workers—in fact more usually concerned simply with maintaining real income in Brazil's inflationary economy.

In order to obtain the implementation of the legal codes relevant to the rural workers, the *sindicatos*, and even more the federations into which they were grouped in each state, had to have recourse to the labour tribunals. For this they needed lawyers, whom they employed. And often those lawyers came to occupy a pre-eminent position. Wilkie writes that when the priests who had originally been entrusted by the Archbishop of Pernambuco with the task of organizing the rural unions tried to withdraw into the background, 'the laymen who assumed control of the syndical movement were not so much the peasant leaders as the lawyers'.[27] Originally, then, just as was the case with the *ligas*, the *sindicatos* were organizations stimulated from above and built from the top downwards. They did not arise as a result of an autonomous development of peasant consciousness at the grass roots, or of pressure generated from below. And it is patently clear that those who took the initiative in the organization of rural unions—the bishops, later the priests, and the top laymen employed by the federations—did not regard the *sindicatos* as a means towards the political mobilization of the peasants. It was, early on, very far from their minds that peasant pressure should lead to 'basic structural changes' in the rural areas. Their approach was strictly economic and legalistic: for them it was a matter of the implementation of existing 'rights' and of bargaining within the existing structures. The political use of trade unions, aimed at changing the existing laws, or at the achievement of basic structural changes which would mean a redistribution of wealth and especially of power in the countryside, was essentially ruled out in their scheme of things. Even less conceivable to them was the use of *sindicatos* as the nuclei for a wider revolutionary movement.

The Catholic radicals move into *sindicalismo*

It did not take long before the *sindicatos* founded on the instigation of the church authorities began to move off the course set by their originators. Once they started to spread, bishops, priests, and lawyers could not maintain a grip over the fast growing network of organizations, or keep their ideology under control. When organizations such as SORPE wished to expand their activities, they had to attract people who had some sort of capacity to train and educate illiterate or semi-literate peasants, and who were willing to do this kind of work under the often very primitive conditions of the backlands. Some of the new cadres, of course, wholeheartedly accepted the ideology and working methods of a man like Pe Crespo. But many others who involved themselves in *sindicalização*—mainly students, both from secondary schools and from universities—came to the new task with an ideology made up of much headier stuff, or else developed this while in the field. These were the youngsters from JEC, JUC, and eventually from AP. They entered a wide range of organizations, Christian and non-Christian, depending upon what was available in the different areas,

[27] Wilkie, p. 46.

always choosing those that were most militant and radical—or might become so. In the beginning especially those who adhered to AP's line regarded MEB as too 'soft', and they had no use for the Movement. Gradually, however, in the course of 1963, after MEB had digested the conclusions of the *I Encontro de Coordenadores* and had adopted views which in outline fitted well with those of the other Catholic radicals,[28] the latter increasingly approved of and participated in the work of MEB in the countryside. Its presence there was so important because both the young Catholics who had been moving towards more radical views, and the bishops and priests who were concerned about the 'menace' of the *ligas* and the communists, regarded this organization as an appropriate means for the achievement of their very diverse goals.

The majority of those to whom 'the Catholic church' entrusted the education for rural trade unionism came to look upon the *sindicatos* as a potentially very important means of organization, which could be used to bring about a revolutionary transformation in the first instance of the countryside, and subsequently of the entire socio-economic structure. After the peasants and rural workers had become aware of their rights as citizens, had learned to see themselves as part of the nation and part of society, they would arrive at an understanding of the workings of that society, and of their place in it as a group oppressed and exploited in economic and political terms—the *pólo dominado*, with which those Christians working in *sindicalização* wholeheartedly identified. And by their participation in organizations such as the *sindicatos*, the rural *povo* would develop class consciousness, and begin to think in terms of class action. They would then be fully *conscientizados*.

But it was recognized by the young radicals, certainly by those of them working in MEB, that this transformation of the mind of the peasant was not likely to be an easy process, and that one could hardly hope for class consciousness to emerge overnight. Many steps would have to be taken before the peasant or rural worker could even reach a sense of 'citizenship': hitherto the state had meant little more to him than the armed power of the landowner. It would require much patience to give the peasants a sense of the possibilities for change which existed if they were to unite against those whom they had always regarded as their natural superiors.

In respect of the process of *sindicalização* itself, the Catholic radicals saw no point in setting up numerous local trade union branches before

[28] See below, pp. 152 ff.

peasant consciousness had reached the stage at which these organizations could be used effectively by the peasants themselves. Any other course of action would only lead to new forms of paternalism and *massificação*. Thus they foresaw a rather arduous task of *conscientização* that might take a long time to show results in the form of militant organizations run by the *povo* themselves. Their populist approach, however, had to be abandoned within a year. By the middle of 1963 they were forced to do exactly what they had so condemned in their rivals: they were setting up *sindicatos* everywhere, with little regard for the peasants' own capacity to run them. As populists they had come up against the kind of circumstances which had to lead either to the abandonment of some of their principles and scruples, or of their hope of maintaining an effective grip on the course of events.[29]

This situation was caused by developments in the national political structure, which in turn had resulted from the increasingly apparent breakdown of the politics of compromise. Once President Goulart, especially alarmed at the emergence of non-traditional, non-*populista* politicians such as Arraes in some important states, had embarked upon the course of trying to broaden his power base by extending the operation of the hitherto exclusively urban *populismo* into the countryside, the Catholic radicals were confronted with an entirely new situation. This happened after the passing of the Rural Labour Statute in 1963.

Massificação in the rural areas

For almost ten years Congress had been considering a bill to extend the scope of the existing labour legislation, hitherto only applied to urban workers, so that it would explicitly include workers in rural employment as well. It had been discussed in committees and plenary sessions, shelved, pulled out, and shelved again; its tortuous path back and forth between the Senate and the Chamber ended in January 1963, when the latter essentially accepted the latest Senate version and sent the bill to the President for approval. The Rural Labour Statute was signed by Goulart on 2 March 1963, and came into force three months later.[30] In relation to the concern of this study, the most

[29] See the second general hypothesis on populism, below, p. 268.
[30] Price, pp. 9 ff., describes the bill's long path, from the earliest version sent to Congress by President Vargas in 1954, to the final product of 1963.

significant aspects of the statute, and of the decrees and instructions issued from June onwards to regulate its implementation, were the provisions dealing with the founding and operation of rural *sindicatos*. They put the activities of church-sponsored unions, till that time legally in a somewhat precarious position, on a solid footing. But they also had a different effect. They induced a 'rush' into the countryside of the various persons, parties, and movements interested in utilizing the new possibilities of building up a power base in the backlands— Goulart among them, through the Ministry of Labour.

The labour law specified that in each locality (*município*) there could be only one union for each category of workers: once a union had been constituted and recognized by the Ministry of Labour, its monopoly was ensured and no challenge to the directorate was possible from the outside. Five categories of rural workers were mentioned: workers in agriculture, in cattle raising, and in rural extractive production, independent workers, and small property owners without employees.[31] A *sindicato* could be founded by fifty people belonging to any one of these categories or a combination of them. If workers from three or more categories were present, the *sindicato* was to be a general union of rural workers, but if only one or two categories were represented, the union was to become specific to those occupations.[32] As many peasants were consecutively engaged in various types of activity, and as there was a constant migratory movement especially into areas needing extra hands at harvest time, this legal arrangement almost invited the setting up of ghost unions, especially since the rules made the actual foundation of a *sindicato* extremely easy.

The prize which went with the control of a *sindicato* was considerable. The union tax (*imposto sindical*) was automatically deducted from the payroll, at the rate of one day's wages a year for workers and an additional sum fixed from time to time for employers. Part of it was handed over to the higher federative organizations, but the bulk (60 per cent) went into the coffers of the local union.[33] These financial dispositions, though of course smoothly operating only where the employer's hostility to the very idea of *sindicalismo* had been overcome, further strengthened the position of the founders and first directorate of a *sindicato*; they made this position in practice virtually unchallenge-

[31] Ibid., p. 16. From this official definition it is also clear that the *sindicato* covered both peasants and rural workers.
[32] Ibid., pp. 20 f.
[33] Ibid., pp. 29–31.

able. Beyond the obviously rather limited power derived from the hold over a local *sindicato* lay more exciting prospects for the politically ambitious: the control of the rapidly emerging federations in different states, which would, in turn, eventually have a voice in determining the council of the national federation.

From the middle of 1963 the pace began to quicken.[34] The Ministry of Labour, long the stronghold of support for Goulart, set up the National Commission for Rural Unionization (CONSIR), made up of three representatives of the Ministry, three of the Superintendency for Agrarian Reform (SUPRA), and one peasant appointed by each, though the latter apparently never took an active part in the proceedings. The Commission formulated a grandiose plan for a truly massive effort at unionization, hoping to constitute 1,700 *sindicatos* in the first year of its operation. The idea of the President was clearly to shore up the failing political system by extending the *populista* tentacles of his party, the PTB, through the Ministry of Labour deep into the countryside. But by this time Goulart no longer seems to have been in effective control of his own machine. CONSIR had a minority of Goulart-supporting PTB members; there was an equal number of communists, one member of AP, and one representative of the Christian *sindicatos*—though the latter arrived after all deals had been clinched and found himself virtually without influence on CONSIR's activities.

One of the indications that the government's clientelistic apparatus was being eroded from within was the fact that from the start CONSIR backed the efforts of the PCB-dominated ULTAB (*União de Lavradores e Trabalhadores Agrícolas do Brasil*) to set up *sindicatos* and federations, and to get them formally recognized by the Ministry of Labour. As has already been seen, the communists had till then concentrated their efforts, through ULTAB, on *ligas camponeses* and other associations of rural workers which operated under the civil code. After the passing of the Rural Labour Statute, many of these were swiftly transformed into *sindicatos*, despite the fact that earlier ULTAB had on the whole stayed aloof from the latter kind of organization and

---

[34] The following account is based mainly on various lengthy interviews held late in 1965 with persons who had been prominently involved in the Christian efforts at *sindicalização*, and on documents written by one of them both before and after the coup of 1964. Unfortunately most of the documentary material of this period is not readily available today, and has consequently not been consulted. There is, however, a possibility that much of it will as yet be made public in a study of rural *sindicalismo* in Brazil currently being prepared by Miss Julieta Calazans.

had even struggled against them, as they were seen as the 'instruments of the padres'.

In the meantime it had become patently obvious to the Catholic populists that they could not wait for the slow gestation of peasant consciousness if they wanted to keep a hand in things. Events forced them to climb on the bandwagon, and to try and establish as many *sindicatos* as possible with a leadership which would accept their orientation. This orientation differed substantially from the one given by other organizations of Christian inspiration, who had not been waiting for the peasants to be 'wholly ready' before they had started setting up their *sindicatos*. In the South of the country, in São Paulo, Rio Grande de Sul, or Paraná, the old established Catholic agrarian leagues had a conservative 'solidarist' point of view. Organizations directly linked to the dioceses, such as SAR in Rio Grande do Norte and SORPE in Pernambuco, were perhaps a little more pugnacious and concerned with the formation of peasant leaders. A few of them could, in practice, be quite militant, but their ideology was, as we have seen, far from revolutionary. The only true radicals were the Catholic populists. The differences between most North-Eastern *sindicatos*, constituted by the diocesan trade union organizations, and those established by members of AP and the majority of those oriented by MEB gradually increased. These differences, coupled with other factors of a more personal character, led in July 1963 to an open clash. This occurred at the First National Convention of Rural Workers in Natal. Although actual peasant leaders participated in this Convention side by side with their mostly urban advisers, it was the latter who set the tone of the meetings and engaged in ideological polemics. Relations between the leaders and advisers of the 'clerical' or moderate Catholic *sindicatos* and the Catholic populists were clearly becoming increasingly strained.

Faced with the rush into the countryside, and the resulting free for all, the 'clerical' unions tried to steal a march on the others by founding the National Confederation, thus ensuring a majority for themselves on its council.[35] A confederation could be constituted, according to the law, once three federations had been established and recognized by the Ministry of Labour. By July 1963 five federations existed: three— moderate Catholic ones—in the North-East, one of conservative

---

[35] The idea had been in the air for quite a while: Pe Crespo mentions on p. 64 of the article cited in n. 25, published in the first half of 1963, that the North-Eastern federations 'are at present joining to form the National Confederation of Rural Workers (CNTR)'.

Christian orientation in São Paulo, and only one directed by ULTAB, in Paraná. The Christian preponderance at this moment was an expression of their more long-standing concern with *sindicalização*: though ULTAB had another eight federations in preparation, most of these had not yet been formally established, and none of them had been recognized.

Shortly afterwards the four Christian federations met in Recife and founded the *Confederação Nacional de Trabalhadores na Agricultura* (CONTAG). Paraná did not participate, alleging that the invitation had arrived too late; the organizers, however, maintained that their absence was a deliberate manœuvre to call in question the legality of the founding meeting. A period of massive intrigues followed, during which ULTAB put various kinds of pressure on the four original founders to make them agree that the confederation had not been legally established, or at least that the election of the council had been irregular. In this they were fully supported by CONSIR. Sometime early in November a meeting was held between the Christian federations and CONSIR, from which the member of the Commission most closely identified with the Christian federations' point of view was absent. At this meeting the latter were bluntly told that the papers on the foundation of the Confederation would be filed away, and that no further action to ensure recognition was envisaged.

The Christian federations perhaps demonstrated a certain lack of imagination as to the means by which they might have resisted these pressures. Be that as it may, they saw no alternative but to give in to the suggestion that a new council should be elected at a gathering in Rio on 19 and 20 December 1963, to which all the by then existing federations were to be invited. As a result the 'rush' developed into a veritable race. About a month was left to raise the troops and get them into position for the decisive battle, and the three interested parties made full use of all the possibilities afforded by the new legislation. ULTAB seems to have been particularly adept at constituting *sindicatos* and federations everywhere. They even 'founded' some ten federations which claimed to represent categories or areas already covered by federations set up by moderate Catholic groups. This expedient ensured that the latter were neutralized and that they would not be present in December, as the Ministry of Labour had to sort out the conflicting claims for recognition. And that was a process that needed time.

Eventually CONSIR invited twenty-four federations to the December

9

meeting. Taking place against a background of general political excitement, the meeting was characterized mainly by caucuses of the various groups, who jockeyed for position and bargained over deals deep into the night. ULTAB controlled the largest group of delegates: ten federations in all. Eight federations had a more or less moderate Catholic orientation—though by the end of the meeting two of these had made a deal with the representatives of the six federations whose point of view was broadly identified with AP. In the first instance the non-communist federations had attempted to achieve agreement over policy and the division of offices on the council: together they had a clear majority of votes. But the differences of opinion were too great, and the personal antagonisms too deep. There was no love lost between AP's openly revolutionary spokesmen and the most influential advisers of the moderate Catholics, whose conception of the role of a trade union movement was to a large extent modelled on that of the CIO-AFL, the North American confederation of labour unions, and its Latin American offshoot, ORIT (Inter-American Labour Organization).

With the attempts at co-operation between the moderate and radical Christians making no headway, AP and the communists switched their attention to each other. They came to an agreement on a *frente única* (united front) and decided on the division of the spoils. ULTAB took the presidency and treasury, and an AP man became secretary-general. Each received two further posts. The moderate Catholics were offered the two least significant offices on the council of nine: third vice-president and second secretary. At the last moment they decided to accept this derisory offer. They obviously hoped that once the organization was functioning AP would see the light and co-operate with them in out-manœuvring the communists. But in the three months left before the coup the confederation never really gathered steam, and there is no evidence that the moderate Catholics were making any progress in their efforts to woo AP away from the communists.

AP in the political arena

Nevertheless, AP did, apparently, develop doubts about the *frente única* in CONTAG. It seems that in general united fronts were more often than not rather unhappy experiences for AP, and the movement was far from united on the wisdom or the advisability of such co-operation. AP was very much the junior and less politically sophisticated partner in the wheelings and dealings with the communists. The latter played a shrewd game by which they benefited greatly from AP's support, without having to give much in return. The CONTAG elections came to be seen in this light, and after a thorough post-mortem on these events AP seems to have been getting ready for a reorientation of its relations with the communists, perhaps even for a complete break with them.

This break, forestalled by the coup of April 1964, would have been justified on several grounds.[36] AP resented the manipulative practices of the PCB, which was legally prevented from openly participating in politics. The party, however, frequently seemed to make a virtue out of necessity, and hid its true colour from the masses, for whom communism was to a large extent still a dirty word. The communists played a whole range of roles depending on their ally: from anti-imperialism with the nationalist bourgeoisie to anti-capitalism with the rest of the radical Left. AP also doubted (and with good reason) the willingness of the communists to promote radical change if necessary by really revolutionary means, and began to suspect that they were being pushed into exposed positions by the communists—who did not want to be caught red-handed in case things went awry. At the same time the communists were seen as intending to 'use' the other radical forces in order to achieve their own aim of reaching power. They attempted to dictate policy, always claiming their rights as the oldest revolutionary force in the country, acting 'as a kind of Holy Office of the Brazilian Revolution'. Their attitude, in the view of AP, was based on the premise that any united front was a compromise, a 'temporary alliance with error', permissible only because it would eventually help the party to attain hegemony. The AP leadership concluded that if the movement's praxis had to be linked with that of other political groupings it would be necessary for each constituent party of a united front to have its own clearly defined and openly proclaimed identity. This would lead to a demarcation of interests and differences, and prevent dissimulated manipulation of some by others.

These views were being developed in AP after approximately eighteen months of full-fledged activity, of penetration of existing organizations, state or private, of collaboration with other left-wing organizations, and of a certain amount of success to get members (or

---

[36] The views of AP discussed in the following paragraph derive from information obtained from an informant interviewed in December 1965, who had the opportunity to observe the AP *cúpula* at close hand (without, however, belonging to it), and from a draft paper drawn up by the AP leadership early in 1964, discussing the problems of the *frente única* (typescript).

sympathizers) to occupy positions of political importance. As has been seen, this was especially the case in the rural trade union movement. A few, moreover, had posts in the federal and state bureaucracies—notably in departments concerned with education. Hence, during this period, members and adherents of AP were to a limited extent close to the centres of political power, even though they did not effectively participate in decision-making on a scale that really made an impact.

Nevertheless, this apparent closeness to the foci of politics put a strain on the populist purity of their actions. Thus the scramble for power in CONTAG expressed the degeneration of a movement of potentially great social significance into a fragmented instrument of doubtful efficacy, for use by the politically ambitious. Despite itself, despite the very clear prescriptions to the contrary of its populist ideology, AP participated in the frenzy—felt it *had* to participate. Similarly, the movement came to be organized along lines which were much more 'élitist' than its own ideology could seem to have warranted; in fact *institutionally* AP developed a structure during this period which had almost more in common with that of a Communist Party than with a movement whose main concern was supposedly 'to let the people speak'. Those who became actual members of an AP 'group' were expected to carry out certain tasks according to a 'line' which had been decided at a higher level: they were, in fact, expected to submit to 'discipline'.[37] Understandably, this created conflicts between the *cúpula* and the membership. In fact, substantial over-all tensions were present in the movement almost from its foundation.[38] But with 'infiltration' a favourite activity of all left-wing political movements during the last hectic year of the Goulart government, the leadership of AP must frequently have wanted to forestall a move by those who had few scruples about *massificação*.

The coup made all these considerations quite irrelevant, at least with respect to political activities openly carried out. After 1964 the clandestine and fragmented remnants of AP ranged themselves increasingly on the side of those favouring violent revolution, while the PCB attempted (against the opposition of the Peking-oriented *Partido Communista do Brasil* and other Marxist splinter groups) to maintain a position of

[37] At times such discipline would even extend to a person's private life: one informant told me of a member of an AP group who was told to break off his relations with a girl who belonged to the PCB. Cf. the by now classic discussion of this very phenomenon in Arthur Schweitzer, 'Ideological Groups', *Amer. Sociolog. R.*, ix (1944).

[38] In the years of clandestinity, after the coup, the movement apparently fell apart into various mutually hostile factions.

compromise, and condemned 'adventurism'. As I wrote at the beginning of the previous chapter, after 1964 AP seems to have finally lost its specifically Christian associations. From the start it had shunned institutional connections with the church or Catholic organizations, but in the pre-coup days it still bore the philosophical and ideological marks of its radical Christian parentage. Since then, however, it appears that it has not only fallen apart in various mutually antagonistic grouplets, so that one can no longer meaningfully speak of *an* AP line, but also that the views held by most of the different factions have become wholly anchored in a secular—Marxist, Castroite, or Maoist—radicalism.[39] At this point, then, let us turn to the evolution of the specific subject of this study, the *Movimento de Educação de Base*.

[39] I write this with some diffidence, as it has proved impossible to get really reliable information on the post-coup development of AP.

7

MEB: Its Scope, Operation, and Cadres

The origins of MEB

MOST of MEB's own documents, which include a section on the history of the Movement, begin their story with the understanding reached between the federal government and the CNBB early in 1961, whereby the latter agreed to expand the experience of radio schools in the dioceses of Natal and Aracajú to the whole of the less-developed areas of Brazil. Education by radio had been going on for some years—in the case of the Natal diocese, for instance, since 1958. There it was part of the wide-ranging SAR social-work programme set up by the local bishop, D. Eugênio Sales, under his own close personal supervision.

By 1958 there were a fair number of radio stations owned by dioceses,[1] and in that year a first meeting was held to discuss matters of common interest. At this meeting, which was attended by representatives of thirty-two stations, many of them from the wealthier south of the country, an organization was set up charged with keeping the stations in touch with each other and studying and solving common problems: the *Rede Nacional de Emissôras Católicas* (RENEC). Its first Secretary-General, who had organized the meeting on behalf of the secretariat for Social Action of the CNBB, from the start took a special interest in the educational role of these diocesan radio stations. She was well aware of the fact that a system of radio schools could function effectively only if the people running it were properly trained. Thus short training courses were organized for the prospective cadres of three newly-formed radio-school systems. In these courses the experience of the Natal diocese, and of the earlier established Colombian radio schools centred on Sutatenza, was put to good use.[2] Early

---

[1] Strictly speaking the stations were owned personally by the bishops, as under Brazilian law radio stations cannot be owned by corporate bodies.

[2] The clericalism of the Colombian *Acción Cultural Popular*, was, however, rejected from the start. A brief discussion of the Colombian radio schools may be found in my 'Paternalism and Populism', *J. Contemp. Hist.*, Oct. 1967.

in 1960, after these radio-school systems had been functioning for a while, RENEC summoned those responsible to an *Encontro de Educação de Base* in Aracajú, the capital of the North-East state of Sergipe. Although this meeting mainly concentrated on techniques and organizational problems, some of the wider implications of basic education were also discussed. It was here, apparently, that the question was first mooted of extending the existing work to a national scale.

During the campaign preceding the presidential elections of 1960, on a visit to Sergipe, Jânio Quadros encountered the work of the diocesan radio-school system. Its basic activity was to teach adult peasants to read and write. Quadros seems to have been much impressed, and while visiting Aracajú he met the Archbishop, D. José Távora, under whose responsibility the radio schools were operating. During this meeting D. Távora and Quadros briefly explored the idea that the church should organize this type of education by radio on a wide scale throughout the country.

D. Távora discussed the matter further with the RENEC people in Rio. They felt that by then enough experience had been gained with the training methods to make possible a broad and soundly based expansion. They said that they could undertake to create a network of radio-school systems on condition that the necessary funds could be found. If the federal government were to provide the finance, there should be no insuperable problems. D. Távora also consulted some of his fellow bishops, and especially the secretariat of the CNBB. Its Secretary-General at the time was D. Helder Câmara, then auxiliary Archbishop of the diocese of Rio de Janeiro. D. Helder, a man whose main preoccupation had been in the social field ever since he came to Rio, and who was already at that time a great deal more aware of the deep-seated nature of Brazil's social and economic problems than most of his colleagues, received the idea with enthusiasm. By promoting basic education the church could play a role in development. It could contribute to the raising of the abysmally low living standards of the rural population by making them more capable of helping themselves.

Basic agreement was reached between the bishops and the President right at the beginning of the latter's period of office. D. Távora had formally proposed the idea to Quadros in a letter dated 11 November 1960: the CNBB would provide the people and the organization and do the job, the government would give its secular blessing and foot the bill. Just over four months later, on 21 March 1961, the President signed the decree sponsoring the *Movimento de Educação de Base*, to be launched by the CNBB, which was to organize radio schools in the underdeveloped areas of the North, North-East, and Centre-West of the country.[3] The decree provided for financial collaboration during five years (1961–5), and stipulated that MEB would receive just over Cr$400 m. during the first year—in bi-monthly payments, in advance.[4] In return the Movement would install 15,000 radio schools in that year, and see to an expansion in each subsequent year always greater than that in the immediately preceding year. Provision was made for subsidiary agreements with various ministries, such as those of education, agriculture, and health, and in an important clause MEB was given the right to request the secondment of federal functionaries for services judged indispensable to the Movement. This facility was used on a fairly large scale once the organization got going, also after separate agreements in respect of functionaries of the various states, mainly in order to bring school teachers into the Movement as supervisors, teachers, and so on. The secretary of RENEC became Secretary-General of MEB.

As will be seen, the whole operation was conceived on a monumental scale. All concerned no doubt dreamt of a mass literacy campaign which would in one stroke eliminate rural illiteracy, or at least reduce it substantially below the national average of approximately one in two of those over ten years of age. In the North-East the 1950 average had been well over 70 per cent, a figure that had apparently changed little in the following decade.[5] There had been various such grandiose efforts before, all of which had fizzled out after a short while for lack of funds or personnel, or because of the political atrophy of the sponsoring agency. In the case of MEB there is no need to doubt the honest intentions and the genuine concern of the President or the bishops who took the initiative, and yet it is also hard to escape the impression that other considerations entered the motives of both sides. Illiterates do not vote in Brazil, and it is probable that a govern-

[3] *Decreto Presidencial* no. 50.370, 21 Mar. 1961, published in the *Diário oficial* on 22 March 1961. The final outcome involved a change from the originally intended nation-wide organization, by the exclusion of the more developed areas of the country in the South. In general terms, of course, this made good sense—but it assumed a homogeneity of development which the South hardly possessed. Many rural areas there could have benefited equally well from the scheme.

[4] This represented approximately US$1·7 m. at the time it was promised; in terms of the average value of the cruzeiro during the year it was approximately US$1·5 m.

[5] All experts I have consulted consider the literacy figures of the 1960 census as totally inaccurate.

ment (or President) financing the elevation of the rural masses to voter status hoped for some rewards at the polls—however unrealistic this might seem in retrospect. This may well have seemed especially important to a *populista* such as Jânio Quadros who did, after all, capture the presidency on a wave of popular enthusiasm, without having had much of a political 'machine' at his disposal. For many bishops, on the other hand, the project promised prestige and influence through the ownership of a radio station; and a good number of them hoped to use the basic education programmes for religious instruction and the propagation of the faith.

The radio schools and the *sistemas*

The operational set-up of the Movement which was laid down at the beginning remained in broad lines unaltered through the years. The shifts and changes that occurred related more to the balance of power between the constituent elements than to the overall pattern of organization and work. The Movement, originally a department of the CNBB, later an independent agency in which a Council of Bishops (the *Conselho Diretor Nacional*, CDN) appointed by the CNBB exercised control at the top, was essentially conceived on three levels: local, state, and national.

The basic unit of organization is the *sistema*. It is made up of the *equipe*—the team of remunerated teachers, supervisors, radio announcers, and ancillary personnel who programme the daily broadcasts, execute them, and see them applied in the radio schools—the peasants, and the *monitores*, who provide the bridge between the former and the latter. The number of *sistemas* rose from 11 in 1961—four of which had existed as independent diocesan organizations before the foundation of MEB—to 59 in 1963, declining to 52 by the end of 1965, a result of the political and financial· difficulties following the coup of April 1964. By the end of 1966 37 were still in operation.[6] Some *sistemas* came to work by methods different from radio classes, usually because a promised transmitter or wavelength did not materialize after the unit had been set up, and in the course of time the general emphasis in the Movement's work shifted away from radio teaching. Nevertheless, the most common form of organization and work remained that focused on the radio schools.

[6] The downward trend continued in the following years: in December 1967 there were twenty-one *sistemas* in operation.

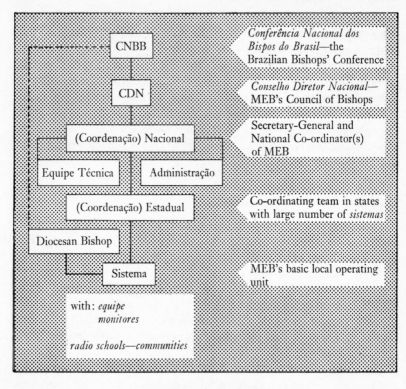

CNBB	*Conferência Nacional dos Bispos do Brasil*—the Brazilian Bishops' Conference
CDN	*Conselho Diretor Nacional*— MEB's Council of Bishops
(Coordenação) Nacional	Secretary-General and National Co-ordinator(s) of MEB
Equipe Técnica Administração	
(Coordenação) Estadual	Co-ordinating team in states with large number of *sistemas*
Diocesan Bishop	
Sistema	MEB's basic local operating unit
with: *equipe monitores* *radio schools—communities*	

MEB'S ORGANIZATION

These radio schools are very simple matters indeed. Though they often operate in a community's school building, itself usually a primitive affair, there are many communities where such a building does not exist.[7] In that case the class, made up of perhaps 10–15 students, most of whom are between 15 and 30 years of age,[8] meets in the dwelling

---

[7] There is a bewildering variety of types of 'community', used here to refer to a rural settlement of families who have some sense of belonging together as a 'locality group' or 'neighbourhood' found outside the administrative 'urban' nucleus of the *município*. For a useful general discussion see Marshall Wolfe, *Lat. Am. Res. R.*, 1/2 (1966), and Lynn Smith, ch. 17.

[8] The proportion of students under 15 in two—not really representative—samples taken in 1963 and 1964 was respectively 24 and 4 per cent. Those over 30 accounted for 15 and 17 per cent respectively. It seems quite safe to say that approx. two-thirds of the students of MEB were aged between 15 and 30 (cf. *MEB em cinco anos*, p. 97).

of the *monitor*, almost always a house of the wattle and daub type, no different from the others found in the area. As Table 1 shows, the number of radio schools reached its peak of just over 7,000 in the third quarter of 1963, after which a decline set in. In the first instance this was occasioned by a forced shift in the time of broadcast, resulting from the introduction of a daily, official hour-long bulletin by the Brazilian government, the transmission of which was compulsory for all radio stations. MEB's programme had to be rescheduled, and the inconvenience of the new time to the peasants—classes were either too early or too late—meant that many dropped out and a quarter of all radio schools were closed, though seasonal fluctuation may have played a part here. A further reduction occurred after the coup in 1964; in many areas MEB was inactive for over three months. Where a *sistema* remained, some schools reopened with reduced numbers, others never started up again. Consequently, between December 1963 and December 1964 the number of radio schools was reduced by another fifth; on the latter date there were about 4,600 left. With the closing down of all *sistemas* operating in Pernambuco, Bahia, Minas Gerais, and Goiás—essentially the result of political and financial pressures—the number of radio schools dropped to about 2,500 by the beginning of 1967. Hence the Movement's decline was greatest in the areas of political tension such as the North-East. Moreover, after the coup, the peasants there lost interest in radio schools which could neither discuss the real problems facing the *povo* nor hold out the promise of a significant political participation for the eventual literates. In the North, on the contrary, in the less 'politicized' Amazon states, the Movement continued to gain ground steadily: this can be seen both in the absolute number of schools and in the proportion of the total.[9]

The *monitor* is one of the most essential cogs in the MEB machine. During the first year of the Movement's operation he (or she) was appointed from above, later he was chosen by the peasants themselves. The *monitor* is always a member of the community. At first he was conceived of as the link between the school and the team running the *sistema*: a person who has had some formal schooling and is at the very least a semi-literate. He is a kind of unpaid auxiliary, relaying the broadcast instructions to the students, checking their exercises, making them come to the blackboard, stimulating the slow ones, and leading discussions. The latter aspect of his duties is the most sensitive

[9] For a further discussion of the implications of this fact see ch. 10.

TABLE I

No. of radio schools, and proportion by region, approx. end of each year, 1961-6

	Dec. 1961		Dec. 1962		Sept. 1963		Dec. 1964		Dec. 1965		Jan. 1967	
	No.	%	No.	%	No.	%	No.	%	No.	%	No.	%
North*	75	3	362	7	500	7	678	15	1,051	23	1,154	45
North-East†	2,586	96	4,956	88	6,464	88	3,604	78	3,280	73	1,332	53
Centre-West‡	26	1	280	5	389	5	316	7	191	4	41	2
	2,687	(100)	5,598	(100)	7,353	(100)	4,598	(100)	4,522	(100)	2,527	(100)

* Amazonas, Pará, Rondônia.
† Maranhão, Piauí, Ceará, R.G. Norte, Paraíba, Pernambuco, Alagoas, Sergipe, Bahia.
‡ Minas Gerais, Goiás, Mato Grosso.

Note. These figures must be taken more as indicating an order of magnitude than as a fully reliable statement of the number of radio schools actively functioning. Some optimistic reporting by *monitores* (and by *sistemas*) certainly took place, especially in the earlier years.

Source: MEB em cinco anos, p. 90, and annual reports.

to his leadership capacities. It was not long before this factor—leadership—became the main requirement for a *monitor*. He gradually came to be thought of in the Movement less as an auxiliary teacher and more as a community leader, with many tasks besides that of providing the link between the radio-teacher and the students for an hour every evening.

This change occurred *pari passu* with that in the Movement's self-image, in which the literacy element, seen as part of basic education, was ousted from its predominant position by a much greater stress on the understanding of the existing social situation, and on organization which might lead to the peasants becoming both less dependent upon the landowners and more assertive of their own interests. In 1963 this resulted, for instance, in a surge of activity aimed at preparing the peasants for participation in rural trade unions, the *sindicatos*. In the same period the *sistemas* began to shift away from broadcasts and radio classes as their primary concern. More attention came to be paid to visits by supervisors to the schools and the communities and to new methods of community co-operation. The *treinamentos*, short training, study, and discussion courses lasting usually about five days, took on added importance as the years went by. In the first two years these *treinamentos* were organized on the assumption that MEB's impact must be made through the actual radio schools. Gradually, however, as the Movement developed a wider view of its task, the emphasis shifted from the radio school to the community, and from the *monitor* as an auxiliary teacher to the *monitor* as a potential community leader.

Treinamentos are altogether nodal elements in the functioning of the Movement. They are also used to prepare the *equipe* of the *sistema*, or to keep them up to date. In the first year of MEB's operation most *equipes* were recruited from people recommended by the local bishop or by priests; later the flow of new members into the Movement became much less dependent upon ecclesiastical initiatives. Most newcomers would find that their first *treinamento* gave them a new perspective on the world. This would be the case for their views on social and economic organization, and might even touch religious matters such as the role of the layman in the church—although this would be more by implication than through explicit discussion. The method by which the local *equipe* was inducted into the Movement then formed the model for the *treinamentos* which they in turn provided for the *monitores*. Conceived in the first place as a training instrument, these courses developed, together with the more formal and less

TABLE 2

Treinamentos for sistema teams (equipes), 1961–6: no. of participants and proportion by region

	1961		1962		1963		1964		1965		1966		1961–7	
	No.	%	No.	%	No.	%	No.	%	No.	%	No.	%	No.	%
North	—	—	—	—	53	16	12	9	2	2	23	28	90	10
North-East	78	84	93	69	187	57	107	81	76	72	59	72	600	68
Centre-West	15	16	42	31	90	27	13	10	28	26	—	—	188	21
Total	93	(100)	135	(100)	330	(100)	132	(100)	106	(100)	82	(100)	878	(100)
No. of treinamentos	4		6		14		6		5		3		38	

Source: MEB em cinco anos, p. 87, and annual reports.

TABLE 3

Treinamentos for monitores, 1961–5: no. of participants and proportion by region

	1961*		1962		1963		1964		1965†		1961–5	
	No.	%	No.	%	No.	%	No.	%	No.	%	No.	%
North	80	7	65	2	205	5	588	19	225	12	1,163	8
North-East	1,052	89	3,458	93	3,220	84	2,071	66	1,455	78	11,256	82
Centre-West	50	4	186	5	445	11	488	15	183	10	1,352	10
Total	1,182	(100)	3,709	(100)	3,870	(100)	3,147	(100)	1,863	(100)	13,771	(100)
No. of treinamentos	36		135		153		111		83		518	

* Approx. figures.   † Incomplete figures.
Source: *MEB em cinco anos*, p. 86.

regular representative meetings of the different levels of the Movement's leadership, into truly two-way flows, where the views of the
bases came to exert as much of an influence on the higher levels as the
other way round. It was there that the principles of non-directiveness
were first worked out, principles which would have such a fundamental
influence on the whole development of the Movement.[10]

From 1961 to the end of 1966, as Table 2 shows, a total of 38
treinamentos were held for the teams of the *sistemas*, by which means
just under 900 trainees were reached. The peak occurred during the
year 1963, when 40 per cent of all the courses were held and 40 per
cent of all the potential team members trained—that was MEB's
period of most rapid and euphoric expansion. Table 3 gives the figures
available regarding *treinamentos* for *monitores*. Until the end of 1965
500 of these were held, in which almost 14,000 trainees participated.
The predominance of the North-East is even more striking for trainee
monitores than for those being prepared for the *sistemas*; the drop after
1964 (both absolutely and relatively) is even more marked.[11] In neither
case did acceptance as a trainee guarantee incorporation into the
organization. But the number of failures was not important, although a
certain amount of turnover in personnel, paid as well as unpaid, did of
course occur.

The figures presented in these tables, in particular those referring to
the *monitores*, certainly provide the most significant quantitative
indicators of the Movement's scope and effectiveness. Though substantial differences existed in 'quality', especially between different
monitores, MEB's impact should be measured by the cadres it formed.
Many of these people became genuine leaders in the rural areas. That
their effect was not very great must be attributed to the relatively short
period of time available for unhampered activity—and learning—in
the rural areas: after the coup almost any kind of peasant leadership was
suspect, and few activities beyond innocuous education were tolerated.

The Movement's statistics regarding the number of illiterates who
concluded a year's course with MEB are much more questionable.
The only figures available are those set out in Table 4 showing the
number of matriculated students still attending at the end of each

---

[10] See ch. 11.

[11] As can be seen from Table 5 the data become less complete after 1964. All that is
known for 1966 is that at least 12 *treinamentos* for *monitores* were held in 6 *sistemas* (464
participants). This low figure reflects both a decline in the number of *treinamentos* due to
financial difficulties, and the administrative (communications) problems of this period.

TABLE 4

Students at end of each year, 1961–6, and proportion by region

	1961		1962		1963		1964		1965		1966	
	No.	%	No.	%	No.	%	No.	%	No.	%	No.	%
North	974	2·5	6,200	5·7	6,902	6·2	9,257	14·5	12,225	19·9	16,448	53·2
North-East	37,374	96·5	99,183	91·3	98,236	88·4	50,248	78·8	46,270	75·3	12,278	39·7
Centre-West	386	1·0	3,188	2·9	5,928	5·3	4,253	6·7	2,905	4·7	1,195	3·9
Total	38,734	(100)	108,571	(100)	111,066	(100)	63,758	(100)	61,400	(100)	30,920	(100)
of which 'advanced' students	17%		11%		24%		30%		41% (est.)		not known	

Source: MEB em cinco anos, p. 92 and annual reports.

school year in December. They rose from 39,000 at the end of 1961 to 111,000 by 1963; then fell back in 1964 to 64,000, with a further slight drop to 61,000 by the end of 1965. In the year 1966, with the closure of so many *sistemas*, the number dropped further to 31,000. The growing importance of the Movement's work in the Amazon region is reflected in a steady rise from 1,000 (or 2·5 per cent) in 1961 to 16,000 (or 53·2 per cent) in 1966.[12] No one in the Movement knows exactly what margin of error these figures contain because of over-reporting; for the earlier years it could easily be between 10 and 20 per cent. Attendance, moreover, does not guarantee result—and no reliable evaluation data are available on the effectiveness of MEB in promoting literacy. The most one can say of figures such as these is that they give an idea of the order of magnitude involved.

Drop-out figures are known for two years: in 1963 and in 1964 about one-quarter of those who started did not persevere. One datum of importance was the growing proportion of 'advanced' students who completed a second or subsequent year's work: it rose from 17 per cent in 1961 (all in the pre-existing radio schools of Natal) to 41 per cent in 1965. It is not unreasonable to assume that the impact—in the broadest sense of the term—of the Movement was correlated with the time spent in its ranks. In any case, with the shift in focus to problems connected with the peasants' social and economic conditions, the actual attention paid to sheer literacy as a sign of effectiveness decreased (outside the Amazon region) as time passed. Nevertheless in MEB's publications the emphasis, in so far as figures were concerned, remained heavily on the literacy side.

Overall co-ordination: *Nacional* and *Estaduais*

In those states where more than two or three *sistemas* are to be found, their co-ordination is undertaken by a separate entity, the state co-ordination or *Estadual*. These teams—they have existed in Pernambuco, Ceará, Bahia, and Minas Gerais—operate from the state capital. In the course of time the formal functions of the *Estaduais* became less important than their role as key elements in the dynamic of the Movement's ideological and structural development. The state leadership was relatively close to the 'bases' and participated in much of the actual work. They thus knew the problems of MEB's

[12] By the end of 1967 there were 27,000 students left, of whom 14,000 were in the Amazon region.

clientèle from personal experience; their thinking on exploitation or poverty was related to concrete evidence. And yet, because they were on the whole quite highly educated people, they could make sense of the more abstract philosophical and ideological language of the central team in Rio, with whom they also had frequent contacts. In this way the *Estaduais*—and the *sistemas* operating from the more important state capitals—mediated between theory and practice, also because unlike the others in the more distant areas, they lived in places where the new radicalism of JUC and later of AP found organized expression. The contrast in this respect with the individual *sistemas* in the North, which were not regionally co-ordinated, and none of which was founded before 1963, was very great.[13] It was largely the vision and the activity of the *Estaduais* and the *sistemas* from the large cities which drove the Movement in a new, populist, direction from 1962 onwards, brought it much more in touch with the people, and made it into an expression more of the latter's view of the world than of that of the bishops.

Finally, at the national level, there are a general secretariat, administration, and technical team, established in the national headquarters in Rio. At first these functioned in the building which housed the secretariat of the CNBB, but early in 1964 the *Nacional* moved to its own home. The *Nacional* provides overall direction to the Movement, gives expression to the national unity which overarches the regional differences, furnishes specialized technical services—such as the preparation of primers, mimeographed texts, instructions and study documents for the *sistemas*, and leadership at high-level *treinamentos* —and maintains contact with governmental and church organizations. At the peak of the Movement's activity there were, including secretarial, administrative, and domestic staff, some fifty people working at the national headquarters; later this diminished to about half that figure. Table 5 presents an overall figure of the Movement's personnel. At the *Nacional* a variety of professions have been represented, ranging from law, through accountancy, to education, sociology, and psychology. Some were university graduates, others were continuing their studies while they worked. Each contributed from his own specialized perspective to the Movement's operation and ideological development; the latter was especially influenced by the various students and graduates in philosophy employed by MEB.

---

[13] Some of the problems engendered by this discrepancy are discussed in ch. 11. The situation in the Amazon region is briefly examined on pp. 205 ff.

TABLE 5

Total no. of paid functionaries, 1963–7, and proportion by region.

	Dec. 1963		Dec. 1964		Dec. 1965		Jan. 1967	
	No.	%	*No.*	%	*No.*	%	*No.*	%
North	43	9	45	10	61	14	74	38
North-East	367	76	315	72	315	71	115	59
Centre-West	74	15	77	18	65	15	7	4
sub-total	484	(100)	437	(100)	441	(100)	196	(100)
Nacional	47		32		29		25	
Total	531		469		470		228	

Source: MEB em cinco anos, p. 83, and annual reports.

At the *Nacional*, too, there were many who had been active in student politics and Catholic Action before they came to MEB. The *Nacional* contained, during the crucial years 1962 and 1963, various individuals who maintained personal links with the vortices of Christian radicalism discussed in the foregoing chapters (including two past national co-ordinators of JUC), without, however, in any sense acting as uncritical 'spokesmen' or one-way transmitters of ideas. On the other hand the Secretary-General and one further highly placed member of MEB's national team had for many years worked in the closest association with the bishops at the Secretariat for Social Action of the CNBB. The *Nacional* became the often uncomfortably tense hothouse in which the Movement's ideology developed; it provided the links with what went on in the outside world, and put the broad new concepts being formulated in Christian circles at the disposal of the organization. But the new ideas were usually hard to understand for the less sophisticated members of the Movement, and the *Nacional's* ideologists hardly ever descended from the lofty heights where sociological analysis mingled with philosophical speculation. This created repeated friction with the *sistemas*, who often reproached the Rio intellectuals their lack of *vivencia*, of real-life participation in the Movement's work.

The *Nacional* also has the overall financial responsibility for MEB: it receives the funds from the government and channels them to the lower echelons. This financial responsibility has proved something of a burden over the years, in the first place, because the promises of the federal government in money matters were always more impressive than its performance. Secondly, because after 1964 MEB's dependence on the government for funds gave the latter great opportunities for putting pressure on the Movement, to bring its work more into line with the views of the new authorities. In the first year of its existence MEB received less than one-tenth of the amount mentioned as the government's subvention in President Quadros's decree—and about half of the money was not remitted till the final week of the year. While the promised support was of the order of US$1·5 m., the sums actually received amounted to no more than US$110,000—though of the amount outstanding a further US$270,000, approximately, were remitted during the following year.[14] Year after year the annual reports complain of the irregularity in the arrival of money. Usually the amount inserted in the national budget suffered some cut in Congress or by government decree as a result of general economy measures; MEB learned to prepare for this by requesting a larger sum than it expected to receive. By dint of the expedient of not paying the full sum allocated till late in the year, or even in the following year, the actual financial burden on the federal government was automatically lightened by the constant inflationary process.

The year-to-year amounts budgeted and received can be recalculated into a meaningful total by making adjustments for inflation and restating the amounts in dollars. It is a somewhat hazardous process, but the following figures will give at least an approximate idea of the problem,[15] and they also provide a forceful warning to anyone inclined to take Brazil's official data very seriously. For the five years 1961–5 of the original agreement between the federal government and the CNBB, the total appropriation for MEB in the federal budget, and passed by Congress, amounted to some US$3·8 m. The total actually received

---

[14] See n. 15.
[15] Calculated from figures given in Annual Reports, and in *MEB em cinco anos*, table on p. 105, where the figures have been expressed in 1961 cruzeiros with the help of the *Tabela de Deflação* of the *Fundação Getúlio Vargas*.

by the organization, on the other hand, did not exceed US$2·2 m., less than 60 per cent of the amount appropriated.

Financial insecurity and attendant planning problems—no plan ever seems to have been fully carried out, and all plans were constantly being revised—have been a feature of the Movement virtually from its inception. It was in the years after 1964 that insecurity took on unprecedented proportions bordering on disaster. In 1966 MEB had requested—no doubt over-optimistically—US$2·2 m., a large but not wholly unrealistic sum in view of the need to renew much of the by then run-down equipment. After enormous efforts, which included various private encounters as well as a correspondence between the Minister of Education and one of the bishops of MEB's National Council (the CDN), the government released in June some US$300,000 as its total contribution for 1966.[16] That the money was made available at all resulted, without any doubt whatsoever, from the authorities' hesitation to provoke an open clash with the CNBB, which remained ultimately responsible for the Movement. But the government did not think twice about fully using its capacity for financial pressure (one is tempted to say blackmail) to attempt to create conditions which would guarantee that MEB would work within the limits set by the 'philosophy' of the post-coup rulers of the country. During those drawn-out negotiations in 1966 the government spokesmen even suggested structural changes in the Movement and in its relationship with the state which could have enabled the latter to exercise more effective control.[17]

Characteristics of MEB's cadres

So far various statements have been made about the kinds of people to be found in MEB at the different levels of the organization. Relatively early on during the fieldwork it was possible to discern a likely pattern regarding the personal characteristics and background of those comprising the Movement's cadres. A mental picture emerged of a group of people not only full of idealism, but also highly educated in

[16] The situation in 1967 was even worse. The Movement was virtually forced to a standstill, and received only US$130,000. In 1968 the position improved, however, after a new agreement with the government had been signed in August 1967, and MEB was enabled to operate on a normal basis in those areas where it survived.

[17] At this time the Minister proposed that the finances should be channelled directly from the government to the individual bishops in whose diocese a *sistema* operated. In this way the *Nacional* would have been cut out, and the authorities would have acquired greater leeway to influence the individual units of the Movement. See the discussion on *diocesanização* below, and in ch. 11, pp. 220 f., 224 ff.

comparison with their environment, who had joined the Movement driven by a well-developed social and political consciousness, often acquired in one of the radical youth movements of Catholic Action.

To test the truth of this impression, which rested more on extra-polating to the whole Movement experience at the *Nacional*, a short questionnaire was issued to a sample of those active in the Movement during the period of fieldwork. That sample of fifty-six persons in all did not turn out to be fully representative of the Movement as a whole. Though it gives an accurate picture of those most directly responsible for MEB's operation at each level, of the actual leadership of the Movement from *Nacional* to *sistemas*, not many conclusions can be drawn from it regarding the bulk of the people working in the *sistemas* as supervisors, etc. Moreover, as the gathering of information occurred in 1966, those who had left the Movement after the coup but had played an important role in the earlier years were automatically excluded. Nevertheless, despite these limitations, the data obtained throw much light on a number of important aspects of the make-up of MEB's cadres, confirming some of the expected results and refuting others.[18]

For purposes of analysis the sample was divided into three groups: the top leadership (*Nacional* and co-ordinators of *Estaduais*), the intermediate leadership (co-ordinators and past co-ordinators of *sistemas*), and the rank and file.[19] Perhaps the most important general conclusion to be drawn from the figures relates to the difference in personal characteristics and background to be found again and again between the Movement's different levels. Thus while the top leadership was preponderantly male (60 per cent), at the other levels women predominated (approximately 65 per cent).[20] Half of those in the top group had entered the Movement during its first two years of operation, against only one-fifth of those in positions of intermediate leadership, and none of the rank and file.[21] The importance of the provision in the presidential decree enabling MEB to request the secondment of teachers is reflected in the high proportion of ex-teachers in the

[18] For a more detailed discussion of the method used and of the limitations of the findings see App. I, which also contains the data presented in the form of tables, and a more precise discussion of the statistical significance of the figures. In the following pages I shall only refer to statistical significance where a comparison between two groups is mentioned which is *not* statistically significant at the 10 per cent level.

[19] See introductory remarks to App. I.

[20] App. I, table 1. Finding lacks statistical significance at 10 per cent level.

[21] App. I, table 3.

Movement: half of those in the rank and file who had worked elsewhere before entering MEB, almost two-thirds of those in the intermediate group, but only one-third of those at the highest level, had
been teachers.[22]

Not surprisingly for education-conscious people, a high level of
education characterizes the entire sample. Only two persons had not
progressed beyond the *ginásio*, the first four years of secondary education. All others had at least spent some time in a *colégio* (the last three
years of secondary education). Most remarkable was the fact that *all*
the people in the top leadership group were either studying at or had
graduated from university: half in each category. For the rest of the
sample, just over half had at least some experience of higher education,
and almost two-thirds of these had in fact graduated, usually from
their local Faculty.[23]

Socially the background of MEB's cadres is very markedly non-
working-class. On a rather crude division of the respondents' social
backgrounds into middle class and working class,[24] only 21 per cent of
the entire sample (12 persons) fall into the latter category. The figure
was highest for the middle-leadership group, but even there it merely
reached 29 per cent. One-fifth of those classified as middle class were
clearly from upper middle-class urban families—those of independent
professionals, large businessmen, or higher civil servants. Only one
person in the top-level group came from an urban working-class
family.[25] Data on fathers' education suggest that middle-class status
is recent and/or precarious for most people in the sample, but here
again the top group forms a conspicuous exception. Among the latter,
two-thirds had fathers whose education included at least some secondary schooling, with more than half of these having completed at least
the *ginásio*; among the other two categories almost 70 per cent of
fathers had never attended secondary school, and a third of these
either had no schooling at all, or had not completed primary school.[26]

We must now look at some data which can enlighten us on the
extent to which those who joined MEB had a history of previous
involvement in the youth movements of Catholic Action. Such involvement may in some cases be taken as *prima facie* evidence of at
least embryonic radical ideas—that would certainly be true for most

[22] App. I, table 4.
[23] App. I, table 5.
[24] See App. I, Questionnaire, note to Q.6, for a discussion of the social class classification.
[25] App. I, table 6. Finding not significant at 10 per cent level.
[26] App. I, table 7.

who had been members of JUC and JEC—while in other cases it should indicate a more diffuse, non-political Christian concern. The overall figures should also give some idea regarding the existence of personal links, facilitating the flow of ideas, between MEB and the circles in which Brazil's radical Catholic ideology was being elaborated.

That such links existed will not, by now, come as a surprise. Exactly half of the people in the sample indicated that they had been (and in a few cases continued to be) members of one of the constituent bodies of Catholic Action. Of these only about a fifth had not at some point participated in one of the ideologically 'radical' movements, JUC and JEC.[27] And once again it is the top-leadership group which stands out. Among them only a quarter did not indicate that they had had personal experience of Catholic Action—as opposed to 59 per cent for the rest of the sample. Among the latter 34 per cent had participated in a 'radical' section of this movement, 7 per cent in a non-radical one. In contrast, 20 per cent of the top leadership had participated in a non-radical section, but as many as 53 per cent had been members of JUC or JEC.[28]

An alternative cross-classification, by date of entry into MEB, also shows a noteworthy differentiation. Of those who entered the Movement in the first two years of operation (fifteen in all), two-thirds had some kind of Catholic Action experience; of these four-fifths had belonged to one of the radical youth movements (over half of the entire intake). In contrast, among those who entered the Movement later, namely after the first period of intensive and careful preparation had made way for the expansive rush of 1963 and early 1964, 55 per cent had had no experience of Catholic Action movements at all. Of this intake one-third had been involved in one of the radical movements.[29] This suggests that in the time of rapid expansion a fairly substantial proportion of those who entered the ranks of MEB were not ideologically motivated. It should, however, be pointed out that it is in this context that distortions are likely to be greatest as a result of some of the most

[27] This identification of JUC and JEC with radicalism obviously oversimplifies matters somewhat. Not all 'constituencies' of these movements were equally radical. I have also not been able to take into account the period during which people were members: as was made clear in ch. 2 the shift towards radicalism only occurred after 1960. But almost all of those in the sample who indicated membership in JUC or JEC are likely to have been members after 1960.

[28] See App. I, table 8. Comparison between 'radical' and 'rest' not significant at 10 per cent level. As very few people who had been members of AP were willing to state this in writing in 1965–6, I have omitted AP from the analysis.

[29] App. I, table 9. Not significant at 10 per cent level.

radical members of the Movement's cadres leaving after April 1964.

An attempt was made to gauge the 'idealism' of the cadres, or their willingness to make sacrifices for the sake of the cause MEB represented, by asking whether joining MEB had involved a cut in earnings. One-fifth of those who had worked in MEB did not answer the question. For those who did reply there was a notable difference between the early joiners and the rest. For 36 per cent of those entering MEB during the first two years of its existence no data are available; of those who answered exactly two-thirds had taken a cut in earnings. Of the others 15 per cent did not reply; of those who did, only just over a quarter had seen their earnings reduced upon entering MEB.[30]

Finally, to look at the ideas to which MEB's cadres were exposed. In order to ascertain which thinkers or thought systems actually exercised a *direct* influence on the Movement (apart from the indirect impact through the Movement's own publications), cadres were requested to list whether or not they had ever read anything by or about Lebret, Mounier, Marx, Sartre, Teilhard de Chardin, and Vaz (the most important intellectual sources of the radical ideology analysed in the two previous chapters). They were also asked about any additional 'important books in [their] lives'.

Lebret, the most down-to-earth author on the list, also the easiest to read and the one most concerned with underdevelopment today and least concerned with philosophy or ideology (the latter are implicit in his Christian humanist approach to economic problems), easily led the field: he was mentioned by 84 per cent of the entire sample.

Next, jointly, came Mounier and Pe Vaz, as has been seen, pre-eminently the sources of radical ideas. Just over half the people in the sample had read them; about nine-tenths of those in the top category, just under one-third in the intermediate group, and just over half of those in the sample who were at the grass-roots (this is one of the clearest and most obvious examples of their unrepresentativeness: in the Movement as a whole the figure must have been much lower). Teilhard de Chardin—probably more read about than read—also had a substantial following at the apex of the Movement: 80 per cent mentioned him. Of the intermediate group 29 per cent were in some way familiar with his work, again surpassed by the third category with 38 per cent. Marx and Sartre came last. In both cases about one-

---

[30] App. I, table 10. The rather large proportion of the early joiners for whom no data are available makes the conclusion statistically dubious. Classification by level in the organization did not produce a clear result.

fifth of the lowest two categories had some knowledge of their work; among the top leadership two-thirds had read (or read about) Marx, and 40 per cent (about) Sartre.[31]

All in all, even though these data do not provide evidence in depth, they do serve to confirm both the intellectual image—and self-image—of MEB, and the fact that its ideas derive from the same sources as those encountered in the documentary analysis of the foregoing chapters. The other authors whose names were written in by respondents did not add much to the intellectual picture, except to confirm the 'soft-heartedness' of MEB's cadres, their concern for their fellow human beings: Saint-Exupéry, Michel Quoist, Khalil Gibraun, figure prominently next to such Brazilians as Celso Furtado and Josué de Castro.[32]

MEB and its bishops

One further aspect of the Movement's formal structure must be mentioned at this stage, because to a greater or lesser extent it has influenced the operation of MEB throughout its existence: the functions of and part played by the bishops in the organization. MEB came about as the extension of limited initiatives taken by a small number of bishops in their dioceses. It originated as a direct dependency of the CNBB—though from the beginning its job was conceived as one for laymen, and laymen were prominent in formulating its tasks. Nevertheless, the basic working unit, the *sistema*, was set up on a diocesan basis. And after the Movement had acquired a separate legal identity this diocesan basis of organization was retained. Despite attempts to clarify the position, undertaken at various moments in the Movement's history, the role of the bishop *vis-à-vis* the local team has always remained ambiguous.

The local *equipes* were quite closely integrated into MEB's regional and national structure. Hiring and firing was the sole responsibility of the lay leadership, and the Movement's working 'line' was, as has been seen, developed through the interaction of the various levels in the organization. There was never any question that the bishop, locally, could or should exercise control over the day-to-day activities of the *equipe*: the latter alone were considered to possess the necessary

---

[31] App. I, table 12. In view of the heterogeneity of data, no statistical test has been applied.
[32] App. I, Questionnaire, Q. 13.

professional and technical know-how as educators. But most bishops in whose diocese a *sistema* operated considered themselves responsible at least for the doctrinal line of the MEB *equipe*—a responsibility made explicit in formal regulations passed in August 1964.

Doctrine is a broad and elastic concept, especially as it includes social doctrine. No one can say with certainty where, in the work of MEB, the line runs between technical or educational decisions, and those which involve an ideological option—although, of course, there are instances where the ideological aspect stands out for all to see. Some bishops left the team in their diocese almost completely alone, usually out of lack of interest, but in a few cases because they were champions of lay autonomy in secular matters. Some supported them actively even during the most radical period. But in numerous cases there was much friction and more than a few incidents, especially with the more conservative bishops who, having accepted the radio schools as a prestige-bringing and catechizing instrument, found that young 'firebrands' were using them to preach radical ideas, which they took to be both ill considered and dangerous.

The tensions expressed themselves locally, and were also reflected in the deliberations of the Movement's directorate, the CDN. It was instituted after the Movement became formally independent from the CNBB, and consisted of eleven members. One of these was to be appointed by the President of the Republic—a provision never effectively implemented—and the remaining ten were appointed by the CNBB. They were all bishops. From August 1964 onwards the Secretary-General became a full member of the CDN, in actual fact its only layman. During the first three years the CDN was little more than a rubber stamp, and most decisions were ratified by the President, D. Távora, who was regularly consulted by the leadership at the *Nacional*. But from late 1963 onwards the bishops began to take their responsibilities more seriously.

An important series of meetings between the members of the CDN and a large number of bishops (ranging from forty-five to ninety), including on the first occasion quite a few who were not 'MEB-bishops' (i.e. did not have a *sistema* in their diocese), was held in Rome, in November 1963, during the second session of Vatican II. Also present were two of the top lay leaders of the Movement, who made a point of speaking personally to as many MEB-bishops as possible. During these conversations several of the more conservative prelates took the opportunity to raise doubts about the Movement's operation—in terms of its political philosophy, its adaptation to the varying conditions prevailing in the country, its position *vis-à-vis* the growing 'demagogic' political climate, its lukewarm attitude (at best) to religious instruction and evangelization, and, finally, the ambiguity in the role of the diocesan bishop towards the *equipe*, and their unwillingness to submit to his authority. Other bishops, however, praised the Movement's cadres, the dedication with which they were pursuing their tasks, and the benefits they were bringing to the people in the diocese.

The individual and collective meetings provided the first significant opportunity for the lay leadership to present the Movement and its problems to the members of the hierarchy, and to gauge the latter's feelings in return. They seem to have been quite successful in moderating the more extreme critics. That this happened in Rome, during what was probably the most decisive session of the Council for the emergence of a collective commitment to renewal in the Church, was certainly a positive factor. Positive in the sense that MEB could benefit from the goodwill generated by the extraordinary atmosphere, and that it found the bishops without the daily preoccupations— including, perhaps, over MEB—with which they were usually burdened when they were actually in their dioceses. Positive, also, in that it made the laymen aware of the resistance which new ideas could generate even among the Brazilian bishops—who, as a group, were among the most progressive at the Council. As the laymen wrote in the report of their meetings in Rome for their fellow members of the *Nacional*: 'The whole church has a long road to travel yet—and that includes the bishops in the vanguard: there is a big distance [still] between ideas and their practical acceptance.' And if the encounters had any negative aspect, it was related to this point: views expressed and ideas accepted in Rome did not guarantee their implementation back in the less rarified atmosphere prevailing on the bishops' home ground.

The bishops of the CDN, who did represent, if not a random sample of the Brazilian episcopate, at least a fairly representative group of those who fell within the range from moderately conservative to very progressive, became more directly involved in the affairs of the Movement from early 1964, when MEB suddenly found itself openly accused of being 'subversive'. The first instance of public trouble occurred in February of that year, when the then governor of Guanabara, Carlos Lacerda, impounded *Viver é Lutar*, the new reader for advanced students, at the printer's, after having been informed that it was 'communist' in nature. The personal intervention of D. Távora led to a compromise, which was hardly to the liking of many of the more militant elements in the Movement.[33] Shortly afterwards, however, repression began in earnest. With the coup of April 1964 widespread attacks were made on the Movement; in many places its leaders were interrogated and even imprisoned. The many bishops who defended their local *equipes* with vigour did so, however, more often by means of privately exercised influence than through public statements supporting them.

A little over a month after the coup the CDN met for a series of important discussions, during which substantial disagreements emerged on past policies, as well as on future plans. Various of its members directed their criticisms especially at the laymen's past 'radicalism', the bishops' lack of control, and the failure of the Movement to be truly—or explicitly—Christian in its activities. But even though a good deal was said during those meetings which disturbed the Movement's lay leadership, the CDN came out with a strongly-worded defence of MEB, which was sent to the CNBB. From then on the CDN met at more regular intervals, and the business it transacted became more substantive. While early in 1964 various of its members, perhaps even a majority, had been in favour of full independence of the Movement from the hierarchy (something pressed for with increasing insistence by many of the laymen ever since the *I Encontro de Coordenadores* in December 1962), the turn of events after April convinced everyone that it was only thanks to its formal links with the church that the Movement survived at all. The issue of 'laicization' was quietly dropped. In its place there occurred, in effect, a significant reduction of the hitherto almost total autonomy which the Movement's laymen had enjoyed.[34]

In the first place the CDN as a whole, and one or two of its members in particular, began to play a more active role in MEB's relations with the authorities. They became a kind of buffer between a hostile government and a group of embattled and often harassed laymen, acting as go-between in the negotiations over money (as already stated, none too delicately pursued by the authorities), defending the Movement to the authorities, and explaining—though rarely approvingly—the latter's views to MEB's laymen. All in all a very difficult job which they handled with tact, yet not always to the liking of the laymen, and

[33] See ch. 8.
[34] See the further discussion below, pp. 193 ff.

without being able, or at all times wanting, to prevent the need for a clear-cut adaptation of the Movement to the new circumstances.

In the second place, a shift occurred at the level of the *sistemas*, which gradually gave greater power to the diocesan bishop. I have remarked before that the demarcation of functions and responsibilities between *equipe* and local bishop had never been very clear, a fact which had from the start led to friction in various *sistemas*. Already in Rome many bishops had raised this point, and had demanded a greater say in the running of the Movement. Such demands had, however, been resisted by D. Távora; nevertheless they had been sympathetically received by some members of the CDN. The attacks on MEB after the coup, though fended off by the bishops, made them nevertheless more conscious of their supposed—but badly defined—responsibilities, and gradually in the period that followed these were not only sharpened, but also more effectively upheld.

It is true that both before the coup and afterwards the CDN tended to back the lay leadership in the case of differences of opinion with a local bishop, but slowly the voices grew louder in the CDN for greater independence of the *sistemas* from the centralized leadership of the *Nacional* (and of the *Estaduais*), and greater 'integration' of the *sistema* in the diocesan structure. The laymen strongly resisted this edging towards the Movement's *diocesanização*, but in fact some watering down of the 'national unity' started soon after the coup. At the local level the result was in some cases the adjustment of MEB's theory and practice to the new political circumstances, with bishop and *equipe* agreeing to concentrate on a less 'dangerous', more purely educational, line. In others the differences of view between a radical *equipe* and a cautious, if not conservative, bishop led to tensions which made continued operation of the *sistema* impossible. As a result various *sistemas* were closed down. This also occurred in a few cases, notably in the North-East, where bishop and laymen both agreed on the desirability of continued work, guided by pre-coup radical ideas, and on the impossibility of carrying this out under a repressive military regime.

The Movement as a whole, however, soldiered on. Despite great pressure exercised—mainly at the financial level—by the government, it survived the coup which led to the disappearance of virtually all other expressions of lay Catholic radicalism (or to their metamorphosis beyond recognition), and which paralysed almost the entire effort of the different movements and organizations concerned with reaching and 'awakening' the peasantry. Of course, *if* it wished to survive, MEB had to make certain inevitable adjustments. In the next chapter the shifts in the Movement's ideas under the impact of these and of earlier external circumstances will be followed in detail. But at the outset it should be noted that certain very important general principles remained essentially unchanged throughout. These principles had to do with the commitment of MEB to the peasantry, the exploited *povo*, and with the need to make this *povo* aware of its potential as an active 'agent in history'—through co-operation with and frankness towards each other. The expression of MEB's populism in the genuine spirit of humilty and equality with which its cadres approached the peasants—whose life experience had always placed them in positions of inferiors in a world where *patrões* kept people in their place—was perhaps the aspect which could justify the continued operation of the Movement after 1964. For despite the fact that only strictly limited tangible results can be expected where the military and the landowners are constantly on the look-out for 'subversion', it can be argued that any operation which boosts the so sadly lacking sense of human dignity and pride of the peasantry, and undermines their passivity, is valid in its own right. It may even prepare the ground for an eventual challenge, by the peasants, of the structures which now still ensure their oppression and exploitation.

8

Aspects of MEB's Development until April 1964

Earliest formulations of MEB's aims and methods

THIS chapter is mainly concerned with examining the ideological evolution of MEB until April 1964 through a discussion of various documents which are informative of the aims and methods of the organization, and through an analysis of the circumstances under which they were formulated.

At the time of the first contacts with President Jânio Quadros early in 1961, the task at hand was essentially conceived as consisting of the extension of the two or three existing radio-school systems run by individual bishops, to become a national organization. Literacy training was to be the main objective, though from the outset this was set in a wider context. Basic education should approach the peasant as a total human being (*homem integral*), and aid him to develop himself fully. In order to achieve this, the Movement was to concern itself with community development, literacy training, sanitary and agricultural education, and an introduction to democratic practices. A spirit of initiative was to be fostered, which would help prepare the peasants for the 'indispensable basic reforms, such as that of the agrarian structure of the country'. Moreover, basic education was to

watch over the spiritual development of the people, preparing them for the indispensable upsurge of the underdeveloped regions, and helping them to defend themselves against ideologies which are incompatible with the Christian spirit of nationhood.[1]

The Movement was never to come closer to explicitly inscribing anti-communism in its banner. The phrase was incorporated into the first draft of the *Regulamento Interno*, prepared at about the same time, but it had disappeared from that document when it was published in its final form a few weeks later.

[1] *Instruções Gerais*, drafted early in 1961, and sent as *Objetivos* to President Quadros.

A defensive attitude, which expressly contrasted MEB's point of view with that of other groups or organizations, had obviously not been acceptable to the Movement's future leadership, even at that early stage. A positive approach, focusing on the need to help the peasant create for himself the means by which he could forge his own destiny, was present from the beginning. This is clear on the first occasion when the embryonic Movement is mentioned in print, in a monthly bulletin of the CNBB. In that article the stage is set by a discussion of the problems of underdevelopment in the Brazilian countryside, and a description of the sub-human living conditions of the peasants and their lack of the rudiments of formal knowledge. The article then moves on to the need for basic education,

which has the power to awaken man to his own problems, and to help him find his own solutions. Through basic education he can learn how to eat well, how to protect his health, and how to maintain good relations with his fellow men. He will come to stand on his own feet, decide his own destiny, and seek his civil, moral, economic, social, and spiritual improvement.[2]

Various of these phrases were to recur, with only slight variations, in almost all subsequent formulations of the Movement's basic aims, but the context in which they were placed changed over time. Modifications in that context were to reflect the changing circumstances of operation of MEB, as well as variations in the influence of different sections of the Movement, and of different sources of ideas outside it.

One such modification occurred even before the Movement had actually got off the ground. In the first draft of the *Instruções Gerais*— the document eventually sent to President Quadros—there is an enumeration of what is to be included in basic education. One of the items there is 'Christian education' (*formação*). This is also found in an early draft of the *Regulamento Interno*. But the religious element in MEB's task disappeared in the course of re-drafting: it was not included in the final version of either document. In the *Instruções* it was transformed into a phrase which speaks of watching over the spiritual development of the people; in the *Regulamento* it became the provision of moral and civic education. It thus appears that an early intention of giving the Movement an explicitly Christian character was dropped before MEB got under way.

The main pressure for this particular deletion came from the federal government, which would have found it difficult to square the financing

---

[2] *Comunicado mensal da CNBB*, Jan.-Feb. 1961.

of a venture with a specifically religious character with the lay nature of the Brazilian state. But that pressure coincided with, and was reinforced by, a viewpoint held within the nascent organization. The laymen involved in the earliest contacts encountered much enthusiasm among the hierarchy in areas where a *sistema* of MEB might be set up. But it soon appeared that the enthusiasm of many diocesan bishops for the new organization was caused mainly by the vistas of prestige (and power) *vis-à-vis* the local upper class, and the prospect of mass catechization opened to them by the chance of owning and operating a radio station. It was obvious that if such views had been put into practice by means of the organization then being planned, they could have resulted in a substantial distortion of the Movement's primary task. Hence, despite the fact that the laymen active in this earliest phase were not only devout Catholics, but also people who had been working in various bureaux or commissions of the CNBB, MEB did not, according to the original formulation of its aims, plan to fulfil any *specifically* Christian functions. As will shortly be seen, these were incorporated later, after the 1964 coup, when the 'balance of power' between bishops and laymen had changed, and the government had become suspicious of the promotion of social change to an even greater extent than of religious overtones in federally-financed ventures.

The *Regulamento Interno* remained the only *official* source for the Movement's ends and methods of operation until after the April coup.[3] Other documents of a less formal nature must therefore be used to follow the ideological development of MEB. The first of these which is of relevance is the Annual Report for 1961, which was written in the second half of the following year. Its style betrayed the fact that those responsible for this report had as yet neither had much contact with the peasants and their life situation, nor fallen deeply under the influence of the new ideas already then spreading like a bushfire among the younger Catholics. It was rather lofty and in parts very abstract: the first signs had appeared of the tendency of the *Nacional* to fly off into higher philosophical spheres, leaving behind in baffled bewilderment those at the bases of the Movement.

Basic education, it stated, must confer three benefits on man: a conception of life, making him conscious of his own physical, spiritual, moral, and civic worth; a style of life, which guides behaviour in the

---

[3] Formal statutes of incorporation were written late in 1963, when MEB became officially independent from the CNBB. They were, however, formulated in broad legal terms, and are hence irrelevant to the tracing of the Movement's ideological evolution.

personal, family, and social spheres; and finally a mystique of life, which acts as an inner force ensuring dynamism and enthusiasm in the fulfilment of duties and the exercise of rights.[4] Basic education must teach the peasant about the human condition, social behaviour, work, the family, and civic and political organization. The first of these items would seem, to the outsider, a rather overwhelming task; it is to give answers to such questions as: who am I, why do I exist, what is a human person, in what direction is the world developing, and how can it realize its destiny? Less abstract were the problems related to social behaviour—such as knowledge of one's milieu, the value of mutual help and solidarity, of temperance, property, and family—or to work: human labour and its history, labour and capital, organization and nobility of labour, occupational and class consciousness, and trade union organization.[5]

MEB radicalizes: the *I Encontro de Coordinadores*

The foregoing paragraphs clearly suggest that in mid-1962, once the statements had descended from the theoretical clouds, the practical tasks set by the *Nacional* placed the Movement in no way beyond the progressive sector of those accepting the church's traditional social doctrine. But it was not to be long before MEB was jolted from that position. Early in December of 1962, while Brazil's bishops were in Rome at the first session of the Vatican Council, the *Nacional* called a meeting in Recife of the co-ordinators of all the then existing *sistemas*. This meeting, which lasted for a week, brought face to face for the first time all the leaders of the organization appointed since its inception. Some of these people knew each other, but even they had until then not had any formal contacts in their capacity as MEB cadres, no opportunity to discuss the problems encountered during those euphoric but often rather chaotic early months. What each knew of the situation in other *sistemas* had come to him indirectly, mainly through contacts with the *Nacional*. The discussions at the *I Encontro Nacional de Coordenadores* showed that several *equipes*, especially those operating from the more politicized state capitals, had developed increasing feelings of unease about the sense and direction of their work, feelings also shared by various members of the *Nacional*. As the meetings progressed a far-reaching reinterpretation of the role, aims, and methods

[4] *Relatório anual*, 1961, p. 1.
[5] Ibid., pp. 2 ff.

of MEB took shape. It set the seal on MEB's own 'discovery of Brazilian reality', and marked its entry into the mainstream of Catholic radicalism in Brazil—a couple of years after the first explosions in JUC, and about six months after the founding of *Ação Popular*.

At the time of MEB's first *Encontro* the views propounded by the new Catholic radicals were very much in the air, and it is obvious that some of the most persuasive participants in the *Encontro* were strongly influenced by the new ideology. Moreover, various people who were clearly identified with Catholic radicalism addressed the meeting during its opening phase; their remarks made a profound impact. One of these visitors placed MEB's work in a theological perspective. His analysis made the participants familiar with ideas on the Christian meaning of history, and on historical consciousness as involving man in an active transformation of the world, which had been elaborated mainly by Pe Vaz and which provided the theological—and philosophical—basis for the ideology of JUC and AP. After this introduction the *Encontro* was presented with a lengthy study document. Its discussion, in study groups, revealed that almost no one had really considered the implications of his membership in MEB, that there was certainly no clear idea of the paths which the Movement was to follow henceforth, and that collectively no particular path had consciously been chosen. From those discussions the idea gradually emerged that education, the *raison d'être* of MEB, should be considered as communication in the service of the *transformation* of the world.

Another important document was that introduced by a member of the *Nacional* who had until recently been active in JUC; his views provided a direct link with the analysis of 'Brazilian reality' current at the time among the Catholic radicals. His use of the concepts *pólo dominante* and *pólo dominado* aroused violent argument among the participants—especially because this suggested that MEB's work led *ipso facto* to the Movement's identification with and commitment to the 'dominated pole'. Traditional Catholic social doctrine made the idea of MEB's involvement on one side of a class struggle repugnant to many; and yet the *Encontro* as a whole took a very long step in that direction. There is no doubt that this was facilitated by the participants' experience of actually having worked with peasants and landless labourers—something that was still quite exceptional in those days among the adherents of the new Christian radicalism.

Thus there is a great deal of difference between 'the value of mutual help, solidarity, temperance, property, and family' stressed only months before in the Annual Report for 1961, and the general objective which emerged from the December meeting:

To contribute in a decisive mode to the integral development of the Brazilian people,[6] taking into account the full dimensions of man and using all authentic processes of *conscientização*. This should be undertaken from a perspective of self-promotion and lead to a decisive transformation of mentalities and structures. That transformation seems to us, at the present moment, both necessary and urgent.[7]

This is certainly quite a strong general formulation; even so it is not more than a pale reflection of some of the things said during the actual meetings.

The conclusions of the preliminary discussion groups must have left the participants a little startled by their new-found daring and the strength of their feelings.[8] Of course in any organization, and especially one of the nature of MEB, many often contradictory things are said during small group discussions. Those different, and perhaps extravagant, opinions are subsequently ironed out in the plenary sessions. Hence the notes taken of those discussions do not represent positions to which MEB as such ever subscribed, but they are valuable in that they provide an insight into the 'raw' currents of opinion which were flowing through the Movement.

One of the more cautious groups, after asking whether MEB was not up to a point a mere palliative, had concluded that the whole orientation of MEB in relation to the needs of Brazil required rethinking. They should come to 'a complete revision of positions taken up to now, which have probably been conditioned by an individualistic and conservative viewpoint (*consciência*) which is gradually losing historical relevance'. A second group concluded that Brazil would need a global transformation which could only be violent—as evolution was impossible. Only time could tell whether that violence implied a bloody revolution. In all this MEB's position was ambiguous. As an organization it was formally linked to the government and to the 'clerical bourgeoisie', who had started it as a palliative, while its personnel (they themselves, and their colleagues) identified themselves fully with the oppressed—with the dominated pole—and had the

---

[6] The word actually used is *povo*. This is the first time that this term appears in MEB's vocabulary.

[7] MEB, *I Encontro de Coordenadores, Conclusões/1*, Preamble.

[8] The two following paragraphs are based on the notes taken during the *Encontro* by rapporteurs.

wish to form revolutionary cadres. But a third group did not share this interpretation. Having asked themselves whether MEB was a revolutionary movement, they replied in the negative: 'its personnel', they concluded, 'is petty bourgeois, has attitudes of false prudence and fear, and is personally involved with the bourgeoisie'. Thus they proposed a retraining and new selection of supervisors with a view to developing a revolutionary mentality.

At the end of the *Encontro* these different views were brought for discussion to a plenary assembly. There the conclusion was reached that all should have broken with the bourgeois mentality; hence MEB was 'in no way ideologically compromised with the bourgeoisie'. On the contrary: its line was a revolutionary one. This profound change had many implications. One of these, a participant remarked, was that the government might be led to withdraw its financial support. That premonition was all too well founded, but it was to take until 1964 for it to become a real threat.

The *Encontro*, then, was clearly a watershed in the development of the organization's ideology and programme for action. As a result of the discussions a small commission was set up to prepare a *cartilha* (primer) really relevant to the life of MEB's clientèle. This led eventually to the publication of *Viver é Lutar* (To Live Means to Struggle), which was immediately to cause so much trouble, as will shortly be seen. The year 1963 brought the most intensive as well as extensive development of MEB's activities, its entry into the field of *Cultura Popular*, and in particular its increasing involvement in the building up of rural trade unions. The Movement came to be criticized by a growing chorus of the less radically inclined from without as well as from within (a substantial number of diocesan bishops and one or two members of the CDN), but it went ahead undaunted on the path it had chosen and sincerely believed in.

The Annual Report for 1962, written towards the end of the following year, took over many of the phrases which had been coined during the *Encontro*. *Conscientização* figures prominently among the aims of MEB, as presented in that report. The process of education takes place through *action*; it helps man to 'become conscious of what he is, what the others are, what all *can* be' (my italics). Education implies developing 'man's consciousness in the face of history. 'The future is not a simple moment. It is man developing himself, to the extent that he continually renews himself and continually transforms the world.' Thus man must be the maker of his own history, and education is to

help achieve this capacity for action; it must 'take as its point of departure the needs and longings of the *povo* for liberation'.[9]

The affair of the 'subversive *cartilha* of the bishops'

Viver é Lutar, the primer prepared in the course of 1963 by a commission of supervisors from various *sistemas*, especially from the
North-East, was printed in January 1964. Three thousand copies of
this textbook destined for MEB's more advanced students were impounded at the printer's late in February by order of the then Governor
of Guanabara, Carlos Lacerda, after he had apparently received information that 'communist textbooks were being printed for the
Ministry of Education'. The incident caused an uproar in the press,[10]
and brought MEB into the public eye—under very unfavourable
circumstances—for the first time. It sharpened the division between
the bulk of the Movement's lay cadres and the more cautious bishops.
It heightened the sense of unease among some of the leading members
of the *Nacional*, who felt that the Movement's course was becoming
more and more unpredictable. In the last months of the Goulart
government no external constraints seemed to be operating on the
povo, and its *conscientização* could lead to truly unforeseen results.
The precise details of method and content of that *conscientização*
therefore took on substantial significance; they became, in fact, the
touchstones of radicalism in the Movement.

Viver é Lutar was part of a *conjunto didático*—an educational en-
semble. The actual textbook consisted of thirty lessons, realistically
illustrated with photographs, geared to the experience of the peasant
and his actual life situation.[11] The rest of the *conjunto* was made up
of a further three mimeographed booklets, meant only for those who
were engaged in the production of MEB's radiophonic programmes.
The first was called *Mensagem*, which elaborated the spiritual message
of *Viver é Lutar*, referring to texts from the Gospels and making suggestions for links with programmes of catechization. This booklet
was the most overtly Christian publication ever to come from MEB.

---

[9] MEB, *Relatório anual*, 1962, all quotes from *Apresentação*.

[10] One of the more graphic headlines (*A Notícia*) read: 'Subversive *cartilhas* seized yester-
day belong to pink bishops'.

[11] In this respect it started from assumptions very similar to those of Paulo Freire's
method, though no actual survey of the vocabulary and phraseology preceded the writing
of the textbook. From late 1962 onwards a certain amount of mutual influencing appears
to have occurred, particularly in the North-East.

It attempted to cut the ground from under the feet of those who would argue that *Viver é Lutar* lacked a Christian spirit (a criticism made regardless). The second booklet was called *Fundamentação*: that was concerned with the philosophical basis of the process of *conscientização* by means of *Viver é Lutar*. Its language was extraordinarily dense and obscure; one *equipe* wrote back to say that this philosophical tract was unnecessary for those who had studied philosophy, and wholly incomprehensible to those who hadn't (they were right!). Like *Mensagem* it provided a lesson-by-lesson commentary. The same procedure was used by *Justificação*, by far the largest of the booklets. This contained empirical background material, taken from a wide variety of sources such as official statistics, sociological monographs, legal documents (especially on trade union organization), or economic publications of ECLA. It was a truly remarkable achievement, a kind of mini-textbook on Brazilian society.

From the time of the apprehension of the textbook by Carlos Lacerda's police, less than a month and a half before the April coup, much was made by MEB of these complementary booklets in its defence against the charges of 'subversion'. But, as a friendly critic wrote to one of the members of the *Nacional* a week before the army took control of the country, 'the *cartilha* is most likely to be read without the relevant accompanying material'. This was no doubt true: the other booklets were destined only for members of the *equipes*, not even for the *monitores*. Hence the essential impact of *Viver é Lutar* would come from its own text: that would be the 'instrument' which reached all peasants, the basis for their *conscientização* and the inevitable starting point of their discussions. From a 'conservative' point of view, *Viver é Lutar* could, indeed, only be called 'subversive'—that so conveniently vague term with which to stigmatize any instrument of unwelcome change.

But people who had a year before (at the *I Encontro de Coordenadores*) declared that they were in no way ideologically compromised with the bourgeoisie did not mind being called subversive, nor did they have the slightest intention of pulling their punches. D. Távora, MEB's President, tried in the first place to smooth over the incident by means of a face-to-face meeting with Carlos Lacerda (whom he knew well personally). In this he was successful, and at a press conference called the day after this meeting he was able to announce the incident formally closed. His handling of the affair was considered too 'soft' by many in the top echelons of the Movement's leadership, and his

statement at the press conference did indeed have a rather defensive
character. He harped on the extensive training of the *monitores*, who
would lead the communities through transformations 'based on
Christian principles'; he said that all of MEB's work had a Christian
orientation, and was carried out by people who realized that 'a materia-
list solution would be disastrous for Brazil'.[12] On the other hand he
hardly minced his words in the written declaration sent two weeks
later to the Commissioner of Police in charge of the case. Having taken
note of the fact that ideological doubts had been cast on MEB's work,
that it had even been suspected of being at the service of communism,
he remarked:

More than anyone we, as bishops who represent the church, know how to
distinguish between communism and Catholicism ... But we are also
aware that the living conditions of the rural population are so grievous, their
socio-economic situation is so precarious and unjust, that merely describing
this reality, or even showing pictures of it, can appear subversive. Nevertheless, it is a common-sense conclusion that describing this reality is not
subversive, while the reality itself is.[13]

It was this subversive reality that *Viver é Lutar* spoke about. Its
technique was essentially that of raising questions, and occasionally
providing very general answers; basically it was a textbook meant to
stimulate discussions among the peasants about the things that
'really mattered' to them. Lesson 1 read as follows:

> Eu vivo e luto.
> Pedro vive e luta.
> O povo vive e luta.
> Eu, Pedro e o povo vivemos.
> Eu, Pedro e o povo lutamos.
> Lutamos para viver.
> Viver é lutar.[14]

A few further examples will be sufficient to convey the flavour of the
book.

The seventh lesson speaks about God. 'Man does not live by bread
alone. A house and wage are not enough. Man needs God. God is

---

[12] Press conference, 27 Feb. 1964, quoted in MEB, *O conjunto didático Viver é Lutar*
(mimeo.), July 1964, which presents the entire documentation on the episode, and reprints
all press commentaries.
[13] Ibid.
[14] 'I live and struggle. Pedro lives and struggles. The people live and struggle. I, Pedro
and the people live ... and struggle. We struggle to live. To live is to struggle.'

Justice and Love. God wants Justice between men, and Love.' But even a little homily such as this can be highly 'subversive' when men live under conditions which are the incarnations of the very opposites of Love and Justice. The message becomes direct when we read:

Pedro came back enlightened from the *treinamento*. He came back knowing that the government is there for all. The whole people must participate in government. Some men have more than enough, while many have nothing at all. Some make too much. Many work and their work is exploited by others. A lot of things are wrong in Brazil. A complete change is needed in Brazil.[15]

Or again, a few lessons later, after speaking of the rising cost of living:

Who decides on the price of merchandise? When wages rise, prices go up even more. Why? Why doesn't the worker get the fruits of his work? Who's making a profit out of this? The people of Brazil are an exploited people. Exploited not only by Brazilians. There are many foreigners exploiting us. How can we free Brazil from this situation?[16]

The ideas expressed in lessons such as these did, indeed, fit perfectly with the ideology with which the Catholic radicals outside MEB confronted the world. To a very large extent the social analysis underlying such ideas was empirically unexceptionable. No moderately objective observer could quarrel with this:

What are elections like in Brazil? Many voters vote for the candidate of the *patrão*. Many give their vote in exchange for shoes, clothes, or medicines, others for a job or for money. Should this situation continue? The vote means consciousness. It means freedom. Consciousness can't be sold. Freedom can't be bought.[17]

But some of the earlier-quoted phrases were more open to criticism. One did not have to oppose radical change to feel uneasy about unconditional generalizations such as 'the people are hungry and sick', 'The worker can't get a thing for his wage: he suffers injustice like the peasant.'[18] As one critical bishop wrote: 'generalizations are half-truths, more pernicious than errors'; they are, he argued, the stock in trade of demagogues, who exploit the ambiguous promise

[15] Lesson 16.
[16] Lesson 26.
[17] Lesson 20.
[18] Lessons 6 & 10.

held out in slogans such as 'the whole people must participate in government'. Another letter in the files pointed out that the message could well lead to 'violence by misunderstanding; when the time comes you can't quickly print another booklet saying: "the Portuguese store-owner shouldn't be lynched; the *fazendeiro* must not be hanged".' And it continued: 'the *cartilha* as a whole doesn't seem to me to augment the quota of love in the world—quite the contrary'.

Those who regarded *Viver é Lutar* less as an expression of human solidarity and love than as one of class conflict were no doubt right. By mid-1963 MEB had opted for identification with the *pólo dominado*. It was developing many of the characteristic features of its populism. The view was already spreading that it was inherently wrong to provide specific answers to the peasants' problems; the people themselves should decide how their troubles should be overcome and what kind of structures should be built to replace the present unjust ones. Hence no one in the Movement was unduly worried by the lack of precise directives in *Viver é Lutar*.

But outsiders increasingly were, and the Movement was brought especially in conflict with those churchmen (collaborating with MEB or wholly outside it) who were convinced that Christian social doctrine had clear answers to all problems. *Viver é Lutar* was thought merely to make people rebel against their situation, 'while giving no answers'. Even two and a half years later, a Vatican diplomat, who had lived through the whole period, exclaimed (more hurt than angry):

The church does have the answers to these problems—the social doctrine of the church gives the answers. So why not teach the students these answers? . . . The main task of the church is not to make peasants revolt against their situation; it is spiritual guidance and care of souls.[19]

The charges of over-simplification or generalization, however, were harder to deal with. But here again most of MEB's cadres were not greatly perturbed. The intellectual niceties and scruples of middle-class reformers would be lost on ignorant peasants. *Conscientização* has to deal with those aspects of the situation that must change. It must lead to and be confirmed through action—and as action of this kind will be opposed by the forces representing the *status quo*, it will have to take on the character of a struggle, and a revolutionary one at that. Revolutions are not made by people who are all the time reminding themselves of the other side of the coin; hence the need for a bold

19 Interview, 6 Sept. 1966.

approach. *Viver é Lutar* was a clear expression of MEB's deeply radical perspective in those days, and it was no accident that after the coup the book was taken out of circulation by the Movement. It was replaced by a primer called *Mutirão*.[20] With its heavy emphasis on peasant co-operation *Mutirão* could help to engender intra-class solidarity, but it could hardly be said to provide a stimulus to inter-class conflict. The formulation of the peasant's woes in dialectical terms had disappeared: the 'class enemy' was dropped from sight.[21]

There are, however, indications that this change of emphasis was under way *before* the coup, that sections of the Movement's leadership were beginning to be concerned about the unpredictable consequences of untrammelled radicalism. Towards the end of 1963 misgivings about the Movement's 'line' were beginning to appear in internal documents at the *Nacional*. It was not that those responsible for overall co-ordination doubted the correctness of MEB's opposition to the existing social order, but they seem to have taken over some of the objections of the *cartilha*'s critics to the use of ambiguous slogans and facile catch-words. There was also growing concern about the fact that friend and foe alike were beginning to speak of MEB and AP in the same breath. The problem came to be formulated in terms of the need to avoid committing the Movement *as such* to a political line, when in a personal option one decided to become involved with a specific political group. MEB, it was said, as an educational movement engaged in a particular historical reality, needs an ideological justification, but it cannot proclaim itself openly in favour of one or another social system, such as socialism.[22]

Many of these doubts were brought into the open in January 1964 during a study week of the *Nacional* with a number of outside experts (prominent was Pe Vaz), meant as a preparation for the *II Encontro Nacional de Coordenadores*, planned for April. The notes taken during the discussions, summary though they are, show a considerable degree of perplexity regarding such fundamental questions as the meaning of *conscientização*, what it was supposed to lead to, and the way in which that process would be influenced by the *conscientizadores'* ideology. Much of the meeting's time was taken up, however, with extremely abstract discussions during which the concepts presented

[20] A *mutirão* is a mutual-aid party of peasants, usually to help one of them to tackle a task beyond his own physical means (building a house, clearing a field), also for communal activities such as repairing a road.

[21] See below, pp. 201 ff.

[22] Preliminary document for the planned *II Encontro de Coordenadores*.

by Pe Vaz—such as 'reflex-ideology', 'historical project'—were bandied around without much apparent clarity or practical result. It is obvious that considerable points of tension were appearing in the organization around the relationship of MEB's educational task to its possible practical involvement in undeniably controversial political activities. It is not easy to work at the revolutionary *conscientização* of the masses and then to wash one's hands of involvement in setting up the instruments of struggle against the 'dominant pole'—particularly if one holds strong political opinions and sees the danger of opponents reaping the fruits of one's educational labours. These tensions were most in evidence around the problems of rural *sindicalismo*, fully discussed at that preparatory meeting which occurred so shortly after the fateful elections for the council of CONTAG. The 'coalition' between AP and the communists, which had been the dramatic climax of those confused events, had evoked an angry response from Pe Crespo of SORPE, in the form of a circular letter condemning AP —and MEB—for its refusal to co-operate with the moderate Christian *sindicatos*. After the study week the firm decision was reached, at least at the *Nacional*, that henceforth the cadres should concentrate exclusively on the educational aspects of *sindicalismo*. As this entanglement of MEB in the drive to organize the peasants and rural labourers into trade unions was so central a feature of the Movement's activities before the coup, a more detailed examination of these developments seems warranted.

MEB and the *sindicatos*

MEB, it must be recalled, was set up by the CNBB. In the first years of the Movement's operation that body still took a fairly active, though largely indirect, interest in the Movement, which was essentially regarded as a pliable tool at the disposal of the bishops. When the bishops developed a collective concern for rural *sindicalismo*, when, from the middle of 1962 onwards, the CNBB's central committee explicitly began to promote the idea of Church-sponsored rural trade unions,[23] MEB was seen as the obvious educational instrument for the preparatory phase. With its radio schools, *monitores*, and supervisors covering much of the area in which rural trade unions should be fostered, MEB represented for the hierarchy an excellent means to

[23] See CNBB, 'Plano de emergência para a igreja do Brasil', *Cadernos da CNBB*, no. 1 (Rio, 1962), pp. 14, 48.

ensure the penetration of the countryside by Christian social doctrine. The peasants with whom they had already established contacts were to be educated by the Movement for trade union activities, and prepared for the time when *sindicatos* of Christian orientation could be set up. MEB's Council of Bishops, the CDN, therefore thoroughly approved of the organization's move into the field of *sindicalização*. And its cadres, despite some doubts about the readiness of the Movement for this kind of work among MEB's top echelon, saw in this new task an excellent opportunity for *engajamento*, for commitment. No bishop could have objected to their enthusiasm. But many, indeed, would from the outset have objected to the growing radicalism of their ideology, had they been truly aware of it and understood its implications.

In mid-1962 the bishops, concerned at the growing number of unconnected diocesan efforts in the field of *sindicalismo*, entrusted the task of their co-ordination to a young lawyer, who had played a prominent role in JUC during its critical transition phase in 1960. He was to make his headquarters at MEB, and also aid the Movement in preparing its cadres for the task of *educação sindical*. This appointment must be seen as a significant turning point in the Movement's work. It occurred in the same period that AP was formally launched, a few months before MEB held its momentous *I Encontro de Coordenadores*, during the time that criticism of the conditions in Brazil's rural areas was growing by leaps and bounds. With a person at MEB *Nacional* directly concerned with *sindicalismo*, a focus was created for the now fast developing impetus among the Movement's cadres to work in a way which was directly relevant to the promotion of drastic structural change. That this person was someone who had helped put JUC on its new course was important in two respects. It strengthened those in MEB whose views were collectively to have such a profound influence on the line which emerged from the *I Encontro de Coordenadores*. But it also helped to overcome the doubts about MEB, even hostility to it, that had hitherto prevailed among the more committed *JUCistas*, who had looked down upon the Movement as 'clerical' and excessively church-bound. A number of them subsequently entered MEB.

From the beginning of MEB's work in the field of rural unionization it had been fully understood that the Movement would occupy itself with education for *sindicalismo*: it would use its radio schools and other methods of reaching peasant communities to awaken an interest in the idea of *sindicalismo* and to convey the basic contents of its theory and practice. All this was to happen within the wider context of *con-scientização*. *Sindicalismo* was to be brought up slowly and naturally, if and when the peasants began to express a wish for organization and action. It was thus meant to be—and indeed became—part of MEB's activities in, and contact with, the community: a facet of the work, important certainly, but not to be isolated from such matters as literacy training or co-operativism. Special *treinamentos* which focused on rural *sindicalismo* were organized for emerging peasant leaders, 'in order to enable the formation of *sindicatos* truly led by the peasants themselves'.[24] One thing and another enabled MEB to bring into the Movement a large number of peasants who had hitherto been no more than on the periphery. It also led to a dramatic shift in the sex ratio of the *monitores*: before the beginning of the work on *sindicalismo* there had been a great preponderance of women.[25]

But not all of MEB's activity in this field was merely educational. In actual fact there were many *sistemas* which entangled themselves far more deeply in the process than could be justified by a purely educational effort. The Annual Report for 1962 had already mentioned that various persons, both at the *Nacional* and in a number of *sistemas*, were specifically charged with advisory functions on *sindicalismo rural*; it added, rather casually, that various *sistemas* 'in the absence of others, also took direct responsibility for help in the creation and foundation of *sindicatos*'.[26] Effectively this meant that in those localities where MEB was the only outside influence, where none of the various other 'parties' interested in organizing the peasants had yet established a foothold, the peasants wishing to proceed with the foundation of a *sindicato* had no one to turn to for advice but the MEB supervisors. Even semi-literate peasants, capable of being stimulating *monitores* and effective community leaders, cannot without expert guidance go through the fairly complex procedures which eventually lead to recognition of a *sindicato* by the Ministry of Labour. Unless there exists someone with the necessary literacy skills and with knowledge of the appropriate administrative and legal formulas, processes, and channels, the *sindicato* will never get off the ground.

The dilemma for the MEB cadres was clear, especially once the politically-motivated 'rush' into *sindicatos* and federations began. They could either let the development of the most important instru-

---

[24] *Relatório anual 1963*, p. 62.
[25] *Relatório anual 1962*, p. 13.
[26] Ibid.

ment of '*conscientização* through action' languish because of scruples about overstepping the limits set both by the populist views which were rapidly spreading among them at this time, and by a role defined in educational terms. Alternatively they could help, and inevitably become involved as 'advisers' whose advice was likely to determine the course of action at the more crucial moments. That advice would be particularly significant where a *sindicato* had to be represented at a higher level, in a federation or at a congress such as the one held in Natal in July 1963 (the *Convenção Nacional de Trabalhadores Rurais*), where problems were discussed and decisions taken which went far beyond the life experience and understanding of all but the most accomplished peasant leaders. Had the 'rush' not occurred, the *sindicatos* could have gathered steam more slowly, with the advisers' role less prominent from the start. A judicious mixture of further educational efforts and action-oriented help for the peasant leaders, designed to create increased awareness of problems and growing confidence in their own capacity to exert power, could have resulted in a gradual disappearance of the need for outside advice. But in the actual circumstances the pressure on the advisers to act was simply too great. Moreover the people in MEB specifically charged with *sindicalização* feared the entrance of others into their communities, others who would 'massify' from conviction rather than from necessity.

In some states, such as Sergipe, the initiative to use MEB cadres for *sindicalização* had come from the hierarchy. Elsewhere the decision to go ahead in this field came from within the Movement itself, whether from the local *equipes* or from the national co-ordinator for *sindicalismo*. According to the Annual Report for 1963 'specialists' on *sindicalismo* were, in fact, attached to state or local *equipes* in eleven states: Pará, Maranhão, Piauí, Ceará, Rio Grande do Norte, Pernambuco, Sergipe, Alagoas, Bahia, Minas Gerais, and Goiás.[27] They were often people especially recruited for this job. A significant proportion of them seem to have been active in the Catholic student movement and partly also in AP. They jumped at the opportunity of making their broad ideological convictions concrete in a specific context, of implementing them in the framework of a well-established organization. They were no doubt delighted to find that MEB lacked strong patterns of centralized authority and was committed to a basic method of work (non-directiveness) which permitted much freedom of action at the grass-roots. In fact in some areas virtually the whole time of the MEB *equipe* was

[27] MEB, *Relatório anual, 1963*, p. 62.

taken up with work on *sindicalização*. Thus while the intention may well have been to keep this formally separated from education, for the peasants the identification of MEB with the efforts at promoting *sindicatos* was complete—as it was for a number of others, who looked upon the whole business from the outside.[28]

As 1963 progressed, the objectives became more and more narrowly defined in terms of creating power bases for the control of the higher echelons of the union structure. Cases occurred in which MEB was being blatantly used for the promotion of the political goals which members of MEB *equipes* subscribed to as individuals. When in discussing the December 1963 meeting of CONTAG, Leonard Therry speaks of 'the AP-controlled unions of MEB', he is guilty of exaggeration and of over-simplification.[29] MEB as such 'had' no unions, nor did AP 'control' them. But it is true that in certain instances where all the groundwork for the founding not only of *sindicatos*, but also of federations, had been done under the aegis of MEB, a member of the MEB *equipe* in question was sent as the federation's representative to the 'second founding' meeting of CONTAG in December 1963: this was the case for six of the twenty-four federations present. Four of these federations could, indeed, be described as following a line of action which was clearly oriented on, if not by, AP; the two other federations whose representatives came from a MEB *equipe* were part of the moderate Catholic group.

One can only repeat, in conclusion, the observation that by the time of this scramble for power in CONTAG the main thrust of *sindicalização rural* had been deflected into a struggle between groups with conflicting ideological views for the bureaucratic control of a national organization of doubtful efficacy for the peasants. It is patently impossible to say how things would have developed had the coup not intervened shortly afterwards. But in MEB, early in 1964, there were widespread misgivings about the direction in which matters then appeared to be going. A return to a much more clearly delimited educational role was being advocated at the *Nacional* and would almost certainly have been implemented in practice.

However, any hesitations that might have remained were 'resolved' at one stroke by the coup. Though education for *sindicalismo* (subsumed, usually under the wider term *associativismo*) continued to figure among the tasks MEB set itself, in practice the Movement had

[28] See, for instance, Therry, in *J. Inter-Amer. Studies*, Jan. 1965.
[29] Ibid.

little to do, after April 1964, with an area of activity which was both fraught with political dangers and apparently of little practical effect under the existing circumstances. On a very limited scale others carried on this work, trying to strengthen the precarious foundations laid in more auspicious times. In some cases, especially in the North-Eastern sugar zone, the *sindicatos* and federations, though clearly severely limited in the scope of their actions, notched up occasional successes in struggles over wages and living conditions. But for the large portions of the countryside where trade union organization had barely begun in 1964, the statement seems generally valid that the coup, in virtually denying the *sindicatos* a legitimate role, condemned them to a somnolent existence with a dwindling, passive membership.

Notes on *sindicalismo* in one *sistema*

It may be illuminating to examine a report on the experience with *sindicalização* of one MEB *sistema* which covered a state in the far North-East. A retrospective document on the development there of *sindicalização* was drawn up in September 1964 by the co-ordinator of the *equipe* and sent to the *Nacional*, where it was found in the files. Its tone is balanced and objective, and its remarkable insights seem to square well with the general picture presented above. MEB started activity in that state in 1962. *Treinamentos* led to the setting up of an *equipe* in anticipation of a transmitter becoming available for the broadcasting of basic education programmes, but in fact the transmitter never materialized. Rather than sit around and wait at the local headquarters, the *equipe* began to consider other methods by which to reach the communities. It was here that the ideas were spawned which eventually led to the integral approach of *Animação Popular* (AnPo).[30] The method was developed under the name of *caravanas populares*, with the *equipe*, acting as a kind of roving agent of *conscientização*, trekking from place to place in their jeep. Even though these *caravanas* were supposed to stimulate the community into a wide range of activities aimed at tapping its resources through organization and at mobilizing the members in the defence of their common interests, *sindicalização* soon became the main concern. The *sindicato* was seen— no doubt rightly—by *equipe* and peasants alike as providing the most appropriate form of community organization under the existing circumstances of the absence of educational broadcasts on the one

[30] See below, pp. 212 ff.

hand, and the need for a collective attack on the power of the land-owners on the other.

The first community in the state to be reached by MEB was 'Tapiranga', where a *treinamento* for potential community leaders was held in September 1962. This community, therefore, was reached by MEB well before the beginning of the 'rush' into *sindicatos*; its decision to found a union was not made under the pressure of extraneous considerations. The main economic activities in Tapiranga were cattle raising and rice growing; the rice was exported from the area through the intermediary of a few important *comerciantes*.[31] These either were themselves the most significant landowners and local politi-cal bosses (*coronéis*), or had personal links with them. The *sindicato* resolved to set as its first goal the administrative redefinition of the area from one primarily used for cattle raising to one where the main activity was agriculture, something that had in fact been true for many years. But it had suited the landowners to maintain the cattle-raising status of the area: this meant that protection of cultivated plots was the responsibility of the tenants. Cattle had free range in territory thus defined, and no cattle owner could be held responsible for damage done by his cattle to peasants' crops. In practice the matter came down to the question of who was going to erect a fence and pay its cost; of whether the cattle should be fenced in by the cattle owner, or fenced out by the peasant. Under the prevailing administrative definition the burden was on the peasants. It was a burden most of them could not, or not effectively, shoulder; and the hazards of cattle straying into plots and ruining the crops were ever present.

Once the membership of the *sindicato* really started to rise, the local *coronéis* attempted to incorporate it into the existing clientelistic structure. They invited the leaders to become part of the locally dominant party, and to commit their members to its support. Not surprisingly the peasants refused. After that, all means were used to fight the *sindicato* and its leaders. The request for change in the administrative status of the area was denounced as an act of rebellion, both locally and by the *coronéis*'s political friends in the state Secre-tariat of Justice. Then cattle were intentionally let loose on the *roças* (subsistence plots) of the peasants. Enraged, some of the peasants killed a few head of cattle. This provided a pretext for police action against the peasants—the police, of course, being controlled by one of the *coronéis*. Many peasants were beaten up, all hunting arms were

[31] Tapiranga was thus a typical area of peasants, rather than of a rural proletariat.

confiscated, the seat of the *sindicato* was closed and its leaders subjected to all possible legal and extra-legal harassments. The president of the *sindicato*, for instance, though gravely ill, was summoned to appear at the district police station. He was carried there in the midst of a throng of peasants clamouring for justice and better treatment, circumstances serious enough in the eyes of the authorities to arrest him and throw him in jail on a charge of endangering national security. And all this happened well before the April coup.[32]

So much for developments in the first community reached by MEB in the state—developments which provide an insight, limited though it is, into the kinds of conditions under which the newly founded *sindicatos* had to operate. By October 1963 five *sindicatos* had been formed in the state under the auspices of MEB. They were all faced with problems of a similar nature, and were locked in battles with landowners or intermediaries when the storm of the unionization 'rush' broke over them. It broke at the end of that month, when a national organizer of ULTAB passed through the capital of the state, and contacted MEB with the suggestion that they should jointly found a federation. ULTAB had been active in the rural areas of the state for a somewhat longer time than MEB. According to the report, ULTAB's activities 'represented an important phase in the struggle for better conditions' (e.g. through the mobilization of public opinion), but ULTAB 'remained without deep roots, because it acted from the top downwards', and with a few exceptions no true peasant leaders arose from its ranks. Co-operation with such an organization was not much to the liking of MEB's populist leaders, who replied in the first instance to the communists' suggestion that 'decisions on this matter depended completely on the peasants themselves'.

Then, however, the *equipe* apparently examined the possible consequences of their position. It occurred to them that an insistence on non-intervention and non-directiveness could well be self-defeating. The leadership of the federation might fall into the hands of people who were neither peasants, nor loath to use the organization for extraneous ends—people much more experienced in this kind of *sindicato* politics than the leaders of the unions fathered by MEB. The most acceptable compromise seemed to be to call the 'best' leaders of the MEB-sponsored *sindicatos* from the different areas to a *politização*

---

[32] The story has an unexpected and surprising ending: after the *Revolução* the district police chief was arrested on various counts of arbitrary exercise of authority. The president of the *sindicato* was set free, and the charges against him were withdrawn.

meeting, which, though focused by the *equipe* on the political problems involved, would still leave the final decision to the peasant leaders themselves. Before they had actually met news came from the *Nacional* about the decision of the CONSIR to call the December meeting to reconstitute the CONTAG directorate. That letter also touched upon the expected final 'rush' to found *sindicatos* and federations.

The *politização* meeting was duly held. The peasant leaders who participated, after having been briefed and after discussing the issues at length, resolved to go ahead and to found, there and then, a federation, i.e. without calling in the unions affiliated to ULTAB. A directorate—made up entirely of officers of the MEB-sponsored unions—was elected; the necessary documents were drawn up and dispatched to Rio. But soon afterwards the *equipe* discovered the facts about the political complexion of CONSIR and its wholly pro-ULTAB stand. The relevance of this lay in the way CONSIR would handle the documents of an 'all-MEB' federation, if faced shortly afterwards with those of a rival effort sponsored by ULTAB: there could be no doubt that the latter's claim to official recognition would be supported and upheld. The newly-elected directorate of the federation set up through MEB thereupon reversed the original decision of the *politização* meeting, and opted for co-operation with the ULTAB unions. But the original founding documents had been sent off, and would soon land on a desk at CONSIR, complete with the names of the all-MEB directorate. An attempt to set matters straight by sending the *equipes'* co-ordinator to Rio failed. Despite her explanation, CONSIR refused to send out the air tickets for the federation's representatives to travel to Rio. In any case the commission seemed determined to annul—for technical reasons—the foundation of the original federation. And so this state was not represented at the December meeting.

By the end of the year the *equipe* and the peasant leaders involved had agreed to start again from scratch, and to take the ULTAB unions into the federation. All this led early in 1964 to the state's own 'rush' into *sindicatos*, and then to squabbles between the *equipe* and the president of the preparatory commission, a representative of ULTAB. These became so violent that the *equipe* resolved formally to turn the work over to AP; in the end the latter walked out of the joint founding meeting and once again bundled the *sindicatos* started by MEB into a separate federation. That is where the matter stood on 1 April 1964.

A few of the reflections on this course of events found in the report are worth reproducing. There was, it is stated, a serious and positive attempt truly to live up to the idea of self-promotion of the peasants, to be non-directive at meetings and only to offer information when requested to do so. And yet the often-used terms *sindicato dos padres* (of the priests), *do MEB*, *do PC*, *da AP*, and so on, did frequently correspond to the reality 'in which this or that group manipulates the rural masses for ends alien to rural unionism'. In a way MEB itself rather underestimated this. Excessive attention was paid to educational problems and to the persuasive aspects of a type of leadership which basically accepted the followers' wishes. What was wholly neglected were the 'techniques of leading larger groups and the methods of getting such groups where and when necessary to take political decisions with the requisite speed'. The document here points to the fact that this frequently left leaders and groups *conscientizados* by MEB at the mercy of political operators and demagogues, whose presence was not taken into account. It is a mark of the realism of these reflections that the writer faced up to this position at a time when in much of the Movement unbridled populism seemed to be running amok.[33] And it suggests that utopian populist purity must be tempered at least by some consideration of expediency, if the utopia is not to be inexorably doomed by the actions of the wicked people in the wicked world around.[34]

[33] See below, pp. 219–20.
[34] A point raised by Nettl (pp. 110–11) is relevant in this context. In discussing mobilization from above he remarks: 'A manipulated mobilization... which encompasses its purpose quickly and relatively honestly in the pioneering circumstances of, say, Ghana, Egypt or Tanzania, is perhaps to be graded higher than a mobilization decked out with the myth and symbols of participation, like a British or Swedish general election.' What Brazil's Catholic populists were trying to achieve was a mobilization *truly* based on participation. But they often disregarded something which the writer of the document under discussion saw quite clearly, namely that effective wholly 'genuine' participation was hard to secure. In the words of Irving Louis Horowitz: 'It is manifestly untrue that to reveal to a person his "true interests" guarantees his participation in ... the mass society or the modernization process. The line between action and interests is far from straight' (*Three Worlds of Development* (New York, 1966). p. 295). They also forgot that some partly manipulated mobilization might be preferable to none at all.

9

Some observations on the *Zona da mata*

MEB frustrated

WITH the remarks in the final sections of the previous chapter on MEB's involvement in rural *sindicalização*, the first part of the discussion has come to an end. As will be seen in subsequent chapters, the events of April 1964 presented no less a dramatic watershed for MEB than for Brazil as a whole. Under the pressure of external forces (government and military authorities) as well as internal ones (those bishops who had formal responsibilities and powers in the Movement), MEB's cadres not only dwindled but were also constrained gradually to shift the focus of their work and even of their aspirations. It was at a time when the effects of those pressures were beginning to be clearly visible that the fieldwork was undertaken on which this study was based. As I pointed out in the Introduction, most of my time was spent in Rio, and in the two relatively 'traditional' areas of Franqueira and Fernandópolis. The material collected in the latter areas refers largely to the post-coup period, and will therefore be discussed after a more general examination of the effects of the political changes of 1964 on the Movement's work. The present chapter is something of a hybrid. It deals with the *zona da mata* after the coup, but it is primarily relevant to an understanding of MEB as it was, and thought of itself, until the military took over the government, and of the tensions within the Movement during the transition period to the configuration which took shape late in 1966.

In the *zona da mata* the rising tide of socio-political activity between 1960 and 1964 (especially by means of the foundation of *ligas* and *sindicatos*) had coincided with steadily increasing pressure on the peasants, as more and more land was taken into cultivation by the sugar plantations in the wake of the exclusion of Cuban sugar from the Western hemisphere. MEB's *sistemas* in that area had contributed greatly to the development of the Movement into a truly radical organization before the coup—so much so that at times they had to be reminded by those from other regions that the *mata* experience was not universal.[1] Until 1964, therefore, a quite aggressive approach had come to characterize MEB in this area, an approach reflected in the primer *Viver é Lutar* which had been drafted with the conditions in the *zona da mata* very much in mind. Radio lessons had spoken bluntly of exploitation, misery, and drastic change; discussions had centred on various forms of organization and class action.

It should cause no surprise that this picture changed profoundly after April 1964. Most *sistemas* in the area remained closed for a number of months after the coup, when the relatively friendly political milieu of 1962–3 made way for a military regime of particular toughness in this region which had been repeatedly described as a 'powder keg'. The majority of the hierarchy in the *zona da mata* continued to provide support (if MEB had not been formally under their aegis, the authorities would not have allowed it to start operations again); but the North-Eastern bishops were now themselves frequently under attack for their outspokenness on social and economic conditions and for their criticisms of the government. For MEB, the only 'radical' organization which had been working in the rural areas to survive into the period of fieldwork, caution was therefore the order of the day. To be cautious meant essentially to fall into line formally with the official change in orientation coming from the *Nacional*: to abandon all open attacks on the nature and structure of society, all overt activity directed at undermining the *status quo*, and all visible involvement in the organization of the rural masses for 'class action'. Such things could no longer be discussed over the radio, though they could still be raised in the now infrequent face-to-face meetings in the countryside, or at MEB's headquarters. These were the only occasions on which frank discussions could take place to help maintain the conviction among *monitores* and other activists that MEB 'was still on their side'— despite the appearance of its having become a 'mere palliative'.

More and more, however, the affirmation that MEB was not a 'mere palliative' was being questioned by the members of the *equipes* themselves. They had continued to work in MEB, despite the restrictions, because in their view MEB was the only 'honest' organization left to operate in the countryside, and because the work of MEB could give them a legitimate reason for travelling and maintaining contact with what was left of the peasant leadership. In the first half of 1966 there had been a good deal of (inconclusive) debate among MEB's cadres in

[1] Cf. the interaction of the Franqueira *equipe* with the *Estadual*, discussed on pp. 232–3.

the region about the extent to which one could justify keeping the Movement alive for the sake of these and possibly other activities, such as a 'radio-school committee' which had been set up by between thirty and forty of the more radical *monitores* in the *zona da mata* who planned to use the network of MEB in the countryside to keep in touch with each other, thus breaking the dependence of all upon the *equipe* for communications.

The conviction did, however, increasingly spread among the *equipes* in the area that the possibility of doing any politically significant work among the peasants was virtually non-existent. MEB was finding itself once more almost exclusively engaged in basic education, most of it literacy training, and it was becoming clear that this could no longer arouse much enthusiasm among the rural workers. Before the coup they had been motivated to study at night by the hope that knowledge would aid their autonomous organization, and by the prospect of political participation through elections, open only to literates. By 1966 these incentives had obviously lost credibility. When I arrived in the region in May of that year,[2] frustration was rife among the *equipes*; interminable, and not very fruitful, discussions took place about the present and future, and relatively little was being achieved in this area, previously seething with enthusiasm, hope, and radical fervour.

The lack of positive achievements was not, in the *zona da mata*, a result of the limitations of *conscientização*. The rural proletariat, exposed to manifold political influences before April 1964, subjected to strong (especially cyclical) economic pressures, and yet clearly better off than before the formal expansion of the labour legislation to the countryside in 1963,[3] had become quite aware of the social and economic structures of which they were part. If class-consciousness and a practical awareness of the nature of class confrontation existed anywhere in rural Brazil, it was among the rural workers I met during my stay in this region. The lack of achievements in 1966, and the frustrations among the members of MEB's *equipes*, were clearly the result of the repressive measures taken by the authorities against those who held views considered 'subversive'; and bland programmes harping on co-operation in an area full of people thoroughly enlightened about exploitation were bound to be received without enthusiasm.

I came to the conclusion that there was little to be gained from a

[2] I spent about three weeks altogether in the area, during two periods in May and July.
[3] They were thus in the typical socio-economic situation which has again and again been shown to lead to radicalization: things were getting better, yet pressures persisted.

detailed analysis of the position of MEB in the *zona da mata* in 1966: already at the time of my stay the situation was clearly a transitory and unstable one (the *sistemas* were closed down later in the same year). Instead, I decided to concentrate on gathering some first-hand data on the life and work situation of the plantation workers in the area. The following pages will deal with this, and even though this discussion makes no direct reference to the operation of MEB, it does provide the context necessary for a fuller understanding of MEB's pre-coup development, and of some of the virtually insurmountable obstacles subsequently encountered when continuing to try and help the rural workers help themselves.

A North-Eastern sugar plantation

It should be said at the outset that in much of the North-Eastern sugar zone the specifically 'proletarian' condition of the cane workers is a fairly recent phenomenon. In the past, the 'relations of production' on the sugar plantations were much more traditional, and workers were given substantial plots of land on which to grow their own crops. Large areas belonging to the plantations were not planted with sugar cane, although one can discern cycles of expansion and contraction related to the price of sugar in the market.[4] Though ever since the end of World War II there had been a trend for plantations to take land— which had previously been leased out to individual peasants—back into cane cultivation, the great squeeze in the North-East did not start until the beginning of the 1960s.[5] At that time the sudden change in established world marketing conditions which resulted from the Cuban revolution, and from that country's difficulties with the United States, led to undreamed-of opportunities for Brazilian sugar. Sugar-cane was planted wherever it would grow, and all but the smallest plots of land were taken back by the plantations. The sugar workers thus became a true rural proletariat, completely dependent upon their wages. In the process, they had often been pushed out from the interior of the plantations, now given over entirely to sugar cultivation, and had settled—closer together, in more direct contact with each other—on the periphery. In this new situation peasants did not have to be *conscientizados* into seeing that the old-established social relations were not fixed for eternity: they had manifestly broken down for all to see. The path was clear at the very least for a transfiguration of patron–

[4] See de Andrade, p. 108.
[5] See Furtado, *Dialética do desenvolvimento* (1964), pp. 143 ff.

dependant relations, with *ligas*, and especially *sindicatos*, taking over some of the roles previously fulfilled by the *patrão*. But these outside agencies did bring an awareness of rights under the law, and stimulated the beginnings of a civic consciousness among the plantation workers. Simultaneously, the latters' participation in union activities, and their growing awareness of a common fate, laid the foundations—here, if anywhere in rural Brazil—for a consciousness of class.

Some personal familiarity with the situation on the sugar plantations seemed most desirable. I was most fortunate in being enabled, as the result of the helpful intervention of an acquaintance, to visit a plantation which had been expropriated by the federal government to serve as a 'pilot project for agrarian reform'.[6] The plantation was administered by the Brazilian Institute for Agrarian Reform (IBRA). My visit was admittedly short—altogether no more than a working week was spent there—but nevertheless led to insights of some importance into the social mechanism at work on a *usina*.[7]

The Usina São Pedro was expropriated in mid-1964, after having been economically on the downgrade for many years. The equipment in the central sugar mill was fairly old, and the productivity of the *engenhos*, of which there were just over a score attached to the *usina*, was low. In the first six months of 1966 the agricultural working population fluctuated between 1,400 and 2,400 depending upon the point in the cycle of production; in April–May 1965 the total population of the *usina* engaged in agriculture (i.e. excluding the mill workers)[8] had

[6] Personally, I regard Jacques Chonchol's definition of agrarian reform, 'a massive, rapid and drastic redistribution of the rights over land and [irrigation] water', as the most appropriate for the majority of situations in Latin America (see his *El desarrollo de América Latina y la reforma agrária* (1964), p. 91). The proposed measures of the Brazilian authorities on the plantation in question—the redistribution of lands in family-sized plots to selected workers of the plantation—may have been interesting for the workers concerned and valuable as a pilot project, but in themselves hardly amounted to an 'agrarian reform'.

[7] *Usina* (lit: factory) is to be distinguished from *engenho* (lit: mill). The *engenhos* consisted, before the coming of steam power, of plantations with their own small sugar mill. When the large mechanized sugar mills (the *usinas*) were developed, the *engenhos* stopped manufacturing sugar and sent the cane to the central mills. Still later the *usinas* acquired many of the *engenhos*, thus becoming integrated enterprises. The word *usina* has thus come to be used both for the actual sugar mill and for the entire agro-industrial complex comprising *engenhos* and *usina*: cf. Usina São Pedro. The corresponding dual-purpose word in English is plantation: it refers, in contrast, at times to the area where cane is grown (the *engenho*), at times to the whole enterprise.

[8] The distinction between rural workers (cane cutters etc.) and mill workers (factory hands in the sugar mill) is important. The latter are in fact industrial workers living in a rural area. Many of them are semi-skilled. They have more settled working conditions, are better paid, and have a stronger union than the rural workers.

been just over 4,000 persons, distributed over 840 families.[9] Almost all men were wage workers (93 per cent), three-quarters of them without any skill; 63 per cent supplemented their wages by subsistence agriculture on a piece of land for which they did not have to pay rent in cash or in kind—but for two-thirds of these the plot was truly minute (under 0·6 acres). Two-thirds of the heads of households made less than the legally established minimum daily wage; 15 per cent received that amount, which was then approximately US$0·90, and only 5 per cent received a higher wage. Three-quarters of the family heads, and 80 per cent of the entire population over seven years of age, were illiterates; 83 per cent of the children of school age were not going to school. Membership of the *sindicato* was mentioned by 80 per cent of the heads of households. This high percentage has only limited significance in view of the fact that all workers were automatically members and had their dues deducted from the pay packet. One-third of those said they 'always' participated in meetings, half did so 'rarely', and the rest 'often'.

The first concern of IBRA was to get the plantation back to a more efficient pattern of production, so that it would not continue to make a loss during the period of preparation for the allocation of plots to selected plantation workers. The management of the *usina* and the supervision of the *engenhos* was entrusted to men with experience of those jobs—and the men appointed had learned the ropes in other commercial plantations in the area.[10] What they brought to São Pedro was not merely a set of techniques related to the operation and management of an integrated sugar mill: they imported equally the attitudes and modes of behaviour towards the plantation and mill workers which prevailed in the region's agro-industrial establishments. Two years after the take-over by IBRA the 'relations of production' at São Pedro had hardly changed from the general patterns prevalent in

[9] These and the following statistical data derive from an unpublished survey conducted by IBRA sociologists, in Apr.–May 1965 when all heads of households were interviewed as part of the preparatory work for the division of the land.

[10] I shall be using the following terminology when referring to different members of the administrative and production hierarchy at São Pedro:
General Manager or Superintendent: *Superintendente*
On production side (sugar mill):
    Works Manager: *Gerente da Usina*
    Chief Engineer: *Chefe mecânico*
On plantation side (*engenhos*):
    Manager of the *engenhos*: *Gerente do Campo*
    Field manager, responsible for one *engenho*: *Administrador*
    Plantation foremen: *Cabos*

the *zona da mata*. Not that the highest regional functionaries of IBRA lacked awareness of this fact: it was deplored, but nevertheless considered inevitable, as there were no 'capable' plantation cadres with a more 'modern' mentality.[11]

The superintendent (general manager) of São Pedro, Dr Carlos, was a man in his mid-40s, with a degree in law, who himself owned a relatively small *engenho* which grew cane for one of the large sugar mills. Early in our first talk, which took place during the two-hour car journey to the plantation, he made a statement which revealed a good deal about the relations of production in the *zona da mata*. He suggested—and it is of limited relevance from our point of view whether his story was entirely true or not—that since the passing of the Rural Labour Statute in 1963 the previous trend towards integrated sugar mills had been reversed. The Rural Labour Statute had led to improved conditions for the rural workers and higher costs for the enterprise; the integrated *usinas* had found it difficult to control the costs on their plantations and had thus begun to lease out the sugar-growing side of the enterprise. The lessees were usually persons who had in the past owned and/or personally supervised an *engenho*. In contrast to the field managers employed by the integrated *usinas* to administer an *engenho*, 'semi-literates who don't care, because it's not their own property', the lessees are 'people who have done this for their whole life, even for generations—better educated men, cultured people'. Pressed to give an explanation why more cultured lessees should be more effective at controlling costs, Dr Carlos agreed that it had something to do with the actual supervision of the work in the field. He explained: 'when in an integrated *usina* a worker comes up to the field manager and says: "This job is too much, I can't do it", the man will reply "That's all right *meu filho*, just do half of it".' A lessee, on the other hand, would realize that his own money was involved, and would not be so lax.

The available accounts of the relations of production on the sugar plantations in the *zona da mata*, the conditions at São Pedro itself, as well as those apparently prevailing in surrounding plantations all contradict this almost idyllic picture of the relations between the field manager and the rural workers. But a statement such as that by Dr Carlos—a man whom various informants from MEB and 'progressive' functionaries at IBRA characterized as a person of goodwill, intellectually prepared to accept change and reform, even though emotionally

[11] Two high functionaries at regional headquarters of IBRA independently gave this view.

with deeply ingrained conservative feelings—is nevertheless of interest as an indication of the reaction of the sugar-cane industry to the prospect of improved conditions for the rural worker. That reaction seems to have consisted of an attempt to safeguard the (admittedly precarious) profitability of the industry by exploiting to the hilt the employers' monopoly power, based on the lack of alternatives available to the workers, through reverting to a greater measure of direct, face-to-face confrontation between agrarian capitalists and their labour force. And the coup of April 1964 had made 'squeezing' relatively easy for the employers. It had resulted in a dramatic swing in the overall power balance against the rural workers. Their trade union organizations were emasculated by constant threats of suppression for 'subversive activities', and in mid-1966 they were only just beginning tentatively to try new ways of operation under the changed circumstances.

Difficulties between *usina* and *sindicato*

At São Pedro there had in fact been a major clash between IBRA's administrators and the largest of the local *sindicatos*, which was far from wholly resolved by mid-1966. An aspect of the activities of the *sindicatos*, as important at São Pedro as elsewhere, had always been the rendering to the workers of various personal services, such as legal aid in their relations with employers, and especially a rather rudimentary form of medical aid. With the atrophy of the bargaining and defensive functions of the *sindicatos* since 1964 these *assistencialista* aspects had taken on even greater weight, although the existing circumstances had made it impossible to broaden or improve the services rendered in any way. But at São Pedro medical assistance had been provided not only by the *sindicatos*: the *usina* itself had been running a medical service, which it was obliged by law to operate for the benefit of the mill workers.

The trouble between the *usina* and the *sindicato* had started early in 1966, when the management proposed that the *usina*'s medical facilities should henceforth be available also to the rural workers (who had so far had recourse only to the surgery hours of the *sindicato*), and that this extension should be financed by allocating 50 per cent of the rural workers' union dues to the *usina*'s medical fund. Dr Carlos had in private justified this proposal by saying that the *sindicato* in any case did nothing useful with the dues: it used them merely to provide a salary for its president and a jeep in which he could 'tour around' on the plantations. Although it has to be admitted that his view had more than a grain of truth in it—the president, Bernardo, was a well-meaning but rather timid man, a former treasurer of the *sindicato*, elected to the presidency after having been appointed 'interventor' elsewhere by the military authorities—the administration had of course no *right* to act in the way it did and ignore the existing legal dispositions.

Not surprisingly the *sindicato* protested at this threat to its easy-found financial independence. The management's response was to stop deducting *any* dues, and to hold a ballot among all rural workers to make them choose between *usina* and *sindicato* for medical care. That ballot was little more than a sham. Workers were called into the offices of the *engenhos*'s field managers, where they were presented with a form which read: 'I agree that my employer will not deduct the contribution to the *sindicato*'. Their choice was to comply, and sign, or to refuse to do so; the latter entailed taking an open stand of defiance. The form had the forbidding appearance of an official document, and had to be counter-signed by two witnesses, in most cases the field manager and one of the plantation foremen—hardly circumstances likely to lead to the free expression of a preference. The *usina* obtained a vote of 85 per cent against deductions. Bernardo, the *sindicato*'s president, then consulted the regional federation. About a week later he went back to São Pedro and drove around the *engenhos*, distributing his own ballot papers to the workers he found in the fields. In this way he collected, in a matter of hours, 330 pro-*sindicato* declarations—almost all from people who had earlier 'signed their rights away'.

This procedure brought down the wrath of the administration, who decided to ban the man from the grounds of São Pedro. He was sent a letter informing him that henceforth he was *persona non grata*, in view of the fact that he had been 'inciting people against the existing order and implanting disobedience within our jurisdiction'. Dr Carlos also wrote a long letter to the local judge; its flavour is adequately conveyed by the following extracts:[12]

You know well, Sir, what this region which is now under your direction was like before IBRA took over. Everything was unsettled and unstable; there was social injustice, hunger and despair. Then a presidential decree brought us here to initiate the pioneer model for agrarian reform in this country.

[12] I was lent photostat copies of the relevant letters by Bernardo during my first visit to the *sindicato* on 22 May 1966.

In this difficult and arduous task, above all a question of experimentation, we began to give the rural worker a true sense of his human condition, paying him a fair wage, allowing him leisure on holy days [*sic*], giving him a weekly rest, a thirteenth month's wage, essential medical assistance, dental care, hospital and pharmaceutical facilities, and opportunities for education and amusement. All this was because we recognized that he, with his capacity for work, represented the major vehicle for the progress and greatness of our common Fatherland. Thus his lot was improved, while his standard of living was safeguarded by our labour laws and social-security legislation. If work contracts were made between us and our fellow workers, they were carried out within the guiding principles of social justice, according to the dictates of our judicial labour processes. Then, with the noble intention of better serving our fellow workers in the countryside, we entered into contact with the local *sindicato*. We wanted to sign an agreement with it, which would lead to the provision of wider and more effective assistance to our country dwellers. Our suggestion was immediately accepted, only to be rejected soon afterwards without the slightest justification.

Now, to our surprise, the *sindicato* appears, in the person of its highest leader, seeking to disturb the order and discipline reigning in our environment where we struggle and labour, and work hard at recuperation. It stirs up the workers against the administration, wanting to force them to become members of the *sindicato*. But faced with the inefficiency and lack of capability of the union machinery, they had earlier quite clearly refused (by an average of 85 per cent) to join the above *sindicato*. We hold the undeniable proof of this assertion. It can be substantiated by documents signed completely voluntarily by these workers, which state that they do not want such a connection with the *sindicato*. . . .

What is happening in this enterprise, Judge, can be regarded as an attempt to return to that state of affairs which has been so disturbing to the Brazilian nation. It is the wish to restore a *modus vivendi* contrary to human dignity and to the sacred principles for which we have struggled obdurately, as they form part of our own Christian and anti-materialist upbringing. The subversion by the president of the *sindicato* of the order and discipline implanted among us has been made evident in the last few days through spiteful and anti-patriotic insinuations—which incite the ill-informed minds of our rural dwellers—that we are torturers, that we are doing nothing for their good, that we are exploiting them, and denying them their most basic rights, guaranteed by law.

Bernardo retorted with a two-page document to the judge, drawn up by a lawyer from the regional federation. One of the most important points was that the workers of São Pedro had

constantly complained to this *sindicato* about the illegal actions of that
13

enterprise, which consisted in forcing the workers to sign the annexed document . . . under threat of loss of employment, change of work, or the improper increase in daily tasks.

The cane workers

In general, one may legitimately question whether in São Pedro any more than in the surrounding plantations the cane workers were given a square deal in terms of work, whether the officially agreed *tabela*, linking the piece-work rates to the daily minimum salary, was being fairly applied in the fields. This problem had first come to my notice some weeks before my stay at São Pedro, when I had been taken on a Sunday to the offices of the *sindicato* concerned by a member of the local MEB *equipe*.[13]

Our visit took place on the occasion of a meeting at which a lawyer from the regional federation was due to explain the agreement reached with the administration of São Pedro, which had resolved the conflict over the non-deduction of union dues. We arrived at around 10 o'clock, when the meeting was supposed to start. The rooms were overflowing with cane workers. But the lawyer did not turn up until 2 p.m., by which time most workers had left. Meanwhile we sat next to Bernardo's desk and spent the time talking to the workers and listening to them as they came up to speak to the president of their *sindicato*.

Bernardo, a vast man who sat authoritatively behind his desk, in his dark suit looking more like a *patrão* holding court than a union leader, did at first tend to react by giving paternal advice to the workers and establishing a certain social distance between them and himself. A man who wanted help from the *sindicato* but had no card to prove his membership was treated to a five-minute homily on the need to carry documents, at the end of which Bernardo pulled out a wallet bulging with papers and spread an impressive array of identity cards on the desk. When specific complaints about the situation on the sugar plantations began to come up, Bernardo at first responded with a further series of sermons, expatiating on the fact that workers too were humans, and Christians, and had rights. But gradually he fell silent and listened, merely occasionally explaining why the *sindicato* was powerless to do anything under the existing circumstances. He spoke of the failure of the labour courts to function on behalf of the workers: irregularities in payment or unjust dismissals were duly noted, but the first hearing

---

[13] The person in question had been active in *sindicalização* before the coup and was apparently completely trusted by Bernardo.

usually did not occur until three or four months later. Legal action, he said, was the only kind of action that could be taken—he did not once discuss the possibility of collective responses such as strikes, despite repeated promptings by my companion from MEB—and legal action was obviously of little use if delays of this length occurred.

The complaints of the workers (and it was in the nature of the meeting that many workers came from São Pedro) almost all referred to the various ways in which the *cabos* (plantation foremen) prevented the men from making a full day's wage for a full day's work. Slight negligence—such as not cutting the cane close enough to the ground—meant that the area in question was not counted at all. Over-allocation of work seemed another favourite complaint. The plot to be finished in a day was measured in the morning: by 'jumping' with the measuring stick, the *cabo* might push up the effective yardage to be cut or cleaned by 20 or 30 per cent. On the whole many workers seemed to be given tasks which they could not finish even by working for as long as ten or twelve hours, or by getting one or two members of their family (usually wife or son) to help them for part of the time. A group of workers from an *engenho* adjacent to São Pedro showed me a letter which they had brought to the meeting and intended to hand to the lawyer from the federation. I copied it on a typewriter, watched for five minutes in absolute silence by those standing around, no doubt promoted in their minds to a *doutor* who was going to resolve their problems. It is here faithfully reproduced, with only the spelling mistakes not 'translated'—a document which probably conveys the situation of these people better than any number of general descriptions. The contents also show quite clearly that these rural workers were no longer simply dependants hoping for favours, but men with a sense of citizenship, aware of the protection that the law might offer them.

Illustríssimo Senhor Advogado,
We workers from the *Engenho* X comes by this letter to ask from you a declaration on the labour laws and on what has been happening in the Y enterprise.
　1. We pays 5 per cent of deduction for the medical fund and we don't have rights to consultation for our families, and afterwards we have to pay whatever they say for the medicines. We want measures taken in this case.
　2. We are given 130–150 *braças*[14] to do for Cr. $1800; it takes you two days to cut because 8 hours are not enough to cut it they makes us work 8 hours in the fields and if you don't finish you don't make anything.

[14] 1 *braça* = 2·20 metres; the reference is here to a plot of e.g. 10 × 13 to 10 × 15 *braças*.

This way we all ends up tubercular at the end of the year because without eating we don't have any resistance, we eat dry cornflower during work because we have to work 10 and 12 hours to cut this amount and even so very few finish it that's why we workers want to know from you whether this is of the Law, if this is not of the Law we want measures taken in this case.

We can't even plant a bed of potatoes because we leaves in the morning and only gets home in the evening weak with hunger. And the rest you know its not even necessary to say.

With nothing more right now,

[Signatures of 14 peasants from X].

The result of situations such as these is not only that cane workers work 6 days to receive at the end of the week a payment equivalent to the minimum salary for 4 or 5 days—they also find themselves not paid for Sundays as they 'haven't worked the full week'. One day on which he falls, say, 10 per cent short of the given task, is enough to lose the worker his rights for Sunday pay, which, in the view of the administration, is a 'reward' for work properly done, as is payment for a public holiday. Failure to reach the targets set also diminishes a worker's chance of being paid the thirteenth month to which he is entitled at the end of the year: in the books he appears as someone who has not worked 'regularly'.

I made an attempt to verify the average payment received by the workers at São Pedro, by comparing the figures for the total number of workers on the books of the enterprise with the total amount paid out in wages (excluding salaries to administrative personnel) for one out of every two weeks from January to mid-June 1966 (total 12 weeks). The figures were supplied by the São Pedro office, and I did not have an opportunity to make an independent check. As I have some doubts about their accuracy (more because of probable clerical errors and/or misunderstandings than because of intentional misrepresentation), I shall not reproduce them in full. Taking them at face value they would lead one to conclude that during this period the average weekly wage— which even included the salaries of the field managers and plantation foremen—fluctuated between Cr$6,500 and Cr$9,100, the overall average being Cr$7,300. The official minimum weekly wage (including payment for Sunday) during this period was Cr$12,600.[15]

Another approach to the problem was made by using an available list of all those who, since the beginning of the IBRA administration, had used the services of the dispensary. A sample of 1:20 was taken,

[15] In April 1966 Cr. $2,220 = US $1.

and for each the amount of total wages received during a seven-week period (25 April–26 June) was supplied by the office. After elimination of 2 field managers, the sample consisted of 24 workers. Of these 3 had received no wages at all from São Pedro. Of the others, 9 had received an average weekly wage of under Cr$5,000; 5 between Cr$5,000 and Cr$10,000; 4 between Cr$10,000 and Cr$12,600, and 3 had made Cr$12,600 (the minimum weekly wage) or more. The overall average was Cr$4,300. If we eliminate those who made less than an average of Cr$5,000 per week, a category likely to have consisted in part of people who had 'voluntarily' worked substantially less than most others, in part of people who had been prevented from working by sickness, the mean is still no higher than Cr$6,500.

The significance of figures such as these is limited, as they cannot be interpreted unambiguously. The sample data do not refer to the plantation's entire work force, but only to those who had bought medicines for themselves or their families. In the seven weeks examined, about one-quarter of the total labour force did so. Probably the best gloss on these figures is that they refer to that part of the rural workers which is in greatest difficulty to ensure survival. The aggregate data include very disparate sections of the work force and, like the sample data, they give no indication of the actual number of days worked for the plantation. All data, moreover, refer largely to the slack period in the sugar cycle, which further restricts their significance. The following paragraphs should elucidate this point.

Activity on the sugar plantation is greatest from August to December, smaller until March, and there is least work from April to July, when the only job to be done consists of the cleaning of the cane fields. In the latter periods the migrant workers who come in from the *agreste*[16] during the busy season have gone home, but even so there is not really enough work for the entire labour force of *moradores*, namely those permanently living on the *engenhos*. While on the one hand the plantation cannot afford to shoulder the full wage bill due to the permanent labour force, on the other hand wholly undisguised unemployment could mean that part of the workers decided to move away from the plantation for good—and that would endanger the availability of the necessary labour during the period from August to the beginning of the new year. The plantations, then, must try to retain their labour force at minimum cost. This is done by requiring

[16] The transition zone between the *zona da mata* and the *sertão*, the arid highlands of Brazil.

the performance of extra large tasks, which have no bearing upon cultivation needs; tasks so large that many workers cannot complete them in the time allowed.[17] As has been seen, these people do not receive a full week's wage on pay-day. The enterprise also economizes through those other workers who, in refusing to accept the large tasks, remove themselves *temporarily* from the pay-roll, and try to make ends meet by working elsewhere or cultivating their subsistence plots.

The manager of the *engenhos* at São Pedro gave an account which was similar in general outline, but differed in respect of a number of significant details.[18] Between March and July, he suggested, approximately 40 per cent of the *moradores* in the *engenhos* seem to settle down to working for São Pedro. The rest prefer to work at least part of the time for themselves on their own *roça*, or they go to *engenhos* where work is considered less arduous. Not to work for the plantation is, in the eyes of the manager of the *engenhos*, the result of a genuine personal choice: though he did not mention the often-heard phrase 'because they're lazy', he reasoned that workers considered the work unpleasant, didn't feel up to it, or preferred to work on their own plot—even though this was hardly ever large enough to provide subsistence.[19] Though some absences reported due to illness were genuine, many workers, he said, alleged illness as an excuse for not turning up for work.

In contrast to an outsider, such as the earlier cited IBRA agronomist, the plantation's management did not recognize that the workers' behaviour was determined by structural conditions rather than by personal choice. Statements such as 'the workers prefer to seek work on other *engenhos*' are best regarded as mystifications: broadly speaking, all the plantations in the area were subject to the same conditions. The management might have agreed that elsewhere the law or the collective contracts were broken, but they denied that this was ever the case on their own domain. Thus the manager of the *engenhos* remarked that on other plantations people were often given too large a daily task in the slack period. Not, however, at São Pedro: 'here we stick strictly to the *tabela*'. Though he recognized that perhaps a quarter of those who did work for the plantation did not finish their daily tasks, the fault for this lay, according to him, with the workers themselves. It may be noted in passing that this manager was regarded

[17] From interview with chief agronomist at IBRA regional headquarters, 4 July 1966.
[18] Interview 7 July 1966.
[19] See above, p. 177, for data from the IBRA survey.

by plantation workers as well as by officials of the *sindicato* as a 'decent' man, who did not act unjustly towards the workers or put excessive pressure on them. In negotiations with the leadership of the union federation he had supported the rights of the workers to stand up against 'squeezing practices', and at the time he had been willing to admit that they occurred at São Pedro. But the blame for these he had placed on the plantation foremen, who had somehow been acting 'without authority'.[20]

It is not easy to draw hard and fast conclusions from this contradictory evidence. The truth seems to be that structural conditions in the sugar industry lead to behaviour on the part of the plantation owners which compels workers to work harder for less pay; that the pay which can be earned is below the agreed minimum wage, and for many families below the minimum need for subsistence; that in the face of such a situation workers often react by withdrawing their labour, not in order to obtain better conditions elsewhere (they are not obtainable), but out of anger, frustration, apathy, or despair; and, finally, that while a proportion of those who continue to work for the plantation manage to complete the heavier tasks, others attempt to do so but fail, and a third part—probably the smallest—never actually try. The overall result is that during the slack months most workers on the sugar plantations live under appalling conditions. The earlier mentioned average-wage figures must be interpreted in this light: though they cannot be taken as an exact indication of the earnings of rural workers in this period in view of 'voluntary' withdrawal from work and supplementary earnings elsewhere, they do point to the extremely precarious economic conditions of the North-East rural proletariat.

Lack of leadership and intimidation

Despite all this, on the surface there was little overt expression of dissatisfaction in 1966. People complained a great deal, but they took no action to rectify the situations about which they were complaining. Two interrelated factors would seem to account for this: the weakness of grass-roots leadership on the one hand, and undisguised intimidation on the other. After April 1964 many of the workers who had been militants ('leaders') without being union officials had been fired by their employers, and for the most outspoken ones among them a kind of regional blacklist, which kept them from being employed anywhere in

[20] Interview with leadership of the regional federation of *sindicatos*, 8 July 1966.

the area, was reputedly in operation. Many local union leaders had been forced out by the military on charges of subversion, to be replaced with less conspicuously militant officials. At the level of the federation the lawyers predominated even more after April 1964 than before, and activities were almost exclusively conceived in juridical terms. The federation's main legal adviser remarked with great emphasis: 'The *conscientização* of the rural worker must involve him in understanding his juridical dimension.'[21] Union action was again—as in the earliest days—conceived almost exclusively in terms of seeking compliance with the law: not once during my discussions with union officials were wage claims spontaneously mentioned. Thus the *sindicatos* no longer represented the same kind of independent power base outside the plantations which could support the workers in their struggles with the owners. Nor, of course, did the state government now intervene on behalf of the workers, as had been the case before the coup.

The other factor leading to passivity was direct intimidation of the rural workers themselves.[22] There was the apparently widespread method of greeting openly voiced complaints, for instance about the allocation of work, with accusations of agitation or communism, and it was known that a sufficiently well-established reputation of being an agitator or communist would lead to most unpleasant encounters with the authorities. Workers also believed that any 'trouble-maker' would find his work-load increased or, worse, his very job endangered—and potential trouble-makers were very closely watched. The physical environment of a sugar plantation greatly facilitated such vigilance: the movements of its inhabitants were easily checked and, when suspicious, reported back to the *casa grande* by one of the lower-level participants in authority dotted around the *engenhos*. I have described my personal experience with that authority structure in Appendix II. It was slightly frightening, but most instructive.

It is, then, evident that since the pre-coup days matters had greatly changed. The authorities no longer intervened on behalf of the workers, and the *sindicatos* had lost their sting. I was told at a discussion after a class of MEB at the *usina* that although the president of the Federation was 'O.K.', he was all too eager to see the point of view of the

[21] Interview, 4 July 1966.

[22] For obvious reasons it was impossible to obtain more than 'hearsay evidence' of these practices. But they were mentioned on so many occasions that one had to conclude that they were part of the workers' definition of the situation. Consequently, true or not, *belief* in them left the workers intimidated and passive.

usina. He was reluctant to defend the workers without hedging his remarks in a manner intended to make them seem reasonable and to please management. And when he came down from the capital he would always stop first at the *casa grande* 'and go into a huddle with the administration'. Such practices may have been 'politic' under the existing circumstances. But because of them the *sindicatos*, with their stress on the law and on gentlemanly understandings between the lawyers of the federation and the management of the *usinas*, came perilously close to conforming to the image of appropriate union behaviour held by the *usina* administrators: the unions should make it their business to 'create a climate of co-operation and harmony, and not go about being subversive'.

Few rural workers in the *zona da mata* would have been able to give a coherent account of the economic and sociological factors responsible for their plight. But most were well aware of the fact that theirs was a precarious position, which was likely to remain so until the employers were in some way forced to give in to collective pressure, or until the whole structure of ownership and control in the sugar-producing areas was drastically altered. Widespread *sindicalização* and political activity during the years leading up to the 1964 coup had resulted, in other words, in substantial *conscientização*: rural workers in this area knew well enough that there was nothing God-given about things as they were. They had had experience of the positive results of strikes and other collective action, and they had begun to see that through political choices they could express their own interests. In the *zona da mata* those engaged in *sindicalização* (and they included the cadres of MEB) had seen this process as a first step to wider class consciousness, which would lead to a fundamental challenge to the existing agro-industrial structure and its relations of production. There is little doubt that many problems inherent in the very nature of that agro-industrial structure were not being adequately analysed by the challenges of pre-1964 days, and the difficulties glossed over by those preaching a massive agrarian reform were formidable. But at least a start had been made by the formation of rural *sindicatos*, intended to defend the interests of the workers from within the existing structures. It was the emasculation of those organizations of class interest, the damper put by the coup on any expression of pugnaciousness by those making up the *pólo dominado* that so fundamentally changed the setting in which MEB had to operate. What happened in that new setting to the Movement is the subject of the following chapters.

10

MEB after the Military Take-Over of 1964

The April coup and its repercussions: the bishops step in

THE political upheaval of April 1964 caused a virtually complete standstill to MEB's activities in almost all *sistemas*, varying from about a week to over three months. The military invaded or closed various local offices of MEB, schools were shut down by landowners, material was destroyed or confiscated, members of almost a dozen local *equipes* were either arrested for brief periods of time or called before military inquiry boards (IPMs). *Monitores* were threatened, imprisoned, or dismissed from their jobs in half a dozen states, teaching staff on leave from posts in state schools were recalled to their posts, and a number of supervisors resigned because of the accusations levelled against them by civil or military authorities. Three diocesan bishops virtually disowned MEB. A rather limited number publicly defended the Movement (though they usually weakened their defence by adding some ambiguous statement such as 'human failures are unavoidable in any organization'). Various bishops used their personal influence behind the scenes to secure the release of MEB personnel who had been arrested or to calm down over-zealous searchers for subversion. Three bishops who were members of the CDN had an audience with the new President of the Republic some three weeks after the coup. When they raised the subject of MEB, Marshal Castelo Branco apparently promised to take measures to stop the persecution. The promise had no noticeable effect. Late in May the CDN met in a series of stormy sessions in which the critics of the radical line were very vocal, but the meeting ended in approving a document sent to the CNBB which defended MEB in ardent terms.

This vigorous defence of MEB (in private) by its bishops apparently sufficiently influenced their colleagues on the CNBB to lead to the insertion of some positive phrases on the Movement in a document in other places warmly praising the new military rulers. Twenty-five archbishops and bishops, after an extraordinary meeting called by the CNBB, put out a declaration on 29 May 1964, which said in its opening paragraphs:

In response to the general and anxious expectations of the Brazilian people, which saw the quickening pace of communism's rise to power, the Armed Forces came to the rescue in time to avoid the implantation of bolshevism in our country. . . . Immediately after the victory of the *Revolução*, a feeling of relief and hope could be discerned. This was the case especially because, in the face of the climate of insecurity and almost of despair in which the various social classes or groups found themselves, Divine Protection made itself felt in a tangible and straightforward manner . . . . In offering our thanks to God, who heeded the prayers of millions of Brazilians and delivered us from the communist peril, we express our gratitude to the Military. These rose up in the name of the supreme interests of the Nation, with grave risks to their lives, and we are grateful to them for co-operating to liberate the Nation from the imminent abyss.[1]

The bishops recognized that the military would have to 'consolidate their victory by means of a purge of the causes of the disorders'; they asked, however, that defendants be given 'the sacred right of defence' and that no one would become the 'object of hatred or revenge'.

They went on to state that 'even in movements of a Catholic orientation there may have been recklessness or abuses on the part of one individual or another who escaped our attention, or of others who were victims of their own idealism, of their ingenuousness or inadequate understanding of the facts'. Then, however, the bishops proceeded to defend organizations such as MEB:

On the other hand we do not accept, nor shall we ever be able to accept, the damaging, generalized or gratuitous accusation, whether veiled or explicit, that bishops, priests, and laymen, or organizations such as, for example, Catholic Action and the Movement for Basic Education (MEB), are communist or fellow-travelling. This accusation springs at times from the tactics of the communists themselves, at other times it emanates from certain individuals who cannot accept the open and courageous attitudes which clergy and laymen hold as true apostles of the Church, who preach the sound doctrine, whether against communism or against gross social injustices and against foci of corruption and the degradation of moral values.

---

[1] These, and following, quotations from CNBB, *Reunião extraordinária dos Metropolitas: Declaração*, 29 May 1964.

The latter phrases were more influenced by the view of the progressives among the hierarchy, the people who later felt more than mildly embarrassed when the issue of the wording of this declaration was raised; those who had been the driving force behind the Easter message which the Central Commission of the CNBB had published only a year before.[2]

In MEB, progressive as well as conservative bishops, but the latter more than the former, now became concerned to take steps to eliminate the ambiguities in MEB's aims, tighten up the structure, and in general take a firmer grip on the ultimate direction of the Movement.

The man charged by the CDN with drawing up a draft for the new directives, the *Diretrizes para o Funcionamento do MEB*, was Mons. Tapajóz, appointed during the May meetings as permanent adviser to the CDN. An early draft of his project was discussed at a meeting of the *Nacional* with the state co-ordinators held early in June 1964, the first contact of the top lay leadership after the coup. It was a meeting of much significance, in that the issues facing MEB in the new political situation were discussed with great concern and passion. The Movement was under heavy fire, and many bishops were inclined to join in the chorus of those condemning not only past activities, but also the whole commitment of MEB's cadres to the cause of the peasants, their identification with the *pólo dominado*.

At this meeting in June the laymen stood firm. They concluded that the very nature of MEB's educational work, concerned as it is with the rural areas

where the social problems are more acute and inequality and misery greatest, so that more radical changes are required, leads to a reaction of the more favoured classes. Such a reaction also occurs among a clergy accustomed neither to seeing laymen take on a task in the church, nor to finding the values of the Scriptures explicitly embodied in the social field, as well as among the public at large, which has not been prepared for the kind of work developed by MEB.[3]

They stressed once again the fundamental importance given to the people themselves. No one regarded the *povo* any longer as MEB's 'clientele', as students to whom something was to be given, for whom

---

[2] See above, p. 84.

[3] From the report of the meeting of *Coordenadores*, 8–15 June 1964. At the time this report was not distributed, not even to the *Estaduais*, as this was considered politically dangerous. The report was kept for the record in the archives of the *Nacional*. It was released to the participants in the *III Encontro de Coordenadores* in April 1966.

something was to be organized by a separate entity receiving directives from above. MEB's task was related to the necessity of rapidly and radically changing a social reality which brings man into subjection and impedes him in creative activity—but this *promoção* of man had sense only if he shouldered it himself. Thus the conclusions were reached that the Movement cannot be satisfied with occasional or superficial contacts with the people, and that the *povo* themselves must become the agents of the required changes.[4] 'This implies their participation in the elaboration of MEB's work. The Movement's structure should be more open to the presence of the *povo* in the various phases of its activities, so that this participation can become more effective'.[5]

Mons. Tapajóz's draft had been written in a very different spirit. He was new to MEB and had no experience at all of the problems at the grass-roots. He had approached the task from his professional perspective, as a canonical lawyer requested to set things straight by the bishops of the CDN. He had started from the premise that the organization set up by the CNBB was neither exclusively 'of the hierarchy' nor solely 'of the laymen': it was a Movement in which the two participated 'in relations and functions of subordination and collaboration'. MEB's structure should be adequate to the *juridical* structure of the church; hence he proposed a complicated organization with parallel 'lines of command' for the clerical and lay functions.

The co-ordinators at the June meeting found themselves in profound disagreement with the abstract and legalistic nature of Mons. Tapajóz's draft. To them it was a decided step backwards. Against the very trend emerging at the Vatican Council, which pointed towards increased lay responsibility and independence in secular, professional matters, the draft proposed to curtail the role of the laymen in MEB. And yet Tapajóz's ideas were not out of tune with the realities facing the Movement. There was no denying the fact that the new political situation had substantially increased the power of the bishops *vis-à-vis* the laymen. Everyone, including the bishops themselves, realized that the government had not hit out harder against MEB precisely because of the Movement's links with the CNBB. Not surprisingly, then, the bishops felt that if they were seen by the outside world as being responsible for the Movement, they had better assert

---

[4] This foreshadows the central place which *Animação Popular* will acquire in the Movement. This is discussed in the next chapter.

[5] Report of the meeting of *Coordenadores*, 8–15 June 1964.

that responsibility on the inside, a responsiblity which had in any case always been formally theirs.

The laymen, for their part, were realistic enough to see that the period of well-nigh untrammelled freedom of action was over. They understood that the extreme situation had resulted in the 'calling back' of the hitherto rather diffusely distributed power to its *formally* ultimate source, namely to the CDN. MEB had, in fact, gone through a development not uncommon in large voluntary organizations, whereby the internal dynamic of the organization runs ahead of changes in its formal structure. When this occurs, changes in the 'organization chart', which legalize a new *de facto* distribution of power or even a wholly new basis of power, often come about without much resistance from those hitherto in formal control. But if a crisis intervenes *before* such an adjustment has been made, the formal authority which seemingly had been superseded or had atrophied is called upon to exercise its final power—a situation in which heightened tensions are almost inevitable.[6] This occurs for various reasons. No one below the formal pinnacle of authority structure dares, or feels entitled, to assume responsibility for the unusually important decisions which now have to be taken. Moreover, those in the formally highest echelon themselves feel that they are expected to assume responsibility and reassert their authority. And lastly there is the fact that outside agencies (such as the government, in the present case) expect, under such circumstances, to have dealings only with those who are formally in control.

All these factors operated in the case of MEB. Just before the coup, when the bishops were increasingly uncertain about the Movement's 'line', there had been a good deal of talk about the possibility of making MEB wholly independent of the CNBB. But such a development had become unthinkable after April. By mid-1964, with the bishops throwing their weight about (and formally they were totally justified in this), the laymen had been forced into a defensive position. In the new circumstances they had to try and maintain as much as possible of the power which had previously been theirs *de facto*, to try

[6] I follow here the analogy of power and money so persuasively developed by Talcott Parsons: in the same way as a crisis (of confidence) leads to a disintegration of the credit system and a move back to hard cash (a run on the banks), a crisis involving power, seen as a generalized means of achieving goals, leads to a move from the lower levels which had been creating 'power credit' back to its 'ultimate' source (and possibly to the use of 'ultimate' means of enforcement). See his paper 'On the Concept of Political Power', *Proc. Amer. Philos.' Soc.* cvii, (1963). See also my further discussion below, ch. 14, nn. 1 & 2.

and influence the tightening up of the Movement's official regulations in such a way that in the final analysis very little would change. Thus the state co-ordinators argued on the one hand that the hierarchy's task should mainly be to watch over the *doctrinal* aspects of the Movement's work. On the other hand, while they accepted the reality of the bishop's power, they attempted to draw its sting by suggesting that the overall orientation of the Movement should emerge from constant dialogue between hierarchy and laymen, and should be the expression of their co-responsibility in and for MEB.[7]

The difficult dialogue with Mons. Tapajóz did result in some important modifications in the general lines of this second major formal document of the Movement. The draft of the *Diretrizes* presented to the CDN at the beginning of August 1964 had abandoned the concept of parallel lay and hierarchical lines of control, and was generally less inspired by a simple view from the top, an undifferentiated attempt to assert the ultimate authority of the hierarchy, whether through the CDN or through the diocesan bishops. The CDN, having made a few minor modifications, basically approved the draft unaltered.[8] In the end the document's main importance lay in the spelling out of organizational tasks, responsibilities, and powers. Partly this led to clarifications of real significance—those confirming the Secretary-General's powers of hiring and firing, for instance. But partly the give and take that had occurred in the course of drafting and redrafting had failed to resolve certain profound differences of opinion. In the new document these crystallized into a number of highly ambiguous paragraphs, especially in the area of the relationship between the diocesan bishop and the local *equipe*, which contained the germs of further conflicts. And the *Diretrizes* effectively neutralized the potential consequences of the laymen's new orientation to the *povo* by failing to mention even in the most general terms the peasants' possible active role in the Movement's structure.

How, then, do the aims and methods of the Movement emerge in the *Diretrizes*? The most striking departure from previous formulations (formal, as well as informal) is the sudden prominence of religious phrases and ideas. The opening statement reads: 'MEB is a Catholic entity, whose aims are pre-eminently social and educational, in the

[7] Two years later, in yet another organizational crisis involving that time mainly the diocesan bishops (as opposed to those of the CDN), the concept of co-responsibility would occupy the very centre of the stage.

[8] MEB, *Diretrizes para o funcionamento do MEB*, 3 Aug. 1964.

interest of all men without distinction of creed or ideology.' It continues, much in the same vein:

The essential aim of MEB is to co-operate in the *formação* of man (adult or adolescent) in the underdeveloped areas of the country. This is meant in the sense of leading him to become conscious of his dignity as a human being, made in the image of God and redeemed by Christ, Saviour of the World, and consequently transforming him into an agent involved in the creation of an original culture of a people.[9]

The immediately-following elaboration of the concept of *conscientização* states that it involves 'the affirmation of a God, the Creator, on whom all depends, and to whom all are subordinated', and 'the affirmation that man has a value in himself, a value superior to the whole temporal order and subordinated to God'. Later in the document the means are stated to include catechesis and religious instruction, 'without which man does not possess the basic conditions for knowledge and life compatible with his conditions as a Christian'.

These phrases clearly indicated that there had been a change in the Movement's *official* orientation. For a while a part of the lay leadership had no doubt always *personally* accepted the validity of these religious views, only very few had ever subscribed to them in the context of the work of MEB. Catechism was an activity quite alien to MEB's cadres, one for which they had no competence or preparation, and in fact no one took any action on the newly inserted subsidiary aim of the Movement. The changed formulation did little more than express the view of MEB's bishops after the coup, and resulted from the assertion by the CDN of its final authority.[10]

But other aspects of the document show the influence of the laymen: they reaffirm and even strengthen the socially radical line of the Movement defended by the meeting in June. Thus the third paragraph on *conscientização* reads that this involves 'the affirmation that all men have the same essential value, and that differences between them are admissible only in so far as these are not transformed into the domination of one man over another'. 'MEB', so it continues, 'wants the peasant to be aware of his right to acquire living conditions which enable him to realize his human dignity and to teach him the value of co-operation and communal activities.'

[9] Cf. the emphasis placed in the *Método Paulo Freire* on this aspect of culture.

[10] Just over two years later the laymen called in question the appropriateness to the Movement of this specifically religious task thrust upon them by the hierarchy (see below, pp. 209–10).

It has been seen that the text finally approved by the CDN did not take any steps to enlarge the role of the *povo*, of the peasants reached by MEB, in the formal structures of the Movement. But MEB's increasingly explicit populism did find expression in a very significant new note, sounded towards the end of the *Diretrizes*: '[the peasant's] integration in the community must come about through conscious and free options, the range of which must be shown to him, while none in particular may be imposed upon him'. The well-nigh explosive potentialities of this statement were apparently lost on the members of the CDN. But this phrase should be viewed not only in the context of populist ideology, but also in relation to the idea of freedom of conscience then very much in the air. The Vatican Council's Schema on Religious Liberty had already been circulated among the bishops, and had been formally introduced during the second session in November 1963. The bishops of the CDN were well aware of the shift in Catholic thinking on this matter, and the phrase on MEB's approach to the peasants therefore must have had a familiar ring. That the earlier paragraphs, which extolled Catholicism and church, seemed to breathe less of the new spirit of freedom,[11] merely serves to emphasize the relevance of the specifically Brazilian circumstances, and is a reminder that the document represented a compromise between the substantially different points of view of the bishops and of the lay leadership.

The latter's desire to see specific reference made in the *Diretrizes* to the concrete 'historical conditions' in which the Movement was working was also not fulfilled: aims and means were phrased in general terms, applicable anywhere, at any time. There was no reference to inter-related dominating groups and structures, not a word about the futility of much community development work if carried out in isolation from the wider economic and political reality, no mention of *sindicalismo*.[12] Quite apart from its own doubts on these matters, the CDN obviously considered that in the existing political climate, four months after the coup, with MEB still under a cloak of suspicion, it would not have been prudent openly to stress the very matters which had so recently brought about the allegations of playing into the hands of communism.

The laymen's conception of MEB in mid-1964, tempered by their reaction to the new political circumstances but undiluted by compromises with the bishops' point of view, was expressed in another

[11] Cf. also the discussion of Pope Paul's conception of dialogue, below, pp. 198–9.
[12] In contrast to the laymen's document of 'witness', analysed below.

14

document of importance, conceived during this same period. It arose in the first place out of the June meeting of the *Nacional* with the state co-ordinators, which had agreed upon the skeleton outline of a statement of 'witness'. The statement was presented to the CDN at its meeting in August by the *Nacional*, who had written the document from the suggestions left with them. After discussing the document the bishops took note of the statement, and suggested that after some changes in form, but not in substance, it should be published as a testimony to MEB's work as seen from the inside. The statement was further discussed at the *II Encontro Nacional de Coordenadores* held in mid-March 1965, and though critical voices were raised against the language and style ('incomprehensible to the grass-roots'), it remained fundamentally unaltered, and was distributed in mimeographed form in May 1965.[13]

This important document, in its published version, begins with a long theological section dealing in general terms with the task of the church in the world and in Brazil. Turning to the specific position of MEB, it distinguishes the Movement's educational task from an evangelizing—and especially catechizing—mission. Somewhat ambiguously it states that although MEB has never felt any inhibitions in respect of evangelization, and even though in a Christian attitude it has always desired 'that men reach an adult faith, freely and consciously accepted', these matters have not constituted the prime objectives of the Movement. The ambiguity returns in a later paragraph, whose pluralistic spirit seems neither complete nor wholehearted:

Our educational effort is directed at a population which in its majority is Catholic. But it is Catholic neither in its totality, nor in the fully authentic sense. Therefore our efforts must show a deep respect for the intermediate steps which, necessarily, lead to the final goal: the acknowledgement of God and the church.[14]

The document continues by stating that MEB's work is guided by the ideas on dialogue expressed in Pope Paul's first encyclical, *Ecclesiam Suam*, from which it quotes: 'It is not from the outside that we shall save the world. . . . It is necessary for us to identify ourselves up to a point with the forms of life of those to whom we bring the message of Christ' (para. 21). But Paul's conception is very different indeed from

[13] *MEB: Sua origem, sua ação e seu conteúdo*, May 1965.
[14] Ibid., p. 2.

the populist's whole-hearted openness to the people. One cannot read this encyclical without becoming rapidly convinced that dialogue, there, is for Paul a method of conversion, a means to convince others of the truth held by the church, an expression of Christ's last injunction to his disciples: 'Go ye therefore, and teach all nations' (Matt. 28:19).[15] To some extent MEB's use of the Pope's words may have been merely a tactical device to give strength to their arguments, but it does appear from the wording in the document that some awareness existed of the 'conversionist' nature of Pauline dialogue, and that it was approached—and accepted—with the kind of ambivalence which we have noted earlier. Accepted a little naïvely, perhaps even somewhat *à contre cœur*, because the section ends by reiterating MEB's own pluralist and non-directivist position.

MEB's work is lived consciously, in the face of a people who stand before various options. It is not our task to impose any one of these, nor is it our task to force the *povo* towards the Christian faith linked to the Catholic church, although we must provide them with opportunities to know the faith.[16]

The second section of the document deals with MEB's educational tasks. Here one encounters the by now well-rehearsed view that education is possible only through *conscientização*, followed by a new idea linking *conscientização* to action, to being *engagé* in practice. In the distance, but very recognizably, one hears the Marxist cry on the unity of theory and practice, come to us via the echo-chamber of AP. In MEB it sounds like this: with *conscientização* one must 'bring man to an engagement in his own world, in his culture, in his historical situation, so that he can be a creative agent within this world'.[17] The third section is the most explicitly radical and assertive one. It concerns MEB and the *povo*, and squarely faces the problem of domination, vested interests, and class conflict in Brazil. As Christians MEB's cadres cannot admit that class struggle is a norm of evolution; they are not Marxists, and do not elevate this kind of conflict to a predominant, even less to a desirable, fact of history. But they have to 'accept the reality of the facts without losing objectivity', they cannot gear their entire activity to the prevention of conflicts.[18] They cannot become the

---

[15] *Ecclesiam Suam*, para 60. I cannot make the case in greater detail here. A reading of ch. III of the Encyclical will be rewarding for those who wish to follow up this point.
[16] *MEB: sua origem, sua ação e seu conteúdo*, pp. 2–3.
[17] Ibid., p. 5.
[18] Ibid., p. 6.

manipulators of the people for the sake of an (illusory) social peace:
'we must not fall into the error of paternalism, which regards the *povo*
as the recipient of such things as will prevent them from becoming
a cause of conflicts'.[19]

Most of the Movement's documents published after the April coup
show a great deal of reticence in discussing conflicts and injustice, as
well as the methods to overcome them, in anything but the most
general and abstract terms. Here, however, towards the end of this
lengthy analysis a robust defence is mounted of MEB's uncompromis-
ing position. 'MEB does not cause conflicts: [they result from] the
Brazilian social structure itself, which is unjust.' So long as those
organizations which defend the interests of other groups will not
collaborate, MEB's action 'which cannot be innocuous', dedicated as
it is to the defence of the rights of the less favoured classes, will arouse
resentment—especially among the big landowners, the industrial
bourgeoisie, and the middle classes, most of whom are hardly prepared
for attitudes 'in conformity with the principles of justice'.[20]

The second *cartilha*

The views expressed in the documents just discussed adequately
convey the state of the Movement's ideology in the twelve months
following the coup. The *Relatório Anual* for 1963, prepared towards the
end of 1964, added no new points of view. The already-mentioned
II Encontro de Coordenadores produced no published—or unpublished
—documents of basic importance; it was mainly a meeting which tried
in various ways to evaluate the strengths and weaknesses of the current
work and the existing *sistemas*. The only really interesting aspect of
the report of this meeting was the aggressive reproach of the *sistemas*
that the *Nacional* lacked *vivência* of the problems at the grass-roots:
unless they acquired this, 'MEB could well become an institution or
enterprise like any other one'.[21] Certainly the most important development of that year was the refinement of the concept of *Animação
Popular*, which embodied MEB's own version of populism. That will
be discussed in the next chapter. But also of considerable interest, as a
reflection of the new balance of power in the Movement between

[19] Ibid., p. 7. Cf. the phraseology used by Cardonnel five years earlier, quoted above,
p. 65.
[20] Ibid., p. 8.
[21] MEB, *Relatório do II Encontro Nacional de Coordenadores*, 8–18 March 1965 (Rio,
Apr. 1965, mimeo.), p. 7.

bishops and laymen, was the process of elaboration of MEB's new *cartilha*, *Mutirão*.

Despite the quite vigorous defence which the Movement had put up when *Viver é Lutar* was first attacked, the new political circumstances had made it inconceivable to continue utilizing that text. Too many cases had occurred of zealous military searchers for subversion using possession of the booklet as evidence of a person's dangerous ideological views. Hence the need for new teaching materials which would not lead to such hazardous complications. The central concept of struggle was abandoned; in its place came co-operation.

The final drafts of the new booklets—the first volume was strictly for illiterates, the second volume corresponded to *Viver é Lutar* in that it was meant for more advanced students—drawn up at the *Nacional* had been approved by the *II Encontro de Coordenadores*. They were discussed at the simultaneously-held meeting of the CDN, and unanimously approved after a number of not very important modifications. Nevertheless, 'taking into account previous experience with MEB's *cartilhas*, the Council considered it appropriate to solicit the views of the bishops in whose dioceses MEB has been acting'.[22] It is important to realize that by adopting this line, the CDN more or less washed its hands of the responsibility for the new texts. Its members were, of course, aware of the fact that many of the diocesan bishops were conservatives of one shade or another. The CDN must, therefore, have known that by submitting the new booklets to them for approval, they were virtually inviting a considerable watering down of the text. And this is precisely what happened. In the preparatory stage of *Viver é Lutar* the draft text had also been sent to some bishops. But whereas at that time the more conservative comments were simply ignored, now the new texts underwent a large number of changes. Most of these taken in isolation did not amount to very much. But together they resulted in an end-product from which even the few more or less veiled references to class conflict or exploitation had been eliminated. In the end nothing was said on these matters at all.

There were very few bishops indeed who were troubled by this fact. Out of twenty-six bishops who replied only three made suggestions which would have given the *cartilhas* a more radical content.[23] One of these simply said that he was against them because 'the previous *cartilha*, *Viver é Lutar*, was much more educative'. The second was a very radical churchman from the North-East, who had been outspoken on many occasions. He approved, but commented:

Mutirão seemed to me timid in respect of *conscientização* for development, and in respect of *politização*. I am still convinced that one cannot build up democracy without the conscious and organized participation of the people, which demands basic education. I consider MEB as the privileged field of commitment of adult Christians *together with all others who respect human dignity*. Therefore I can see no adequate reason for an institutional link with the Hierarchy. [Italics in original.]

The third, another prominent bishop from the North-East, wrote:

The book could give more hope by speaking explicitly about agrarian reform. *Mutirão* [i.e. co-operation] needs roots if it is to be successful, and those roots imply the change of the agrarian structure. As long as the Christian message is clearly present we can be firmer in pointing to the evils.

The views of the second bishop quoted, who believed that MEB should become a wholly independent lay organization, were apparently shared by no one else—or at least they were not openly expressed at this time by other diocesan bishops. On the contrary: seven bishops— among them the one last quoted—demanded that a greater amount of Christian content be introduced into MEB's programme and text-books. One of them (who thought the texts too radical) remarked: 'It seems to me that a greater effort of the authors of these texts was directed towards the *politização* of our peasants than towards their *cristianização*.'

One lesson especially was singled out for comment by these bishops. It contained a short verse which read: 'Each has his own way to reach God. God loves all people and made us so that we should love each other.' This was seen as an invitation to religious indifference. One bishop remarked that it might create 'the false notion that all religions are equally good in the eyes of God'—hence he proposed to change the first line of the verse to 'each person has the duty to walk towards God.' The ecumenical spirit had obviously descended more upon the laymen than upon the bishops. Apparently it was not easy to dislodge: in this case the laymen basically stuck to their guns. They gave in a little, but not very much. The final version became:

> Quando Deus criou o homem
> foi p'ra ser feliz e amar.
> Todos têm, pois, o dever
> de ao seu próximo ajudar.

Mesmo quando um cidadão
é de outra religião,
nós devemos respeitar.
Se êle faz um mutirão,
devemos, de coração,
a nossa ajuda lhe dar.[24]

Here the compromise seems perfectly reasonable. But in other cases
the result of yielding to the diocesan bishops meant changing the very
character of the final product. This was especially true in the case of
the objections of a more directly political nature, put forward by the
nine bishops who regarded the texts as too radical. A few examples
will make this clear. Various bishops objected to the second lesson in
the first textbook, which read: 'The owner has the field. The *povo*
has the hatchet. The field belongs to the owner. The *povo* lives. The
hatchet belongs to the *povo*.' One of them wrote: 'This verse is somewhat dangerous, as it could lead to further designs'. His point was
accepted, and the lesson was changed. In its place we find texts dealing
with co-operation and with the benefits brought by machinery.

Another bishop had given the texts for study to two school teachers
in his diocese. Their lengthy and rather pompous opinion, approved
and subscribed to by the bishop, read in part:

We consider it risky to submit illiterate persons, who are simple and credulous, to these very strong contents . . . Human enhancement . . . must be
brought about without the use of unconscious mechanisms of revolt or
vilification of one's neighbour. These, once given, will become conditioned
reflexes in the minds of simple and credulous people.

Thus, the 'very strong contents' were diluted. Lesson 7 of the first
book had said: 'The *povo* has rights. The *povo* needs to live decently.
The peasant needs land. The land needs to be ploughed. With a
plough the land yields more. The *povo* has the right to live off the
land.' After revision, the closest equivalent was found in two lessons:
'Donato works as a share-cropper. He works for his family. The whole
family needs Donato's work. Brazil needs the work of all', and

All people have the right to ownership and use of the land *to cultivate their
roçado* [subsistence plot]—as they've been created by God [my italics]. If

---

[24] God created man so that he would be happy and would love. Therefore all have the
duty to help their neighbour. Even when a citizen (fellow) is of another religion we have to
respect him. And if he makes a *mutirão* we have to give him our help from all our heart
(*Mutirão*, ii, lesson 14).

all think together, a way can be found. All *povo* who help each other live united and in better circumstances.[25]

Despite these changes the two volumes of *Mutirão* were not wholly devoid of material usable for *conscientização*. There were various lessons on the need for organization, and the *sindicatos* were explicitly discussed. A couple of lessons looked at the formal processes of democracy, elections, and voting; amazement was expressed at 'the people who vote without knowing what they want'. 'The vote is a sacred matter for him who understands it. Freedom can't be bought, consciousness can't be sold.' And yet, the limitations of *Mutirão* are forcibly brought to one's attention by this direct quote from *Viver é Lutar*.[26] Much was made in the Movement of the way in which *monitores* or supervisors would be able to use the texts as starting points for discussions which went well beyond their overt content and meaning. But it would need great skill and a highly developed social and political consciousness to extract, from texts which all the time stressed the benefits of co-operation, elements leading to an awareness of the limits to such co-operation posed by the power of *patrões* and the ideology of the military rulers of the country.[27] It would be equally difficult to shift from an explanation of hunger, disease, or inequality which focused upon *personal* ill will on the part of *some* landowners,[28] upon lack of co-operation among the peasants, and especially upon the results of ignorance, to one which saw the peasants' problems arising out of general 'built-in' characteristics of iniquitous *structures*.

MEB's textbooks thus came remarkably close to the classical positivist viewpoint that individual errors and *personal* immorality must be held accountable for the evils of the world. Especially since it was in no way the Movement's intention that this inference should be drawn from its texts, it is remarkable to see how pressures and the need to compromise could imperceptibly lead to a modification of

[25] *Mutirão*, i, lessons 7 & 10.

[26] See above, p. 159, for the rest of the lesson in *Viver é Lutar*, not reproduced in the new text.

[27] For a wider discussion of this issue, see below, pp. 260–6 ff.

[28] Cf. lesson 36 in *Mutirão* ii:

Some people, when they share, take the best piece.
Some people, when they sell, cheat and sell the worst.
They forget comradeship, and show egoism.
Can there be a greater sin?

The picture above this verse showed a rather sinister-looking *patrão* figure making off with a bundle of banknotes.

the entire basis on which the discussion of societal matters rested. The categories and concepts central to *Mutirão* were adequate to the comprehension of a world without conflict, or without gross inequalities of wealth and power; they certainly were not relevant to *conscientização* as it had come to be understood in the Movement. The new texts thus reflected the overt adjustment of MEB to the post-coup situation.

MEB's centre of gravity shifts to the North

There was, however, no question that the ideology implicit in the new texts was initially subscribed to by the Movement's cadres. The major loss of old-timers among MEB's personnel did not occur until the closure of the *sistemas* of Pernambuco late in 1966, and of those of Bahia, Minas Gerais, and Goiás early in 1967; certainly until that time much of the actual work carried out in the rural areas did at least try to be true to the views and the spirit of the pre-1964 days. After these extensive closures, however, the Movement faced a situation substantially different from the previously predominant one. In the first place, the broad *national* perspective on the social, economic, and political causes of the peasants' plight, which the Movement had developed as a result of operating *throughout* the underdeveloped areas of Brazil, lost much of its compelling character. In the second place, the coup led to a significant shift in the centre of gravity of the Movement. Late in 1965 the North contributed 23 per cent of all radio schools, 20 per cent of all students, and 16 per cent of all the local personnel (i.e. not counting those working at the *Nacional* in Rio). Two years later, after the shrinking of the Movement to 21 *sistemas*, the radio schools in the North had come to constitute 75 per cent of the total, the students there 53 per cent, and the 80 functionaries in the area 44 per cent of MEB's personnel outside Rio.[29]

I have already referred, in the previous chapter, to the situation prevailing in the *zona da mata* of the North-East, and I shall subsequently turn to the more traditional areas of Brazil's interior (the areas in which I undertook fieldwork during my stay in Brazil). As it did not prove possible to acquaint myself personally with MEB's work in the Amazon basin, I can do no more than present a few paragraphs to give the flavour of the different circumstances encountered by MEB in the country's vast Northern region.

'Geography' and natural conditions account for a large proportion

[29] See tables 1, 4 & 5, above, pp. 128, 133 & 136.

of the differences which exist between the North and the other areas
in which MEB operated. Any discussion must begin by mentioning
the region's sheer immensity, combined with the very exiguous system
of communication and transportation. The co-ordinator of an *equipe*
stationed in a *município* in the southern part of Pará reported at a
meeting in 1966 that their supervision was done partly on horseback,
partly by motor-launch, and partly by plane (the latter method was, in
certain circumstances, the cheapest); the nearest bank was an hour
away by air. Leaving aside the Indian aboriginal tribes and the population in the 'urban' nuclei which are, by definition, not the concern of
MEB, people provide for their subsistence in various ways.

In the Amazon region a man may be a fisherman, a herdsman, a gatherer of
nuts or extractor of rubber; all these various categories . . . do not, however,
break the fundamental unity of Amazônia: man's isolation in the dense and
closed forest, and his predatory extractive activity.[30]

Isolated and primitive, poor, and even more devoid of educational
facilities than the peasant in other parts of the country, the inhabitant
of the Amazon is largely left to fend for himself, without the support
of near-by neighbours. His techniques of cultivation are of the simplest
kind. He is essentially a gatherer of products of the tropical forests and
rivers (timber, nuts, rubber, fish), and he does this with the help of
only the simplest of tools.[31]
  The *latifúndio* is represented in the North by the large rubber
operations. There are hardly any true man-made 'plantations', as most
rubber derives from rubber trees growing wild in the tropical forest.
But in *social* terms the relations between the rubber gatherers and the
owners of the land on which the rubber trees grow are fairly similar to
those between landlord and sharecropper on the traditional *latifúndio*.
The rubber gathered is handed in at the *barracão*, the local river-side
trading post. Here the *seringueiro* (rubber gatherer) is credited for his
production in the books of the company, receiving in return foodstuffs
and other necessities for the following week or fortnight. As a result
almost all *seringueiros* remain perpetually in a state of virtual debt

[30] Manuel Diégues Jr., *Regiões culturais do Brasil* (1960), p. 221.
[31] On the occasion of the agricultural census in 1950 virtually all agricultural establishments in the North operated without the use of any means of animal or mechanical traction
(97.6 per cent of the approx. 80,000 establishments were reported to be without ploughs or
tractors). This was by far the highest proportion in the country; the average for Brazil
as a whole (including, of course, the much more developed South) was, at that time, 72.2
per cent (see Clóvis Caldeira, *Mutirão*, (1956), p. 88).

slavery.[32] But this indebtedness is somewhat tempered by the continued existence of the benevolent aspects of the traditional patron–dependant relationship in the Amazon region. The people living close to a particular trading post regard the trader as *patrão* and *compadre*, 'the trader–collector relationship is not merely an economic bond', and both parties develop sentiments of personal loyalty.[33] Nevertheless, one can hardly argue that these people are not 'exploited'—often they are worse off than many a peasant in the *sertão* of the North-East. As there appears to be very little awareness of this fact in the region, *conscientização* obviously has a role to play. And although, in view of the extremely low educational level in the North, the *form* of the 'message' brought by MEB to that area might have had to be somewhat different from that which was presented to peasants elsewhere in the country, its *focus* should clearly have been the same. Their predicament resulted from lack of economic (and political) power; they were the *pólo dominado* in a structure that reached well beyond the local trading post. What Wagley has written of Itá, the community he studied in the Lower Amazon, is applicable to the situation of many Amazon dwellers, and fits well with MEB's pre-coup perspective:

The people of Itá alone cannot modify the orientation of their economic system. They are caught in a commercial system and a credit system which have developed as a concomitant of the Amazon extractive industry. To change this, there must be changes throughout, from the exporter in Belém to the trader in the rural areas and the individual collector.[34]

Rubber, however, no longer has the dominant position in the economy of the Amazon which it held at the beginning of this century, and men make their living in many other agricultural pursuits. Vast areas have not yet been 'appropriated', and in various places the government has sponsored colonization schemes of smallholders—usually peasants brought from drought-ridden areas of the North-East. In many places the gathering of forest products other than rubber is predominant. It was with these types of relatively independent subsistence activities that most of the peasants reached by MEB eked out a living in this region. They depended less on a landlord-*patrão* than on a trader-*patrão*, and it was not fanciful to suggest that the application

[32] See Charles Wagley, *An Introduction to Brazil* (1963), p. 62; cf. also Orlando Valverde, *Geografia agrária do Brasil* (1964), pp. 275 ff.
[33] Wagley, p. 109.
[34] Wagley, *Amazon Town, a Study of Man in the Tropics*, new ed. (1964), p. 274.

of better methods of agriculture or greater co-operation could significantly increase their productivity and decrease their forced indebtedness to the *comerciante*. This was perhaps especially true in relation
to problems of transportation and marketing. When these peasants
were threatened it was often by speculators, moving in where new roads
were being opened, who cheated them of their tenuous property titles;
here again with some enlightenment, education, and co-operation,
positive results might be achieved. Stress on the benefits of co-operation
had particular significance in view of the isolation of one peasant
family from the next. In Amazônia, according to Clóvis Caldeira,
collective endeavours have not only economic importance but respond
—one would say in true Durkheimian manner—'to the necessity which
[the isolated individuals] feel of renewing contacts and reaffirming the
sentiments of solidarity'.[35] And, finally, for many colonists coming
from areas where *some* form of public education, however defective,
existed, MEB presented the only hope for their children of acquiring
any formal learning at all.

In the North, then, it was far from absurd to harp on the benefits
to be reaped from co-operation. The shift, after April 1964, from a
concern with the general nature of class relations in rural Brazil, and
with *conscientização* of the *pólo dominado* in its struggle with the *pólo
dominante*, to a stress on the benefits of *mutirões* and community
improvement, was followed by a shift in the area of operation of MEB
which made the new orientation—though no doubt one-sided—relevant in a way it could not have been before.

MEB settles down to new realities

By 1966 the Movement's post-coup situation had been more or less
stabilized, at least from an ideological point of view. The enormous
financial difficulties severely limited the number of *treinamentos* at
all levels and of supervisory visits to the communities, and the continuing hostile political climate made 'valid' work with the peasants
extremely difficult. The determination of a significant number of
MEB's bishops to get a firm grip on the Movement and to steer it in
the direction which they desired made 1966 into a rather inward-
looking year, with the trial of strength between laymen and hierarchy
over the changes in the Movement's structure as the dominating feature.
Despite the precarious state of MEB's finances in 1966 the Movement

[35] Caldeira, p. 102.

called its co-ordinators to Rio twice in that year: the *IV Encontro de Coordenadores* was held late in October 1966, the *III Encontro* had been held in May. On both occasions the episcopal pressure for *reestruturação*, aimed at giving the diocesan bishops a much greater direct say in the Movement's day-to-day operation, and at reducing the *Nacional* to a sort of service organization to the individual *sistemas*, was the main item on the agenda. On the whole the laymen contented themselves with reiterating their own, hitherto prevailing, conception of MEB. But on one count they formulated a reasoned challenge to an already-incorporated episcopal point of view: they proclaimed that MEB should not concern itself with catechesis.

It has been seen that catechesis was introduced as one of MEB's secondary aims into the *Diretrizes* of 1964. It was never accepted as a legitimate task for the Movement by its cadres, nor was it ever carried out; and in October 1966 the laymen made this clear to the bishops. More than a third of the contents of the document they sent to the CDN after their discussion of the proposed structural changes gave an unsolicited view on this question.

It appears that the use of the term catechesis among the secondary aims in the present *Normas e Diretrizes* leads to misunderstandings and friction within the Movement. On the one hand it does not satisfy the *equipes*, because they do not identify the work in which they are engaged with this term. On the other hand some diocesan bishops, when they read that catechesis is one of MEB's secondary aims, expect the *equipes* to teach the catechism in the traditional way.[36]

Catechesis, they continue, is concerned with the transmission of doctrinal teachings to those who wish to be taught. But the people reached by MEB cannot properly demand such teaching: Brazil's rural population, though formally Catholic, is caught in a web of superstition, and they even at times identify religion with the injustices of the social structure. Hence the main task for MEB is to help these people 'to reach an adult Faith, freely and consciously embraced'. MEB, therefore, considers itself to be active in the sphere of pre-evangelization, that is in the creation of conditions without which a man cannot make any meaningful choices in his life—including the choice to be religious. Having made this point the laymen suggested that MEB might help to train those people in the dioceses who were

---

[36] MEB, *Documento dos Coordenadores sôbre reestruturação do MEB*, Nov. 1966 (mimeo.), p. 10.

to be specifically charged with catechesis of the peasants. They could teach them the techniques of working with groups; 'in this way, by means of an activity proper to the Movement—the training of personnel—MEB would be collaborating with the global pastoral plan of the diocese'.[37]

It can be argued that on this last occasion before the closing down of the *sistemas* which had always constituted the very core of the Movement, MEB's laymen read the bishops this lesson in personalist philosophy, and rejected their role as catechizing agents with such determination, not merely because MEB's cadres had had a role forced upon them for which they did not feel adequately prepared, but also because the issue of the teaching of religion had become both a symbol and a touchstone. Restructuring the Movement in accordance with the bishop's wishes would have made each *equipe* much more a tool in the hands of the head of the diocese—and what many of these were most interested in was not basic education or *conscientização*, let alone stimulating the peasants to demand fundamental structural change, but religious instruction of a more or less pre-conciliar type. No one in the Movement was willing to see MEB turned into a Sunday school by radio. By insisting at this time on the change of one of MEB's subsidiary aims, and by using five pages of foolscap to argue the case for substituting one word (*catequese*) by another (*preevangelização*), the laymen served notice on the bishops that they rejected the new perspective which the latter were apparently trying to impose on the Movement, whatever was to come of the controversial reorganization.

A survey such as the one begun in Chapter 5 and concluded in the present one of the interaction between the Movement's theory and ideology, and the changing social situation in which it had to operate, almost inevitably leaves out much of the 'fuzziness' of reality. Hence it might create the impression that in each phase positions were wholly crystallized, and that these successive positions represented a logical progression of unambiguous views held unanimously and with full conviction by all concerned. In reality, of course, developments were much less neat: in the flux of events there always remained unanswered questions, disputed formulations, and internal tensions. Not that the Movement's cadres would have given the impression of over-confidence: MEB was imbued with an authentic spirit of humility, and there was a constant awareness that the right solution—if *right* solutions existed—had to be genuinely searched for. In that sense, as in many

[37] Ibid., p. 2.

others, Christian love for their fellow man, especially together with populist convictions honestly held, helped guard them against easy satisfaction and unwarranted pride. A remark written down after the meetings with the bishops in Rome, late in 1963, seems to me to catch this human element in an admirable manner:

Our life in this work is going to be, and will have to be, one of a constant struggle. In this *critical* formative phase ... we are all searching for the proper form for our own ideas, for a valid formulation—especially by working together. We will have to continue discovering the road, and that we will try to do with honesty and courage [italics in the original].

In the following chapter it will be seen that it was around the development of the Movement's ideas on non-directiveness that this search for the right approach concentrated much of the time. And it was in this area that MEB's populist character eventually found its most characteristic expression.

The Fusion of Populist Ideology and Non-directive Techniques

Animação Popular (AnPo)

THE previous chapter described how the aims and methods of MEB underwent a gradual transformation. From 1963 onwards the *povo* and their self-promotion slowly emerged as the central theme around which the organization tried to gear its activities, and after the coup this orientation was strengthened, despite occasional appearances to the contrary and despite the reservations of the bishops. The importance of 'conscious and free options', the range of which was to be shown to the peasant without any one in particular being imposed upon him, became a central tenet of the Movement's ideological orientation; gradually MEB's personnel saw themselves as moving to the sidelines—leaving the *povo* to run their own affairs. The implication was that the cadres of MEB should not provide the actual leadership; the most they could do was to advise. And advice itself was to be given not in the form of directives for action (or thought), but in the form of data and techniques to which the peasants had not, so far, had access. The people themselves would choose and decide: it would not be up to any outsider to question that choice.

It is tempting simply to attribute the shift in MEB's orientation towards self-promotion of the peasants to the emergence of the populist ideology which MEB came to share with the other sectors of the radical Catholic movement in Brazil. But in reality things were a little more complicated. Two specific internal developments in MEB, which were *not*, in the first place, ideological at all, helped to prepare the ground for the acceptance of populism. In both cases they were matters of technique rather than of broader values, though in both cases the techniques adopted could be said to have had an intrinsic 'fit' with populist ideology, which later provided a most persuasive set of political and intellectual rationalizations for these techniques. The first had its origin in certain kinds of work at the grass-roots level, with the peasants: it was to be known as *Animação Popular*. The second, on the contrary, was developed in the context of the *treinamentos*, in the first instance at the top of the Movement: it was to go under the name of non-directiveness.

Already at the *I Encontro Nacional de Coordenadores* in December 1962, the word *animação*[1] had been used (it is best translated as 'stimulation'), but it was not until some two years later that AnPo became a key concept in MEB. Early in 1965 a paper was drawn up at the *Nacional* in preparation for a seminar on the subject, in which members of various *equipes* participated. AnPo was defined there as a 'process of community structuring, which is progressively undertaken by the community members themselves'; also it was said to be 'the global process of the enhancement of Man by means of his own action'.[2] These definitions are somewhat abstract, and they are not untypical of the veiled wording characteristic of the Movement after the April coup, brought about on the one hand by the need for circumspection in the face of a hostile environment, on the other by the continuing divorce of the thinkers in the *Nacional* from the day-to-day concerns at the grass-roots. But even though the name possibly was, AnPo in itself was not the brainchild of part-time philosophers in Rio: as an invention it was little more than an exercise in induction, which had supplied a generic term for discrete experiences of a similar nature. These experiences had been taking place especially in two *sistemas*, one in the North-East, and one in the Centre-West; they consisted of methods of stimulating community activity not connected with radio schools.

As my experience of the *sistema* in the Centre-West is examined in greater detail in Chapter 13, the developments in the *sistema* in the North-East are briefly considered here. That *sistema* had been without a radio transmitter ever since MEB had begun to operate there in 1962, and the *equipe* had had to discover alternative methods of running the classes. They had started out with a kind of touring school, the *caravana*.

---

[1] The word was a translation from the French *animation*, used in French Africa (especially Sénégal) for the programmes for rural development and education. The leadership of MEB was familiar with the work done there, through personal contacts and seminars in France—especially at *Peuple et Culture* in Paris, and the *Centre Universitaire de Coopération Économique et Sociale* in Nancy—as well as through the literature, such as IRAM, *Animation et participation des masses au Plan Quadriénal du Sénégal* (Paris, 1961). The English-language equivalent is 'community development'.

[2] MEB, *Animação popular* (1965, mimeo), pp. 4 & 5.

But without daily radio programmes in between the visits of the *caravanas*, all activity had to revolve around members of the local communities themselves. In those circumstances teaching was extremely difficult—although a semi-literate peasant full of goodwill might be able to act as a link between the radio-teacher and the class, he was hardly capable of organizing a literacy programme by himself, without being directed via the radio. The *equipe*, therefore, had quite naturally tried to develop other activities, which could be more easily sustained during their absence, and their work evolved into a programme of community development and leadership training. They found a justification for this in the general trend of thinking in the Movement away from 'mere' literacy work and towards *conscientização*.

In this *sistema* four-day training courses *in the communities* were held as early as mid-1963. Typical headings of the different sessions or discussion groups included

economic reality: *latifúndio-minifúndio*; lack of agrarian credit for the small producer; imperialism and trusts: exploitation of region by region and country by country. Political reality: why do only people with money get elected? Social reality: reactionary and progressive forces. The latter: peasants, workers and students.[3]

Further discussions focused on agrarian reform, rural trade unions, and peasant struggles. All this was not yet, at that time, called *Animação Popular*, and in some important respects there were substantial differences from the full-blown product—especially in the conscious avoidance, later on, of the imposition on the participants of a quite specific programme.

But AnPo was actively pushed beyond the necessities of one or two *sistemas* without a transmitter, and it should by now be more than evident that various feed-back processes were at work in the Movement, whose elements—populist ideology, AnPo, and non-directiveness, shortly to be discussed—led to the wholesale reorientation of the Movement on the *povo*. The community was supposed to take over, not merely the activities, but also the very decisions on what to do.

In no circumstances must we take the leadership of any group or community in which we have been acting. . . . Our work will be that of advising. We must confine ourselves to making available to the community, through its leaders, those data and techniques to which they have not, so far, had access. . . . Thus the changes will not be brought from the outside, by strangers to the

[3] From a contemporary document of the *equipe*.

community, but will derive from a movement from within, the result of a stand taken by the members of the community themselves.[4]

MEB's personnel must not be tempted into taking over the role to be played by the community's own leaders: during discussions or planning sessions they may help by giving information—but the final decision of the group or community must be respected, even if the supervisor disagrees.[5]

The introduction of non-directive techniques

Perhaps even more important than the development of programmes and activities under the heading of *Animação Popular* were various non-directive techniques introduced right from the start into MEB's *treinamentos*. Those reponsible at the CNBB for the earliest training courses for radio-school *sistemas*, held shortly before the decision was taken to set up MEB on a national scale, began to experiment with these techniques, developed in the United States within the framework of group dynamics. They had been made familiar with the work in this field through a young Brazilian social psychologist who had returned in 1960 from studying in France. Together they had formed a small working group with a view to introducing these techniques into Catholic Action and other relevant organizations linked with the CNBB.[6] They encountered much opposition.

These official Catholic organizations always had been rather paternalistic and rigid. People who joined were more or less told what to do and even how to do it. The result was a lack of autonomy, independence, and open-mindedness on the part of the members. This situation was conducive neither to successful learning, nor to the development of a critical approach to the world. The new basic education efforts could hardly hope to operate effectively with such people. Hence the concern, right from the beginning of basic education by radio, even before the plan existed to cover the entire country through one national organization, to ensure that those working in this field would be adequately prepared to fulfil their tasks in harmony with the new 'basic education outlook'. That was already then clearly different from the

---

[4] MEB, *Seminario de AnPo: conclusões sôbre fundamentação* (1965), p. 16.
[5] Ibid.
[6] The following discussion on the historical origins of non-directiveness in MEB is based on various interviews with members of this working group, who later became part of the top leadership of MEB.

one prevailing in the traditional Catholic lay organizations. It was in this context that certain of the findings of social psychologists regarding the dynamics of small groups seemed relevant, and the following ideas came to constitute the theoretical basis for the *treinamentos* of MEB.[7]

When the members of a small group are allowed to interact in a totally unstructured manner, solving problems or reaching a consensus is often a long and tortuous process. During this process the members of the group lay bare to the trained observer—the discussion leader—personality traits or defences which often hinder the accurate perception of reality or the establishment of relationships. *Ex-post-facto* analysis of the group's interaction by the leader and the group members will frequently bring to light the reasons for earlier blockages, difficulties, and conflicts. One of the central ideas of group dynamics, whether concerned with learning or with therapy, is that actually living through these difficulties helps group members to understand them, and to integrate new behaviour patterns and attitudes into their personality structure. This idea, as various others in group dynamics (such as that of the importance of transference phenomena between members of the group and its leader), is adapted from psycho-analytic theory.

The leadership of MEB did not turn to group dynamics because they intended, or desired, to subject all new recruits to a process of psycho-analytic group therapy. They were, in fact, aware of the danger that these techniques could set in motion psychological processes among the participants, which would be hazardous to their mental health if not controlled by a competent psychologist or psychiatrist. Consequently the kinds of situations likely to encourage the emergence of problems from the deepest and most central core of personality were consciously avoided—and certainly at no *treinamento* was the *exploration* in a group of basic psycho-analytic patterns encouraged. For MEB the lessons of group dynamics were lessons in *learning* theory; non-directive methods helped ensure a fuller comprehension of one's defences against new ideas or new ways of acting, and ultimately led to a fuller acceptance of them. If a group had been left to muddle through hours and hours of discussion, getting completely bogged down, the eventual discovery by the group itself of why this

[7] They were derived, *i.a.* from the following sources: A. P. Hare, & others, *Small Groups* (New York, 1955); M. B. Miles. *Learning to Work in Groups* (New York, 1959); W. R. Bion, *Experiences in Groups* (London, 1959).

had happened would be of much greater help to understanding and learning than early interference and advice.

Non-directive techniques were first employed at the very top of the Movement, in the *treinamentos* which preceded the setting up of new *sistemas*. The next step was a logical one: to use the same methods at the *sistema* level, when preparing the *monitores* for their share in the work. Finally non-directiveness was also to become the MEB-sponsored norm governing the discussions in the communities, when the peasants examined some aspect of their life-situation in the presence of the *monitor* or of a supervisor. So gradually the Movement developed a set of techniques, applied at all levels of the organization, which derived from group dynamics, and which MEB came to regard as peculiarly their own. In the training of *monitores*, for example, the local *equipes* were urged to use a whole series of group techniques. There were to be round-table discussions, where each participant spoke in turn for a few minutes; 'socio-dramas',where the participants were required to act out various social roles which seemed relevant to their future work; panel discussions, which divided the trainees into a 'verbalizing group' and an 'observing group', with the former discussing a theme and the latter afterwards evaluating their discussion—followed by an inversion of the roles; small study groups; and, finally, the 'assembly', to bring together towards the end of the *treinamento* the various experiences of the participants. Prominence was also given to audio-visual aids, and to evaluation techniques.[8]

The changing interpretation of non-directiveness

There can be little doubt that during the first year or two of MEB's existence—say, at least, till the time of the *I Encontro de Coordenadores* in December 1962—these techniques were used by the leadership to achieve very specific goals. They were means to more effective learning and to the incorporation of newcomers into the Movement. But with the increasing acceptance in MEB of the new populist ideology, which said that only the wholly conscious and free choices of the people had moral (and political) validity, things that had hitherto been matters of technique alone were invested with a more profound meaning. The consequence was the gradual appearance of certain contradictions in the new position which could not be satisfactorily resolved. Though these contradictions were widely experienced as problems,

[8] MEB, *O Monitor* (n.d.), pp. 6 ff.

they were on the whole not clearly understood in the Movement. They revolved around the incompatibility between strongly held moral and political views about 'Brazilian reality' and philosophical views about the nature of man and (desirable) society on the one hand, and the prescription of full freedom of choice for the *povo* on the other, and in a parallel fashion around the differences between non-directiveness as a means to an end and non-directiveness as a goal in itself.

The logical implication of non-directive populism was that the cadres of MEB were obliged fully to accept whatever was decided by the people after they had been helped to discover the various courses of action open to them. Thus the earlier-quoted pre-1964 pamphlet on the *monitor* mentioned the following among the aims of the *treinamento*:

To supply data which will make it possible for the trainee to verify his personal responsibility and his role of agent in history. This will enable him to choose between *either accepting the existing situation*, or attacking at the roots the unjust and inhuman set-up under which he is suffering [my italics].[9]

Obviously no one in MEB seriously expected the peasants to prefer the *status quo*, and the suggestion that this was a realistic alternative smacked of self-deception. Openness on the *kind* of change the *povo* would choose was, however, another matter. There is no reason to doubt that there were people in MEB who were genuinely relativistic about this, though often the corollary was the (manifestly unwarranted) assumption that the *povo*, once they had understood the facts, would inevitably choose a course of action which was in some inherent sense 'good' or 'right'. But many others, and especially those who held elaborate and quite specific views regarding the working of the present system and the desirable shape of things to come, must have found it more difficult to maintain a position which left the future entirely open, which postulated the people as the sole source as well as arbiter of wisdom and change. Hence the emergence of a disturbing tension between the ideal of the fully self-promoting man, and the desire to present an interpretation of reality which would 'open a revolutionary perspective', a phrase which immediately preceded the quotation from the pamphlet on the *monitor* just given.[10]

[9] Ibid., p. 5.
[10] 'To open a revolutionary perspective' could be seen as the first step of political mobilization, which 'supplies some of the critical minima of information' (Nettl, p. 199). Nettl adds: 'The information in question will, indeed must, be crude, and the manner of communicating it blaring and repetitive if it is to succeed in fulfilling its purpose.' Adherence to populist non-directiveness makes political mobilization extremely difficult.

It seems that at first the tension was simply ignored. The *equipes*, who used non-directive techniques during *treinamentos* or visits to the communities, also presented many facts about the peasants' political and socio-economic position, and about the wider national or even international context. When faced with the new 'demands' of populism, they acted as if those facts were always quite 'objective', wholly free of choice-restricting implications. They therefore chose to disregard the unmistakable evaluations built into them, and the way these evaluations inevitably set the peasants on a particular course. This 'resolution' of the dilemma was occurring before the coup, when *conscientização* meant very specifically the 'opening of a revolutionary perspective' and when the hope of actually seeing the revolt of the *pólo dominado* was widespread—and from the vantage point of those days one can well understand that the revolutionary element dominated the non-directive one.[11]

Gradually, however, the populist objections to this ultimately directivist procedure gained the upper hand. The heart-searching on revolutionary tactics began soon after the Christian *débâcle* at the founding of the National Confederation of Workers in Agriculture, in December 1963. Then the coup wholly removed any remaining obstacles to fully fledged populist non-directiveness, as, for all practical purposes, it diminished the chances of revolutionary success to zero—at least for the foreseeable future. It is more than likely that this fact in itself explains to a large extent why the balance swung the other way. And so the next attempt to resolve the unresolvable dilemma came close, for a time, to sacrificing *conscientização* altogether. This occurred when the concept of non-directiveness, in the beginning applied only to the means used to achieve certain goals, then extended to the goals themselves, was finally stretched to cover the contextual facts as well. MEB's cadres became increasingly stingy with facts: they, too, had to be 'discovered' in a free-floating learning process; to supply them unrequested also came to be seen as *massificação*.[12]

Facts may be neutral, but in most contexts their assertion is not. Nevertheless, some are better—more 'objectively'—established than others. And it is only when certain kinds of fact are available that certain kinds of decision become possible. Being stingy with facts can be 'functional' for learning; things discovered after a great deal of

[11] See the first general hypothesis on populism, below, pp. 267–8.
[12] An awareness of this was just emerging during the period of fieldwork among some of the more acute observers within MEB.

effort are more valuable to the individual, less likely to be forgotten, and more likely to be used. But the acquisition of new knowledge *about* the world is much less subject to the psychological processes of defence and rejection than the learning and unlearning of beliefs and attitudes, which relate the individual personality *to* the world. And with the former 'cognitive' type of learning it is not very long before the waste of time, the confusion, and the inefficiency of the round-about methods start weighing heavier than the gains to be had from non-directiveness. In the case of MEB, the excessive populist scruples over facts made *conscientização* substantially more difficult—and that at a time when the political circumstances in the country made it far from easy to begin with. Perhaps this was in some unexpected sense 'functional': it kept meetings muddling along rather aimlessly—but it kept them going—when there was very little that could have been accomplished in any case.

MEB only slowly learned that it had to live in some way with the contradictions which sprang from its desire for change and its com-mitment to populist non-directiveness, that no solution to the dilemma was possible beyond some kind of compromise. In the rest of this chapter and in the following two chapters, a range of situations will be examined, some encountered during the actual fieldwork, some reconstructed from interviews and documents, which illustrate the very central problem which the dilemma inherent in non-directive *conscientização* constituted for the Movement, from the highest level of the organization down to the lowest.

The *III Encontro Nacional de Coordenadores*

In April 1966, during the period of fieldwork for this study, a full-scale meeting of *coordenadores* took place (the first after the coup), with a view to discussing developments since 1964 and examining the future of the Movement. The situation at the time of this meeting was extremely serious. On the one hand it had become apparent that the Ministry of Education was increasingly reluctant to finance an effort considered 'subversive' by many, both in the armed forces and in the SNI (*Serviço Nacional de Informações*, the Brazilian counter-intelligence service). On the other hand there existed a growing desire on the part of the hierarchy to subordinate the *sistemas* more directly to the respec-tive diocesan bishops, at the expense of the control hitherto exercised by the *Nacional*: a development referred to in the Movement as its *diocesanização.* Were this latter development to come about, it would result, so the argument ran, in the loss of the common perspective, ideology, and programme of action—it would break up the Movement into a number of *MEBzinhos* (little MEBs), each with its own outlook on the task in hand. It had been hard enough to maintain something of the radical drive in the Movement after the coup; with the power of the *Nacional* reduced, many local bishops could be expected to impose an orientation which would be hesitant, careful, paternalistic, and emphatically anti-revolutionary. MEB would once again be reduced to what it had fought so hard to escape: a palliative.

About a week before the *Encontro* was to begin, discussions were initiated at the *Nacional* regarding the mechanics of the meeting, which was to last for at least a week. It was soon agreed that at an early stage of the *Encontro* information would be needed from each *sistema*, regarding the relations with the civilian and military authorities and with the church, the current evaluation by the local cadres of their effectiveness in the field and of the main obstacles to the fulfilment of their task, and, finally, the present attitudes of the peasants towards MEB. But from there on, these preparatory discussions—in which I participated, together with all members of the *Nacional*—produced a good deal of disagreement about procedure. That disagreement revolved essentially around the issue of non-directiveness. Some, mainly the more radical members of the *Equipe Técnica*, interpreted non-directiveness from the perspective of populist ideology. In the circumstances they wanted minimum 'interference' by the *Nacional*; they argued, moreover, that especially in view of the gravity of the crisis the participants should undergo the 'educational experience' of gradually discovering for and by themselves the essential and inescapable facts about MEB's current situation. Others pointed to the limitations of this procedure, and to the 'costliness' of being over-stingy with facts.

Almost all believed that the *Encontro* would have to choose between winding up the Movement and continuing to work under the constant threat of having to give way on a growing number of principles for the sake of survival. They agreed that this decision would have to be based on a clear understanding of the hopes of MEB till 1964 and the frustration of many of these hopes during the two years that had lapsed since the coup, and the question was raised whether the meeting should not be presented with a 'schema' for discussion in order to achieve that understanding. Although this idea was set aside by the *Nacional* after much argument—the radicals objected to it as the first step on the road to *massificação*—there remained much concern that too unplanned a meeting might get bogged down before it could begin serious consideration of the really important questions.

During the preparatory discussions account was also taken of the expectations attributed to the participants. Especially for those who had been in MEB from an early date, these were likely to flow from the identification of the techniques of non-directiveness with the very essence of the method peculiar to MEB, and one might add: underpinned by an ideological commitment to populism. Thus the suggestion was made that the representatives of the *sistemas* and perhaps even of the *Estaduais* would probably consider any ordering of the discussion by the *Nacional* as a limitation of their freedom to decide themselves how to run the *Encontro*. All their *treinamentos* had conditioned them to expect this freedom; if plans regarding the order of the meeting and its agenda were to be presented to them ready-made, they would surely complain of *massificação*. Here again, however, those preparing the *Encontro* reminded themselves that important business would have to be transacted. *Massificação* or not, the participants were sure to complain at the end if the *Nacional* allowed the meetings to degenerate into disorder.

These, then, were unmistakable signs of the tension between the requirements of efficiency and the exercise of a minimum of authority from the top on the one hand, and the demands of MEB's non-directive ideology, of the vision of MEB as a 'way of life' rather than a bureaucratic organization, on the other. These tensions were, incidentally, also present within the *Nacional*. Some expressed the view in private (also during the preparations for the *Encontro*) that the final decisions were in any case taken at the top and that the whole business of consultation and joint policy-making in the end foundered on the authority of the CDN and the Secretary-General. Nevertheless, it was impressive how constant attempts were made by all those involved honestly to resolve these obviously insoluble dilemmas, to reconcile authority with populism, or efficiency with participation. It is, moreover, worth remarking that the striving to be true to the Movement's practical and theoretical principles, as seen in these preparations, was in no way exceptional. On the contrary: it was encountered at all levels in almost all situations I witnessed during the period of fieldwork.

While the concern with non-directiveness was general in MEB, the people most likely to do battle for full freedom and democracy from below, and to raise the hue and cry of *massificação* whenever they regarded a proposal or disposition of the leadership as running counter to those principles, tended to have certain distinctive characteristics. On the one hand they were those who, even if they had never actually been members of AP, at least whole-heartedly subscribed to its pre-1964 populist viewpoint. On the other hand this extreme non-directiveness was usually proclaimed with most forcefulness by those who were not, at any particular level or on any particular occasion, in a position of ultimate responsibility. This seemed to be true despite the fact that at the state and local levels there was a good deal of rotation of functions, and fully democratic decision-making within the *equipes*.

At the actual *Encontro* this two-way correlation was clearly visible. The opening was performed by one of the members of the *Coordenação Nacional*, with a speech stressing the need for information and help from the *sistemas*, represented at the meeting by about twenty participants. Then a timetable and broad agenda were presented and a brief statement was made about the gravity of the decisions to be taken (whether to continue the Movement or to wind it up); within half an hour from the start of the proceedings the timetable and the agenda had been accepted virtually without discussion. Then *coordenadores* from two *Estaduais*, people whose usual task on their home ground was to keep things moving, made suggestions which would have imposed a tighter order on the meeting than the proposals of the *Nacional*. Immediately two members of the *Equipe Técnica* justified the original free set-up, referring to the need for spontaneity and the requirement of bringing out the many different facets of MEB's local reality. To this the *coordenador estadual* retorted: 'That is psychologically beautiful, but is it really useful and viable in the present circumstances?' The meeting quickly agreed to put a discussion schema on the blackboard, but the *Equipe Técnica* insisted that all should feel free not to follow it. A list of the data needed, as discussed in the preparatory meetings of the *Nacional*, was then displayed on the board; in effect, that schema came to be followed in the presentation by each *sistema* of its report on the situation in its area. This development much upset those members of the *Equipe Técnica* who had most strongly rejected the original suggestions of structuring, and during the first day of the *Encontro* there was a good deal of resentment on their part, which found expression in frequent allegations, made mainly in private, of *massificação*.

The *Encontro* lasted ten days. Looking back over its deliberations one has to conclude that an effective balance was struck between imposed structure and populist anarchy, leading to achievements which were quite considerable, though perhaps less impressive when seen from the vantage point of hindsight. During the first three days each participant presented a survey of the situation in his *sistema* or state. This brought into the open (a fact well known at the *Nacional*) the substantial differences in approach and circumstances between *sistemas* operating in the various areas of the country. These variations were a result of time-lags in the establishment of the *sistemas* and the consequent lack of experience and sophistication of the more recently-founded *equipes*. They were also related to differing social and political conditions, including the views of the local bishops, and to conditions which in turn had affected the extent to which the equipes had espoused political radicalism and populism and had emancipated themselves from close clerical supervision.

The main division in the Movement was that between the more recently-established *sistemas* in the North, and the older *sistemas* of the North-East and Centre-West. The former had been working in areas where the *latifúndio* and its associated social and political structures were relatively rare and where there had been comparatively little political agitation before 1964. The latter had mainly been operating in places where the exploitation of the peasants was more severe; they had been deeply involved in the radicalization of the Movement during the last two years before the coup, and had, during those years, flung themselves body and soul into the 'opening of a revolutionary perspective'. Their representatives were most concerned during the *Encontro* with the restrictions on MEB's work and the erosion of its influence; they were the ones least willing to compromise with the authorities, whether civilian, military or ecclesiastical; they were most adamant about the need for national unity and most outspoken in their rejection of *diocesanização*. Most of the *coordenadores* from the North, on the other hand, started out by being much more inclined to stress the educational aspects of the Movement's work, in contrast to seeing *conscientização* as the first step towards structural change. They also gave prominence to past achievements and to the continuing potential future benefits of MEB's work, including those for individual radio-school students who might achieve social mobility through their attainment of literacy. They were, finally, a good deal less worried about the probability of a growing frustration of radical aspirations.

At the end of the presentation by each *sistema* of the survey of its achievements and difficulties, one of the members of the *Equipe*

Técnica presented a summary of the findings; then the plenary divided into four smaller groups. It was there that the participants were really confronted with each other for the first time, and the principles of non-directiveness found most active expression. The discussions ranged widely for a day, and although the conclusions of the four groups all pointed in the direction of the wish to continue the Movement's activities, not all of them demanded equally strict safeguards for MEB's ideological purity and practical freedom of action. This divergence resulted at least in part from a fact which became obvious during further plenary sessions: most of the newer recruits among the *coordenadores* had clearly not fully digested many of the more general principles of the Movement's *Weltanschauung*—and this was particularly true of the views in which MEB's populism found practical expression. As a consequence substantial time had to be spent at the *Encontro* in attempts by members of the *Nacional* and by one of the *Coordenadores Estaduais* to clarify these matters, especially those regarding the commitment of MEB to basic transformations in Brazilian society. These more recently recruited leaders from the North (significantly one of them was a priest and another a nun, a very exceptional situation in the Movement)[13] also found it difficult to understand the dissatisfaction of many others in the Movement with the structural links with the hierarchy: in contrast to those others, they did not feel that they were dependent upon bishops on the whole much more cautious than they were themselves.

On the fifth and sixth days of the *Encontro* it thus became visible that there were considerable differences of opinion in the Movement regarding certain essential questions. These differences emerged all the more clearly once the *Nacional* and the *Estaduais* effectively stopped intervening by means of information and guidance, letting the meeting find its own way, true to the central principles of non-directiveness. The participants, in a sense, turned inwards; and the voices of dissent —represented mainly by the two clerical *coordenadores* from the North —for a while dominated the proceedings. The result was a truly awful muddle, a complete lack of clarity as to any decisions about the future that might come from the *Encontro*. Further small group meetings and more direct personal confrontations ensued, interspersed with plenary sessions.

By this time it had become possible to discern in the concrete reality

[13] There was another priest at the meeting, representing a *sistema* in the North-East; all others in positions of leadership in the Movement were laymen.

of the *Encontro* the benefits as well as the practical limitations of non-directiveness. As one session had followed upon another, a consensus slowly emerged among the Movement's top leadership (the *Nacional* and the *Estaduais*) that the *Encontro* should move towards the adoption of some formal statement. That statement should make plain to the bishops of the CDN—still very much the ultimate authority in the organization—the views of the lay cadres of MEB on its future. It should spell out in so many words the conditions in which they would be willing to continue staffing the Movement—conditions rejecting *diocesanização*, and reaffirming the Movement's task as that of helping, by way of *conscientização* of the peasants, to bring about basic structural transformations in Brazilian society.

But the emergence of a consensus on the need for such a statement did not attest a common view of its consequences. Some of those in the highest ranks of MEB, mainly people directly familiar with the situation in the regions where the post-1964 reaction had been fiercest, had come to the conclusion that only a miracle could save the Movement and that closure had become virtually inevitable. To their manner of thinking continued operation of MEB, according to the basic ideas which had been developed in the Movement's five years of existence, had been made impossible by the political conditions in the country. For them, the projected statement would serve to reaffirm MEB's principles in the face of by then overwhelming odds, uphold its sense of integrity, prevent compromises which they considered shameful, and be the prelude to the closing down of the Movement as a national organization.

Others in the top leadership, however, were most reluctant to see this course followed. They either believed MEB could still play a genuinely positive role, or that the perpetuation of a national body in touch with the peasantry was so useful in itself that it mattered little if it had few direct results. For them, the formal statement was aimed at staving off further erosion of MEB's capacity to act; at the very least it was to serve the function of a bargaining instrument *vis-à-vis* the bishops or the Ministry of Education. Both groups, however, realized that the meeting would not produce such a statement if left to find its way non-directively.

Hence guidance seemed to be called for, and this despite the fact that the discussions of the last days had brought greater mutual understanding between the two currents which had emerged among the representatives of the *sistemas* at the *Encontro*. On the one side were the *sistemas* which felt that without the backing of the strong central authority of the *Nacional* their activities would be deflected by the local ecclesiastical powers towards a more politically neutral line, and towards greater emphasis on religious instruction. On the other were the *sistemas* (mostly from the North) who believed that much useful work could be done even if, as *MEBzinhos*, they were to be on their own. The former, as a result of those interminable discussions, had come to a more genuine understanding of the very different conditions under which the Northern *sistemas* operated, and had consequently become more tolerant of their approach, while the Northerners had slowly learned to identify themselves with the Movement as a whole, and had thus moved towards a willingness to join in any likely demands for the maintenance of national unity and central lay executive authority. But, it must be repeated, without positive steering, such a demand would not have come to be articulated.

On the eighth working day of the *Encontro* a conclave of the *Nacional* and the *Estaduais* analysed this situation. They examined the *de facto* absence of national unity, and discussed at length whether, and if so how, the *sistemas* could be persuaded to accept a common statement unanimously. During this conclave various strategies were discussed, in spite of the protests against this threatened *massificação*, especially from two members of the *Equipe Técnica*. These kept saying that the participants should 'discover' the right course of action wholly by themselves, and that any guidance or gentle persuasion from above would leave the meeting without 'true' agreement or 'full and conscious' adherence to the ideas expressed. This viewpoint was perhaps extreme, but it influenced the other sufficiently to result in a compromise in which the non-directive element was once again given prominence. It was decided that the *Encontro* would be split into three groups, more homogeneous in terms of outlook than those that had been formed before, to discuss, in the presence of members of the *Nacional*, exactly what was meant by national unity and how it could be defended. But before they started their deliberations the groups were given guidance regarding the need to reach a strong and united position *vis-à-vis* the CDN, a piece of not altogether overt persuasion on behalf of the national leadership which was brought off admirably by one of those who had most tenaciously held out for the maximum degree of non-directiveness.

The compromise paid off: the three groups came up with remarkably similar conclusions, which formed the basis for an easily drafted and whole-heartedly endorsed statement to the CDN. That statement is worth reproducing in full. It read as follows:

1. We understand MEB to be an educational movement, which identifies itself with the aspirations, of the Brazilian people, and is based on a national unity of structure, methodology, and line of work.
2. We consider:
   (a) that within MEB's present structure basic contradictions exist, in respect of the interpretations of its objectives and the utilization of its means, between the hierarchy and the laymen professionally engaged in the Movement;
   (b) that the interpretation of MEB's line, as lived by the *equipes* and consolidated in this *III Encontro de Coordenadores*, can be secured in the *sistemas* only if these can count on the cover and support of the existing national structure;
   (c) that this national structure ensures that the Movement is recognized, nationally as well as internationally, as a force;
   (d) that it is certain that MEB's experience—which has been a response to a global set of problems of national scope—will not be fully pursued, nor its objectives realized, if the Movement breaks up into local efforts.
3. Therefore, we conclude that it is necessary to maintain national unity regarding line of work, structure, and methodology, though not necessarily in respect of [sources of] finance. This unity should be realized through a *Coordenação Nacional* which would maintain its overall administrative autonomy, and which would guarantee centralization of effort, and a unified perspective of work.

The results of ten days' hard work, with hours of involved, often seemingly senseless and repetitive, discussions was the forging of a unity of purpose, common commitment, and sense of identity among the score of *coordenadores*, many of whom had begun with an almost exclusive preoccupation with the problems of their own *sistema*. It also produced the laymen's most direct challenge to the bishops so far in the Movement's history.

But after all the hard work, the achievement was to turn out to be rather hollow. This resulted in part from the ambiguity that remained in respect of the *purpose* of the statement: it has been seen how at least two interpretations were put on the probable (and desirable) consequences of sending this message to the CDN. Unity in the Movement did not go so far as to achieve clarity or agreement on the manner in which to proceed in the future, and as a result the course eventually taken by events was one which was not in accordance with the hopes of the proponents of either interpretation. Within a few months after the *Encontro* the Movement had shrunk almost beyond recognition. And it was the *sistemas* in the North-East and Centre of the country that disappeared, those which had been the foci of radicalism in the Movement, those which, at the *Encontro*, had been most adamant against sacrificing any of MEB's principles—in theory or practice—for the sake of survival. Within a few months, too, the diocesan bishops had pushed the remainder of the Movement a long way on the road of *diocesanização*.

In the end, all the efforts of the *III Encontro* made very little difference to the course of events. Although its participants had opted against further compromise, they had *also* chosen to continue, and not to close down there and then, as a national organization. But, as was seen at the conclusion of the previous chapter, once the *sistemas* of the North-East and Centre-West had been eliminated, the centre of gravity shifted to the North. And that brought with it a change of emphasis in the kinds of ideas stressed and activities undertaken by the Movement —a change that in the light of the deliberations at the *Encontro* cannot but be regarded as a compromise. For MEB's survival that compromise was necessary; in the process, however, the Movement lost some of its most salient pre-1964 characteristics.

Non-directiveness in decision making, and true participation of all levels in the formulation of policies, must somehow be reconciled both with internal authority structures and with external circumstances. A lack of awareness of the weight of these can lead to a deceptive feeling of achievement; but in itself the manner in which decisions are reached does not guarantee that they can be implemented. In the end, it was the institutional structures, and especially the relative power of the bishops, the government, and the laymen, which determined the future of the Movement. And despite very significant continuities, the course followed after 1966 clearly meant the sacrifice of past ideas and commitments.

12

Populism and Non-Directiveness at the Grass-Roots, I

A view of Franqueira

To examine the way in which populism and non-directiveness were implemented by the people actually working with the peasants, and the practical difficulties they experienced, it is necessary to turn to a rather detailed discussion of the experiences of one *sistema*, situated in the *sertão* of the North-East, operating from a town which will be called Franqueira.

Franqueira, a *município* with an area of over 2,000 sq. miles, had, in the mid-1960s, a sizeable urban centre, with over 15,000 inhabitants. It lies in a region still largely characterized by more or less traditional patron–dependant relations, which continues to be a stronghold of *coronelismo*. The town's life is dominated, politically and economically, by one family, the Barretos. They own the only two substantial local factories, which employ between them a few hundred people, and the largest trading establishment in town—which, in the absence of a bank, also fulfils important credit functions. They own the town's public-address system, which blankets Franqueira's central area with a continuous stream of music, publicity, and news, and have the local press in their pockets. They are involved in various further ventures, including the main building and engineering firm. Needless to say, the Barretos are also very large landowners. They are prominent in politics, occupying positions of power at the municipal, state, and even national level. The family's ramifications in the public domain are worth relating *in extenso*.

The core of the clan consists of a number of brothers. At the time of the fieldwork most of them occupied some position of public power. One brother, the managing director of the family industry, held the post of secretary of the regional development board—a federal institution. One was mayor of Franqueira. One was president of its town council. One was deputy for Franqueira in the state Assembly, and finally one was prominent and influential in politics at the state level. They were surrounded by a number of outer 'satellites', some relatives, some not. These included a brother-in-law, the head of the town's building and engineering firm (who had been mayor of the town a few years before), and two sisters, first cousins of the Barretos: both were teachers, and between them they ran the town's educational system— one was head of Franqueira's primary school, the other was in charge of all secondary education.

Non-directiveness at the *equipe* level

MEB Franqueira[1] was organized during the second half of 1962.[2] It was subordinated to the region's *Estadual*, which organized the *treinamento* for the original *equipe* and which generally acted as mediator with the *Nacional*.[3] During the early stages of operation non-directiveness as a technique or populism as an ideology had not yet grown deep roots in the Movement. At first members of the *equipe* were being appointed at the behest of priests or bishops; *monitores* were selected by the *equipe* because of their supposed teaching gifts (quite a few were local school teachers), and without meaningful consultation with the members of the community concerned. The latter were primarily regarded as potential pupils. During the first year activity was concentrated on literacy training and 'general knowledge': a mixture of hygiene, domestic science, agricultural techniques, and civics. It soon became apparent, however, that people were not responding to broadcasts on these subjects. The content of the general

[1] The decision to spend a fortnight working with the *equipe* of MEB Franqueira was made after a good deal of discussion with members of the *Nacional* and of the *Estadual* concerned. This decision was reached not because the *sistema* was considered to be 'typical' or 'representative' of the whole Movement in 1966: no *sistema* could be typical of MEB as a whole, with its diverse experiences. But the conclusion seemed justified that MEB Franqueira presented many characteristics which would throw light on some of the most interesting and important questions: relations with the civil and ecclesiastical authorities, development and difficulties of the work with the *povo*, and the extent of identification with the nationally-proclaimed line of theory and action.

[2] The following historical account is based mainly on two collective interviews with the *equipe*, of about three hours each, held towards the end of my stay on 2 June 1966. Checks for reliability were later made by means of inspection of documentary evidence (letters, minutes of *treinamentos*, etc.), and by means of further individual interviews.

[3] No one of the *Nacional* had, in fact, visited MEB Franqueira in the almost four years that had passed between its foundation and mid-1966: all contacts with members of the *Nacional* had taken place either during *treinamentos* at the *Estadual* or during individual visits of members of the local *equipe* to the state or national headquarters.

knowledge lessons did not appeal to them; it did not relate to felt needs, nor did it stimulate any new interest. The immediate worries of the communities were different from those discussed over the radio.

The situation was changed in stages. First the local *equipe* had to learn more about the necessity to take account of the peasants' 'real needs', and to interpret these in the light of the existing social, economic, and political institutions. This happened mainly as a result of *treinamentos* conducted by the *Estadual*, where the 'discovery of Brazilian reality', and the necessity to see this reality from the perspective of the peasants—essential foundations of populism—were given emphasis from early 1963 on. Simultaneously the lessons of group dynamics were being assiduously followed in these *treinamentos*. This was so at least in terms of the rather self-conscious application of certain techniques used in order to achieve the (predetermined) goal of getting the *equipe* to share the views of the *Estadual*. One thing and another alerted the local *equipe* to the need for a change in orientation. The teaching of general knowledge was dropped. Instead the *equipe*, through personal contacts, cultivated a receptiveness towards the different problems of each local community, and a willingness to help these communities organize themselves for action to change their circumstances.[4]

But the shift towards community orientation, populism, and non-directiveness did not occur without difficulties. During most of 1963, and in the early months of 1964, there was recurrent dissension between MEB Franqueira and the *Estadual*. Most of the latter's experience derived from the *zona da mata*, with its proletarianized rural workers, its grossly exploitative agrarian capitalism, its fast-growing *sindicalismo*, and its total lack of land for the peasants. The members of the *Estadual* could hardly help being greatly influenced by their more immediate surroundings. Their most frequent contacts were with others operating among the sugar-plantation proletariat, or with people working among the thousands of migrants in the cities' shanty towns. Hence the core problems of 'Brazilian reality', in so far as they were not seen as pertaining to foreign exploitation, were often couched in terms relevant to the structure of the *zona da mata*, and derived from the needs or demands of the peasants there. Change was seen to be intimately linked with agrarian reform, unionization, and especially politicization.

For the *equipe* of Franqueira all this was rather remote. But in the

---

[4] It is worth remembering that in the Movement at large this was the period when education for rural *sindicalismo* was beginning to take on greater importance.

first year of operation much of it was non-directively rammed down their throats in *treinamentos* by the *Estadual*. As a result, the first change from the unsuccessful general knowledge lessons was an approach to the peasants which turned out to generate equally little enthusiasm—because it completely failed to refer to the 'reality' they were experiencing. Gradually—in the second phase—the local *equipe* began to resist the approach of the *Estadual*. They maintained that the concerns of the peasants in their area were, as yet, remote from aggressive unionism or agrarian reform, and that much groundwork had to be done before these matters could be effectively broached to the peasants and even more before they would be spontaneously raised by the latter themselves. As a reward for their efforts the *Estadual* called MEB Franqueira 'alienated'.

Though wrong, that appreciation was at least understandable. In this period the primary interest of the *Estadual* was to transmit to others the awareness of the structure and dynamics of 'Brazilian reality' which they themselves had only very recently arrived at (it must be remembered that the significant collective experience in MEB in that regard was the *I Encontro Nacional de Coordenadores*, of December 1962). The fusion of group dynamics and populism had not yet taken place, mainly because the latter was only just emerging as an articulate ideology, though *massificação* was already beginning to be a term of abuse. The Franqueira *equipe*, looking back on those times, remembered how members of the *Nacional*, participating in *treinamentos* at the *Estadual*, were placing ever greater stress on non-directiveness as the end of 1963 approached. To the *Estadual*, however, non-directiveness in those days still seems to have been little more than a collection of techniques learned from the *Nacional*, which were imputed to have beneficial effects on *treinamentos*. One of the means involved was the panel method.

They would make us sit down in a panel, and tell us to discuss some topic or idea, often something we knew hardly anything about. Like: 'Discuss the concept of bourgeoisie'. What the hell did we know about the bourgeoisie? So we all got very fed up with those panel discussions. And the worst thing was that the freedom of those discussions was only apparent: those who were holding the *treinamento* knew exactly what they wanted to get to, and we obligingly arrived at their predetermined conclusions.[5]

But the local *equipe* fought for their own viewpoint, and for their

[5] From the collective interview on 2 June.

right to be different in the light of the realities of the *sertão*, realities which had been discovered in a dialectic with the ideas, deriving from the *zona da mata*, expressed by the *Estadual*. In this way they slowly moved towards a genuine understanding of the situation of the *povo* in their area. They also moved to an integration of the ideas of non-directiveness and populism, mainly as a result of the confrontation with the *Estadual*, sometime before the latter had developed in that direction. No doubt a significant factor in this connection was the less explosive nature of the situation in the Franqueira area, and the consequently less intensive commitment there to revolutionary change on the part of MEB's cadres, who could more easily accept the implications of populist non-directiveness.[6]

As a result of the clashes over these matters between the *Estadual* and *Franqueira* (and no doubt other *sistemas* as well) the former's approach was modified in turn: the attempts at manipulation decreased from early 1964 and soon ceased completely. Here again the political circumstances after the coup must have greatly facilitated this shift, which had been given its first real impetus when the negative aspects of the (very directivist) rush into *sindicatos* had sunk in. This thrust from below over non-directiveness was reinforced from above by the populist ideology, which reached full maturity in the Movement shortly after the coup. Over the next two years the horror of *massificação* increased until it assumed the overwhelming proportions (even 'facts' were to be discovered or asked for) examined in the previous chapter. To a large extent this also occurred in Franqueira. Despite the difficulties that arose in the attempts to implement the ideas of non-directiveness among the cadres of the Movement, the overall results were no doubt positive. A group of people had come into being who had learned to think for themselves and to let others do the same. That group was incorporated in an organization which had increasingly managed to ensure a genuine two-way flow of ideas, constantly keeping the channels of communication open, and to maintain an overall unity of views which was quite remarkable considering the vastness of the territory covered and the great differences in background among its members.

Some attention must now be devoted to the experience with non-

---

[6] This fact is consistent with the first and second general hypotheses on populism, as formulated below, pp. 267–8. The Franqueira political context gave little hope for an early participation in power, nor was there any real 'threat' from non-populist ('massifying') radicals.

directiveness at the last and most crucial level, that of the *povo* them-selves. For the different *equipes*, local, state, and national, the basis of non-directiveness was to be found in the techniques deriving from group dynamics. The relevance of the populist ideology had really been indirect—it had, in a sense, reinforced the commitment to non-directiveness by a kind of halo effect: everybody at a lower echelon became *povo* for those higher up, and the *povo*'s wishes, views, and ideas had to be respected. At the very grass-roots, on the other hand, populism was the primary consideration. There what really mattered was to 'let the people speak', and to let them decide for themselves; the techniques of non-directiveness became the tools for the implemen-tation of this ideological prescription. In the following pages the measure in which this emphasis on non-directiveness worked under various circumstances, and the extent to which it aided or hindered the achieve-ment of a significant amount of 'speaking' and 'deciding' on the part of the people, will be examined.

Peasants and landowners in the Franqueira area

Franqueira presented an environment where traditional beliefs and attitudes were still widely held by peasants and landowners alike. The region had hardly been touched by the social and political ferment of the early 1960s. The peasantry, though poor, was not destitute; in the *sertão* few men were landless wage-earners, and no concentrations of population existed like those of the sugar-cane workers in the *zona da mata*. *Sindicatos* had come into being here and there, but their activities were hampered by the complex nature of tenure and labour relations in the area, and no simple pattern of bargaining over wages or working conditions could emerge. The problems of the peasants varied greatly. Often they revolved around the terms on which land-lords were willing to put land at their disposal. Renting of plots was fairly widespread, but the more usual method was some form of share-cropping, a burdensome arrangement for the peasant. Though the landlord financed the purchase of seeds, fertilizer (if any), etc., the tenant was charged for his share of the costs at harvest time. The yield was also divided between landlord and tenant, most frequently in equal shares; if the harvest failed (far from unusual given the difficult climatic and primitive technological conditions of the area), the peasant's share in the costs was carried over to the next year. This resulted in widespread indebtedness of peasants to landlords—a convenient way of ensuring the permanent availability of a labour force.

In many parts of the area, where cattle-raising is the most important large-scale economic activity, peasants also complained of damage done to their crops by the free-roaming cattle of the landlords. Responsibility for fencing in the tilled area devolved on the tenants, but poverty prevented them from using materials such as barbed wire, and wooden fences were both hard to erect and less effective. Naturally, there was a good deal of grumbling about these matters, but most peasants continued to regard them in 1966 as part of life, immutably fixed in the order of things, situations one just had to endure. From time to time a personal complaint, better perhaps a humble request for consideration, would be lodged with the landlord concerned: few had any illusions about the effect. Usually nothing happened; sometimes the occasion would be used for a show of force (for example when the landlord removed his cattle, but raised the rent next year to a level which the peasant involved could no longer afford); only seldom was the result a happy one for the tenant.

Conscientização, the process of making the peasants aware that existing structures, traditional modes of life, and long-accepted oppressive or exploitative practices are not God-given or immutable, is a most difficult task. But occasionally situations occur which stir even long-suffering peasants to seek redress. The outcome of such protests are of great importance in determining their general receptivity to any message of change through their own efforts, in a direction freely determined by themselves. If protests over such 'traumatic' events bring no favourable results to them, they cannot really be expected to become convinced that change is possible in the even more widely accepted aspects of life.

A concrete case from the Franqueira area may serve as an example. Sometime late in 1961 one of the large landowners, a member of the Barreto family, started to fence in a tract of land of several thousand acres, which had hitherto been freely used by the peasants living in the district for cattle grazing and free passage. As rainfall is scarce in the *sertão*, a great asset of the tract had been the fact that it contained over thirty lakes. The enclosure brought an outcry in the adjoining communities. It resulted in the necessity of making vast detours— something not to be made light of where people go from place to place largely on foot, and at best by mule—and had substantially reduced the area in which the cattle owned by the peasants could be put to graze.

The matter was taken to a local priest, who brought in a lawyer from a church-sponsored rural advisory organization in the capital of the state; events culminated in a public discussion meeting, at which various Barretos and their lawyer made an unexpected appearance. The meeting ended in pandemonium, with both sides waving sheaves of paper at each other to 'prove' ownership or rights of usage. But in the end no further action was taken by the peasants' lawyer, and the enclosure remained. The explanations I was given for this fact ranged from intimidation by the Barreto family to the wise dropping of an impossible case, depending on the social status and political views of the informant.

It is certainly probable that no peasant could have produced documentary evidence acceptable to a court of law to prove that he had clear rights in the area. Contracts had in the past more often than not been made orally, and most of the few titles to land held by peasants in Franqueira were not very firm. But it is equally probable that the Barretos rode roughshod over customary rights, and similarly would have stood no chance of proving their ownership in a court of law. There was only one important difference between their situation and that of the peasants. The Barretos had the means rapidly to erect a wire-mesh fence, and the economic and political power to ride out a challenge to the legality of their action: they were never confronted by a (state) government determined to support the case of the peasants by legal or political means. By 1966 the fence had been a *fait accompli* for a number of years—and no one any longer expected the *status quo* to change. By that time a good deal of bitterness still existed over this affair; its main effect, however, had been to reinforce the peasants' view that you could not really fight the *patrões*.

All this is merely to set the scene for the efforts of MEB Franqueira at *conscientização*; at helping the peasants to cut themselves loose from the habit of thinking in terms of requesting personal favours from the locally powerful; at teaching them to formulate their own problems and find their own solutions without waiting for directives from above or outside (whether *patrões* or MEB); and at making them see that united they could achieve much that was impossible to isolated individuals. Given circumstances such as those described, no one should be under any illusion that the task of MEB was easy. Not only were they trying to establish a wholly new mentality, but they were doing so in the face of overwhelming proof to the peasants that the *patrões* would in any case have their way whenever they wanted to.

The *patrões* remained in power, and they were determinedly opposed to any kind of 'agitation' which would 'provoke the less favoured to revolt against those who own something'. One of the spokesmen for the Barreto family (the mayor of Franqueira), declared:

The ideal would be for each person to lead the life of his dreams. But the opportunity to do so varies in relation to a man's financial capacity, his intellectual capacity, and his capacity for initiative. These are not equal for all—so that naturally some must lead a better life while others have to lead a life which is, well, less affluent, a simpler life, more humble, with more difficulties. This is right and proper, this is the way it has been since the beginning of the world. Christ himself didn't succeed in changing the mentality of people, in bringing a situation of equilibrium, of equality for all. So why should we now imagine that this should come about in our time?

He recognized that the peasant in the area was really wholly defenceless: 'He needs more information, he needs someone who helps him to think, who will show him that the world in which we live today, with its machines, is no longer the world in which he lived twenty, thirty, or forty years ago.' But when asked whether the peasants, in spite of these limitations, were satisfied with their situation he said:

Our peasant is a man who is absolutely accommodated, an individual who, thank God, has not yet been caught up in the political disturbances which were stimulated in the country before the *Revolução*. He is a most peaceful and orderly man. He is not aggressive and does not wish to own what doesn't belong to him.[7]

And in regard to the majority of peasants he was, no doubt, right— even for many of those reached by MEB. Nevertheless a first dent had been made in the solidly traditional structures of thought of some of the more receptive among them, either because they were more intelligent and perceptive, or because they exhibited that evasive quality 'leadership'. They had become aware that even if things were not changing, they did not exist *by right*.

We are now at least beginning to know that certain things aren't legal, things we knew absolutely nothing about before the arrival of MEB and the radio school. We were simply deceived by them [the *patrões*], now we are beginning to know how and to whom we can complain.[8]

Here one encounters the stirrings of a sense of citizenship, the first

[7] Interview 31 May 1966.
[8] The remarks of peasants quoted in the rest of this chapter were all made in various meetings during the last fortnight of May 1966, in two communities in the Franqueira area.

but very important step away from wholesale integration in the pattern of patron–dependancy. And yet it was clear during these meetings in the communities of the traditional *sertão* that the number of people who had so far been at all shaken was still very small, and that in those cases the change that had come about did not go very deep. These peasants were, after all, a people exploited for generations, wilfully kept in ignorance and stupidity, and sorely in need of knowledge of the world.

Once substantive issues from the peasants' life experience had been raised, they would talk quite freely about their problems, and virtually everywhere it was possible to piece together from their own remarks a fairly complete (though obviously not completely accurate) picture of the forms of land tenure and labour relations, the exercise of economic power, and the operation of the local political system. Although that political system was still traditional, the political loyalty of the dependants was no longer an aspect of the relationship simply taken for granted: it had to be bought with special favours. This was so despite the fact that in this area the *patrões'* ultimate monopoly position had remained unchallenged. But there was often a shrewd awareness of the (traditional) possibilities inherent in pre-election situations for individuals or communities. At the time of the field-work, a few months before elections were scheduled, 'Seu João', one of the community leaders in the Franqueira area, explained in a discussion that he had just requested the authorization of the president of the municipal council to proceed with his plan to get people together to clear a road that had been badly neglected in recent years. The Barreto in question had agreed and would pay the men for the job—though characteristically João had no idea whether that money would come out of Barreto's own pocket or out of the municipal treasury.

In contrast, there were few illusions among these peasants about promises made at election time which are supposed to take effect after polling day. 'They come and promise us the moon when they want our votes—but when the time comes to fulfil them nothing happens.' Then they do not dare complain, individually or together, because, so they say, 'the result would be that we'd end up in jail, or get beaten up'. It is immaterial whether or not this is true: these are the expectations. And, of course, at the next election, these communities deep in the backlands again vote for the same people, despite all the broken promises. The explanation for this fact is not merely, as one woman said, 'because we're stupid and let ourselves be taken for a ride'. It is more related to the fact that the areas covered by the local polling stations usually coincide with these small communities; and that a massive rebellion against the *patrão*'s local candidate would be immediately noticed where the total number of ballots in an urn may be no more than fifty or a hundred. The economic (and of course political) monopoly position of the 'humiliated' candidate (or his *patrão*) could ensure that life in the community concerned would be far from pleasant.[9]

The community which had been involved in the protest over the enclosure thus experienced the harsh consequences of their 'rebellion'. They were totally cold-shouldered in their requests to the Barreto-dominated municipality for at least three years after the incident—and this despite the fact that in the election immediately following the affair, the Barreto candidate had polled 100 out of 130 votes in that community. Political, legal, and economic power are too intimately intertwined for a piecemeal challenge to be successful.

We can't complain, because if we complain we're even worse off. If we'd wanted to complain we'd have to do so, say, to a judge. But that judge, or whoever we should complain to, is the same person, or at least the same *kind* of person, as the fellow we want to complain about. So why complain? We've just got to put up with it.

Conscientização in a discouraging environment

Faced with this kind of defeatist (but possibly quite realistic) reaction of peasants still enmeshed in largely traditional patron–dependant relations—replete with exploitation—MEB's cadres would try to make the peasants believe (almost against all available evidence) that things might be different, especially if only they would start to behave like a community rather than as a number of wholly isolated individuals. After that outburst on the futility of complaining, the group was gently prodded into considering the possibility of a *joint* protest. At first no one saw the point; then one man said: 'One man alone is very small and weak, but many together can solve more. With unity things are easier. But lots of people here don't understand that.'

Unfortunately, but in the circumstances almost inevitably, those who do understand often have no more than an abstract notion of the value of unity, a notion that can be activated by the appropriate (non-directive) question in a discussion, but which in practice means very

---

[9] Because of this maintained monopoly position one could not speak of a development towards patron–*client* relations in this area.

little indeed. Even the most *conscientizados* in these far-off communities often lacked the knowledge of how to translate these general conceptions into concrete deeds. For a time, during the period of excessive concern with non-directiveness (i.e. facts shouldn't be 'imposed'), the *equipe* became almost blind to the need for straightforward factual enlightenment and practical help for people who were supposed to set out on ventures which were quite new to them—with corresponding results. Thus even though some peasants in the Franqueira area had, for instance, a certain amount of hearsay understanding of the value of various types of co-operatives and of *sindicatos*, they lacked all knowledge of the mechanics of those organizations, and there was an equally obvious lack of confidence—even on the part of the informal leaders—in their own capacity to get something of this nature started. 'Somebody who understands things better than we do has to help'— a viewpoint which echoed the earlier cited statement of the mayor of Franqueira, but for which there was, at the time, little sympathy among the MEB *equipe*, who regarded it as running counter to the prescriptions for self-knowledge and self-help.

It would appear that there is no reason to assume that abstract and generalized notions on the value of communal action, developed in discussion groups, will come automatically to be translated into concrete deeds. Old patterns of behaviour can exhibit an amazing tenacity, even though they embody the very opposite of *apparently* learned or understood new ideas. Thus someone who can be quite articulate in the abstract about the need for unity in the community, may not see at all that a particular situation calls for precisely such a (new) communal response.

'Seu João', the man we have met earlier, seemed typical. In the case of the road-clearance job, he had acted *individually* and on his own initiative when he went to the local politician with his request. On another occasion, during the fieldwork, when various problems had been discussed in a meeting held after the daily radio class, he did suggest a *communal* response, but in a situation in which no one was faced with the need to do anything concrete there and then. The problems concerned the likely reaction of the community to a possible closing down of MEB by the government—and various of those present, including João, were inclined to face that hypothetical situation with a communal response. 'If the government loses interest in MEB the people of the community can take an interest, and help, in whatever way they can, so that MEB wouldn't wind up—help, that

is with money, or in any other way.' It is true that some of the others
at the meeting were sceptical of the willingness of their neighbours
to co-operate in this way, but at least some of the peasants more
influenced by MEB did suggest a community-oriented solution. The
point to note, however, is that this was a hypothetical problem, and
that the hypothetical solution was arrived at in the presence of MEB
personnel (a supervisor and myself), who stimulated its emergence by
asking certain questions. These, though non-directive—e.g. 'Did you
hear the programme last Saturday on MEB's financial difficulties?',
'What have the politicians you have elected done for you?', 'Is there
anything you people could do yourselves?'—turned the attention to the
possible alternative courses of action, and brought forth, at least from
some of them, a set of non-traditional responses.

Consider, however, the matter that almost accidentally came up
shortly afterwards in the same meeting. The local schoolteacher, a
girl whose parents lived in Franqueira itself, did not much like to be
away from home for more than a few days at a time, and so she had
been cutting classes on one or even two days of every week since the
beginning of the year.[10] This was a matter of much concern to the
community, but despite the fact that it had by then been happening
for some five months, no attempt had been made to change the situation. João merely remarked at the meeting that he had been *thinking*
of going to the mayor to complain, or to ask for a new teacher. Now this
meeting had just been discussing the need for persuasion, co-operation,
and communal action—and yet it occurred to no one present that the
parents in the community could get together, and jointly approach
first the teacher, and if that failed, the authorities. In this case the
presence of MEB personnel did not even induce a hypothetical non-
traditional response: the relevance of community discussion and action
had to be raised in very direct terms by those representing the Movement—though once suggested, it was fully accepted by the peasant
leadership. No doubt the question had been the subject of gossip in
the community, but that is a far cry from discussion in a kind of
embryonic Parent–Teachers' Association.

A few preliminary conclusions may be drawn from the material

---

[10] Cutting classes is still very widespread in the Brazilian educational system, and
especially so outside the larger towns. On the two occasions when I visited the local high-
school in Franqueira there were various classes milling around with the teacher absent.
Even one of the members of the local MEB *equipe*, a young man full of ideals and commitment, who was a part-time teacher in the high-school, saw nothing strange in twice missing
a class in order to accompany me on a visit to one of the communities.

presented so far. In the first place, there were, apart from the *monitor*, usually only a mere handful of people who participated at all in the discussions in these communities—those people had attuned themselves, up to a point, to the approach of MEB's supervisors (an approach on the whole shared by the *monitores*) and would respond hesitantly but positively to neutral questions about their problems. Of course, the mere possibility of talking about themselves to sympathetic outsiders was a relatively new experience for them, especially as those outsiders had most of the trappings of the *patrões*—they lived in town, were educated, drove a car—and yet acted in a totally different manner, treating the peasants as equals and encouraging them to express themselves freely and honestly. Any evaluation of MEB, of the tasks it set itself and the extent to which it carried them to a successful conclusion, would be meaningless if it did not take account of this important human—or rather humanizing—factor. MEB's cadres approached the peasants with whom they came into contact as equals, as people whose opinions were of great importance, and who were dignified by their life and labour. One must recognize the moral value of this type of encounter, even when the peasantry does not rapidly acquire a wholly new mentality or different social attitudes towards those who do not treat them in an egalitarian manner. It was consequently not surprising that often the discussions started, for my benefit, with a veritable paean to the *equipe*, 'who have helped us to become a community, set us on the road to development', but who also constituted a group of people up in town to whom one could turn in case of personal need, who would help you, say, to find a doctor.

It would, nevertheless, seem legitimate to suggest that the distance which the peasants had travelled 'on the road to development' was, as yet, quite short. MEB's populist orientation and its non-directive methods had, apart from their 'humanizing' aspect, helped lay the basis for the emergence of a sense of citizenship (focused on rights under the law), and for a new community orientation, and had helped to develop at least among some of the peasants a certain capacity for raising problems in the presence of MEB personnel. But it appeared doubtful whether the peasants were visibly moving towards a capacity for relatively independent decision-making—so that they neither required the constant presence of members of the *equipe*, nor passively awaited their endorsement of any decision taken—or were moving away from a situation still in many ways similar to one characterized by deference to the *patrão*. Traditional attitudes continued, in practice, very strongly; *conscientização* was strictly limited, and one could not point to many *specific* achievements in the community.

In the next chapter material from another area, where MEB was notably more successful and made substantial inroads into traditional attitudes and patterns of behaviour, will be examined. But there, too, the Movement came up against conditions which blocked the process of change. In both cases there is little doubt that much of the blame for the lack of greater success must be placed on the contextual conditions, on the broader social and political structure. Where all challenges, however small-scale, to the established system consistently fail, one cannot expect people to continue making them. Even less can one expect the peasants to be convinced by populist intellectuals, however sincere and accepted, that a wholly new kind of society is going to arise in which the peasants themselves will make all the important decisions in their lives, when hitherto, at all crucial points, others have made those decisions for—or rather against—them.

The kinds of communities discussed in the present chapter could be pulled out of their total social and political dependence only by sustained change at a higher level of the political system. Such change might come about, short of a social revolution, if peasants in areas of less complete traditional domination were sufficiently *conscientizados* to vote for a new type of candidate for high office—that is, after all, how men like Julião and Arraes were elected in 1962. As a federal deputy Julião may not have made much impact on his electors' lives, but as a state governor Arraes certainly did. Had he been given time, he would no doubt also have come to make his influence felt in those communities where the peasantry were, perhaps realistically, not yet willing to take the risk of directly challenging the local powers. Hence Arraes, or others like him, were *not* given time.

From April 1964 challenges to the *patrões* became less advisable than ever before. Since the coup, therefore, it is again necessary to pay at least some attention to the point made by Bertram Hutchinson: the rural reformer—if it is *reformer* one wants to be—

must use the patron–dependant relationship as a means of introducing agrarian novelty. Either ... innovations must come to the people with the full support and exhortation of the traditional patron; or the reformer must himself so organize matters that he appears as, and plays the part of, a new and powerful patron to whom the *camponês* can with confidence turn for help, advice, and assistance in emergency.[11]

[11] Hutchinson, in *Sociologia ruralis*, vi/1 (1966), p. 26.

13

Populism and Non-Directiveness at the Grass Roots, II

Fernandópolis and Lagoinha

EXAMPLES such as those discussed in the previous chapter can easily be adduced from other areas in which fieldwork was undertaken. They strengthen the impression that many obstacles must be overcome before the peasants are really capable of 'standing on their own feet', of understanding anything about the 'topography' of the area in which they are supposed to stand, or—even more—of mastering the art of walking by themselves through this newly discovered land. But, of course, there are success stories too. One of these, concerning a community in the Fernandópolis area, will now be examined, devoting special attention to the factors that seem to account for early positive achievements as well as later difficulties. In Fernandópolis, a fast-growing city in the central highlands of Brazil, MEB operated from the start in an atmosphere favourable to its ideas. This *sistema* was chosen for fieldwork because it was generally regarded in the Movement (and especially at the *Nacional*) as one which had not only successfully fallen in with the developments in the Movement's ideology and methods, but had, in fact, itself made substantial contributions to those developments. This will become evident in the following detailed account of the impact of MEB Fernandópolis on one community, Lagoinha.

Lagoinha is a small dispersed settlement of some seventy families, fairly typical for the area, where most of the land is owned by three large landowners. At the time of the fieldwork one of them was the mayor of the *município* in which Lagoinha is situated. Another, a physician, was living in Fernandópolis, and the third, Valentino, was a local man with no formal political position. They were related to each other either by birth or by marriage. The two former had, so it seems, frequently made life difficult for their tenants, for example by exacting the largest possible rent or share of the crop—just short of forcing

245

17

them to move. They expected strictly traditional deferential behaviour. Valentino, on the other hand, was widely regarded as a very good *patrão*. He was fair and approachable: a man who took his traditional duties seriously (he was god-father to many children) but was not afraid of change.

The land-tenure system in Lagoinha was mainly based on share-cropping. Peasants in the community would eagerly talk on any available occasion about the abuses this system gave rise to, especially with the two less benevolent *patrões*. They were well aware of the fact that more often than not it was the landlord who stood to benefit from the arrangement, especially as, in this area, where mixed crops were planted, he could take his 'half' by demanding at will different proportions of the various crops (e.g. half the rice, no beans, 80 per cent of the corn). Security of tenure did not exist, and a peasant could be expelled from the land at short notice if, according to the landlord, the occasion warranted this. The peasant's situation could, short of this, easily change from one year to the next: as will be seen, there were various less abrupt ways of getting rid of unwanted tenants. Nevertheless the peasantry as a whole was probably not too badly off in comparison with other areas of the country: the land was relatively fertile and living conditions, as well as standards of consumption, were higher than those found, for instance, in the Franqueira area.

MEB's involvement in Lagoinha dated from late in 1962.[1] The developments there were not untypical of the general experience of MEB Fernandópolis.[2] The first *monitores* were chosen by the *equipe*, upon the recommendation of the parish priest in the near-by small town, effectively without reference to the peasants. At first the school was fairly successful, but once the novelty had worn off interest in the set lessons—literacy, agriculture, hygiene, etc.—began to decrease. Greater emphasis then came to be placed on the analysis of 'Brazilian reality' especially in *treinamentos* in which the *monitores* participated. The whole effort, however, remained for a long time conditioned by the concept of change through literacy, and directed at revitalizing the radio schools and at motivating members of the community to participate in the classes. The radio school remained the focal point of MEB's activity, and the only 'instrument' of *conscientização*.

---

[1] The following historical discussion is based on interviews with members of the *equipe*, as well as on a profusion of contemporary documents in the *sistema*'s archives.

[2] These were also in many respects similar to those of the Franqueira *equipe* (see above, pp. 231 ff).

But participation continued to be very limited, here as in other communities. Supervision ascertained a lack of enthusiasm among the students, and back at MEB Fernandópolis the problems were discussed in such a way as to question increasingly some of the basic assumptions on which the *equipe* had been operating. Contemporary documents show this process in operation: the *equipe* was most conscientious in making reports on visits, keeping minutes of discussions, putting in writing any conclusions reached, even tentative ones. Slowly an awareness emerged that the schools were in fact isolated from the communities, and that supervision limited to the experiences of teaching and learning should be replaced by a wider concern with stimulating community interaction, spreading socio-economic and political knowledge, and fostering community organization. This happened in the course of the second quarter of 1963, after the conclusions of the *I Encontro Nacional de Coordenadores* had sunk in and had settled MEB's new emphasis on education for structural change (leading to the massive drive at *sindicalização*). In the same period many efforts at reaching the urban and rural masses sponsored by other groups and organizations had got under way, and MEB Fernandópolis co-operated with a number of these. Especially the local *Centro Popular de Cultura*, with its various politico-cultural activities such as sketches depicting typical and socially significant aspects of peasant life, helped create a climate in which MEB could make the switch from school-centredness to community-centredness. This happened gradually via a period during which the community activities were essentially conceived as leading to an improvement in school attendance.

Animação Popular in Lagoinha

In September 1963 the *equipe* tried out a new method of making contact with a community. They sponsored a sort of *fête champêtre*, which took place on a Sunday and embraced discussions about the local socio-economic situation, 'dialogues' converging on MEB's view of man and his dignity, sketches *à la Cultura Popular*, relating to some aspect of ignorance and learning (serving as the basis for further discussion) and straight entertainment (song, dance). The meeting was a great success, both for MEB Fernandópolis, which had discovered a new tool with which to reach the peasants, and for Lagoinha itself, as virtually the entire community participated. Similar meetings were held in other communities near-by. During these meetings the communities increasingly expressed an interest in more formal organizations which could defend the cause of the peasants—especially *sindicatos*. Some of these already existed in the region, but in the communities with which we are here concerned nothing got off the ground before April 1964.

The new circumstances after the coup reinforced the populist aspects of MEB's work. They led to the further change in the character of non-directiveness and to the new emphasis on *Animação Popular*.

In July 1964 the *Nacional* organized at MEB headquarters in Fernandópolis an AnPo *treinamento* at which the new trends found expression. This *treinamento* confirmed the greater emphasis which MEB-Fernandópolis had recently been placing on non-directiveness. They had been discussing certain concrete changes in the approach to the community meetings, hitherto largely organized by the *equipe*. Though the peasants had, of course, actively participated in these meetings, they had so far had little opportunity to take the initiative, to decide what was to be discussed or presented. Henceforth the communities themselves were to take over the planning and organization of the meetings: the *equipe* would merely help when and where requested.

The first of these new-style community meetings was held in Lagoinha during the actual AnPo *treinamento* and was a resounding success. This was partly due to the presence in that community of three brothers, the Carvalhos, two of whom had unusual capacities for leadership. Literate themselves, and somewhat better off than the average peasant in the community, they had shown a keen interest in MEB from the start, and had constituted the main channel of communication between the community and the *equipe*, by-passing the rather ineffectual *monitores* of the radio schools.[3] They had regularly drawn attention to aspects of the community's life not related to the radio schools, and had thus in a sense helped to prepare the *equipe* for the switch from literacy training to community development; simultaneously they had increased their own self-confidence and ability to take initiatives. And the innovation of the self-organized day-long community meeting was grist to the mill of the Carvalhos.

---

[3] Between February 1963 and June 1965 (a month or so before they left the community) one of them wrote thirty and the other thirty-five letters to the *equipe*, informing them of local developments, asking for advice, or just gossiping away. There were only a handful of letters from others during the same period.

The brothers, however, were not content to 'animate' their own community: they wanted to share this experience with others. They turned their attention to the neighbouring community of Itapauá which had a rather languishing radio school, and about a month later a letter arrived at MEB Fernandópolis suggesting that Lagoinha should organize such an event for the community of Itapauá.[4] The *equipe* agreed to the idea and arranged for a discussion with the leadership group of Lagoinha, which included the *monitores* and, of course, the Carvalhos. According to the report, this was a completely open-ended discussion, totally non-directive, during which the question of the future meeting 'came out normally, interspersed with other bits of conversation'. At the end of that discussion the Lagoinha group proposed the following schema of objectives, to serve as a basis for the preparations:

(a) To get the people to know MEB ('what we want is that the *povo* here know you, like you, and will feel the same friendship for you as we do: because that way there won't be discouragement or lack of trust').

(b) To strengthen the radio school—to increase the matriculation and frequency of attendance.

(c) To strengthen the leadership of the *monitor* of the community.

(d) To get the people of the community themselves to shoulder the responsibility for the work.

The meeting itself went off very well. It was announced as 'a presentation of the community of Lagoinha to the community of Itapauá,' though the *monitor* and students of Itapauá had been drawn into the planning and took an active part in the proceedings. The *equipe* from Fernandópolis was also present, as was a group of local musicians (fiddlers), whose participation was sufficient to ensure a complete turn-out of the community. There was singing and dancing, there was serious speech-making about MEB, but above all there was a great effort to involve the peasants from Itapauá in the events. A central place in the programme was given to a couple of sketches, devised by the *monitores* from the two communities, and performed by them and the students from Itapauá. The first concerned a girl who had received a love letter; but, as she was illiterate, she had to ask someone else to read it to her. The second dealt with the problem of an illiterate peasant

[4] The following information on the community meeting in Itapauá derives from a (mimeo). *Relatório de AnPo*, MEB Fernandópolis, Oct. 1964, and to a smaller extent from interviews with two members of the *equipe*.

faced with a landlord demanding the rendering of accounts. Both touched—with a good deal of humour—on highly sensitive aspects of peasant 'honour', and initiated heated discussions among the spectators about the need for literacy. The 'animation' of the community had succeeded.

In Lagoinha other initiatives were taken. Increasingly the 'active' peasants, those in one way or another associated with MEB, began to meet in informal gatherings, to discuss local problems. These discussions frequently resulted in action. An instructive example was the case of the local school and school teacher. The building was too small and the teacher very old: the need for a renewal in both respects was blatant. Mauricio Carvalho, the eldest of the three brothers, attempted to get the teacher replaced—but the local authorities would not hear of it. According to the peasants, this was because the appointment had been made to pay off a political debt—in keeping with the almost universal practice in respect of appointments to municipal and even state teaching posts in the country's interior. In May 1965 the community decided during a meeting in the house of Valentino, the 'good' *patrão*, to pool resources and construct a new and larger school, to which they hoped to get a new teacher appointed. Three months later the members of the community, by their own efforts, had completed the building, on land made available by Valentino. Apparently MEB's part in the whole business was minimal: the idea did not come from them, nor did they play any role in the organization of committees, division of labour, purchase of materials, and so on. The *equipe* merely made encouraging noises when they first heard of the idea—and found that between one visit and the next (visits to any community usually occurred at intervals of many weeks if not months) the new school had become a reality. About six weeks before the October elections of 1965 the local politicians suddenly became responsive to the request for a new teacher, and the candidate for mayor saw it to that a young woman was appointed. Hardly had he been elected, however, than she was once more removed—not to reappear till about a year later, when (state) elections were in the offing. In the interim the community had, for part of the time, brought in a girl teacher at their own expense.

The contrast in all this between Lagoinha and Franqueira is striking: the school problems were not dissimilar in the two areas and yet in the *sertão* community a constructive response had been totally lacking. On the available evidence, it is difficult to do much more than suggest a few factors that may have played a part in the Lagoinha success. Living standards there were a little above bare subsistence level, and this left some leeway for discretionary spending. The presence in the community of at least one co-operative *patrão* may also have made a difference, *vide* the remarks of Hutchinson quoted at the end of the previous chapter. Finally, there was the element of leadership provided by the Carvalho brothers: in the relatively favourable circumstances, they supplied the drive which enabled the community to test out, in various forms of concrete action, the idea learned from MEB that things did not have to remain the same, and that change depended on their own efforts. In Franqueira the peasants had never got to that point. On the contrary: their one venture into action (the challenge to the Barreto enclosure) had 'proved' that things *did* remain the same, however hard you tried to change them.

Lagoinha runs into trouble

Shortly after the school was finished the three brothers left the community. Mauricio had acquired a piece of land of his own near-by, and his younger brother accompanied him. Chico, the middle one, had been a long-standing tenant of one of the traditional landlords: he moved out at the same time as his brothers after having his allotment of land reduced for the second year in succession. When I spoke to him a year later, he was in no doubt that this was a deliberate act, aimed at ridding the community of an increasingly influential and 'dangerous' upstart, whose ideas about community organization could lead to a challenge to the hitherto accepted social and economic structure. Events which happened after his departure lend credibility to this interpretation, as will presently be seen.

The departure of the three brothers left the community without leaders. Soon, however, a number of peasants began to take a more active interest in community affairs, and within a few months a small group was crystallizing which was once more providing the community with leadership. They still lacked the self-assurance of the Carvalhos, but none the less initiatives were forthcoming.[5] Early in 1966 they were considering the establishment of a first-aid post in Lagoinha, and requested that someone from MEB should come down

[5] The following section on Lagoinha is based on two collective and two individual interviews with members of the Fernandópolis *equipe*, held in September 1966, and on contemporary documents and reports from the files of MEB Fernandópolis.

for a discussion. This was a period of the most acute financial difficulties for the Movement: the *equipe* lacked even the money to pay for
petrol. When this became known, the community (i.e. those actively
in contact with MEB) decided to pay the expenses: they reasoned that
help from MEB was still needed to give their initiatives a 'solid basis'.
The meeting was held in mid-February. Further developments,
despite their meanderings, again demonstrate the advantages of the
non-directive approach, but they also once more draw our attention
to the obstacles to *conscientização* constituted by adverse political
circumstances.

While discussing the mechanics of setting up that first-aid post, the
new leadership group discovered that, for all the talk of co-operation,
they were woefully ignorant of the workings of co-operative institutions. Knowledge about these, they felt, might help them approach
many problems besides that of the first-aid post in a new way. So they
shelved their immediate project and suggested that MEB should
organize a day of study on co-operativism; they set their sights higher
and were hoping that in due course it would prove possible to start
a co-operative in Lagoinha. One of the members of the *equipe* had
recently attended a course on this subject,[6] and the requested study day
took place a fortnight later.

The study day began with a general discussion of the main ideas
underlying co-operatives. Then the eleven participants, who included
Valentino, the landowner, split up into two groups. After further discussion one of the groups opted for 'going ahead, not just talking, starting now with ourselves and getting the others in later'. But the other
group took the view that things should not be forced upon the community, and that the idea of starting a co-operative, exciting as it
might seem to them, did not necessarily respond to the needs most
acutely felt in Lagoinha. Pushing ahead would mean by-passing
problems which worried their fellows more deeply; the result might
be a failure to get the co-operative started. The latter point of view
was later accepted by all, and they agreed that the real worry in
Lagoinha was hookworm.[7] The study day ended with the decision not
to press ahead with the co-operative for the time being, but to call a

---

[6] This fact may well have had some bearing on the emergence of an interest in the
subject during the first meeting in Lagoinha—and indicate the 'human' limits of non-
directiveness.

[7] A parasitism caused by the larvae of hookworms, which enter the body through the
skin, usually the soles of the feet of people walking barefoot over soil infected by the faeces
of bearers of the disease.

meeting on the health problem and to proceed from there. The *equipe* undertook to contact a couple of sympathetic medical students, and to bring them to the new meeting.

The meeting in Lagoinha was held and was very well attended, and all present agreed on the urgency of the health problem. The medical students arranged for a sample of each person's faeces to be collected and analysed by fellow students from the pharmaceutical faculty; the disease was diagnosed, and appropriate medicines (consisting of free samples) were distributed in the community.[8] But the lasting success of the health campaign depended upon the adoption of preventive measures to avoid a recurrence of the disease. To get people to wear footwear at least presented no economic problems in an age of cheap plastic sandals. But to avoid the infection of the soil by human faeces was, also in economic terms, no mean task in a community where no dwelling (not even Valentino's house) had a latrine. As these had to be built for each family, MEB sought the aid of the federal agency for rural public health (the DNERu), which agreed to supply the building materials.

Now, however, the story took a new turn. When the DNERu arrived in the community with the building materials, no landowner—not even Valentino, who had obviously been persuaded by the others—would consent to a latrine being put up on his land. This refusal was justified for various reasons, none of them at all convincing: the land was already being eaten into by other means; the goodwill of the *patrões* was being abused; allowing the building of latrines would give the peasants 'a foot in the door': soon they would demand that land should be made available for other purposes. The end of the road would be communism. . . .

The landowners' real reason for refusing permission to build latrines was no doubt to be found in their interpretation of a legal disposition stipulating that a *morador* should be paid some compensation by the landowner if the latter forced him to leave a plot of land to which the *morador* had made certain lasting improvements.[9] 'Lasting improvements' referred not only to the planting of permanent crops (e.g. banana trees), but could also consist of things like tiling the roof of the *morador*'s dwelling, or building a 'permanent structure'. A latrine

[8] The *equipe* was very proud of having managed to interest the medical students: their involvement had given them not only diagnostic and clinical experience, but had brought them face to face with the social causes of disease. It was indeed an example of *conscientização* through action.

[9] Brazilian Civil Code (Law no. 3071 of 1 Jan. 1916), art. 516.

might well fall within that category, and in order not to run the risk—obviously rather remote in the circumstances—of being faced with a demand for compensation, the landowners decided to veto the scheme. The DNERu refused to interfere: they would put up the latrines if the landowners gave permission, but it was not within their competence to take active steps to resolve the now developing conflict. MEB, in true non-directive style, felt that the decision about how to proceed should be taken by the community itself. Moreover, shortly afterwards the *equipe*'s activities in the community had come to be hampered by a rumour that the Movement was communist, probably started in the entourage of the mayor. His wife had ordered the radio school to close ('communist schools won't function in our *município*'), an order with which the peasants had promptly complied.

For a few months relations between the peasants and the landlords were very tense. The issue of the latrines remained unresolved; the peasants had accepted the landlords' refusal as a *fait accompli*. No attempt was made to discuss the matter on behalf of the community with any of the landlords, and that despite the fact that at least Valentino could have been expected to be willing to listen to a reasoned case. Nor did his special relationship with MEB induce the *equipe* to make any move: they stuck to their non-directiveness, and to the general principle of never getting involved with *patrões* as *patrões*. By September 1966 the position which was 'formally' acknowledged by both sides had not changed, even though one or two peasants, who were dependants of Valentino, had erected a latrine at their own expense—and with no deleterious results. In Lagoinha, then, despite notable achievements and obvious changes in peasant outlook, the peasants did not react when their interests as a community clashed with those of the landlords.

Peasants and politics

The limits of *conscientização* also became visible through the way in which the community reacted to a minor internal crisis which was developing during the period of fieldwork in September 1966. This community, like others in the area, had hardly been subjected to explicit attempts at political mobilization on the part of organizations outside the traditional political structure. But occasionally such attempts had occurred; before 1964 quite openly—after the coup, of course, *sub rosa*. Adalberto, the PCB organizer in the seat of the *município*, had been making overtures to various members of the community, and had attempted to get them to co-operate with his 'group'. This had happened just at a time when a 'group' of AP in Fernandópolis, whose socio-political views could then still be called essentially populist, was reorganizing itself after two years of quiescence, and had succeeded in getting a foothold in Lagoinha through one of the newly emerging leaders, Luís. But the differences in orientation between these two political organizations were understood by no one in the community, and that effectively included the two protagonists, Luís and Adalberto. Luís came to Fernandópolis to inform the *equipe* of MEB of the difficulties which had arisen: he did not know how to handle the potential split in the community, now that some seemed to want to 'follow' him and others were inclined to accept the lead of Adalberto. It was agreed that someone from MEB would come down to the community a few days later, in order to be present at a discussion with some of the people involved.

This visit took place on the second day of my stay in Fernandópolis. We, that is two of the members of the *equipe*, Isabel and Gilda, Heitor, a young recently graduated professional who was not of MEB, and myself arrived by jeep in Lagoinha in the late afternoon, and went straight to the house of Luís, who had provided a veritable banquet by local standards.[10] Luís was, like the Carvalho brothers, somewhat better off than the average peasant of Lagoinha: he had recently managed to scrape together enough money to buy himself a few acres of land and to make some structural improvements to the house which went with it. According to his own account, he had been particularly stimulated to take this step because his ex-landlord had been raising objections to the community's activities ever since the beginning of the affair of the latrines, and had forbidden the holding of meetings on his property.

Gilda began the discussion by saying that we all knew what we had come together for, so there was no point in beating about the bush— let's start with 'the problem'. But nothing of the sort happened: the first half-hour was spent by the various peasants present describing the hard life which they had to lead, their troubles with the landlords, and so on. Gilda then made another attempt to deflect the discussion to the community's political problems, and raised the matter specifically

[10] A sense of the patriarchial nature of peasant society here—confirmed for instance, by the fact that it was extremely rare for women (apart from female *monitores*) ever to take an *active* part in the MEB-sponsored discussions or community meetings—was conveyed by the fact that the men (seven were present altogether) and the guests ate first, watched and waited upon by the women and children, who followed suit after we had finished.

in terms of the 'group of Adalberto'. There was little reaction, however, beyond discussing Adalberto in personal terms. One or two expressed their lack of understanding as to what he was trying to get at. Luís kept fairly quiet; the others had nothing to say that took the matter any further. One of them wanted to know where MEB stood in all this. The girls explained that MEB was an *educational* movement, which could only involve itself and take a stand up to a certain point: if they wanted to go further, and act *politically*, they would have to do this through some other group. This is where Adalberto and Luís were relevant.

But, so asked one of them, what then did these groups stand for? Thereupon Heitor, after some hesitation, launched into a long explanation of the objectives of the communist party; his remarks—about the abolition of capitalism, the dictatorship of the proletariat, and so forth—seemed to make sense to no one. Though I suspected as much from the start, it now became clear that Heitor was involved in AP. AP was then described as an organization which was concerned to discover the road together with the peasants, and as interested in deciding jointly upon action, while the communists were said to believe that the road was given and had merely to be followed. To the peasants, however, it all seemed to mean singularly little. They remained passive during most of the evening; the occasional question merely demonstrated their lack of political knowledge and experience. That is not really surprising, as this was one of the first attempts in the community at straight 'politicization'. But I doubt whether even more sustained efforts would have led to spectacular results. It is extraordinarily difficult—I do not say impossible—effectively to impart political knowledge in conditions such as those which existed in Lagoinha in 1966, when no opportunity presented itself to gain the political experience needed to base such knowledge on solid foundations.

It is worth just saying a few more words about the actual circumstances in which this first MEB-involving attempt at political enlightenment took place in Lagoinha. Two strangers were introduced simultaneously into the community by the girls from the *equipe*. One of them (myself) was presented as a friend from MEB *Nacional*; the other was not introduced at all. The girls and Heitor began to interact fiercely when the latter was describing AP, elaborating and improving on each other's explanations: soon their points of view, and their political identity, merged in the eyes of those present. When at one point Isabel did remark that not all the members of the *equipe* of MEB would discuss these matters in the same way, that not all had opted for action along political lines, the peasants expressed bewilderment about this lack of unity among the *equipe*. Isabel then elaborated, and said that the *equipe* disagreed neither on the need for change, nor on the direction it should take; some, however, had gone farther than others in *personally* committing themselves to action. Unfortunately, this did not really provide the necessary enlightenment: the peasants obviously were not capable of making sophisticated distinctions of role, of separating the 'total person' from his 'qualities' as MEB supervisor or as member of a political organization.

A few days later, at another day-long visit to the community, an opportunity arose to observe once more the way some community members reacted to these political questions and to discuss them in greater detail. Gilda and I went first to the home of Luís where—rather to our surprise—we encountered Adalberto busily trying to convince Luís that all difficulties would be solved if only they could arrange a meeting between their respective 'leaders': the local PC directorate and the *equipe* of MEB. We had hardly entered when Adalberto put this proposition to us. He said that he understood quite well what our 'group' was about and made approving noises about our 'work' in the community—without, apparently, knowing precisely what he was talking about. Adalberto had moved from Lagoinha to the neighbouring town eight years earlier, and had therefore never had any direct contact with MEB. The next half hour or so was spent by us—*not* by Luís, who was nervous and silent during most of the time—in explaining the nature of MEB to Adalberto. We pointed out that MEB was not a political organization, did not enter into direct contacts or negotiations with political groups, and was trying by educational means to help people understand their situation better so that they could consciously make choices, including those of a political nature. Then Adalberto invited Luís and ourselves to accompany him to his house in town. There he showed us some PCB news sheets and a May Day manifesto denouncing the military dictatorship. We talked a little more about the two 'groups' and suggested to Adalberto that it might well be the case that the peasants who had participated in MEB were not inclined to get involved with the PCB: they might feel that it denied many of the things they had come to believe in.

After that encounter with Adalberto we—that is Gilda, Luís, and myself—returned to Lagoinha, to the home of João Batista, also one of the more active members of the community. There we settled down to a wide-ranging discussion which lasted for over three hours, in which another four members of the community participated. We soon returned to the political problems, and now, with Adalberto out of the way, Luís wanted us to say whether 'Heitor's group' was indeed more 'in line with MEB'. Gilda simply placed the ball back in his court, and Luís responded that they would not want to affiliate with a group which, because of its activities, might endanger all they had achieved in the community. 'If we want to free the peasant, save the peasant, work for an easier life for the peasant, we have to follow Heitor's group', he said. But, significantly, he added: 'Now I want to know whether Adalberto's group has the same line.' This question was bandied to and fro indecisively and in fact left unanswered. Gilda only said that MEB had never told the community what to do, a statement emphatically agreed to by Luís, who remarked that 'MEB merely opened our eyes'. Their response to Gilda's question, whether MEB ought to continue in the community if and when they got more involved in some political group, was interesting. 'Even if you work with a political group', said one, 'you should continue to participate in MEB.' Another remarked that MEB's kind of community work could be done together with, or at least with the knowledge of, the *patrões*; these, however, had to be kept completely out of political work, as 'we can't have everybody in a political group'.

We then again asked those present what *their* view was of the aims of the Adalberto group, or of its pre-1964 predecessor, the then communist-dominated *sindicato*. 'They say they want agrarian reform, but they really want the hammer and sickle ... communism', said João Batista, who had been a member of that *sindicato* before the coup. He continued:

One thing I would like to see is a book that really explains communism, the law of communism. I should like to understand it; now it's not much more to me than a word which is used by the *latifundiários* for anything they don't like. That fellow who ran the *sindicato* was a great communist. He worked a lot with the people here. He helped them a lot, took sick people to hospital, women and children. He was a great communist.

A great communist—a great man. What made him so in the eyes of João Batista was not his adherence to one doctrine or another. He was not remembered as one who had encouraged the expression of 'the people's will', nor had he objected to manipulation or *massificação*. But he had delivered the goods: he had provided services which were of concrete benefit to the people.

Politics in Lagoinha and populist non-directiveness

I shall postpone to the next chapter a discussion of the more general conclusions that may be drawn from the material presented in this and earlier chapters. These conclusions will revolve around a fact which has been a central issue in MEB's short history: the extent to which the Movement's approach should be centred on the state of affairs arising out of the unequal distribution of scarce resources, and on the social and political mechanisms which either maintain that unequal distribution or can be expected (radically) to modify it, or should concentrate on the promotion of co-operation within the peasant class, on the development of more effective institutions in the peasant 'community'. The course of events in Lagoinha will surely have raised some doubts about the efficacy of an exclusive concentration on 'community development'. Yet even community development was frequently regarded with suspicion in post-coup Brazil.

Before I end this chapter, I should like to draw attention to one small but interesting point which arises out of the data here discussed. It refers to one of the 'natural limitations' on the possibility of accepting the full logic inherent in a populist position, which has already been alluded to in general terms in Chapter 5. On the different occasions in Lagoinha when members of the MEB *equipe* discussed 'political matters', a sincere attempt was made to represent the various political views with fairness. But during the community meeting with Heitor, as well as during the conversations in the community a week later, it proved impossible to maintain a rigorously populist or non-directive attitude over the very issue of non-directiveness in politics. The communists were, after all, seen not merely as ideologically misguided, but as 'massifyers', who by their very manipulation denied the people an honest choice. It was hardly satisfactory to leave the peasants 'free' to choose between one option which had been 'pushed' by all possible means, and another which they would have had to 'discover' for themselves. The result was a retreat from the full rigour of MEB's populist position—a phenomenon that is in line with the hypothesis discussed below, that populism gets diluted as its adherents have to operate among other anti-*status-quo* groups, who have few inhibitions about manipulating the people for their own ends.[11]

---

[11] See first general hypothesis, below, pp. 267–8.

14

Conclusions

IN THE final pages of this book I shall not try to present a general summary of all the findings. I shall merely attempt to draw attention to some implications of the data, and especially to certain theoretical generalizations, which might otherwise go unnoticed. As the material presented in the previous two chapters has not yet been adequately analysed from this point of view, it will be as well to start from there; the questions raised by that material in any case refer back to the general problems of rural social structure examined in Chapter 1. One should, however, note at the outset that any general conclusions reached from an examination of the fieldwork data must be somewhat provisional: the fact that they are based on only two areas, as well as the limited amount of time spent in each, must make them so.

Community development and class confrontation

In a system based on patron–dependant or even patron–client relations, such as still prevails in Franqueira and Lagoinha, the essential nexus in a peasant's life is the one binding him to his *patrão*. In such a system one would expect that—short of a situation of drastic (revolutionary) change—the peasant would await the initiative of his *patrão* to introduce innovations in the structure of the system, or at least await the approval of the *patrão* for innovations initiated elsewhere. In Lagoinha, as has been seen, during much of the earlier period of *animação* no opposition was forthcoming from the *patrões* as a group, while one of them, Valentino, actively participated in the promotion of various community ventures. I have also argued that it is probable that these ventures could get off the ground because the economic situation of the peasants in Lagoinha left some leeway for discretionary spending, and because the Carvalho brothers were capable of supplying the initially needed leadership resources. These three factors together created a situation in which certain kinds of change (i.e. initiatives by the peasants themselves) came to be regarded as permissible: the peasants could come to accept the view (of MEB) that change was possible, because it was confirmed by the success of their actions.

While all three factors thus seem to be necessary conditions for the crystallization of community action, the data suggest that leadership, certainly after the first steps have been taken on the road of peasant initiative, is a fairly flexible resource. The new leaders who emerged after the Carvalhos had departed may not quite have had the latter's drive, but they succeeded in getting things done none the less. They succeeded in getting things done, however, only for as long as Valentino maintained his support: once his blessing was withdrawn, once he and the other landowners became hostile and would have had to be opposed, their efforts very rapidly ground to a halt. That development seems to be consistent with the data from Franqueira. Not only did an early attempt to oppose the *patrões*—to challenge them on the enclosure —fail miserably; it also produced some very unpleasant after-effects for the communities involved. Trying to change things thus became identified with failure rather than success; moreover, no open-minded *patrão* helped the peasants along, no outstanding leadership was forthcoming, and economically things were precarious. After the first failure, testing out of new views on social organization simply stopped, and the understanding of what community action was all about remained abstract.

There is a pattern to these failures and successes which should by now have become almost too obvious. That is that in the prevailing political circumstances in these still relatively traditional areas no community has been able to organize itself successfully against the will of the *patrões*, let alone in such a way as to present them with a direct challenge. This points to a significant general distinction which must now be examined in some detail. It is the distinction between activities which can be loosely grouped under the heading of 'community development', and those which more specifically involve a confrontation with the existing social and/or political structures within which these communities are inserted. Lagoinha's successes in self-promotion consisted in the evolution of a rudimentary community organization, in which two successive sets of leaders played a crucial role. These people, with the help of MEB, began to wean the peasants away from their fatalistic acceptance of the *status quo*, with life flowing in more or less predetermined channels. All those channels had connected individual peasant families to a dominant *patrão*; they had left the

18

community for all practical purposes virtually atomized. The various innovations introduced first by the radio schools, then by community meetings, the organization of a football team, the building of a new school, and the initiative on the health problem created new types of links in the community which *supplemented* rather than *superseded* the patron–dependant nexus. Their success helped to bring home the important idea that change would come as a result of common effort and that life could be better if all were willing to unite and agree to co-operate.

No problems, therefore, arose as long as the peasants' initiatives had no repercussions outside the peasant community itself. During that stage the peasants developed certain new forms of organization and co-operation: in fact, *community development* took place. Even though the new structural elements in the community were little more than rudimentary, they made a striking difference in the capacity of the community first to formulate certain collective goals, and then to take purposeful action to try to realize them.[1] The local leaders in Lagoinha helped to transform vague individual wishes into collective goals, and then to bring about positive action. The goals generated were collective aims, on whose desirability there existed a consensus.[2]

But the events in the Franqueira and Lagoinha communities also demonstrated the limits of community development. In the Franqueira case the community mobilized its resources to fight the landlords in the affair of the enclosure. But instead of enlarging the community's alternatives it resulted in their being narrowed down (no help from the politicians for about three years). In Lagoinha the community discovered no effective response to the forced departure of Chico Carvalho, to the landlord's (temporary) closing of the radio school, or to the adamant attitude of the landowners in refusing permission for the building of latrines—in fact it did not respond as a community at all. In all those cases a limit seems to have been encountered at which the willingness to engage in some kind of action to help in the achieve-

[1] If, with Talcott Parsons, we regard power as 'generalized means' available for the attainment of collective goals, including control over the environment in the widest sense of the term, the kind of community development that occurred in Lagoinha was a dramatic case of the extension of the 'fund' of power of a collectivity through organizational innovations. Increasing the fund, or the level, of power widened the range of alternatives open to the community, made it possible to get certain kinds of things done which had hitherto simply been beyond consideration. See Parsons, *Proc. Amer. Philos. Soc.* (1963), p. 255.

[2] One can call the means, the capacity, available to achieve these goals *consensual power*. Community development usually involves the expansion of consensual power. For a further elaboration see my 'Conflict and Power in Society', *Int. Soc. Sc. J.*, xvii/3 (1965).

ment of a collective goal ceased to operate.[3] The common element in these cases was the fact that they all concerned situations in which performance that was related to a collective goal, a common interest, would have had reverberations in areas where interests were no longer common, goals no longer collective.

One must remember that (especially in a traditional community) some peasants are more likely than others to feel that they have something to gain from ingratiating themselves with their *patrão*, and more to lose from opposing or even merely upsetting him. When the collective goal in Lagoinha was to 'fight hookworm', and nothing else, the community was quite easily united. When, however, in fighting hookworm the landlords too had to be fought, performance was no longer forthcoming. There is no doubt that this was in part related to the fact that while no one needed to curry favour with the hookworm, at least some people were concerned about their standing with their *patrão* because of the acceptance of the traditional obligations of a dependant to his patron. But the breakdown of the initiative on health resulted at least equally from the fact that peasants and landlords also had other, conflicting, goals, and it had much to do with the superior power which one party, the *patrão*, had at his disposal to enforce performance which was to his benefit, but to the peasants' disadvantage.[4]

Lagoinha thus demonstrates that community development may go a long way before it comes up against the inequalities inherent in the wider social structure. But these will eventually set the limit to what can be achieved by that approach, a limit that may leave the most important and fundamental aspects of the peasants' lives, those that have the most far-reaching implications, say, for their life chances,

[3] From the community's point of view, the capacity to secure the *performance* of the actions necessary to pursue those goals, had evaporated; even worse, nothing seems to have occurred to try and elicit any performance at all. Parsons, in his analogy of power and money, calls this situation one of 'inflation': (power) credit commitments, which have been entered into in the expectation that they can later be 'cashed in' (i.e., will result in performance), lose their original 'value' (Parsons, *Proc. Amer. Philos. Soc.* (1963), p. 256.).

[4] Once goals conflict, once interests are incompatible, once the aim of one party becomes the widening or maintaining of its alternatives of action at the expense of those of the other, power becomes a 'zero-sum' concept. A's plus is B's minus—and the increase in power available to one side decreases that available to the other. I prefer to call this the exercise of *coercive power*. The problems in this realm are as different from those relating to the mobilization of consensual power, as those which concern the distribution of a fixed amount of resources (land, food, money) are different from problems of economic growth. It is in this respect that I fundamentally diverge from Talcott Parsons's analysis. See my 'Conflict and Power', *Int. Soc. Sc. J.* (1965).

essentially untouched.[5] There is no automatic transition from 'community development', from a capacity to perform in respect of consensual commitments, to the different kind of performance needed to present someone, such as a landlord, with a common challenge. The latter might result from determined efforts on the part of people such as the cadres of MEB to help the peasants to draw the lessons from the failures of community development, and to shift their perspective to that of confrontation. If, however, nothing comes of such confrontations—the case of the enclosure in Franqueira—no real learning (no *conscientização*) is likely to take place.

Let us recall, in this connection, another general point made in earlier pages. It will be remembered that Gerrit Huizer distinguished between the 'traditional following' and the 'rational following', and that in the discussion of those concepts I argued that a number of people who, jointly, have freely chosen to follow a particular leader, may gradually become aware of the existence of common interests among themselves.[6] What can be learned from the present analysis is that a group of peasants may be becoming aware that they share common interests in some respects—in relation to initiatives of community development—without, however, developing class consciousness or engaging in class-based confrontation. One should point out, moreover, that consciousness of *class*, and action flowing from it, depend upon an awareness of common interests of peasants *in general* in opposition to landlords *in general*. Peasants see themselves as a class only once they understand that beyond their own community and its local 'adversaries' lie other communities which find themselves in a situation similar to theirs, and that change in their situation will not come about through action directed merely against those with whom they are in face-to-face relationships. Even a sense of citizenship, with demands for the implementation of rights superseding requests for the granting of favours, will not necessarily result from the development of common interests in community co-operation: many legally recognized rights may be denied by the locally powerful. In the areas studied, such rights were increasingly *known* to the more 'awakened' peasants. But they only had a restricted meaning in the peasants' lives: in the absence of an active struggle they largely remained a dead letter.

[5] Just as a theoretical analysis focusing on consensual power, and neglecting problems of coercive power, misses some of the most important aspects of empirical reality.

[6] See above, pp. 29–30.

This finding takes us back to the analysis of the emergence, and impending breakdown, of *populismo*, presented in Chapter 2. The policies of Vargas and his followers had revolved simultaneously around the bestowal of 'rights' on increasingly broad strata of the population, and around the attempt to reconcile the interests of the various classes in society by politics of compromise. After Goulart's extension of the labour laws to the rural areas it was clear that their *effective* implementation would have required the state to support, everywhere, the interests of the peasants and rural workers against those of the landowners. Hence *populismo*'s identification of the *povo* with the nation broke down, as the nation turned out to be made up of mutually antagonistic groups, some of which did not hesitate (with the coup of April 1964) to mobilize their power to prevent any further challenge to their vested interests. Subsequently, in those parts of the country where prior to the coup the authorities had been conscious of and oriented to the problems of the *pólo dominado*, many of the earlier achievements were eroded.[7] 'National' political mobilization from above had become impossible, as the cleavages inherent in society became visible, and the pursuit of sectional interests took over. Then those threatened by the least privileged put a stop to mobilization altogether, and Brazil entered a period in which politics itself became taboo.

It is, in relation to the foregoing pages, of substantial importance not to lose sight of the fact that the areas dealt with in the last two chapters were areas of relative stability in terms of economic structure. No large-scale modernization had been carried out, no 'rationalization' or mechanization of production adversely affecting the living standards of the peasants or changing their status into that of a landless proletariat. It has been repeatedly pointed out that in conditions such as those prevailing in the *zona da mata*, peasant consciousness does change; their awareness grows, radical responses do emerge, and the (landless) peasantry becomes 'organizable'. In this context, too, the distinction between (class) confrontation and community development is a useful one. In those areas where the peasantry are caught in the mill of change, landowners are forcing through modifications in 'institutionalized', time-honoured arrangements. It is no wonder that *conscientização*, which involves the view that things are not necessarily static (or legitimate), can take place in a situation where new modes of operation, diminishing peasant well-being, are being introduced.

[7] The material on the *zona da mata* presented in ch. 9 has a good deal of bearing on these points.

And in those circumstances no amount of 'community development' which skirted the issue of class confrontation could give anyone
the feeling that the problems which had arisen were being adequately
dealt with.

Populism and power

Until the coup of 1964, ever since the views of the other Catholic
radicals had been assimilated by MEB at the *I Encontro de Coordenadores* in December 1962, the Movement's orientation, its ideology, and
the prescriptions for action flowing from them had had as their central
focus not only the identification with the *pólo dominado*—that remained
equally strong after 1964—but also the need to strengthen the latter
in its struggle with the *pólo dominante*. The Movement had shown its
awareness of the reality of class conflict in the primer *Viver é Lutar*.
Such awareness was maintained by many among its cadres long after
the coup. But, as has been seen in Chapter 10, under the indirect
influence of the wider post-coup political circumstances, and in response
to the direct pressure exercised by MEB's bishops, the concept of
co-operation almost entirely replaced that of *conflict* in MEB's written
statements and guidelines—the new primer *Mutirão* being the most
conspicuous example. And gradually this change in emphasis came to
be adopted by the members of the *equipes* in the field.

I have earlier argued that with the shift of the Movement's centre
of gravity to the Amazon region such a new orientation was far from
absurd. But in areas such as Franqueira or Lagoinha—where MEB,
incidentally, ceased its activities shortly after the period of fieldwork—
and even more in the *zona da mata*, the lack of orientation towards
problems of class confrontation and the concentration upon community
development and co-operation was a procedure far more difficult to
defend on objective grounds. In those areas—and it has to be repeated
again and again—MEB's presence did have a profoundly significant
'humanizing' effect. In promoting community initiatives, and in
changing peasant consciousness at least to the extent of creating an
awareness of the benefits of co-operation, MEB may even have contributed to preparing the ground for an eventual wider active role of
the peasantry. But the evidence of the previous two chapters does seem
to suggest that the transition from 'community development' to 'class
confrontation' is far from automatic, and that it is unlikely to come
about without some stimulus from outside the community.

In these concluding remarks I also want to remind the reader once again of the development of populist non-directiveness in MEB, and to attempt to draw some wider inferences on populism from this and other material presented in previous chapters. In Chapter 11 I pointed to the tension which existed, before the coup, between the objective of contributing to a very specific social transformation (the 'Brazilian Revolution') and the populist prescriptions of non-directiveness, enjoining all to let the *povo* find its own solutions. Before 1964 this tension seems to have been resolved by leaning in the direction of the 'opening of a revolutionary perspective'. The high-water-mark of MEB's populism, the period during which *equipes* seem to have been hesitant to give any kind of guidance or information to the peasantry, in contrast, occurred after the coup, when all revolutionary hopes had been dashed, when all thought of political mobilization of the peasantry had become absurd. What was relevant was the very hopelessness of the situation, hopelessness, that is, in terms of the perspective of class confrontation and widespread structural change which had hitherto been prevalent. This drove MEB's *equipes* into the extremes of non-directiveness which made any achievement virtually impossible.

However, after the emphasis on class confrontation had made way for a stress on community development, and particularly once the Movement had pulled out of those areas in which the latter could not be expected to lead to significant results (i.e. after the shift to the North), the 'excessive' interpretation of non-directive populism fell off, and the need for the giving of information to the peasants was once again recognized. Obviously, within the new circumstances and with the new aims, the content of that information could no longer be what it had been before the coup: instead of data relating to the unequal distribution of income or wealth, or the power of the landlords (let alone that of the military), the peasants were now mainly given information which concerned various co-operative endeavours.

These findings regarding MEB, as well as the earlier documented fact that, before 1964, AP was significantly less populist in its organization and praxis than its ideology would have led one to expect,[8] suggest a *first general hypothesis* regarding populism which seems to warrant further investigation. It relates to the influence which the exercise of, or participation in political power, or even the perceived likelihood of achieving such participation through radical structural change, has on the ideology and especially on the activities of populist movements.

[8] See espec. p. 120.

Closeness to power, and with it institutionalization, seems to push such movements away from the conception of the people's will and hegemony, and towards some form or other of mass mobilization and even manipulation. Populism is unlikely to thrive when it is harnessed to political mobilization. It is as if only marginality and remoteness from power can guarantee a pristine populist people-orientation; the obverse soon brings out the tensions between responsibility for action and true openness to the people. Apparently this tension tends to be resolved in favour of the former, and 'doing the will of the people' easily degenerates into mere rhetoric.[9]

There is another aspect of the political context which apparently has an influence on the extent to which populist movements can translate their principles into practice. No political movement operates in a vacuum, and inevitably some account will have to be taken of the *modus operandi vis-à-vis* 'the people' of others in the political arena. These may either be connected with the government, or they may be other oppositional groups. With the scramble for power in CONTAG late in 1963, and the resulting rush to found *sindicatos* and federations, the Catholic radicals—including MEB—were sacrificing their populist principles for the sake of maintaining some grip on a social and political tool which they regarded as being of the greatest importance. This occurred when they were faced by 'competitors' with a most unpopulist approach, Communists and *PTBistas* intent upon using the embryonic trade union structure for their own political ends.[10] The material presented thus suggests a *second general hypothesis* on populism: there is an inverse correlation between the *effective* populist 'purity' of *ideologically* populist movements, and the extent to which other movements or organizations operating among the people have fewer inhibitions about manipulating the people for their own ends. Thus populism will tend to be weak in a contest of widespread efforts at political mobilization.

Despite all this, MEB in practice did maintain a fundamentally populist perspective, not only after the coup, but also before it. This may seem rather surprising. I should like to suggest that this fact is

---

[9] On this point it may be helpful to consult, apart from the already cited papers by Hennessy and Saul in the Ionescu and Gellner volume, the following remarks in section II of the summary of the Populism conference in *Government and Opposition*, Spring 1968: Peter Worsley (p. 157), Hugh Seton-Watson (p. 161), Franco Venturi (p. 162), Emanuel de Kadt (p. 163), Leonard Schapiro (p. 164), and Angus Stewart (p. 166).

[10] See pp. 113 ff., 120, 165, 169 ff. & 254 ff., regarding the influence of the presence of 'massifying' groups; p. 234., for the reverse situation in Franqueira.

related to yet another general characteristic of populist movements briefly discussed here, and which also merits further examination in the future. In its pre-coup concern with class confrontation the Movement was concerned with matters such as stern action by the state against law-breaking landlords, redistributive measures, and agrarian reform. These entailed problems which transcended the local community, and action which was somehow inserted in a wider network of relations and activities in the regional or even national spheres. An orientation to the regional and national class structures, or even to international political and economic relations, though largely lost after 1964, was central to MEB's outlook before the coup. The Movement developed this concern as part of its educational effort, and its attempts at *conscientização*. But only during the most hectic days of *sindicalização*, in the period of the rush to found *sindicatos* and federations in preparation for the CONTAG elections, did MEB ever come anywhere near actually attempting to integrate the activities of different communities. That was when the Movement indirectly participated in the jockeying for power in the *movimento sindical* as a whole. However, as will be remembered, this experience was on the way to being repudiated by MEB even before the coup, when the decision was in the pipeline to retrench the Movement's activities in that field by concentrating once again on education for *sindicalismo*—the task with which it had been formally entrusted.

There is little doubt that, also before 1964, successful defiance of the forces entrenched in the existing structure could not have come about without a co-ordination of local activities.[11] But before the coup MEB at least provided the peasantry with some cognitive or ideological orientation to the wider structure. Nevertheless, despite the fact that until the contraction of its operations in 1966-67 the Movement operated in many different places, it never pretended to *co-ordinate* the processes of *conscientização* in, and even less the initiatives for action of, the communities. Particularly since 1964, MEB approached essentially the isolated community. The implication was that the Movement could make no more than a minimal contribution to any challenge to the wider society in which these communities had to operate.

[11] The Franqueira community, which feared retaliation after voting against the candidate of the Barretos, *could* have unseated the man had they acted in consort with others. A (half-conscious?) awareness of this on the part of the *patrões* may well have been behind both the intensified promises at election time and their extreme distrust of rural *sindicatos*.

But then MEB, as an educational movement, did not consider the actual intervention in the processes of (class) confrontation to be one of its tasks. Not even in its most radical days, and despite the inclinations of some among its cadres, did the Movement lose sight of the distinction between educational activities and those of a 'political' movement in the broadest sense of the word, for which precisely the co-ordination of action is of the greatest importance.

MEB's abstinence from such co-ordination also greatly facilitated the maintenance of populist purity. Its experience suggests a *third general hypothesis* on populism: the maintenance of populist purity is inversely related to the size of the movement, or rather to the scale on which the movement as a whole, or any of its constituent units, operates. It is relatively easy to maintain the view that the *povo* will always choose right if the *povo* does not have to deal with issues beyond the local community.[12] Earlier I suggested that the *populista*'s claim to represent the entire *povo*, and his attempts to balance the interests of its various sections in politics of compromise, proved to be a sham when these interests turned out to be irreconcilable. MEB, as a result of its engrossment in the local community, never had to face the equivalent difficulty that the 'will of the people' may be much less homogeneous than populist ideas would have us believe, or the fact that the problem of reconciling conflicting 'wills' may be incapable of solution within a populist framework.[13]

By way of epilogue

It must be obvious that anything one could say at the conclusion of this book by way of evaluation has to be highly tentative. The people and the movements that have been discussed here have operated in political conditions of great stress and even greater contrast; the hopes and ideas prevalent during the days of Goulart were largely historical relics in the days of Costa e Silva. Their emergence has been followed mainly in the university milieu of the early 1960s; their decline mainly in MEB. If one were to adopt the point of view of MEB's own radicals —most of whom left the Movement between 1964 and 1967—there is little else but to conclude that MEB's history since the coup is

[12] Cf. also Hennessy's remark: 'As the area of conflicting interests widens so the populist dream fades as manipulative techniques become necessary to mobilize the masses in countering opposition' (Ionescu & Gellner, p. 51).

[13] In this connection the similarities between the populist and anarchist dilemmas are quite striking.

one of betrayal and compromise. For them the only right course of action would have been to close the Movement down, if possible with a strong blast at hierarchy and government alike. But others have struggled with all their might to keep the Movement going, somehow and somewhere, even without harping too much or too insistently on the fundamental transformations that Brazil's countryside obviously still needs in 1969 as much as it needed them in 1963. For them, among a peasantry that remains exploited by its landlords and forgotten by the authorities, so much useful work can and has to be done, so much is to be gained by giving the peasants a sense of human dignity and an awareness of some of their potential capacities, and nothing can be lost by attempting to help them raise their living standards through better methods of agriculture, greater awareness of matters of hygiene and health, or stronger co-operative institutions. Can anyone say that either point of view is wholly wrong, or wholly right?

From a broader perspective than that provided by MEB alone, questions remain as to what has happened to the Catholic radicals of the 'generation of 1962'—taking that year as the crucial one in their development—and what has become of the ideas they defended. The former question cannot be answered with any precision. All that can be said is that while a large proportion of the young Catholic radicals have become *embourgeoisés*, accommodated to the existing situation, if not wholly at peace in it—a far from exceptional development for student revolutionaries—others have pushed the views they held before April 1964 to extreme positions, abandoning not only their links with institutional religion but also their very faith, and have embraced a secular revolutionary position of one variety or another. A third group, in size probably somewhere in between the relatively large group of *acomodados* and the relatively small one of revolutionaries, has continued to deepen their faith, to explore new dimensions in 'theology for development', and to seek new forms of activity through which they can give expression to their Christian radicalism even in the new circumstances.

As for the ideas of the 'generation of 62', those ideas that were so widely attacked from within the church, there is no denying that they have had a considerable influence *after* they had been denounced by the post-coup authorities. Perhaps this was precisely *because* these ideas were so vehemently attacked and repressed, and because the views that came to be officially sanctioned were the very antithesis of those of the pre-coup Catholic radicals. While no body or group connected with the Brazilian Catholic church has (publicly) proclaimed itself to be their heir, has taken over their ideas lock, stock, and barrel, a considerable shift towards a more progressive position has occurred in the church as a whole, with new expressions of radical opinions coming from groups in the church which had hitherto kept themselves in the background. One of these groups, perhaps the most notable one, has been the clergy itself; throughout 1967 and 1968 cases have been reported of 'manifestos' signed by scores or even hundreds of priests, nuns, and theology students who usually denounced first the archaic structure of the church, then the social conditions in the country, and finally, openly or by implication, the government which was apparently indifferent to those conditions it allowed to persist. The first example was the open letter of approximately 300 priests late in October 1967, who denounced, among other matters, the church's paternalism, *assistencialismo*, and commercialization of the faith, the priests' divorce from the people through their middle-class style of life, and the lack of real openness to the ideals and values of the *povo*; then came the open letter of 75 priests and ministers and 400 theology students from São Paulo denouncing 'the *real* agitators in the country, those who hold power and ill-gotten money'; and this was followed by the truly radical manifesto signed again by some 300 priests on the occasion of the CNBB's preparatory meeting for the Latin American bishops' conference in Medellin.[14]

But it has not only been the clergy who have stood up for radical change in Brazil after the coup. Among the movements of Catholic Action, ACO and its youth branch JOC, as well as the rural youth movement JAC, have taken up the banner previously carried almost exclusively by JUC. The Pernambuco branch of ACO, with the support of virtually all other branches of Catholic Action in that state, published in April 1967 a long analysis of the situation in the North-East. They stated that the region's substantial economic growth through the implantation of infrastructure and industry has been based to a large extent on the presence of a vast army of unemployed peasants and workers, who are kept in that state in order to provide a pool of cheap, immediately available labour, which nevertheless does not diminish because the new industries are capital intensive.[15] A few months later JOC's national council launched a manifesto which was also con-

---

[14] I have used the reports which appeared respectively in *O Estado de S. Paulo*, 27 Oct. 1967; *Correio da Manhã*, 21 May 1968; and *Diário de São Paulo*, 16 July 1968.
[15] *Ultima Hora*, 28 Apr. 1967.

cerned with the working and living conditions of Brazil's masses, and the 'marginalization of the working class in the development process';[16] within a year it had published another one denouncing the social, economic, and political situation in the country—'a society resting on violence'—and demanding that 'deep, radical and urgent changes' be 'brought about by the *povo*, through its organization and its struggle'.[17]

No wonder the authorities became worried about this new radicalism from *within* the church, and even though the government itself tended to remain aloof from direct attacks upon the church, powerful underlings, especially among the military, were always ready to search for 'subversive activities' of servants of the church—stimulated greatly in their endeavours by articles in, 'investigations' by, or open letters to, the conservative press. A major crisis erupted late in 1967, when a French deacon working with one of Brazil's progressive bishops was arrested by the military; as a result the Central Commission of the CNBB issued its most strongly worded statement since the April coup. They rejected the attempts by those outside the church to delimit its functions, demanded respect for human rights, stated that 'the abuse of economic and political power . . . [was] . . . subversive of the social order', and proclaimed their faith in youth and the need for an open dialogue with them.[18] Major and minor confrontations between the authorities continued throughout 1968. There was the major role which Rio priests, nuns, and their bishop played at the time of the student demonstrations after a fellow student had been shot by the police in April of that year. There was the reported attempt by the government, apparently successful, to get the plenary meeting of the CNBB in July to water down its final statements. Then came the scandal caused in December by the arrest in Belo Horizonte of three French priests and a Brazilian theology student on accusations of 'subversion', which provoked massive new protests from among the clergy and the laity, widely reported in the press.

It seems fairly clear, then, that by the end of 1968, with the political system emasculated, it was from within the church that the most articulate opposition was being expressed to the social structure supported by Brazil's rulers, and to the repressive actions of those rulers themselves. Even though one should not make too much of that

[16] *Vozes*, 61/10, Oct. 1967.
[17] *O Jornal*, 18 June 1968.
[18] *O Globo*, 1 Dec. 1967.

opposition, or equate it with the most radical Catholic views of pre-1964 days, its significance cannot be doubted, nor the fact that those pre-1964 radicals had provided much of the impulse which resulted in the church's marked shift away from an all-too-cautious middle-of-the-road position. After the clamp-down of December 1968 the authorities did not proceed to move directly and openly against the church in the way they moved against the opposition intellectuals and against the organs of opposition opinion.[19] But it was surely not without reason that one of the most stringent rules applied by the censors was the one against *any* publication of news or opinion relating to critical social, economic, or political attitudes held by members of the hierarchy, the clergy, or Catholic organizations. One can hardly think of a better testimony to the *potential* role of the church in preparing Brazil for the necessary changes in its least developed areas and among its most exploited population groups; or of a better memorial to the Catholic radicals who have been the centre of attention in these pages.

[19] When this book was in proof, well-substantiated reports were widely published in the Western press of widespread torture in Brazil, the victims including members of the clergy, nuns, and theology students. Though the Brazilian government still maintained (or pretended to maintain) a neutral position towards the church, increasingly powerful subordinate police and army commanders showed, by subjecting men and women religious to torture, that they regarded the church as dangerous, and as an appropriate target for intimidation.

Appendix I

Results of the survey of MEB's cadres

INFORMATION on the personal and social background of the cadres of MEB, and on some of their attitudes in respect of the Movement's work and ideology, was of importance for a proper evaluation of the dynamics of the Movement. This was particularly so for an understanding of the process of radicalization from the bases upwards, and of the personal links that existed between the cadres of MEB and other radical organizations, especially the youth movements of Catholic Action. Consequently it was planned to draw up a mail questionnaire and to distribute this among the entire personnel. But during one of the first general discussions at the *Nacional* it was made quite clear to me that no meaningful response to a questionnaire of this kind could be expected in the Brazil of those days—even if such a questionnaire came from the *Nacional* itself. There was a widespread fear of mail censorship. What is more, people were in general very reluctant to entrust their views on subjects, which might conceivably have political implications, to pieces of paper over which they lost personal control. As a result the idea of a mail questionnaire was dropped.

I went ahead, nevertheless, to try and gather as much of this kind of background information as was possible under the circumstances, giving up the hope of a census, or even of true representativeness through a random sample. A simple questionnaire was drawn up (see below), which was administered individually and informally to all the members of the *Nacional* (Nov-Dec 1965). It was also filled in by all the people participating in the *III Encontro Nacional de Coordenadores* (April-May 1966), by those participating in the *Encontro Estadual de Coordenadores* in Pernambuco (May 1966), and by almost all members of the Franqueira and Fernandópolis *equipes* (respectively June and September 1966).

Questionnaires were distributed and explained, but the respondents were left to fill in the forms by themselves. It would no doubt have been preferable for me to administer the questionnaires personally—this would certainly have eliminated, or at least diminished, misunderstandings and incomplete replies (especially on some of the 'tricky' questions, such as those regarding remuneration or past adherence to political associations). At the *III Encontro Nacional de Coordenadores* and at the Pernambuco

Encontro time for this was lacking; in Franqueira and Fernandópolis I followed the same procedure as that used at the *Encontros* for the sake of uniformity. Consequently in some respects the outcome is more like that which might be expected from a mail questionnaire inquiry—with 100 per cent response—than like that from a survey with scheduled interviews.

The total number of people reached was 56. This number included *all* the persons in the *coordenação* and *equipe técnica* at the *Nacional*, and *all* the state co-ordinators. For purposes of analysis these (15 in all) have been grouped in one category: they are obviously 'wholly representative' of themselves and moreover constitute the group with the widest responsibilities in the Movement. In the tables at the end of this Appendix they will be referred to as group A.

The second category (numbering 28) is made up of all co-ordinators of individual *sistemas* who attended either the meeting in Rio or that in Recife, those supervisors from Franqueira or Fernandópolis who had previously fulfilled the function of co-ordinator, and those who worked at an *Estadual* without being the co-ordinator. The category therefore excludes the co-ordinators of *sistemas* from Minas Gerais, Bahia, and Ceará, who were represented at the Rio meeting by their respective state co-ordinators, and whom I did not meet at a subsequent occasion (in contrast to the co-ordinators from Pernambuco). This category is probably reasonably representative of the people who in 1966 were responsible for the running of the *sistemas*; they will later be referred to as group B.

The final category, in the tables designated group C, are the 13 members of *equipes* (almost exclusively of Franqueira and Fernandópolis) who had never fulfilled the function of co-ordinator. This category is not only very small but is also the least 'meaningful' or representative one. It is made up of people from *sistemas* founded in the first year of the Movement's operation, certainly very different from those started more recently (particularly in the North). Both—especially Fernandópolis—had a more than usually sophisticated *equipe*. Although some suggestive comparisons can be made between these people who are close to the grass-roots as well as far from the centres of Brazilian intellectual, political, and ideological ferment, and the other sub-groups of our sample, such comparisons must be regarded as providing no more than tentative indications. In general, I have tended (in the text) to take groups B and C together, and compare them jointly with the top leadership group. The problem of statistical significance is discussed below, after the (marginal) totals for each question have been given.

One further general point must be made. Some of the most radical people in MEB left the Movement shortly after the coup. Our data refer to 1966; they present the personal characteristics of some of those then still in the Movement. A margin of uncertainty exists when we make inferences from these data, e.g. to MEB's ideological development: the composition of the

Movement's leadership in 1962–4 *may* have been in certain respects significantly different.

An outline of the questionnaire, with the marginal totals for each question, follows below.

MEB QUESTIONNAIRE

QI *When did you join MEB?*
1961–2	13	(23%)
1963–April 1964	34	(61%)
After April 1964	9	(16%)
	56	

Q2 *What positions have you held?* (Highest mentioned)
Member of *Nacional* or Co-ordinator of *Estadual*	15	(27%)
Member of *Estadual* or *Sistema* Co-ordinator	28	(50%)
Sistema Supervisor	13	(23%)
	56	

Q3 *Are you working in MEB full-time?*
Yes	39	(70%)
No	17	(30%)
	56	

If not, what other work are you doing?
Studying	6	(35%)
Teaching	5	(29%)
Other	6	(35%)
	17	

Q4 *Did you work before joining MEB?*
Yes	48	(86%)
No	5	(9%)
N.A.	3	(6%)
	56	

19

Q 4   (a) *If yes: in what?*
      Teaching   26   (54%)
      Civil Servant   6   (13%)
      Other   16   (33%)
                    ———

                    48
      (b) *Was your previous salary more, less or the same?*
      More   19   (40%)
      Less   14   (29%)
      Same   5   (10%)
      N.A.   10   (21%)
                    ———

                    48

Q 5   *What education did you receive?*
      Ginásio   2 ⎫
      (some not completed)   ⎬ 19   (34%)
      Colégio   ⎪
      (some not completed)   17 ⎭
      University   17   (30%)
      (not completed)
      University Graduate   20   (36%)
                    ———

                    56

Q6   *Social class background*[1]
      Middle class[2]   40   (72%)
      Working class   12   (21%)
      Not known   4   (7%)
                    ———

                    56

[1] The respondents were classified into 'middle class' and 'working class' in the first instance on the basis of father's occupation. All manual occupations (including shop assistants) were considered working class. All managerial, professional, self-employed commercial, entrepreneurial, and white-collar occupations, as well as smaller medium farmers (as opposed to peasants or agricultural labourers), were considered middle class. Where an ambiguous category was used by respondents, father's education and/or mother's occupation or education were taken into account.

[2] Of these one-fifth (8) were urban upper-middle class.

Q7 *Father's Education*

Primário	31	(55%)
Ginásio	10 ⎫	
		(29%)
Colégio	6 ⎭	
University	5	(9%)
N.A.	4	(7%)
	—	
	56	

Q8 *Mother's occupation*

Housewife	51	(91%)
Teacher/Civil Servant	5	(9%)
	—	
	56	

Q9 *Mother's education*

None	3	(5%)
Primário	38	(68%)
Ginásio	10	(18%)
More than *ginásio*	5	(9%)
	—	
	56	

Q10 *Do you belong to any association of Catholic Action now?*

JUC	3	(5%)
Other Catholic Action	1	(2%)
None stated	52	(93%)
	—	
	56	

Q11 *Regardless of whether you belong now, have you ever belonged to any (other) association of Catholic Action?*

JUC	11	(20%)
JEC	11	(20%)
Other Catholic Action	12	(21%)
None stated	28	(50%)
	—	
	56	

Consolidated Membership of Catholic Action Groups
(at any time, eliminating overlap)

Radical (JUC, JEC)	22	(39%)
Non-Radical only (AC, JIC, JOC, JAC)	6	(11%)
None stated	28	(50%)
	—	
	56	

Q12 *Have you read any article or book of the following authors?*

Lebret	47	(84%)
Marx	19	(34%)
Teilhard	25	(45%)
Sartre	15	(27%)
Mounier	29	(52%)
Pe Vaz	29	(52%)

Q13 *Other books which impressed you* (write in).

Saint-Exupèry	*Le petit prince*	15	(27%)
	Terre des hommes	8	(14%)
Michel Quoist	*Construir o mundo e o homem*	8	(14%)
	Poemas para rezar	6	(11%)
Khalil Gibraun	*O profeta*	6	(11%)
Thiago de Melo	*Faz escuro mas eu canto*	6	(11%)
	porque a manhã vai chegar		
Celso Furtado	*Dialética do desenvolvimento*	6	(11%)

Q14 *Sex*

Male	23	(41%)
Female	33	(59%)
	—	
	56	

Q15 *Age*

20–25	17	(30%)
25–30	25	(45%)
over 30	14	(25%)
	—	
	56	

Q16 *Marital Status*

Single	44	(78%)
Married	11	(20%)
N.A.	1	(2%)
	—	
	56	

With such small numbers cross-classifications soon became statistically meaningless—i.e. the differences found between sub-groups could have occurred by chance. I have therefore limited the analysis mainly to the respondents' place in the three levels of the organization as set out in the opening paragraphs of this appendix. I have, in a few additional tables, used date of entry into the Movement as an independent variable. As indicated in Chapter 7, almost invariably it is the top leadership group (alternatively the group of earliest entry into the Movement) which is contrasted with the rest; tests of statistical significance have hence been applied to such dichotomous comparisons. As will be seen from the tables, even though rather few of the differences are significant at the—conventional—5 per cent level (i.e. the distribution actually encountered is likely to occur by chance not more than 1 in 20 times), most of them stand up to the less rigorous 10 per cent level of significance.[1]

The organizational levels are indicated by A, B, and C, as follows:

A: Members of *Nacional* and Co-ordinators of *Estadual*
B: Members of *Estadual* and Co-ordinators of *Sistema*
C. *Sistema* supervisors.

Table 1. Sex, by organizational level

	Sex Male	Female	Total
A	9 (60%)	6 (40%)	15
B	9 (32%) } 34%	19 (68%) } 66%	28 } 41
C	5 (38%)	8 (62%)	13
Total	23 (41%)	33 (59%)	56 (100%)

$.2 > p > .1$ not significant at 10% level

Table 2. Age, by organizational level

	Age 20–25	26–30	over 30	Total
A	3 (20%)	5 (33)%	7 (47%)	15
B	7 (25%) } 34%	15 (54%) } 49%	6 (21%) } 17%	28 } 41
C	7 (54%)	5 (38%)	1 (8%)	13
Total	17 (30%)	25 (45%)	14 (25%)	56 (100%)

under 30—v—over 30: $.1 > p > .05$ significant at 10% level

[1] The tests used have been χ^2 (with Yates correction for continuity), or, where some expected frequency was less than 5, the hypergeometrical distribution exact test.

Table 3. *Date of Entrance into the Movement, by organizational level*

	Entrance into MEB			
	1961–2	*1962–4*	*after 1964*	*Total*
A	7 (47%)	7 (47%)	1 (6%)	15
B	6 (21%) } 15%	17 (61%) } 66%	5 (18%) } 19%	28 } 41
C	—	10 (77%)	3 (23%)	13
Total	13 (23%)	34 (61%)	9 (16%)	56 (100%)

61/62—v—rest:
p = ·05 significant at 5% level

Table 4. *Previous work, by organizational level*

	Work before entering MEB					
	No	*N.A.*	*Teach*	*Yes* *Civil Servant*	*Other*	*Total*
A	—	—	5 33%	2 13%	8 53%	15
B	2	2	16 } 64%	4 } 12%	4 } 24%	24 } 33
C	3	1	5	—	4	9
Total	5	3	26 (54%)	6 (13%)	16 (33%)	48 (100%)

Teachers—v—rest:
p = ·1   significant at 10% level

Table 5. *Education, by organizational level*

	Education			
	Secondary	*University*	of which: *University* *Graduate*	*Total*
A	—	15 (100%)	(8)	15
B	13 (46%) } 46%	15 (54%) } 54%	(9)	28 } 41
C	6 (46%)	7 (54%)	(5)	13
Total	19 (34%)	37 (66%)	(22)	56 (100%)

p < ·01   significant at 1% level

Table 6. Social class background, by organizational level

| | Social Class | | | |
	Middle	Working	Not known	Total
A	14 (93%)	1 (7%)	—	15
B	17 (61%) ⎱ 63%	8 (29%) ⎱ 27%	3 (11%) ⎱ 10%	28 ⎱ 41
C	9 (69%) ⎰	3 (23%) ⎰	1 (8%) ⎰	13 ⎰
Total	40 (72%)	12 (21%)	4 (7%)	56 (100%)

Middle—v—working (not known excluded):
·2>p>·1 not significant at 10% level

Table 7. Father's education, by organizational level

| | Father's education | | | |
	none/primary	secondary/university	not known	Total
A	3 (20%)	10 (67%)	2 (13%)	15
B	19 (68%) ⎱ 68%	8 (29%) ⎱ 27%	1 (4%) ⎱ 5%	28
C	9 (69%) ⎰	3 (23%) ⎰	1 (8%) ⎰	13
Total	31 (55%)	21 (38%)	4 (7%)	56 (100%)

none/primary—v—secondary/university (not known excluded):
p>·01 significant at 1% level

Table 8. Consolidated membership of Catholic Action group, by organizational level

| | Catholic Action Members | | Not members of Catholic Action | Total |
	Radical (JUC, JEC)	Non-Radical (AC, JIC, JOC, JAC)		
A	8 (53%)	3 (20%)	4 (27%)	15
B	5 (32%) ⎱ 34%	2 (7%) ⎱ 7%	17 (61%) ⎱ 59%	28
C	9 (38%) ⎰	1 (8%) ⎰	7 (54%) ⎰	13
Total	22 (39%)	6 (11%)	28 (50%)	56 (100%)

members—v—non-members:
·1>p>·05 significant at 10% level
radical—v—rest
p = ·2 not significant at 10% level

Table 9. *Consolidated membership of Catholic Action groups, by date of entry into MEB*

Entry	Catholic Action Members		Not members of Catholic Action	Total
	Radical (JUC, JEC)	Non-Radical (AC, JIC, JOC, JAC)		
1961–2	8 (53%)	2 (13%)	5 (33%)	15
1963– Apr. 1964	11 (33%) ⎫ 34%	4 (12%) ⎫ 10%	18 (55%) ⎫ 56%	33
After Apr. 1964	3 (38%) ⎭	— ⎭	5 (62%) ⎭	8
Total	22 (39%)	6 (11%)	28 (50%)	56 (100%)

member—v—non-member
p = ·2   not significant at 10% level
radical—v—rest:
p > ·2   not significant at 10% level.

Table 10. *See facing page.*

Table 11. *Authors read, or read about, by organizational level*

	Lebret	Marx	Teilhard	Sartre	Mounier	Pe Vaz
A	14 (93%)	10 (66%)	12 (80%)	6 (40%)	14 (93%)	13 (87%)
B	24 (86%)	6 (21%)	8 (29%)	6 (21%)	8 (29%)	9 (32%)
C	9 (69%)	3 (23%)	5 (38%)	3 (23%)	7 (54%)	7 (54%)
Total	47 (84%)	19 (34%)	25 (45%)	15 (27%)	29 (52%)	29 (52%)

Table 10. *Earnings before entering MEB, of those who had worked, by date of entry into MEB*

Entry	more	same	less	N.A.	Total
1961-2	2 (14%)	1 (7%)	6 (43%)	5 (36%)	14
1963-Apr. 1964	14 (50%) } 50%	3 (11%) } 12%	7 (25%) } 24%	4 (24%) } 15%	28
After Apr. 1964	3 (50%)	1 (17%)	1 (17%)	1 (17%)	6
Total	19 (40%)	5 (10%)	14 (29%)	10 (21%)	48 (100%)

less—v—rest (no answer excluded)
p = ·1 significant at 10% level

Appendix II

Notes on Fieldwork at São Pedro

WHILE staying at São Pedro, the sugar plantation taken over by IBRA (see Chapter 9), I underwent the only really disagreeable experience encountered during the fieldwork: I found myself suddenly under suspicion in respect of the true motives of my interviewing and research activities. The account of that episode has no real place in the body of this book, but it seems sufficiently interesting to include it as an Appendix both because of the light it throws on the structure of domination on a sugar plantation, and because it shows, once again, that he who disregards (for whatever reason) by now well-established canons of fieldwork does so at his own peril.

To begin with the latter point. Instead of coming with some kind of formal or official introduction, clearly establishing my identity, institutional affiliation, etc., I went to São Pedro after an informal—and rather hurried—introduction to its general manager by one of the senior officials at IBRA's regional headquarters. Once there, aware of the fact that my time was limited to a working week at most, I found myself short-circuiting the normal process of gradually establishing *rapport* and trust. I jumped almost straight into lengthy interviews, many of them taped, often dealing with questions not usually inquired into by outsiders (the relations with the *sindicato*, the image of MEB, etc). I was led, in retrospect largely unnecessarily, to probe into matters of administrative details, such as the arrangements for the medical fund which had caused a row with the *sindicato*. I was probably the first foreigner to visit the enterprise since it had been taken over by IBRA, and in their place I too might have been suspicious 'of that fellow who comes here with his tape recorder, snoops around, speaks perfect Portuguese, and says he's a Dutchman doing sociological research for an English university'. (The works manager as reported by a sympathetic insider.)

In Chapter 10 I refer to the fact that at São Pedro, as on other sugar plantations, in 1966 people were directly intimidated and closely watched. Anything untoward was reported or noted, especially if it might possibly be interpreted as a challenge to established authority or its currently held views. Inquisitive outsiders such as myself were hardly welcome, especially if they asked awkward and unexpected questions. My problems, I believe, began when at the end of a (taped) interview with the works manager I had remarked to him: 'I see that you are armed. Are many people armed round here?' He was visibly surprised by this direct reference to the pistol at his belt, and as he was formulating his cautious answer, he could hardly hide his suspicion of the questioner: 'Yes, there are certain people who are armed. I feel that I need to be armed, because there are 300 people who work here, each one thinking differently. And then you've got lack of education, that is the ignorant person doesn't want to be respectful—that's why I go about armed. It's not only a question of protection, but it's more a matter of ... well ... it seems that it leads to a bit more respect. And it's also customary: I grew up in this environment in which lots of people went about armed. Thank God till today I haven't used it, and please God I shall never have to.'

From then on I became a potential troublemaker. He watched my movements closely. Anyone with whom I had talked was ordered into his office for a 'de-briefing'. The information he gathered over a couple of days showed that I had been talking to most people about the same subjects—MEB, the *sindicato*, working conditions, and so on—and that I had asked some quite specific and detailed 'administrative' questions. The results of his endeavours were passed on to Dr Carlos, the general manager. Dr Carlos lost no time and proceeded to grill me in public for an hour and a half on the veranda of the former *Casa Grande*. He alleged that whatever it was that I was doing, it wasn't sociology: all those details about administration had no relevance to the broad lines—and only those were of concern to sociologists. ('I know, for I have a brother-in-law, a very intelligent man, who teaches sociology in the [local] *faculdade*.' The brother-in-law, incidentally, was a lawyer.)

He was clearly extremely suspicious of my tape recorder. Determined to make it yield some piece of incriminating evidence, he asked whether I had a recording of my visit of the previous night to the MEB Radio School at the *usina*. To my relief I hadn't. He also wanted to know what I had recorded that morning, when with a team of interviewers of IBRA, not belonging to the plantation administration, I had visited one of the *engenhos*.[1] I had talked there to various *moradores*, but had not taken the tape-recorder along—precisely with a view to the possible consequences for them of a situation like the one I now found myself in. When I said that I had made no recordings, one of those present remarked that he had been told that I had also been using a miniature pocket recorder. Apparently someone had seen me operate a light meter before taking photographs. Despite my explanation, that remark added considerably to the general atmosphere of suspicion.

Most of the recordings had been erased—they were, after all, only used as *aide-mémoire* for the making of field notes—but an interview with the chief

[1] The interviewers were engaged in interviewing all *moradores* to establish their 'capacity' to become independent family farmers under the IBRA pilot scheme of land distribution.

factory foreman made the day before my 'interrogation' was still on the tape. Dr Carlos then demanded that the recording of that interview be played back 'in its entirety'. I lied that the first half had already been erased—but he insisted that they would listen to what was left. I then protested that I could not reveal information given in confidence unless specifically authorized by my informant, whereupon the man in question hastily agreed to the tape being played. It so happened that there was nothing 'incriminating' on the tape. A few of my questions on the administration's attitude to the workers and the *sindicato* were rather embarrassingly straightforward, but I had been given the most non-committal replies, contrary to what I had been led to expect from the man's reputation as a 'friend of the workers'. Only later did it occur to me that by the time of that interview I was probably one of the very few people *not* aware of the factory manager's inquiries and suspicions, while my informant was fully on his guard.

That entire experience was obviously a most unpleasant one: I departed under a cloud of suspicion which was only lifted two days later after a formal and written declaration on my status by the British Consul. The most curious thing about the whole business was the *dénouement*. After I had presented the Consul's letter to Dr Carlos, at IBRA's Regional Head Office, he was silent for a long time. Then he smiled, and asked his secretary to bring in the local newspaper of the day before. On the front page there was a story about an official of the SNI (the Secret Service) sent up from Rio to investigate allegations of fraudulent administrative practices in 'a large *usina* administered by IBRA'. This had appeared the morning after my 'interrogation'. In the *casa grande*, I was told later, the paper had been shown around triumphantly by the works manager: the supposedly English Dutchman had, after all, simply been a Brazilian police snooper. After sorting things out, I returned for another day to São Pedro, 'for the record'.

But the affair had positive aspects too. The workings of the structure of power in the enterprise had been brought out much more clearly than would have been the case under normal circumstances. I had been made to *feel*, rather than simply *understand*, something of the process of intimidation of workers and peasants, and something about the reasons for their passivity in the face of the powers that be. I had become aware of what it actually meant to be living on a plantation: all the time supervised by employers, always seen by or spied upon by the boss, some boss. That boss can make you swallow small and large humiliations, and he can ultimately threaten your very livelihood. I grasped in a new way why the workers were entirely impotent without a power base outside the confines of the plantation, and I discovered vicariously how deeply they must have been affected by the loss of the limited amount of government support that existed in pre-coup days.

Glossary

alfabetização: literacy training.
animação popular: stimulation of community activities and organization among the peasantry reached by MEB.
assistencialismo: welfareism.
assistente: ecclesiastical adviser to Catholic Action organization.
barracão: rural store.
cabo: plantation foreman.
cabo eleitoral: the vote-getter in the electoral district (cf. the precinct captain in US politics).
camponês: peasant.
cartilha: primer.
cédula avulsa: ballot paper for single candidate.
cédula única: ballot paper with all the candidates' names printed on it.
comerciante: merchant, middleman.
consciência histórica: historical consciousness.
conscientização: process of arousing consciousness regarding socio-economic and political conditions.
conscientizados: persons who have undergone *conscientizacão*.
Conselho Diretor Nacional: the highest authority of MEB, composed almost exclusively of bishops appointed by the CNBB.
coronelismo: system of political patronage and bossism by the *coronel* (pl. *coronéis*), the locally dominant figure, especially prevalent until 1930.
cúpula: top leadership group.
diocesanização: process of transferring control in MEB from national organs of decision-making to diocesan bishops.
encontro: meeting.
engenho: plantation.
equipe: team.
Estadual (pl. *estaduais*): state co-ordinating team.
favela: shanty town.
fazenda: large estate.
fazendeiro: large landowner.
Frente Agrária: Peasant Front.

igreja: church.

imposto: tax.

liga camponês: peasant league.

massificação: term used by populists indicating (political) processes in which people are manipulated by the leadership.

monitor: unpaid auxiliary, serving as link between radio teacher and class.

morador: farmhand living (more or less permanently) on a rural property.

município: unit of local government analogous to borough.

mutirão (pl. *mutirões*): mutual-aid party of peasants.

Nacional: national headquarters of MEB, including its general secretariat, national co-ordination and ancillary services.

padroado: ecclesiastical patronage delegated by the Pope to the monarch.

patrão (pl. *patrões*): master, landlord, patron.

politização: process of inculcating grass-roots political awareness.

pólo dominado/dominante: dominated/dominant pole.

povo: people.

promoção humana: the promotion of human well-being.

relatório: report.

roça, roçado: (subsistence) plot.

senhor de engenho: owner of a sugar plantation.

seringueiro: rubber gatherer.

sertão: hinterland, the arid highlands of Brazil.

sindicato: trade union.

sindicalização: process of organizing workers or peasants into trade unions.

sistema: system, basic working unit of MEB, covering one diocese.

tenentes: lieutenants.

treinamentos: training, study, and discussion courses.

usina: sugar plantation and mill.

vivência: real-life participation.

zona da mata: sugar-cane zone.

Select Bibliography

Abbot, W. M., SJ, ed. *The documents of Vatican II*. London, 1966.
Adams, R. N. 'Rural labor', in J. J. Johnson, ed., *Continuity and change in Latin America*. Stanford, 1964.
—— 'Political power and social structures', in Claudio Véliz, ed., *Obstacles to change in Latin America*. London, RIIA, 1965.
Alves, Márcio Moreira, *O Cristo do povo*. Rio, Sabiá, 1968.
Alves, Mario. A burguesia nacional e a crise brasileira. *Estudos sociais*, Dec. 1962.
Andrade, Manuel Correia de. *A terra e o homem no Nordeste*. S. Paulo, Ed. Bras., 1963.
Ávila, Fernando Bastos de. *Neo-capitalismo, socialismo, solidarismo*. 2nd ed. Rio, 1963.
Azevedo, Fernando de. *Canaviais e engenhos na vida política do Brasil*. 2nd ed. S. Paulo, Melhoramentos, 1958.
Barreto, Lêda. *Julião, nordeste, revolução*. Rio, Civ. Bras., 1963.
Barros, Adirson de. *Ascensão e queda de Miguel Arraes*. Rio, Equador, 1965.
Bennet, J. W. and Iwao Ishino. *Paternalism in the Japanese economy*. Minneapolis, 1963.
Bezerra, Almery. Da necessidade de um ideal histórico. JUC, *Boletim nacional*, no. 2: *Anais do IX Conselho Nacional*, Dec. 1959.
Blau, Peter M. *Exchange and power in social life*. New York, 1964.
Borges, Fragmon Carlos. O movimento camponês no Nordeste. *Estudos sociais*, Dec. 1962.
Brazil, Presidência, Serviço de Documentação. *I encontro dos bispos do Nordeste*. Rio, 1960.
Brito, Mário da Silva. *Antecedentes da semana de arte moderna*. Rio, 1964.
Buarque de Holanda, Sérgio, ed. *História geral da civilização brasileira: a época colonial*. S. Paulo, 1960.
Buber, Martin, *Paths in Utopia*. Boston, 1958.
Caldeira, Clóvis. *Mutirão*. S. Paulo, Ed. Nacional, 1956.
Callado, Antônio. *Tempo de Arraes: padres e comunistas no revolução sem violência*. Rio, Álvaro, 1965.
Cardosa, Fernando H. *Empresário industrial e desenvolvimento econômico no Brasil*. S. Paulo, Difusão Européia do Livro, 1964.

Cardosa, Fernando H. Hégémonie bourgeoise et indépendance économique. *Les temps modernes*, Oct. 1967.

César, Waldo A. 'Situação social e crescimento do Protestantismo na América Latina', in César and others, *Protestantismo e imperialismo na América Latina*. Petrópolis, Vozes, 1968.

Chonchol, Jaques. *El desarrollo de América Latina y la reforma agraria*. Santiago, Pacífico, 1964.

Coffy, R. Teilhard de Chardin et le socialisme. *Chronique social de France* (Lyon), 1966.

Comité Interamericano para el Desarrollo Agrícola. *Posse e uso da terrae desenvolvimento socio-económico do setor agrícola: Brasil*. Washington, 1966.

Confederação Evangélica do Brasil, Setor de Responsabilidade Social da Igreja. *Cristo e o processo revolucionário brasileiro*. Rio, Loqui, 1962. 2 vols.

Congar, Yves. *Lay people in the church*. London, 1957.

Crespo, Paulo. O problema camponês no Nordeste brasileiro. *SPES*, xvii (1963).

Cuypers, Hubert. *Pró ou contra Teilhard*. Petrópolis. 1967.

Dale, Romeu. *JUC do Brasil, uma nova experiência de Ação Católica*. 1962, mimeo.

Debrun, Michel. Nationalisme et politiques de développement au Brésil. *Sociol. du travail*, vi/3 & 4 (1964).

De Kadt, Emanuel. Conflict and power in society. *Int. Soc. Sc. J.*, xviii/3 (1965).

—— Paternalism and populism: Catholicism in Latin America. *J. Contemp. Hist.*, Oct. 1967.

—— 'Religion and social change in Brazil', in C. Véliz, ed. *The Politics of Conformity in Latin America*. London, RIIA, 1967.

Detrez, Conrado. Existencialismo e juventude brasileira. *Paz e terra*, no. 3 (1967).

Diégues Jr., Manuel. *Regiões culturais do Brasil*. Rio, Centro Bras. de Pesquisas Educacionais, 1960.

Dornas Filho, João. *O padroado e a igreja no Brasil*. S. Paulo, Ed. Nacional, 1938.

Dulles, J. W. F. Jr. *Vargas of Brazil*. London, 1967.

Dumoulin, Diana C. *The rural labor movement in Brazil*. Madison, Wisc. Univ. Land Tenure Center, 1964, mimeo.

Estevão, Carlos. *A questão da cultura popular*. Rio, Tempo Bras., 1963.

Frank, Andre Gunder. *Capitalism and underdevelopment in Latin America: historical studies of Chile and Brazil*. New York, 1967.

Freire, Paulo. *Educação como prática da liberdade*. Rio, Paz e Terra, 1967.

Freyre, Gilberto. *The Masters and the Slaves*, trans. S. Putnam. New York, 1946.

—— *Sobrados e mucambos*. Rio, José Olympio, 1951.

—— *New World in the tropics*. New York, 1963.

Furtado, Celso. *The economic growth of Brazil*. Berkeley, 1963.

—— *Dialética do desenvolvimento*. Rio, Fondo de Cultura, 1964.

—— 'Political obstacles to the economic development of Brazil', in C. Véliz, ed. *Obstacles to change in Latin America*. London, RIIA, 1965.

Furter, Pierre. L'imagination créatrice, la violence et le changement social. *CIDOC cuaderno* (Cuernavaca, Mex.), no. 14 (1968).

—— Utopie et Marxisme selon Ernst Bloch. *Arch. sociol. relig.*, no. 21 (1966).

—— *Educação e reflexão*. Petrópolis, 1966.

—— Caminhos e descaminhos de uma política da juventude. *Paz e terra*, no. 3 (1967).

Galjart, Benno. Class and 'following' in rural Brazil. *América Latina*, vii/3 (1964).

Gerschenkron, A. *Economic backwardness in historical perspective*. New York, 1965.

Guilherme, W. *Quem dará o golpe no Brasil*. Rio, Civ. Bras., 1962.

Herring, Hubert. *A history of Latin America*. 2nd. ed. New York, 1963.

Hewitt, C. N. *An analysis of the peasant movement of Pernambuco, Brazil, 1961–4*. Ithaca, Cornell Univ., NY State School of Industrial and Labor Relations, Dec. 1966, mimeo.

Hirschman, A. O. *Journeys toward progress*. New York, 1963.

Houtart, François and Émile Pin. *The church and the Latin American revolution*. New York, 1965.

Huizer, Gerrit. Some notes on community development and rural social research. *América Latina*, viii/3 (1965).

Hutchinson, Bertram. The patron-dependant relationship in Brazil: a preliminary examination. *Sociologia ruralis*, vi/1 (1966).

Ianni, Octávio. *Industrialização e desenvolvimento social no Brasil*. Rio, Civ. Bras., 1963.

—— and others. *Política e revolução social no Brasil*. Rio, Civ. Bras., 1965.

Iglésias, Francisco. Estudo sôbre o pensamento reacionário: Jackson de Figueiredo. *R. bras. cien. soc.*, ii/2, July 1962.

Ionescu, Ghiţa and E. Gellner, eds. *Populism*. London, 1969.

Jaguaribe, Hélio. *Economic and political development*. Camb., Mass., 1968.

Julião, Francisco. *Que são as ligas camponesas?* Rio, Civ. Bras., 1962.

Landsberger, H. A. 'The labor élite: is it revolutionary?', in S. M. Lipset and A. E. Solari, eds. *Elites in Latin America*. New York, 1967.

Leal, Victor Nunes. *Coronelismo, enxada e voto*. Rio, Tempo Bras., 1948.

Leeds, Anthony. Brazilian careers and social structure: an evolutionary model and case history. *Amer. Anthropol.*, Dec. 1964.

—— 'Brazil and the myth of Francisco Julião', in J. Maier and R. W. Weatherhead, eds. *Politics of change in Latin America*. New York, 1964.

Leite, Sebastião Uchoa. Cultura popular: esbôço de uma resenha crítica. *R. civilização bras.*, Sept. 1965.

Ligneul, André. *Teilhard et le personnalisme*, Paris, 1964.

Lopes, Juarez Rubens Brandão. *Sociedade industrial no Brasil.* S. Paulo, Difusão Européia do Livro, 1964.

—— 'Some basic developments in Brazilian politics and society', in E. N. Baklanoff, ed. *New Perspectives of Brazil.* Nashville, Tenn., 1966.

Maria, Júlio. 'A religião, ordens religiosas, instituçiões pias e beneficentes no Brasil: memória', in *Livro do centenario (1500–1900).* Rio, Imprensa Nacional, 1900.

Maritain, Jacques. *True humanism*, tr. by M. R. Adamson. London, 1938.

Marshall, T. H. *Sociology at the crossroads.* London, 1963.

Martins, Herminio. 'Ideology and development: "developmental nationalism" in Brazil', in Paul Halmos, ed. *Latin American sociological studies.* Keele Univ., Feb. 1967.

Matos, Almir. Aparências e realidades do panorama político. *Estudos sociais*, Apr. 1962.

Mecham, J. Lloyd. *Church and state in Latin America.* Rev. ed. Chapel Hill, 1966.

Medina, Carlos Alberto de. *A favela e o demagogo.* S. Paulo, Martins, 1964.

Mendes de Almeida, Cândido Antônio. *Nacionalismo e desenvolvimento.* Rio. Inst. Bras. de Estudos Afro-asiáticos, 1963.

—— *Memento dos vivos: a esquerda católica no Brasil.* Rio, Tempo Bras., 1966.

Moore, Wilbert. The utility of utopias; presidential address to American Sociol. Ass., 1966, reprinted in *Amer. Sociol. R.*, Dec. 1966.

Morse, Richard M. 'The heritage of Latin America', in L. Hartz, *The founding of new societies.* New York, 1964.

—— Some themes of Brazilian history. *S. Atlantic Q.*, lxi/2, Spring 1962.

Mounier, Emmanuel. *Le personnalisme.* Paris, 1950.

Nettl, J. P. *Political mobilization.* London, 1967.

Parsons, Talcott. *The social system.* London, 1951.

—— On the concept of political power. *Proc. Amer. Philos. Soc.*, cvii (1963).

Paulson, Belden H. *Local political patterns in Northeast Brazil.* Madison, Wisc. Univ. Land Tenure Center, 1964, mimeo.

Pierce, Roy. *Contemporary French political thought.* London, 1966.

Pike, F. B., ed. *The conflict between church and state in Latin America.* New York, 1964.

Pinto, Álvaro Vieira. *A questão da universidade.* Rio, Ed. Universitária, 1962.

Price, R. E. *Rural unionization in Brazil.* Madison, Wisc. Univ. Land Tenure Center, 1964, mimeo.

Queiroz, Maria Isaura Pereira de. *Réforme et révolution dans les sociétés traditionelles.* Paris, Anthropos, 1968.

Quijano Obregón, Aníbal. 'Contemporary peasant movements', in S. M. Lipset and A. E. Solari, eds. *Elites in Latin America*. New York, 1967.

Rahner, Karl. 'Christentum als Religion der absoluten Zukunft', in E. Kellner, ed. *Christentum und Marxismus—Heute*. Vienna, 1966.

Ramos, Jovelino Pereira. Protestantismo brasileiro: visão panorâmica. *Paz e terra*, no. 6, Apr. 1968.

Sanders, T. G. 'Catholicism and development: the Catholic left in Brazil', in K. H. Silvert, ed. *Churches and states: the religious institution and modernization*. New York, 1967.

Santo Rosário, Irmã Maria Regina. *O Cardeal Leme*. Rio, Olympio, 1962.

Schweitzer, A. Ideological groups. *Amer. Sociol. R.*, ix (1944).

Seganfreddo, Sonia. *UNE: instrumento de subversão*. Rio, Ed. GRD, 1963.

Sena, Pe. 'Reflexões sôbre o ideal histórico, in JUC, *Boletim* 4/1: *Ideal histórico*.

Skidmore, Thos. E. *Politics in Brazil, 1930–64*. New York, 1967.

Smelser, Neil J. *Theory of collective behaviour*. London, 1962.

Smith, T. Lynn. *Brazil, people and institutions*. Louisiana, 1963.

——and A. Marchant. *Brazil, portrait of half a continent*. New York, 1951.

Sodré, Nélson Werneck. *História militar do Brasil*. Rio, Civ. Bras., 1965.

Sousa, Luís Alberto Gomes de. *O Cristão e o mundo*. Petrópolis, Vozes, 1965.

Souza, Herbert José, ed. *Cristianismo hoje*. Rio, Ed. Univ., [1962].

Sunkel, Osvaldo. Política nacional de desarrollo y dependencia externa. *Estudios internacionales* (Santiago), Apr. 1967.

Talmon, Yonina. Millenarian movements. *Eur. J. Sociol.*, vii/2 (1966).

Tarso, Paulo de. *Os Cristãos e a revolução social*. Rio, 1963.

Teilhard de Chardin, Pierre. *The phenomenon of man*. New York, 1961.

Tella, Torcuato Di. 'Populism and reform in Latin America', in C. Véliz, ed. *Obstacles to change in Latin America*. London, RIIA, 1965.

Therry, L. D. Dominant power components in the Brazilian students' movement. *J. Inter-Amer. Studies*, Jan. 1965.

Vaz, Henrique C. de Lima. 'Consciência e responsabilidade histórica', in H. J. Souza, ed. *Cristianismo hoje*. Rio, [1962].

—— O absoluto e a história. *Paz e terra*, no. 2 (1966).

Vilaça, Marcos Vinícios and Roberto Calvalcanti de Albuquerque. *Coronel, coronéis*. Rio, Tempo Bras., 1965.

Wagley, C. *An introduction to Brazil*. New York, 1963.

— *Amazon town: a study of man in the tropics*. New ed. New York, 1964.

Weber, Max. *Wirtschaft und Gesellschaft*. New ed. Tübingen, Mohr, 1956.

Weffort, Francisco C. 'Política de massas', in O. Ianni and others, *Política e revolução social no Brasil*. Rio, Civ. Bras., 1965.

—— Le populisme dans la politique brésilienne. *Les temps modernes*, Oct. 1967.

Wilkie, Mary E. *A report on rural syndicates in Pernambuco, Brazil.* Rev. ed. Wisc. Univ., Oct. 1967, mimeo.

Willems, Emilio. *Followers of the new faith.* Nashville, Tenn., 1967.

Wolf, Eric R. 'Kinship, friendship and patron-client relations in complex societies', in M. Banton, ed. *The social anthropology of complex societies.* London, 1966.

Wolfe, Marshall. Rural settlement patterns and social change. *Latin American Research R.* (Texas UP), 1/2 (1966).

Index

Ação Católica, see Catholic Action
Ação Católica Operária, 60, 73, 272
Ação Popular, see AP
Ação Universitária Católica, 58–9
Acción Cultural Popular (Colombia), 122 n.
Acción Popular (Peru), 97
Africa: populism in, 96; French, community-development techniques in, 213 n.
Agrarian: reform, 25 f., 44–5, 49, 67, 74, 76, 84, 176 n.; — MEB and, 149, 203–4, 214 (*see also* IBRA; SUPRA); unrest, 30–1
Alagoas, 128, 165
Almery, Pe, *see* Bezerra, Pe Almery
Alves, Marcio Moreira, 6 n.
Amazon region, Amazonia, *see* North
Amazonas (state), 128
Amoroso Lima, Alceu, 56 n., 57 ff.
Anarchism, 270 n.
Animação Popular, 167, 193 n., 212–13, 247–50, 260
Anti-clericalism, 51
AP, 47, 66 n.; founding of, 5, 80 f.; students attracted to, 69; Christian element in, 81 ff., 121; activities and ideology, 81–2, 98–101; history of movement: till April 1964, 81–94; — subsequently, 81, 120–1; and MEB, 82 f., 112, 135, 153, 161, 165 f., 170, 199; supporters and membership, 82–3; and bishops, 83–4; philosophy of history, 85–90, 91–4; attitude to *povo,* 90–1; Communists: comparison with, 99–101; — relations with, 118–19, 162, 254–8; and *sindicatos,* 111–12, 115 f., 118 f., 165 f., 170 f.; in politics (1963–4), 119–20; in Fernandópolis and Lagoinha, 255 f.; *see also* Populism
Arantes, Aldo, 70
Army, 35, 39 f., 45; *see also* Military coups
Arraes, Miguel, 48–9, 104, 113, 244
Arruda Sampaio, Plinio de, 43
Assistêncialismo, 36–7, 39, 49, 104, 179, 272

Athayde, Tristão de, *see* Amoroso Lima, Alceu
Ávila, Pe Fernando Bastos de, SJ, 65
Azevedo, Fernando de, 11, 15 n., 51–2

Bahia (state), 127 f., 165, 205, 276
Barreto, Lêda , 26 n., 29
Barreto family, 230–1, 236 ff., 251, 269 n.
Barros, Adhemar de, 36 n., 39
Belaúnde Terry, Fernando, 97
Belo Horizonte, 273; University of, 65–6, 98–9
Berlin, Sir Isaiah, 98 n.
Bezerra, Pe Almery, 62–4
Bishops: after 1964 coup, 6–7, 273; Centro D. Vital and, 58; of NE, 61–2, 74 ff., 173; and JUC, 71–2, 77–80; attitude on social questions, 72–7; and AP, 83–5; and *sindicatos,* 109 ff., 162–3, 165, 197; and radio schools, 122–5
and MEB: foundation of, 122–5; their role, 143–5, 151 f.;—(1964–8), 6–7, 138, 145–7, 190 ff., 208–11, 224 ff., 229, 266; *diocesanização,* 138 n., 143, 147, 195, 209, 220–1, 224, 226, 229; and radical trend in movement, 144 ff., 156, 159–60, 163; and self-promotion of *povo,* 212
See also CNBB
Blau, Peter M., 12 f.
Bloch, Ernest, 64 n.
Borges, Fragman Carlos, 28, 101 n.
Bourgeoisie: national, 41 ff., 99; AP and communist views on, 99–101; challenged by MEB, 154–5, 200
Brandão, Mrs Maria, 82 n.
Brasilia, 41, 44 n.
Brazil, Colony and Empire, social relations and structure, 10–16
'Brazilian reality', 61 f., 65–6, 69, 153, 218, 232 f., 246
'Brazilian Revolution', 62, 69, 232, 267

297

Brizzola, Leonel, 43
Buber, Martin, 64 n., 91
Bureaucracy, 84; see also Estado cartorial

Calazans, Miss Julieta, 115 n.
Caldeira, Clóvis, 206 n., 208
Câmara, D. Helder, Archbp of Recife, 58 n., 72 n., 73 n., 123
Câmara, Card. D. Jaime, Archbp of Rio, 58
Capital, foreign, 40 ff., 100, 156
Capitalism, 16, 66–7, 84, 91 f., 95
Caramuru, Pe Raimundo, 72
Caravanas populares, 167, 213–14
Cardonnel, Fr Thomas, 64 f., 70
Carlos, Dr (Superintendent of usina S. Pedro), 178 ff., 186–7, 287–8
Carvalho brothers (Lagoinha), 248 ff., 260 ff.; Mauricio, 250 f.; Chico, 251, 262
Castelo Branco, Marshal, 2, 44 n., 190
Castro, Fidel, Castroism, 97, 121
Castro, Josué de, 143
Catholic Action, 191, 216, 272; founded, 58–9; JUC and, 77–80; and AP, 84–5; MEB and, 136, 139 ff.; membership of cadres, 279 f., 284; youth organizations, see under their names
Catholic church (in Brazil): and dissenting points of view, 1; power and significance of, 1, 51; during colonial period, 51–2; during Empire, 52–4; since 1889, 54 ff.; resistance after coup, 271–4; see also Bishops; Radical Catholicism; Vatican
Ceará, 128, 165, 276
Centre-West, 107; MEB in, 124, 127 f., 131, 133, 136, 213, 224, 229; states comprising, 127; see also Fernandópolis; Lagoinha
Centro D. Vital, 56–8
Centros Populares de Cultura, 69, 105–6, 247
César, Waldo A., 6 n.
Chesterton, G. K., 81 n.
China, Chinese, 77; see also Maoists
Chonchol, Jacques, 176 n.
Christian Democracy, see PDC
Citizenship, sense of, 27, 37, 48, 112, 264
CIO–AFL, 116
Class:
  Concept, relevance of, 4, 9
  Confrontation, 10; MEB and, 6, 10, 153–62; — after 1964 coup, 6–7, 173–4, 196–7, 199–205, 210; nationalism and, 42–3; concepts of, 43 n.; breakdown of politics of compromise and, 47, 49,

265; Catholic social doctrine as alternative to, 64–5, 151–4, 160, 163, 199–200; sindicatos and, 112; in zona da mata, 173–4, 265–6; see also Community development; Co-operation; Revolution; Viver é Lutar
Consciousness: development of, 9–10, 29 ff.; 37, 43, 47, 265–6; rural unions and, 24–5, 28–31, 112; community development and, 262–4, 266
Cleofas, João, 48
CNBB, 215, 272; founded, 73; and meeting of NE bishops (1956), 74–5; statements (Oct. 1961), 76–7; — (Easter 1963), 84; — (1967), 273; and AP, 84–5; and MEB, 122 ff., 135 ff., 143 f., 146, 150 f., 190 ff.; and sindicatos, 162; and group dynamics, 215
Colombia; radio schools in, 122
Commissão Nacional de Sindicalização Rural, see CONSIR
Communism, Communists, 71, 268; bishops on, 76–7, 191; and cultura popular, 102, 104 ff.; and sindicatos, 108, 115 ff., 162; policy after coup and splinter groups, 120–1; MEB and, 149, 156, 158, 254–9; victimization, 188; peasants' attitude, 256 ff.; see also Marxism; Massificação; PCB; ULTAB
Community: definition of, 126 n.
  Development, 6–7, 30, 149, 214–15, 259; limited potentialities of, 197, 240–4; in Lagoinha, 247, 259; and class confrontation, 260–6; co-ordination of isolated communities, 264, 269; see also Animação Popular
Compadrio, 18, 207, 246
Confederação Nacional de Trabalhadores na Agricultura, see CONTAG
Conferência Nacional dos Bispos do Brasil, see CNBB
Consciência histórica, 70, 87–90, 93, 103 n., 149 f.
Conscientização: theory and practice of, 93, 98, 102–7; and sindicatos, 112–13, 164 f., 167; MEB and, 154–62, 167, 214; — after 1964 coup, 6–7, 148, 196, 202, 204–5, 217 ff., 224 ff.; in zona da mata, 172–6, 183, 188 f.; in North, 207 f.; in Franqueira, 236–44; obstacles to success of, 240–4, 252, 264, 269; in Lagoinha, 246 ff., 252, 254; of medical students, 253 n.; see also Class: consciousness; Non-directiveness

Conselheiro, Antônio, 29
CONSIR, 115, 117, 170
CONTAG, 117 ff., 162, 166, 170, 219, 268 f.
Co-operation in communities: reorientation of MEB after 1964 coup, 6–7, 201 ff., 266 f.; in North, 208, 266; in Lagoinha, 252–3
Corbisier, Roland, 41
Corção, Gustavo, 57 n.
Coronelismo, coronéis, 19–24, 38, 48, 168–9
Costa e Silva, Marshal, 2 f.
Crespo, Pe Paulo, 109, 111, 116 n., 162
Cuba, Cubans, 77, 97, 108, 172, 175; see also Castro
Cultura Popular, 69, 82, 102, 104–7, 155, 247–8

Dahrendorff, Ralf, 43 n.
Dale, Fr Romeu, 77, 79
Dantas, Santiago, 47
Debrun, Michel, 43 n.
Detrez, Conrado, 91 n.
Development policy, 39, 41, 44, 66–7, 75 f., 123
Durkheim, E., 208
Dutra, Gen., 38–9

Ecclesiam Suam, 199
ECLA, 39, 157
Education: Jesuits and, 52; rural, 73 f., 149, 206 f.; at Franqueira and Lagoinha, 231, 242, 250; Basic, see MEB
Eisenhower, Pres., 40
Elections: manipulation of, 19–20, 31–3, 159, 239–40; reform, 19 n., 84; conscientização of peasants, 204, 214, 269 n.
Engelke, D. Inocêncio, Bp of Campanha, 72–3
Esprit, 65
Estado cartorial, 35 n., 45
Estatuto do Trabalhador Rural, see Rural Labour Statute
Estudos Sociais, 100
Evangelical Confederation of Brazil, 5–6
Existentialism, 62, 65, 91, 93, 102

Feijó, Fr Diogo Antônio, 53
Fernandópolis, 172, 245 ff., 255
Figueiredo, Jackson de, 56–7
Frank, Andre Gunder, 17, 44–5 n.
Franqueira, 19 n., 20 n., 172, 230–44; described, 230–1; reasons for study of,

231 n.; activities of MEB, 231–5; landlord and peasant in, 235–40; community action, 240; what MEB achieved, 243–4; Lagoinha compared with, 250–1; conclusions drawn from, 260 ff.; MEB ends work, 266
Freemasonry, 53, 56
Freire, Paulo, 82, 102–4, 107, 156 n., 196 n.
Frentes Agrárias, 76
Freyre, Gilberto, 10, 14 n., 15, 51
Furtado, Celso, 43 n., 47, 143, 280
Furter, Pierre, 64 n., 68 n.

Galjart, Benno, 16 n., 17 n., 19 n., 25 n., 27 f.
Gibraun, Khalil, 143, 280
Góes Monteiro, Gen. P. A. de, 38
Goiás, 16, 127 f., 165, 205
Gomes, Brig. Eduardo, 38 f.
Goulart, Pres. João, 2, 8, 36 n., 41; rural policy and causes of overthrow, 45 n., 49, 265; presidency, 46–7, 49, 84, 94, 156; and sindicatos, 108, 113–15
Greene, Graham, 81 n.
Group dynamics, 7, 215–17, 232 f., 235; see also Non-directiveness
Guanais, Oliveros, 70
Guilherme, Wanderley, 50 n.

Hall, George, 98 n.
Hegel, Hegelianism, 87, 91, 102
Hennessy, Alistair, 97, 270 n.
Herring, Hubert, 10 n., 15
History, philosophy of, 85–90, 153; dialectic, 88–9, 91; man as maker and transformer of, 153, 155–6, 218; see also Consciência histórica; Ideal histórico
Horowitz, Irving Louis, 171 n.
Huizer, Gerrit, 29 f., 264
Hutchinson, Bertram, 9 n., 12 n., 13, 244, 251
Huxley, Sir Julian, 86

Ianni, Octavio, 36 n., 42
IBRA, 176 ff., 286 ff.
Ideal histórico, 62–4, 66–8, 70, 78, 87; see also Consciência histórica
Instituto Superior de Estudos Brasileiros, see ISEB
Integralistas, 57
International Monetary Fund, 39, 41
Intimidation and victimization, 7, 168–9, 187–8, 236 ff., 246, 251, 286–8

ISEB, 41, 43, 62 n., 66, 101 n.
Itá, 207

JAC, 59–60, 76, 272, 280, 284
Jaguaribe, Hélio, 41 ff.
Japan, patron-dependency in, 10 n., 14 n.
Jaspers, Karl, 93
JEC, 59 f., 81 n., 85, 111, 141, 279 f., 283 f.
Jesuits, 51 f., see also Ávila, Pe; Teilhard de Chardin, P.; Vaz, Pe
Jeunesse Ouvrière Catholique, 58
JIC, 59, 280, 284
JOC, 59 f., 272–3, 280, 284
John XXIII, Pope, 84 ff., 91
JUC, 59–80; activities and ideology, 5, 60–8, 98–9; relations with hierarchy, 5, 62, 70 ff., 77–80; — with other student groups, 71; and AP, 5, 80 ff., 85; social work, 62, 65–6; and university reform, 62, 68–9; in university politics, 68–71; and cultura popular, 104; and sindicatos, 111, 115; and MEB, 135, 141, 153, 163, 165; — membership of cadres, 279 f., 283 f.
Julião, Francisco, 25–30, 244
Juventude Agrária Católica, see JAC
Juventude Estudantil Católica, see JEC
Juventude Independente Católica, see JIC
Juventude Operária Católica, see JOC
Juventude Universitária Católica, see JUC

Kubitschek, Juscelino, 41, 44 f., 47

Lacerda, Carlos, 145, 156 f.
Lagoinha, 245–59; landlord and peasant in, 245–6, 251, 253 ff.; MEB operations, 246 ff., 266; AnPO, 247–50; the school, 250; comparison with Franqueira, 250–1; local leadership and landlords' obstruction, 251–4; peasants and politics, 254–8, 259; conclusions, 260 ff.
Laity, role of, 80; see also Catholic Action; JUC; MEB
Lampião, 29
Leaders, leadership: development of, 129, 132, 164–5, 168 ff., 214; in Lagoinha, 248–52, 254; see also Intimidation; MEB: cadres: and Treinamentos; Non-directiveness; Sindicatos
Lebret, Father L. J., 65, 81 n., 142, 280, 284
Leeds, Anthony, 27 ff., 33 n.
Leme, Card., D. Sebastião, Archbp of Rio, 56 ff.

Liga Eleitoral Católica, 57
Ligas camponeses, 24–31, 47, 108, 110, 115–16, 172, 176
Literacy: as voting qualification, 18, 26, 134–5; socio-political aims of campaign, 102–4, 107, 129, 134, 149, 174, 224, 246–7; illiteracy figures, 124, 177; see also Radio schools
Lott, Gen., 41
Lumen Gentium, 80 n.

Machado, Christian, 396
Maistre, J. Bonald de, 56
Manipulation, see Massificação; Mobilization
Maoists, 120 f.
Maranhão, 128, 165
Marcel, Gabriel, 91 f.
Maria, Pe Julio, 53–5
Maritain, Jacques, 57, 63, 81 n.
Marx, Karl, 87, 89 f., 142–3, 280, 284
Marxism, Marxists, 39, 42, 67 ff., 73, 94, 102, 106, 109 f., 120 f.; AP and, 85, 99, 121
Marxism-Leninism, 91
Massificação, 5, 94, 104, 107, 120, 199–200, 222 f., 227, 258 f.; of sindicatos, 113 ff., 165; question of facts, 219; in Franqueira, 233 f.
Mater et Magistra, 76, 85–6
Mato Grosso, 128
Maurras, Charles, 56
MEB: history of outlined, 2–3; author's purpose and method of study, 3–7; evaluation of Movement, 7–8, 132, 173–4, 270–4; student and graduate participation, 69, 135, 140, 277 f., 282; radical Catholics and, 81 ff., 112, 140–2, 143, 152 ff., 165; origins, 122–5; financing of, 124, 137–8, 150–1, 208; — government pressure, 138, 147, 155; — grass-roots support, 252; operational set-up, 125–37; laymen, role of and relations with hierarchy, 135 f., 143–8, 151 f., 154 ff., 162 f., 165, 192 ff., 202, 208–11, 224 ff.; part played by women, 139, 164, 255 n., 281
Aims and methods, 2, 6–7; evolution of until April 1964, 82, 149–62; religious element and catechesis, 125, 143 ff., 149 ff., 156 ff., 195 ff., 202, 209 ff., 227; — preevangelização, 210; radicalization,

MEB, Aims and methods—(*cont.*)
134 ff., 139 ff., 151 ff., 156 ff., 163,
172–3; — retreat from, 147, 229;
political commitment, 161 ff., 166,
267–70; *Diretrizes*, 192–7; statement of
witness, 197–200; *reestruturação*, 209;
see also below Military coup, effect of
Cadres: characteristics and background,
8, 127, 129, 132, 134–7, 138–43; no. of
paid officials, 136; membership of
Catholic Action groups, 139, 140–2,
279–80, 283–4; questionnaire, 139–43,
275–85; level of education, 140, 278 f.,
282 f.; social class, 140, 278–9, 283;
financial sacrifices, 142, 278, 285;
what they read, 142–3, 278–9, 283;
humility of, 205, 210–11
CDN, 125, 138, 144 ff., 155, 163, 190,
192 ff., 201, 222, 226 f.
Co-ordinators, 134–5; two-way flow, 129,
131, 134 ff., 167, 213; *Estaduais*, 134 ff.,
147, 222 f., 225 ff., 231 ff.; *Equipe
Técnica*, 135, 221, 223 ff., 227, 276;
meetings: 1st (1962), 152–5, 157, 163,
217, 247; — (June 1964), 192–5;
— 2nd (1965), 161, 198, 200; — 3rd
(1966), 192 n., 209, 220–9; — 4th
(1966), 209; *see also above* Cadres; *and
below* Nacional
Equipes: in *zona da mata*, 7 n., 173–4;
functions and training, 125, 129 f.,
132; bishops' control over, 129, 143–4,
147, 195, 210; radical attitude, 152;
and *sindicatos*, 165 ff.; after 1964 coup,
173–4, 190; in North, 206; and catechesis, 209; and community development, 213–14; and non-directiveness,
217, 219, 223, 267; in Lagoinha, 245 ff.,
252; and co-operation, 266; in Franqueira and Fernandópolis, 276
Military coup (1964) effect of, 2–4, 125,
127, 129, 132, 138, 146–8, 151, 161,
172–5, 190 ff., 205; situation in 1968–9,
3–4, 273–4; reorientation of policy, 6–7,
147–8, 201 ff., 208, 229, 266 f.; to close
down or to compromise?, 221, 223,
226 ff., 270–1
Monitores, 125, 127, 129, 131 f., 157 f.,
217 f.; after 1954 coup, 173 f., 190,
204; in Franqueira, 231, 243; in Lagoinha, 246, 248 f.
Nacional: functions, 135 ff., 144, 147,
209, 220–1, 228; staff, 135–7, 139; and

MEB policy, 151, 156, 161, 173, 192,
198, 200 f., 212 f., 220 ff., 231, 233,
245; and *sindicatos*, 162 ff., 170
Sistemas, 125, 127, 129 ff., 134 f., 137 ff.,
200, 220 ff., closed down, 125, 127, 134,
173, 175, 190, 205, 229; bishops' control over, 138 n., 143–4, 147, 200, 209,
229; in *zona da mata*, 172–3, 175; and
non-directiveness, 217, 222; in North,
North-East, and Centre-West, 224 ff.,
229
Treinamentos, 129–32, 135, 159, 164, 208,
214; non-directive methods, 215–17;
in Franqueira, 231 ff.; in Lagoinha,
246, 248
See also Animação Popular; AP; Class;
Communism; Community develop-
ment; *Conscientização*; Co-operation;
Cultura Popular; JUC; *Mutirão*; Non-
directiveness; North; North-East;
Populism; Radio schools; *Sindicatos*;
Viver é Lutar; *Zona da mata*
Mendes de Almeida, Cândido, 41, 44 n., 85,
102 n., 105
Messianism, 29
Metropolitano, O, 64
Middle class, 35, 40, 200; background of
MEB cadres, 140, 278 f., 283 f.; *see also*
Bourgeoisie
Military coups: (April 1964), 49–50, 100–1,
265; — effects of, *see under* MEB; (Dec.
1968), 3, 274
Millenarianism, 64, 90
Minas Gerais, 16, 34, 72–3, 127 f., 165, 205,
276
Mobilization from above, 171 n.
Moore, Wilbert, 64 n.
Mounier, Emmanuel, 65, 67, 91–3, 142, 280,
284
Mutirão, 161, 200–5, 266

Narodniki, 5, 94–6
Natal, 65, 105 n., 122, 134
National Commission for Rural Unionization, *see* CONSIR
Nationalism, 39–43, 45
Nettl, J. P., 42 n., 43 n., 171 n., 218 n.
Non-directiveness: MEB's ideas and
methods, 7, 197, 212 ff.; convenient in-
conclusiveness, 7, 220; Radical Catholics
and, 93–4, 98; *narodniki* and, 95; in
treinamentos, 132, 215–17; and *sindicatos*,
165, 169 ff.; and promotion of revolution,

Non-directiveness—(*cont.*)
 218–20; effects of 1964 coup, 219–20;
 267; neutrality of facts, 219–21; 3rd
 Encontro de Coordenadores, 221 ff.; in
 Franqueira,230–44; in Lagoinha, 244–59;
 natural limitations, 259
North, 8, 205–8; MEB in, 7 n., 73, 76, 124,
 127 f., 130 f., 133 f., 136; — after 1964
 coup, 205–8, 224–5, 227, 229, 266
North-East, 6, 26 ff., 35, 156 n.; colonial
 society, 11; water politics, 21; *sindicatos*,
 107 ff., 116, 167–71; radio schools,
 122–3, 127 f., 133; MEB and, 124 f.,
 127 f., 130 ff., 136; — after 1964 coup,
 147, 224, 225 n., 229; — community development, 213–14; ACO report, 272;
 see also Bishops; Sugar plantations; *Zona
 da mata*

Old Republic, 34
Ordem, A, 56 f.
ORIT, 118

Pacem in Terris, 76, 84 f.
Padim, D. Cândido, Bp of Lorena, 58 n.
Pará (state), 128, 165, 206
Paraíba, 128
Paraná, 116 f.
Parsons, Talcott, 194 n., 262 n., 263 n.
Partido Communista Brasileiro, see PCB
Partido Communista do Brasil (Maoist),
 120
Partido Democrata Cristão, see PDC
Partido Social Democrático, see PSD
Partido Social Progressista, see PSP
Partido Socialista do Brasil, see PSB
Partido Trabalhista Brasileiro, see PTB
Paternalism, 18 n., 200, 215
Patron-client relationship, 9, 23–4, 29 f., 32,
 35 ff., 240 n.
Patron-dependant relationship, 4, 7, 9;
 colonial period, 12–13; economic and
 social aspects, 16–18; political aspects,
 18–24; — in towns, 31–3, 37; and rural
 unionization, 24–5, 29 f., 107; AP and,
 101; in *zona da mata*, 175–6; in Amazon
 region, 207–8; class confrontation and,
 260–6; *see also* Franqueira; Lagoinha
Paul VI, Pope, 198–9
Paz e Terra, 6
PCB, 28, 99–100, 104 f., 115, 119, 120–1,
 254–8
PDC, 43–4, 109–10

Pernambuco (state), 48, 62, 109 ff., 116,
 127 f., 165, 205, 272
Personalist philosophy, 67, 90–4, 210
Piauí, 128, 165
Pinto, Álvaro Vieira, 41, 43, 68, 101 n.
Pius XI, Pope, 55, 58, 76
Politics and government: colonial period
 and 19th century, 14–16; traditional system of republic, 15–16; — in rural areas,
 18, 19–22; changes in rural politics, 22–4,
 47–9; urban politics, 31–3; general outline: (1930–45), 34–7; — (1945–54),
 37–40; — (1954–64), 41–50; politics of
 compromise, 35 ff., — breakdown of, 45,
 47, 49, 265; *see also* Mobilization
Politização, 106–7, 169–70, 202, 256
Pólo dominado and *pólo dominante*, 6, 99,
 112, 160, 189, 192, 197, 207, 219,
 265 f.
Populism: term defined, 4–5, 94, 97–8;
 MEB and, 7, 148, 160, 171, 192, 212–13;
 220 ff., 268–70; — in practical politics,
 171, 259; AP and, 82, 120, 223; movements in Russia, Latin America, etc.,
 94–7; and *sindicatos*, 111–13, 116; general
 hypotheses, 267–70; *see also* Cultura
 Popular; Non-directiveness
Populismo, 36–9, 42–3, 47, 49, 96–7, 124–5,
 265; and *sindicatos*, 113–18
Positivism, 54 f., 204
Povo: concept of, 42; Radicals' attitude to,
 90–1, 93–4; contribution to new society,
 93; 'agent in history', 148; aims of education of, 156; self-promotion, 192–3, 197,
 212–15, 218, 235, 267; and class conflict,
 200; ability to make right choice, 218,
 270; *populistas* and, 265, 270; remoteness
 of church from, 272; JOC on, 273; *see
 also* Class; *Conscientização*; *Massificação*;
 Non-directiveness; Populism; *Viver é
 Lutar*
Power, theories of, 194 n., 262 n.
Projeto histórico, 62 n.
Protestant churches, Brazilian, 5–6
PSB, 25
PSD, 38 f., 41
PSP, 39
PTB, 38 f., 41, 43, 115, 268

Quadragesimo Anno, 55, 76
Quadros, Jânio, 36 n., 45–6, 123–5, 137
Quoist, Michel, 143, 280
Quijano Obregón, Aníbal, 24, 30–1

Radical Catholicism: emergence of movement, 1, 57-9; expectations in 1961-3, 45-7, 50; and populism, 97; after 1964 coup, 271; influence of ideas, 271-4; *see also* AP; JUC; MEB

Radio schools, 122-32, 149, 205; statistics on, 126 ff., 132-4; non-directive techniques, 215-16; in Lagoinha, 246 ff., 254, 262

Recife, 82, 103, 105 n., 109; JUC in, 62, 65, 104; University, 82, 103 f.

Rede Nacional de Emissoras Católicas (RENEC), 122-4

Religious liberty, 202-3

Rerum Novarum, 54 f.

'*Revolução*', *see* Military coups: (April 1964)

Revolution: hopes of, 47, 50, 219; attitude of JUC, 79; — of Mounier, 92-3; — of *narodniki*, 95; — of AP and Communists, 99-101; *sindicatos* as nucleus of, 111, 269 n.; MEB and, 154-5, 218 f., 224, 234, 267

Revolution (1930), 34-5

Rio Grande do Norte, 73, 109 f., 116, 128

Rio Grande do Sul, 35, 38, 43, 116, 165

Rio de Janeiro, 104; Catholic University, 70, 77; student demonstrations (1968), 273

Rondônia, 128

Rubber gatherers, 206-7

Rural Labour Statute, 49, 113-14, 174, 178

Saint-Exupéry, Antoine de, 143, 280

Sales, D. Eugênio, 77, 109, 122

São Francisco valley, 73 f.

São Paulo; state, 34-5, 39, 43, 272; city, 55, 104; university, 66, 104, 116 f.

São Pedro, Usina, 176-89, 286-8

SAR, 109, 116, 122

Sartre, J-P., 92, 142-3, 280, 284

Seganfreddo, Sonia, 70 n., 83 n.

Sergipe, 123, 128, 165

Serviço de Assistência Rural, *see* SAR

Serviço de Informações, *see* SNI

Serviço de Orientação Rural de Pernambuco, *see* SORPE

Sindicatos rurais: effect on class pattern 24-5, 28, 31, 269 n.; origins and early years, 47, 110-11; leadership in, 74 n., 110-11, 116, 188; radical Catholics and, 111 ff.; MEB and, 112, 116, 155, 162-71, 197; developments of 1963-4, 113-18;

effect of 1964 coup, 167; *politização*, 169-70; in *zona da mata*, 172, 176; Usina São Pedro, 177, 179-83, 187-9; in Franqueira, 234 f.; in Lagoinha, 247 f., 258; *see also* CONTAG; ULTAB

Skidmore, Thomas E., 34 n., 35 n., 36 n., 38 n., 41 n., 44 n., 46, 47 n., 49 n.

SNI, 220, 288

Social class, *see* Class

Social legislation and welfare, 36, 48-9; *see also Assistêncialismo*

Social sciences, 65-6

Socialism, 92, 95, 97, 99

'Socialization', 85-7, 91

Sodré, Nelson Werneck, 41 f.

SORPE, 109, 111, 116, 162

Sousa, Luis Alberto Gomes de, 80 n.

SUDENE (*Superintendência do Desenvolvimento do Nordeste*), 75, 82

Sugar plantations, 175-87; proletarianization of peasants, 30, 172, 175, 265-6; working conditions, 176-87; *usinas* and *engenhos*, 176 n., 178; wages, 177, 181, 183-7, 188; slack period, 185-7; passivity of workers and intimidation, 187-9, 286-8

SUPRA (*Superintendência da Reforma Agrária*), 115

Tapajóz, Mons., 192 f., 195

Tarso, Paulo de, 43, 44 n.

Távora, D. José, Archbp of Aracajú, 123, 144, 146 f., 157

Teilhard de Chardin, Pierre, SJ, 86-7, 90 f., 142, 280, 284

Tenentes, tenentismo, 35, 56

Therry, Leonard D., 65 n., 66 n., 165

Trade unions, 36-7, 107-9; *see also* CONTAG; *Ligas camponeses*; *Sindicatos*; ULTAB

'Traditional areas', 7, 172, 265

Transformation: by education, 153-4, 155-6; *see also under* History

Truman, Pres. H., 40

Uchoa Leite, Sebastião, 106-7

UDN, 38 f., 48

ULTAB, 115 ff., 169 ff.

UME, 64

UNE, 68, 70, 77, 104

União Democrática Nacional, *see* UDN

União de Lavradores e Trabalhadores Agrícolas do Brasil, *see* ULTAB

União Metropolitana de Estudantes, see
  UME
União Nacional de Estudantes, see UNE
University reform, 62, 68–9
Urban working class, 36 ff., 40 f.
USA, 40, 45, 96; Ambassador kidnapped, 3
Utopias and utopics, 63–4, 78, 87, 89 f.

Valentino (Lagoinha), 245, 250, 252 ff.,
  260 f.
Vargas, Pres. Getulio, 33 ff., 39 ff., 73 n.,
  74 n., 113 n., 265
Vatican: relations with Brazilian church
  and state, 52 ff.; Council: 1st, 152; —
  2nd, 1, 80 n., 144–5, 193, 197
Vaz, Pe Henrique de Lima, SJ, 70, 87–90,
  142, 153, 161 f., 280, 284
Vivência, 137, 200

Viver é Lutar, 145–6, 155, 156–61, 173, 201,
  204, 266

Wagley, Charles, 207
Weber, Max, 4, 9
Weffort, Francisco C., 36, 37 n., 42, 104
Weil, Simone, 81
Wilkie, Mary E., 108 n., 110
Willems, Emilio, 6 n.
Wolfe, Marshall, 21
Worsley, Peter, 97

Zona da mata, 7 n., 172–89; in colonial
  period, 10–13; capitalism introduced, 16;
  Arraes forces reforms, 48; MEB in,
  172–5; 188 f.; effect of April 1964 coup,
  172–5, 179, 188–9; class consciousness
  in, 265–6; *see also* Sugar plantations